A History of Feminist and Gender Economics

This book offers a historical exploration of the genesis of feminist economics and gender economics, as well as their theoretical and methodological differences. Its narrative also serves to embed both within a broader cultural context.

Although both feminist economics and gender neoclassical economics belong to the cultural process related to the central role of the political economy in promoting women's emancipation and empowerment, they differ in many aspects. Feminist economics, mainly influenced by women's studies and feminism, rejected neoclassical economics, while gender neoclassical economics, mainly influenced by home economics and the new home economics, adopted the neoclassical economics' approach to gender issues. The book includes diverse case studies, which also highlight the continuity between the story of women's emancipation and the more recent developments of feminist and gender studies.

This volume will be of great interest to researchers and academia in the fields of feminist economics, gender studies, and the history of economic thought.

Giandomenica Becchio is Senior Researcher of Economics and Professor of History of Economic Thought and Methodology of Economics at the University of Turin, Italy.

Routledge Studies in the History of Economics

Divine Providence in Early Modern Economic Thought
Joost Hengstmengel

Macroeconomics without the Errors of Keynes
The Quantity Theory of Money, Saving, and Policy
James C.W. Ahiakpor

The Political Economy of the Han Dynasty and Its Legacy
Edited by Cheng Lin, Terry Peach and Wang Fang

A History of Utilitarian Ethics
Samuel Hollander

The Economic Thought of Michael Polanyi
Gábor Biró

Ideas in the History of Economic Development
The Case of Peripheral Countries
Edited by Estrella Trincado, Andrés Lazzarini and Denis Melnik

Ordoliberalism and European Economic Policy
Between Realpolitik and Economic Utopia
Edited by Malte Dold and Tim Krieger

The Economic Thought of Sir James Steuart
First Economist of the Scottish Enlightenment
José Manuel Menudo

A History of Feminist and Gender Economics
Giandomenica Becchio

For more information about this series, please visit www.routledge.com/series/ SE0341

A History of Feminist and Gender Economics

Giandomenica Becchio

LONDON AND NEW YORK

First published 2020
by Routledge
2 Park Square, Milton Park, Abingdon, Oxon OX14 4RN

and by Routledge
605 Third Avenue, New York, NY 10017

First issued in paperback 2021

Routledge is an imprint of the Taylor & Francis Group, an informa business

Publisher's Note
The publisher has gone to great lengths to ensure the quality of this reprint but
points out that some imperfections in the original copies may be apparent.

British Library Cataloguing-in-Publication Data
A catalogue record for this book is available from the British Library

Library of Congress Cataloging-in-Publication Data
A catalog record for this book has been requested

Typeset in Bembo
by Apex CoVantage, LLC

ISBN 13: 978−1−03−208679−8 (pbk)
ISBN 13: 978−1−138−10375−7 (hbk)

Contents

Acknowledgements

Giandomenica Becchio, University of Torino, Department of Economics, Social Sciences, Mathematics and Statistics (ESOMAS).

Financial support from the Italian Ministry of Education, University and Research (MIUR), "Dipartimenti di Eccellenza" grant 2018–2022, is gratefully acknowledged. A special acknowledgment to colleagues and staff of the Department of Gender Studies (formerly known as the Gender Institute) at the London School of Economics; Women, Gender, and Sexuality Studies at the Columbia University Library, New York; Wirtschaftsuniversität Wien, Vienna; University of Technology Sydney, and the University of Sydney for their help and feedback while I was there working on this book as a visiting researcher.

Introduction

One hundred and fifty years ago, in 1869, John Stuart Mill wrote a radical book, *The Subjection of Women*, to report on the conditions of women within families and society and to promote the economic, political, and cultural emancipation of women. Mill wrote: "What is now called the nature of women is an eminently artificial thing – the result of forced repression in some directions, unnatural stimulation in others" (Mill 1869 [1970], 22). Inspired by his wife Harriet Taylor and by the Benthamite radical tradition, Mill pointed out that, in the name of family values, the reproductive role of women, glorified for centuries as their 'exclusive' one, was to be intended as the result of social conventions, which were determined by the power relationship between the sexes in favor of men. Even in societies in which citizens are equal by law, some habits, customs, traditions, and institutions – including family – had perpetuated the subjection of women and the relegation to their 'natural' role of wives and mothers. Women's 'natural' role as mothers and wives was a product of a patriarchal society that had denied them an equal access to education, economic independence, and political rights as well as their autonomy in legal issues. In Mill's words: "I consider it presumption in anyone to pretend to decide what women are or are not, can or cannot be, by natural constitution" (Mill 1869 [1970], 57).

Mill's book was not an isolated case: it belonged to a long tradition of the interconnections between 'the woman question' (as early feminism has been labeled) and political economy, and between feminism and economics. The connection between the woman question and political economy, which started during the Enlightenment and it had been developed during the 19th century. In the second half of the 20th century, feminism became a global cultural and political movement in Western society and gender issues emerged within the social sciences. Economics were affected by feminism and gender studies as well, and feminist economics and gender economics emerged and were established as two separate and different research fields.

This book deals with the history of the relationship between the woman question and political economy (19th century, interwar) and with the relationship between feminism and economics (1960s–2000s) as well as with the genesis of feminist economics and gender economics and their theoretical and methodological affinities and differences, which may be summed up by the fact that feminist economics rejects neoclassical economics, while gender economics adopts neoclassical economics. Nonetheless, especially during the last two decades, the term 'gender' had been adopted by the two approaches. To avoid any possible confusion, in this book gender economics is intended to mean gender neoclassical economics.

The adoption of a historical perspective allows us to consider the cultural framework of both feminist and gender neoclassical economics. In fact, any research field is crucially interconnected with its *Weltanschauung*; that is, the cultural vision embedded within its paradigms and models. As Schumpeter clearly explained, the history of a discipline allows an understanding of the strict connection between vision and analysis. This process is valid especially within social sciences, including political economy and economics (Schumpeter 1954). Hence, a glance at early feminism and feminism is necessary to better understand the origin and the development of both feminist economics and gender neoclassical economics. Although a taxonomy of the multifaced form of feminism is not the intent of this book, a brief description of the periodization of feminism may be useful. Feminism belongs to several intellectual traditions: political philosophy, political economy, history, and sociology, which converged in a general definition of feminism as a cultural and political movement whose aim was to promote the emancipation of women from their subjection in any possible sphere of human life in order to reach some equality between genders. The French word *feminisme* apparently was coined by the utopian socialist Charles Fourier in 1837, to promote gender equality in his utopian society. The first documented English version of the word 'feminism' appeared in 1852, and it was used to denote women's conditions in an article titled "Woman and her Needs", published in a business magazine, *De Bow's Review of the Southern and Western States*, printed in New Orleans (Honderich 1995).

Different traditions of feminist scholarship agree in considering that the history of feminism spanned three different periods: the first wave of feminism, also labeled as early feminism or the woman question (1830s–1918); the second wave of feminism (1960s–1970s); and the third wave of feminism (1990s–2000s). The use of the wave metaphor to denote feminism began in 1968, when Martha Weinman wrote an article on *The New York Times*, with the headline "The Second Feminist Wave", to denote the differences between the women's sexual emancipation occurring at that time and the battle for women's rights that had taken place since the early 19th century.

During early feminism (1830s–1918), women fought to gain an equal opportunity to get higher education, which pushed them to require gender equality in legal and economic issues as well as in political issues, which included the right to vote. The second wave of feminism (1960s–1970s) was much more focused on a cultural revolution rooted on the liberalization of women's sexuality, which included the self-determination of reproduction. Grounded on the ideas that men's dominance had forged differences in gender social roles and that traditional education had been biased by sexism, second-wave feminism carried out a cultural revolution against the traditional role of women in society. The third wave of feminism started in the 1990s: it faced many issues that may be summarized in the effort to denounce gender inequality at any level and in any context and to build up a political and cultural agenda able to reduce (and possibly to eradicate) gender inequality. During this latest phase, the fight for gender equality had been adopted by any movement whose intent was to achieve equality for all persons belonging to other gender-related minorities, and for other minorities regardless of their gender.

This book's aim is threefold. The first aim of this book is to show that the interconnection between the woman question and political economy (19th century–early 20th century) as a determinant in the progression of women's empowerment. During the long process for women's enfranchising, the role of political economy had been central, albeit too often neglected. Political economy was a major field for protofeminists (scholars engaged in the woman question in early modern history who lived and wrote between the 15th and 18th centuries) and for early feminists in the 19th century, when the woman question became a central issue within public debates and was especially hosted in economic publications.

The connection between early feminism and political economy implies a double narration: on one side, it is necessary to cope with the specific issues that linked economic theory and the woman question. For instance, the consequence of women entering the labor force, which included the gender wage gap, and unpaid work; on the other side, it is inevitable to deal with the contributions of the first women economists, who were able to get some reputation in economic matters either as free thinkers or as the first women to get Ph.D.s in economics and, eventually, academic positions as faculty members. Nevertheless, a perfect overlap between the two sides of this narration has not always occurred: many women economists worked on the woman question, but not all women economists were specifically interested in the woman question. Hence, this book is not devoted to women economists in general terms, unless they were pioneers of the introduction of the woman question into political economy or did specific research that shaped research fields related to the woman question, such as home economics, household economics, and later feminist economics and gender neoclassical economics.[1] In this book, mainly in Chapters 1 and 2, there are many biographical sketches of women economists and activists; some portraits of the first women entrepreneurs are depicted as well. Their biographies allow the reader to be aware of the fact that the personal commitment of women activists, women entrepreneurs, and women economists engaged in the woman question within political economy had played a fundamental role in the philosophical and cultural battle for women's empowerment as well as in building up the historical roots of both feminist economics and gender neoclassical economics.

The second intent of this book is to display the fundamental role of classical liberalism within the story of the connection between the woman question and feminism and political economy, against the idea that feminism is mainly related to socialism. The first steps of women's emancipation included the right to get a higher education as well as economic and legal independence: these issues were *leitmotiv* within the classical liberal tradition since early modern history. The battle for women's emancipation that involved political rights belonged to classical liberalism as well. In fact, the label 'universal suffrage', used before the First World War, did not include women: this is the main reason the movement of the suffragettes arose. Therefore, the idea that feminism is commonly associated almost exclusively with socialism is partially misleading: socialism was more a matter of class struggle rather than women's emancipation. The woman question and socialism started to be connected only much later, in the late 19th to early 20th century, to vindicate social rights. Socialist activists, who were much closer to the Marxist tradition, usually criticized the suffragette movement, it being a typical bourgeois battle that would have reinforced the split between middle-class capitalists and the lower-class proletariat. Nonetheless, socialist activists who were much more oriented either towards gradual socialism (such as Fabianism in Great Britain) or social democracy supported women's battle to get universal suffrage. In this book, the two traditions of classical liberalism and socialism have been presented in the description of the origin and the connection between the woman question and political economy (Chapter 1) as well as in the description of the emergence of feminist economics (Chapter 3).

The final purpose of this book is to contextualize both feminist economics and gender neoclassical economics in their historical framework and to describe their contents. Although officially recognized as autonomous research fields relatively recently (the American Economic Association officially recognized gender economics as a subfield of labor economics in 1990 and feminist economics as a heterodox economics in 2006 [see Chapter 3]), feminist economics and gender neoclassical economics are rooted in a long tradition that is intertwined on one side with the history of the woman question and on the other side with the history of political economy and economics. Both feminist economics and gender neoclassical economics scrutinize the nature and the effects of gender discrimination in some strategic markets, such as the labor market and entrepreneurship as well as the gender wage gap. Both feminist economics and gender neoclassical economics analyze gender gaps by using specific economic models that may be very different.

Today, feminist economics and gender neoclassical economics are two separate research fields devoted to gender issues within economics. Feminist economics may be regarded on one side as a development of women's studies within economics and on the other side, as a deep critique to the approach of neoclassical economics to gender issues, an approach that is mainly rejected. Contrary to feminist economics, gender neoclassical economics adopts a neoclassical economics approach, often revised or extended to gender issues. In the narrative of this book, the terms 'mainstream', 'standard', and 'conventional' economics are used as synonyms for neoclassical economics. Recently, gender neoclassical economics has been labeled 'economics of gender'. Hence, in this book, 'gender neoclassical economics', and 'economics of gender' are intended as synonyms and as an alternative approach to feminist economics.

This book is structured as follows: Chapter 1 and Chapter 2 aim to describe the emerging woman question within political economy and the place of the first women academic economists, while Chapter 3 and Chapter 4 aim to describe the rise of feminist economics and gender neoclassical economics embedded in their cultural *milieu*. The final appendix provides a timeline of the connections among the woman question, feminism, political economy, and the rise and development of both feminist economics and gender neoclassical economics as academic research fields.

Chapter 1 is devoted to the history of the relationship between the woman question and political economy (late 19th century–early 20th century) within the two traditions of classical liberalism and socialism in three different geographical areas: Great Britain, where both classical liberalism and Fabian socialism were influential in the political economy debate on women's issues; German-speaking European countries (specifically Austria and Germany), where classical liberalism, social democracy, and Marxism had a great impact on the woman question as a political economy matter; and the United States of America, where classical liberal tradition forged both the woman question within political economy and abolitionism. In many other countries, such as France, Italy, or Russia/Soviet Union, the cultural role of Marxism and Leninism was dominant but, as previously mentioned, both Marxism and Leninism did not focus their attention specifically on gender inequality as long as they considered women's emancipation to be a direct effect of the political emancipation of the proletariat as a whole.

During the 19th century, early feminists, mainly women, strongly promoted the necessity to allow women to finally get access to higher education in order to obtain academic degrees as well as Ph.D.s in any field. Their aim was to overcome the traditional pink ghetto's education (*belles lettres*) to which women who were lucky enough to get a higher education were traditionally relegated. Higher education in fields such as law, medicine, and political economy was asked by women activists as a tool to finally reach an economic independence for women and to remove obstacles which had prevented women from entering the public sphere on equal terms with men. Economic independence was seen as the only way able to make women no longer materially subjected to their husbands, fathers, or brothers. Women's economic independence needed to be reinforced by introducing the recognition of equal legal rights within marriage and family: in fact, married women were not allowed to own their own property or to take custody of their children after separations and divorces. The final stage of this long process was the fight to get women's political rights: passive and active suffrage would have allowed the promotion of some welfare measures in order to meet the needs of both working and nonworking women (Dale and Foster 2013).

Early feminists mostly reinforced traditional values: motherhood was still glorified; the burden of housekeeping and the responsibility of family care were regarded as natural tasks for women. The endorsement of traditional values was mainly due to the fact that early feminists, including early socialists (the cases of Beatrice Webb and Sylvia Pankhurst in England, and Lily Braun in Germany, are emblematic) came from middle-class families. After the First World War, two different subgroups emerged inside classical liberal feminism, which split into two groups. In the first group were equal rights feminists, who considered any specific legislation to protect women to be a form of discrimination. In the other group, there were new feminists, as in Eleanor Rathbone's definition (Rathbone 1924), who argued that a specific legislation for women was a necessary instrument to reach equality between sexes, and might be seen as an efficient tool to increase the well-being of the society as a whole (Seiz 2000).

Offen (2000) better specified the phases of women's emancipation by identifying five stages of the process that occurred between 1814 and 1914. At the beginning of the 19th century, women activists asked for an increase of literacy and education for girls.[2] More educated women emerged as active participants in the European nationalistic movements that spread during the 19th century both in Europe and in the United States.[3] Women's increasing involvement in political movements opened the way for a massive request for the economic emancipation of women, especially during the spread of the second Industrial Revolution.

Along with these developments, women asked for a serious revision of their sexual education that was denied until then: a lively debate about women sexual emancipation within and outside of marriage, motherhood, and reproduction started; it was concerned with the question of how sexuality could be regulated or reformed in public and private (Funke and Grove 2019). In the 19th century, the understanding of female sexuality had been carried on by two different positions: by the mainstream women's rights movement, focused primarily on the dangers of sex (underage pregnancy, single motherhood, an elevated number of children to raise, and health issues related to maternity and delivery); and by another perspective that had encouraged women to freely live their sexuality, while failing to offer a radical critique of the dominant male-constructed sexuality (Dubois and Gordon 1983). Offen concluded by affirming that the final stage of the process of women's emancipation was the rising of official several feminist movements, which occurred in different European countries as well as in the United States, as the direct effect of the previous four phases (education, politics, economy, and sexuality).[4] Offen also pointed out that, during the 19th century, early forms of antifeminism spread up along with early feminism: as the woman question increasingly became a political issue, antifeminism developed as a reaction to a new dimension of women within society.

Although I generally second Offen's interpretation of the nature of these five phases in the process of women's emancipation, my intention in this book, as shown in Chapter 1, is to consider the request for women's economic independence a step earlier than the request for women's political rights and to consider the role of getting access to study political economy in colleges as crucial for women's emancipation. Furthermore, the battle for economic independence, which implied the emergence of the first women entrepreneurs, too often neglected, must be regarded as a direct effect of the popularization of some principles of political economy carried on by the first women economists. Many women started to be involved in building up their own professions as well as their own firms. Elizabeth Garrett Anderson (1836–1917) was Britain's first female physician: supported by Elizabeth Blackwell, another English woman who had gained her medical degree in the United States, Garrett Anderson set up the New Hospital for Women. In her hospital, she appointed only women to the medical staff (Elston 2017). Many other examples are provided in Chapter 1.

The access to graduate studies in academic fields that traditionally excluded women gave them the chance to be economically independent from men. Political economy was among those fields: debates around equal pay and around women entering in the labor force allowed the popularization of a broader debate on gender discrimination and played a decisive role in the emancipation of women; the increasing number of women entrepreneurs made women's independence effective as well.

The idea that economic independence for women was ineludible was clearly summed up by Virginia Woolf in *A Room of One's Own* (Woolf 1929). The metaphor of one's own room symbolized the capacity to deliberate independently from an imposed convention led by men, which affected cultural categories as well as language and styles. Woolf claimed that women's emancipation (which includes the possibility to write literature) needed a sort of economic independence, economic poverty being the cause of the intellectual impoverishment of women: she underlined that she started working as a writer only after she inherited enough money to allow her to receive a fixed income. By introducing the fictional character of Shakespeare's sister, Woolf underlined the role of the cultural gender gap in women's potential for independence: she cited the examples of many women, like George Eliot and George Sand, who used pseudonymous male names in order to get some credit in society.

As described in Chapter 1, the role of education as emancipatory has been a transversal *leitmotiv* in any attempt to enrich the social condition of minorities. The access to higher education institutions

> Furnished space for self-development, affording some relief from the constrictions of family life. Further, they gave women access to their peers and to new reference groups, and hence constituted environments in which feminist ideas might be articulated and shared. Finally, and crucially, of course, the new schools and colleges guided an albeit small section of women, each generation, towards high status areas of knowledge and expertise, and hence, indirectly, towards power.
>
> (Dyhouse 2012, 175)

Early feminists were not an exception: the access to any degree of education was fundamental for a real emancipation of women from misogyny, chauvinism, and patriarchy. Classical liberals in the 19th century regarded education as the main tool for a correct understanding of natural rights, which made consistent the battle for the equality between genders, without imposing any countersupremacy from the female side. Socialists in the 19th century considered education to be the most powerful instrument to realize that the middle-class dominant culture exploited the proletariat. Only a few socialist thinkers, influenced by Engels, explicitly compared middle-class dominance with men's dominance over women whose social role and work had historically been underrated or denied in the same way the capitalist class had exploited the working class.

As previously mentioned, the link between the woman question and political economy implied a double involvement of women in economic issues. On one side, women became new entrepreneurs (Gamber 1998): many cases occurred especially in Great Britain and in the United States, but also in *felix* Vienna, Austria. On the other side, women became economists: in the first stage, they were popularizers of the emerging political economy – for example, Sophie de Grouchy, Jane Marcet, and Harriet Martineau – and, in the second stage, when they finally got the chance to be enrolled in Ph.D. programs in political economy, they became economists, either within or outside academia. In the early 20th century, women economists had a chance to get academic positions and their numbers rapidly increased, especially in Great Britain and in the United States. As previously stated, many of them devoted their research to the economic conditions of women, especially labor and wage legislation.

Chapter 2 deals with the emerging of home economics and household economics as academic disciplines in the United States. This process allowed many women to get academic positions. Home economics may be regarded as a peculiar expression of the ideals of the Progressive Era, which spanned the 1890s to the 1920s across the United States and was meant to counteract the negative effects of industrialization in social terms. Home economics was intended as the scientific management of the house and was based on the interconnection between the cult of domesticity and the ideal of social responsibility. The emerging of home economics as an autonomous field in autonomous departments had a double effect. On one side, the gendered nature of home economics was a tremendous tool for women's emancipation and created a formidable chance of an academic career for many women economists who worked on labor and social issues. On the other side, home economics became a niche for women economists and isolated them in a discipline that never raised questions about patriarchy and the traditional role of women in society (Folbre 1991; Hammond 1993; Forget 2011; Apple 2006).

Directly connected with home economics, another research field emerged a few years later: household economics, which was developed during the interwar era at the University of Chicago in Illinois. Like home economics, household economics became a niche for women economists. Household economics copes with the production of the goods and services by the members of a household, for their own consumption, using their own capital and their own unpaid labor. Household economics combined a theoretical approach and an empirical technique that later converged into a new research field, called new home economics, which spread in the 1960s and the 1970s. It represented the roots of what today is called economics of gender. Meanwhile, the old home economics was transitioning towards a form of theory of consumption based on a proper education of family members, which lost its original intent linked with social responsibility.

The new home economics, introduced by Mincer (1962, 1974) and Becker (1981), explained the specialization of households as a direct consequence of the theory of human capital, making implicit some neoclassical methodological assumptions (for example, optimal decisions depend on different skills of different members, the division of labor within households depends on biological and cultural differences between men and women, the allocation of women's time to the household and of men's time to the market is rational, and the gender wage gap is a natural consequence of this specific division of labor between men and women) as well as some patriarchal assumptions (for example, the household's utility function depends on the head of the family, who is supposed to be benevolent; marriage is seen as a long-term commitment to assure that women are protected; and specialized market-oriented investments in boys and household-oriented investments in girls are optimal strategies).

As earlier mentioned, both home economics and household economics allowed many women to get positions within academia: since the early 1930s, the number of women economists working in specific fields such as consumption theory, distribution, and home economics had increased. Nonetheless, a marginalization of women within academia as well as a significant decrease of tenured women economists occurred during the 1950s and 1960s, a trend that was partially limited only in the 1970s (Folbre 1998; Forget 2011). A discussion around the number and the role of women economists within the discipline started in 1971, when the American Economic Association recognized that the economic profession should be more open to women and created the Committee on the Status of Women in the Economics Profession (CSWEP) to monitor the progress of women economists within academic departments and to reduce gender gap in the profession (Madden 2019). This story is described in Chapter 3, which mainly deals with the complex genesis of feminist economics and its analytical and methodological core, with a special focus on the contents of the journal *Feminist Economics*.

Feminist economics emerged as a revision of the field (gender issues within economics) as well as of the discipline as a whole. (Ferber and Nicosia 1972). According to feminist economists, any feminist inquiry will affect the economic lives of children, women, and men, as well as the relationship between genders. The genesis and the development of feminist economics can be seen on one side as an enlargement of women's studies to economics, which occurred during the rise of the second wave of feminism, and on the other side as an alternative to the new home economics approach in dealing with gender issues, which was grounded on traditional gendered stereotypes that ignored the separate identities of the family members and underestimated noneconomic factors.

The introduction of the woman question in economics at the academic level occurred in three phases: the fight for female students to get access to any university and to be enrolled in any academic degree (including research fields that were not traditionally opened to women such as political economy); the actual increasing number of women who got an academic position, including within the economics' departments; and the introduction of women in labor force, women's wages, women's role in household, and so forth, as academic issues.

The introduction of women's studies within academia shaped some new academic curricula that converged towards a form of interdisciplinary which was able to include reproduction, family, fertility, and the introduction of contributions by women in any discipline that had been too often neglected. Feminist economists shared with women's studies scholars the necessity to explore social norms associated with gender, to investigate the origin of social inequalities, and to open up a general debate on the masculine nature of social sciences, which had led to a serious discussion around the role of women within any scientific field (Boxer 2002; Kennedy 2008; Chesler 2018). Feminist economics challenged the *malestream* approach to economics provided by neoclassical economics (Bergmann 1990; Nelson 1992, 1993). Feminist economics shared with both women's studies and with second wave feminism the idea that maleness affected the nature of science within Western philosophy. In the Western cultural *Weltanschauung*, reason and emotions had been dichotomized: the metaphor of a pure and detached masculine thinking and the metaphor of a sympathetic feminine thinking were grounded on the idea that women are emotional beings while men are rational beings. This dichotomy had forged the central role of objectivity within the modern conception of rationality by shaping a masculine notion of rationality that had been incorporated into social science, including neoclassical economics, and its application to gender studies – that is, gender neoclassical economics – while it was firmly rejected by feminist economics.

The initial divergence between feminist economics and gender neoclassical economics covered many issues, which are described in Chapter 3 and Chapter 4. Although many feminist economists have been working within the neoclassical tradition[5] differently from gender neoclassical economics, feminist economics offers political insights into the underlying constructs of the economics discipline and the cultural context of economic knowledge in order to elaborate a critique of the discipline (Ferber and Nelson 1993, 2003; Folbre 1994; Barker 1995; Harding 1995; Grapard 1995; Nelson 1995, 1996; Fraser 2009). Feminist economics stands for a more pluralistic approach within the broad rubric of economics: it is a more politically oriented approach that involves a deep revision of the neoclassical economics as well as a more radical and newer economic thinking that includes the idea that the economy is influenced by gendered social norms and that the economy in households is driven by love, power, and obligations besides the market.

This way of considering economic matters makes feminist economics a heterodox economics' approach. Along with other heterodox economists, feminist economics has been fighting against the 'economic imperialism' of neoclassical economics, a broad process that has discarded a pluralistic approach within the discipline and has made neoclassical economics prevail upon other social sciences. The final paragraph of Chapter 3 deals with a possible convergence between feminist economics and some other heterodox economic theories such as Marxist political economy, post-Keynesian economics, Austrian economics, social ontology, Sen's approach of capabilities, behavioral economics, and economic comparative systems.

Besides their structural differences, both feminist economics and gender neoclassical economics aim to illustrate how the gender gap actually shapes our society on a global scale. Today, the distinction between feminist economics and gender neoclassical economics may be ambiguous if we consider that more recent feminist economics literature has constantly adopted the term 'gender' to denote and to analyze gender economic inequality, which affects all gender identities and minorities in terms of ethnic groups, as an alternative approach to neoclassical economics' treatment of gender issues. Meanwhile, as previously anticipated, the field devoted to gender issues within neoclassic economics has been officially labeled 'economics of gender' by the American Economic Association. Chapter 4 describes the evolution of the gender label within social science, which partially explains the semantic overlap of its use in both feminist economics and gender neoclassical economics. Rooted in the idea that gender has always been a constraint that has shaped social power, gender studies emerged in order to understand the role of gender in explaining social phenomena and to denounce cultural, political, economic, and social distortions and discriminations based on gender identities (Butler 1990; Haraway 1991; Lerner 1986, 1991; Nussbaum 2000; Essed et al. 2009). Any inquiry on the influence of gender on economic matters implies some consideration of individual behavior in economic situations (altruism versus competition; nurture versus nature; risk aversion versus risk proneness) that traditionally had been dichotomized in women's behavior (altruistic, nurturing, and risk-averse) and men's behavior (competitive, aggressive, and risk-prone). Differences in behavior can be originated either by cultural expectations or by social pressure and had been influenced by different education for boys and girls. For instance, entrepreneurship and finance were for boys, education and caring were for girls. Furthermore, any inquiry on the influence of gender on economic matters implies on one side, a microeconomic analysis focused on gender differences in choices and preferences, and on the other side, some reflections on the influence of economics on gendered stereotypes and social roles (Eswaran 2014).

Chapter 4 is specifically focused on the latest developments in gender studies in economics in order to show that the impact of gender as a cultural category within feminist economics has been different from the impact that it has had on gender neoclassical economics. The introduction of gender studies within social sciences occurred in the 1960s and aimed to promote a balance between men, women, and other gender identities into different aspects of the cultural, political, and economic sphere. Although feminist economics always considered the inquiry into the nature of care work, of the gendered nature of social roles, and of gender stereotypes as possible tools able to enlarge and revise the discipline as a whole, the economics of gender adopted neoclassical tools to analyze mainly labor economics and the theory of marriage by developing and enriching Becker's new home economics (Lundberg 2008; Grossbard 2015, 2018; Blau and Winkler 2018; Averett et al. 2018; Giuliano 2018).

Beyond their theoretical and methodological differences, the two approaches converged in pointing out that the persistence of gender inequalities between men and women in the economy still affects the situation of women and other minorities (including the situation of women economists within academia). In the final paragraph of Chapter 4, major gender economic gaps (the gender labor gap, wage gap, and entrepreneurship gap) have been scrutinized by showing off some data that reveal that although women's economic conditions are significantly better off, the road to gender equality and to women and minorities' empowerment is still long and challenging.

Since the publication of Mill's essay, many things have changed in terms of women's empowerment and gender equality. Nonetheless, gender inequality still persists and massively affects the society as a whole.

Notes

1 Some publications, such as Dimand M.A. et al. (1995), Dimand R. et al. (2000), and Madden and Dimand (2019), covered the contributions of many women economists in the history of political economy and economics.
2 During the early modern age, a small number of women were able to get access to higher education. Elena Lucrezia Cornaro (1646–1984) was the first woman to get a college degree: in 1678, she graduated in philosophy from the University of Padua, Italy. In 1732, Laura Bassi (1711–1778) was the first woman to get a permanent academic position at the University of Bologna, after having obtained a doctoral degree in philosophy (Findlen 2003).
3 Feminists involved in the liberal revolutions of 1848 advocated universal suffrage. Many of them grounded their requests on the basis of the principle of 'equality-in-difference', as theorized by Ernest Legouvé: "a concrete program for radically restructuring the institutional arrangements for marriage and women's social roles within the existing bourgeois order of family centeredness and private property, coupled with a celebration of motherhood" (Offen 1986, 457).
4 In 1848, the First International Congress of Women's Rights gathered in Paris. Its main resolution affirmed the equality between sexes, even though the question of women's suffrage was not on the agenda. Other international meetings about women's rights followed in Washington, D.C.; (1888); London (1899); Berlin (1904); Amsterdam (1908); Toronto (1909); Stockholm (1911); The Hague (1915); Zurich (1919); and Vienna (1921). On the eve of the First World War, there were three international associations for women's rights and emancipation in Europe: the International Council of Women, the International Alliance of Women, and the Women's International League for Peace and Freedom (Rupp 1997).

5 Barker (1999) provided a detailed description of any possible convergence between feminist economics and neoclassical economics.

References

Apple R. (2006) *Perfect Motherhood: Science and Childrearing in America*. New Brunswick, NJ: Rutgers University Press.

Averett S., Argys L., and Hoffman S. (Eds.) (2018) *The Oxford Handbook of Women and the Economy*. New York: Oxford University Press.

Barker D. (1995) "Economists, Social Reformers, and Prophets: A Feminist Critique of Economic Efficiency". *Feminist Economics*. Vol. 1:3, pp. 26–39.

Barker D. (1999) "Gender". Paterson J. and Lewis M. (Eds.) *The Elgar Companion to Feminist Economics*. Cheltenham: Edward Elgar, pp. 390–396.

Becker G. (1981) *A Treatise on the Family*. Enlarged Edition. Cambridge, MA: Harvard University Press.

Bergmann B. (1990) "Feminism and Economics". *Women's Studies Quarterly*. Vol. 18:3/4, pp. 68–74.

Blau F. and Winkler A. (2018) *The Economics of Women, Men, and Work*. 8th Edition. New York: Oxford University Press.

Boxer M. (2002) "Women's Studies as Women's History". *Women's Studies Quarterly*. Vol. 30:3/4, pp. 42–51.

Butler J. (1990) *Gender Trouble: Feminism and the Subversion of Identity*. New York and London: Routledge.

Chesler P. (2018) *A Politically Incorrect Feminist: Creating a Movement with Bitches, Lunatics, Dykes, Prodigies, Warriors, and Wonder*. New York: St. Martin's Press.

Dale J. and Foster P. (2013) *Feminists and the State Welfare*. London: Routledge.

Dimand M.A., Dimand R., and Forget E. (Eds.) (1995) *Women of Value: Feminist Essays on the History of Women in Economics*. Aldershot: Edward Elgar.

Dimand R., Dimand M.A., and Forget E. (Eds.) (2000) *A Biographical Dictionary of Women Economists*. Cheltenham: Edward Elgar.

Dimand R., Dimand M.A., and Forget E. (Eds.) (2005) *A Biographical Dictionary of Women Economists*. Cheltenham: Edward Elgar.

Dyhouse C. (2012) *Girls Growing Up in Late Victorian and Edwardian England*. London: Routledge.

Essed P., Goldberg D., and Kobayashi A. (Eds.) (2009) *A Companion to Gender Studies*. Chichester, UK: Wiley-Blackwell.

Eswaran M. (2014) *Why Gender Matters in Economics*. Princeton, NJ: Princeton University Press.

Ferber M. and Nelson J. (Eds.) (1993) *Beyond Economic Man: Feminist Theory and Economics*. Chicago: The University of Chicago Press.

Ferber M. and Nelson J. (Eds.) (2003) *Feminist Economics Today: Beyond Economic Man*. Chicago: The University of Chicago Press.

Ferber R. and Nicosia F. (1972) "Newly Married Couples and Their Asset Accumulation Decisions". Strümpbel B., Morgan J., and Zahn E. (Eds.) *Human Behavior in Economic Affairs*. Amsterdam: Elsevier, pp. 161–187.

Findlen P. (2003) "The Scientist's Body: The Nature of a Woman Philosopher in Enlightenment Italy". Daston L. and Pomata G. (Eds.) *The Faces of Nature in Enlightenment Europe*. Berlin: Berliner Wissenschafts Verlag, pp. 211–236.

Folbre N. (1991) "The Unproductive Housewife: Her Evolution in Nineteenth-Century Economic Thought". *Signs: Journal of Women in Culture and Society*. Vol. 16:3, pp. 463–484.

Folbre N. (1994) *Who Pays for the Kids? Gender and the Structure of Constraint*. London: Routledge.

Folbre N. (1998) "The Sphere of Women in Early Twentieth Century Economics". Silverberg H. (Ed.) *Gender and American Social Science: The Formative Years*. Princeton, NJ: Princeton University Press, pp. 35–60.

Forget E. (2011) "American Women and the Economics Profession in the Twentieth Century". *Oeconomica*. Vol. 1:1, pp. 19–30.

Fraser N. (2009) "Feminism, Capitalism, and the Cunning of History". *New Left Review*. Vol. 56, pp. 97–117.

Funke J. and Grove J. (Eds.) (2019) *Sculpture, Sexuality, and History. Encounters in Literature, Culture, and the Arts from the Eighteenth Century to the Present*. London: Palgrave Macmillan.

Gamber W. (1998) "A Gendered Enterprise: Placing Nineteenth-Century Businesswomen in History". *The Business History Review*. Vol. 72:2, pp. 188–217.

Giuliano P. (2018) "Gender. A Historical Perspective". Averett S., Argit L., and Hoffman S. (Eds.) *The Oxford Handbook of Women and the Economy*. New York: Oxford University Press, pp. 645–671.

Grapard U. (1995) "Robinson Crusoe: The Quintessential Economic Man?". *Feminist Economics*. Vol. 1:1, pp. 32–52.

Grossbard S. (2015) *The Marriage Motive: A Price Theory of Marriage. How Marriage Markets Affect, Employment, Consumption, and Savings*. Dordrecht, Heidelberg, London, and New York: Springer.

Grossbard S. (2018) "Marriage and Marriage Markets". Averett S., Argit L., and Hoffman S. (Eds.) *The Oxford Handbook of Women and the Economy*. New York: Oxford University Press, pp. 55–73.

Hammond C. (1993) "American Women and the Professionalization of Economics". *Review of Social Economy*. Vol. 51:3, pp. 347–370.

Haraway D. (1991) *Simians, Cyborgs, and Women: The Reinvention of Nature*. London and New York: Routledge.

Harding S. (1995) "Can Feminist Thought Make Economics More Objective?". *Feminist Economics*. Vol. 1:1, pp. 7–32.

Honderich T. (1995) *The Oxford Companion to Philosophy*. Oxford: Oxford University Press.

Kennedy E. (2008) "Socialist Feminism: What Difference Did It Make to the History of Women's Studies". *Feminist Studies*. Vol. 34:3, pp. 497–525.

Lerner G. (1986) *The Creation of Patriarchy*. Oxford: Oxford University Press.

Lerner G. (1991) *The Creation of Feminist Consciousness: From the Middle Age to 1870*. Oxford: Oxford University Press.

Lundberg S. (2008) "Gender and Household Decision-Making". Bettio F. and Verashchagina A. (Eds.) *Frontiers in the Economics of Gender*. London: Routledge, pp. 116–133.

Madden K. (2019) "Anecdotes of Discrimination". Madden K. and Dimand R. (Eds.) *Routledge Handbook of the History of Women's Economic Thought*. London: Routledge, pp. 169–190.

Madden K. and Dimand R. (Eds.) (2019) *Routledge Handbook of the History of Women's Economic Thought*. London: Routledge.

Mill J.S. (1869) *The Subjection of Women*. London: Longmans, Green, Reader, and Dyer.

Mincer J. (1962) "Labor Force Participation of Married Women: A Study of Labor Supply". Lewis G.H. (Ed.) *Aspects of Labor Economics*. Princeton, NJ: Princeton University Press, pp. 63–105.

Mincer J. (1974) *Schooling, Experience and Earnings*. New York: Columbia University Press.

Nelson J. (1992) "Gender, Metaphor, and the Definition of Economics". *Economics and Philosophy*. Vol. 8:1, pp. 103–125.

Nelson J. (1993) "Value-free or Valueless? Notes on the Pursuit of Detachment". *History of Political Economy*. Vol. 25:1, pp. 121–145.

Nelson J. (1995) "Feminism and Economics". *Journal of Economic Perspectives*. Vol. 9:2, pp. 131–148.

Nelson J. (1996) *Feminism, Objectivity and Economics*. London: Routledge.

Nussbaum M. (2000) *Women and Human Development: The Capabilities Approach*. Cambridge and New York: Cambridge University Press.

Offen K. (1986) "Ernest Legouvé and the Doctrine of 'Equality in Difference' for Women: A Case Study of Male Feminism in Nineteenth-Century French Thought". The Journal of Modern History. Vol. 58:2, pp. 452–484.

Offen K. (2000) *European Feminism 1700–1950*. Stanford, CA: Stanford University Press.

Rupp L. (1997) *Worlds of Women: The Making of an International Women's Movement*. Princeton, NJ: Princeton University Press.

Rathbone E. (1924) *The Disinherited Family*. London: Edward Arnold.

Schumpeter J.A. (1954) *History of Economic Analysis*. London: Allen & Unwin Publishers.

Woolf V. (1929) *A Room of One's Own*. London: Hogarth Press.

1 The woman question and political economy

The woman question arose dramatically in the 19th century as an application of the principle of the supremacy of individual freedom, which was a milestone within the tradition of classical liberalism, to the conditions of women, who have been traditionally subject to men from a cultural, social, economic, legal, and political point of view. A few scholars, including some women, had previously dealt with the virtuous role of women in the household as a key tenet in the development of a wealthy society. Differently from the French and the British protofeminists, who were much more involved in a vindication of juridical and political rights for women, the Italian protofeminists pointed out the importance of the role of women in economic matters (Ross 2009). Three Italian ladies, Christine de Pizan (1365–1430), Moderata Fonte (1555–1592), and Lucrezia Marinella (1571–1653) were forerunners in focusing their attention on the importance of women's ability to handle the economy of the household as a major achievement for society as a whole. In 1405, de Pizan published a pamphlet, *Livre de la Cité des Dames* (De Pizan 1405 [1999]), to advocate in favor of education for women and to urge women to manage their household in order to get an active role in economic life that would allow them to get some independence in their private life.

During the 17th century, the battle for the equality between sexes was grounded on the debate around the nature of virtues. Supporters of the equality between sexes claimed that virtues were not gender-differentiated: a brave man and a brave woman are equally brave; they actually share the same virtues and they can be equally virtuous in any domain. The scholars who were involved in this debate included Mary de Gournay ([1622] 2002), who was deeply influenced by Montaigne, and the (male) French philosopher Poullain de la Barre (1673). They both insisted on the fact that there were no neurological differences between men and women that would determine different behavior between sexes. Hence, any differentiation between sexes was grounded on an unfair subjection of women. The argument around the nature of virtues was directly linked with the battle for equal education for women, which became the most important goal for the scholars who were engaged in promoting the equality between men and women. The urgency for an equal education between the sexes was directly linked with the request to overcome the pink ghetto of *belles lettres*, which was the only scholarly field women might aspire to become enrolled in if they ever had a chance to get some education.

John Locke was a promoter of gender equality and equal education for both boys and girls (Locke 1693). Locke strongly fought against a long tradition of authors, from Knox to Filmer, who claimed that the subjection of women was natural and in accordance with God's will. John Knox, a Scottish leading Protestant reformer exiled in Geneva, had argued that women were incapable of ruling a kingdom: his pamphlet was directed against the three Catholic queens in charge during his time (Mary I of England; Mary of Guise, Queen Dowager and regent of Scotland; and Mary Queen of Scots [Knox 1558]). A century later, Robert Filmer wrote *Patriarcha, or the Natural Power of Kings* (1680 [1969]). He insisted on the divine origin of monarchical power directly derived from God's will to Adam, who represented the Man and the King. According to Filmer, men being the perpetual symbols of Adam means that husbands are the only legitimate heads of family and that kings are the only legitimate heads of a state. Therefore, women may not have any role in political matters (Butler 1978). Arguing against the detractors of women's ability to be good leaders, Locke underlined that the ability of ruling either a family or a country depends exclusively on intelligence: given that differences between men and women are only physical, Locke denied any differences of mind between the sexes and advocated an identical program of education (Nyland 1993).

The debate around the woman question became central during the Enlightenment, when the promotion of the emancipation of women and equality between the sexes became essential amongst many scholars. In the sixth volume of the *Encyclopedia*, the subjection of women has been depicted as a constructed result of the patriarchy. Women's disadvantages within families and society were publicly recognized, especially within the legal framework and the economic realm, because access to education was denied to women. The debate around the subjection of women led in different directions. First, the emancipation of women was urged in the name of individual natural rights that are equal for both sexes. Second, the peculiarity of some values that were supposed to be feminine, because they were grounded on the emotional sphere, was considered complementary and not inferior to masculine values based on rationality. Third, the role of women as mothers and wives was recognized as fundamental to the development of public utility. In this threefold dimension we can find the roots of what later became the liberal–individualistic version of feminism (grounded on the equality of individuals) as well as the broader version of feminism (based on the specificity of the role of women in society).

During the French Revolution, several associations were founded, such as the *Société fraternelle de l'un et l'autre sexe* as well as the *Société des républicaines révolutionnaires*, and counted more than 200 members, exclusively women.

In 1791, the French feminist Olympe de Gouges (1748–1793) published her *Declaration of the Rights of Woman and the Female Citizen*, and, in 1792, the British writer Mary Wollstonecraft (1757–1797) published *A Vindication of the Rights of Woman*. These two books can be regarded as the first feminist publications in the modern time: their aim was to fight for the juridical and political status of women. They both were milestones in the history of women's emancipation. Fifty years later, John Stuart Mill published *The Subjection of Women* (Mill 1869) for the perfect equality between sexes. Between Wollstonecraft and Mill, the woman question was embedded in political economy: in fact, the battle for women's education started to focus on the necessity to include economic studies. The interconnection between the woman question and political economy spread through two different traditions (classical liberalism and socialism) and specifically in three distinct areas (England; German-speaking countries like Germany and the Austrian Empire; and the United States). Liberal feminism, grounded in the tradition of classical liberalism, was focused on the principle of providing equal opportunities for human beings, indifferently, whether they were men or women: the provision of equal opportunities requires a specific economic and legal framework based on private property intended as a natural right (along with life and liberty).

The literature on feminism has traditionally identified the roots of liberal feminism in the suffragettes' movement in Great Britain and in the abolitionist movement in the United States, while the roots of socialist feminism have been depicted in continental Europe, especially in Germany and Austria, where Marx and his followers mostly influenced cultural elites. This dichotomy is partially misleading. Liberal feminism had a central role everywhere in Europe of the 19th century: from *fin de siècle* Vienna (where a Jewish component with its strong assimilationist tendency strengthened this thread) to Victorian England; from the Second Empire in France to the German *Gründerzeit*. Early feminism was a matter of liberal middle-class women, embedded in their moral and cultural bourgeoisie values, under which both individual rights and social order were incorporated.

The connection between the woman question and socialism mainly arose during the late 19th century, when many feminist activists, influenced either by social democracy or by Marxism, embedded the woman question in a deep criticism of capitalism. Socialist feminism, rooted on the contribution of Saint-Simon and Fourier, was focused on the idea that of the emancipation of humanity from capitalistic structures would have eradicated women's subjection in both private and public life.

1.1 Women economists in Great Britain between classical liberalism and Fabianism

Regardless of their political identity, both classical liberal feminists and socialist feminists intended the role of education on political economy and economic matters to be central in the process of women's emancipation. During the 18th century, women started to join the debate around the nature of political economy, a new discipline that was emerging from moral philosophy. Lady Mary Wortley Montagu (1689–1762) exchanged some thoughts with James Steuart about his book, *An Inquiry into the Principles of Political Economy* (Steuart 1767), and she invited him to admit the possibility that women could be active in economic matters and useful to the prosperity of their country. Priscilla Wakefield (1751–1832) wrote several books to promote women's economic emancipation as a benefit to both women and society as a whole. Wakefield's *Reflection on the Present Condition of the Female Sex; with Suggestions for its Improvement* (Wakefield [1798] 2015) aimed to promote women's education and financial independence and was directly and explicitly inspired by Adam Smith (Dimand 2003).

Mary Wollstonecraft opened up the feminist tradition within British classical liberalism: she was rightly defined as "the first feminist republican" (Halldenius 2016). Unlike other thinkers such as the already-mentioned moralists Priscilla Wakefield and Hannah More (1745–1833), she addressed the inequality between sexes not simply as a matter of morality but as a matter of political and legal rights. In *A Vindication of the Rights of Women* ([1792] 1994), Wollstonecraft replied to Jean-Jacques Rousseau's *Emile*. In his novel, Rousseau proposed that a girl's education should aim to make her supportive of her well-educated husband. According to Wollstonecraft, Rousseau's attitude, grounded on the fact that privileged and educated men systematically denied education and autonomy to women, may be regarded as the major enemy of women's emancipation. Wollstonecraft wanted to destroy the traditional complementarity between the stereotype of an emotional, intuitive, and tender woman and the stereotype of a rational, ambitious, and strong man (Todd 2014; Botting 2016).

Wollstonecraft's legacy was central in Jane Austen (1775–1817): in Austen's *Persuasion*, the author perceived feminine traits (emotions, feelings, and so forth) not as natural, but as the inevitable effects of social constraints. Furthermore, in Austen's *Pride and Prejudice*, the role of education for girls was a central vindication of women's emancipation (Brown 1973). Furthermore, Wollstonecraft influenced 19th-century popularizers of political economy, like Jane Marcet (1769–1858) and Harriet Martineau (1802–1876), who strategically highlighted the fact that gender norms had constantly and systematically reinforced women's subjection by influencing social institutions and had affected the traditional ideals of femininity. For instance, marriage was the only way for women to get access to any kind of resources, but married women were completely subject to their husbands. Following the earlier suggestions by Marcet and Martineau, women economists during the 19th century were specifically focused on the economics of marriage and domestic economy and on women's access to the labor market and professions.

1.1.1 The classical liberal tradition during Victorianism

During Queen Victoria's reign (1837–1901), British women were traditionally forced within the rhetoric of marriage and family as the only way for their fulfilment and were subject to men from any legal and material perspective. The major obstacle to women's economic emancipation was the unequal access to education between the sexes. Women were barred from universities, clubs, and scholarly societies involved in the formation of leadership. Their education was only focused on female accomplishments, which included foreign languages, literature, and art. These topics aimed to prepare future middle-class and upper-class wives and mothers, but had the effect of marginalizing women from public debates on economic and political matters (Rostek 2014; 2019).

The relationship between Victorian feminism and educational reform was very complex: education was a central point in the woman question's agenda before the organization of any official women's movement, but the foundation of girls' school and women's colleges involved individuals who not necessarily claimed the feminist stance. The classical liberal elite was the main promoter of equal education for girls and boys, but in many cases, the battle for higher education did not involve women's political emancipation. The case of Emily Davies (1830–1921) was emblematic: Davies founded the first residential women's college, but she was against female suffrage. However, if not all educational promoters were feminists, all feminists claimed that women need to get a higher education in order to improve society as a whole, by challenging the traditional model of the bourgeois family, which included the stereotypical role of wives who were engaged neither in household nor in professional jobs (Schwartz 2011).

A major aim of women activists during Victorianism was the proposal of a significant reform of young women's education, which included the introduction of boarding schools, the training of women teachers, and the gradual access to university education for women (Mallett 2016a, 2016b). In 1870, the Married Women's Property Act created a major change in 19th-century British property law. The act granted British women the right to own and control personal property and dramatically increased the bargaining power and the amount of properties of married women (Combs 2006). This legal change in married women's property rights facilitated a growing female role in investment. As Robb (1992) pointed out, in England during the 19th century, a consistent group of women made relevant investments in income, capital growth, or a share in the family business. Mostly ignored by scholars, women as investors were especially active in the stock market (Rutterford and Maltby 2006).

Sophie de Grouchy (1764–1822), Jane Haldimand Marcet (1769–1858), and Harriet Martineau (1802–1876) were the first women to explicitly write about political economy. Mainly inspired by Smith, Ricardo, and Malthus, they were engaged in the popularization of the economic principles of the classical school.

De Grouchy, Condorcet's wife, translated Adam Smith's *Theory of Moral Sentiments* into French in 1798 and placed much emphasis on the role of sympathy (Forget 2003). In her *Letters of Sympathy* (de Grouchy 1798[2019]), de Grouchy describes the mechanism of sympathy as relevant in explaining the development of political institutions. Marcet wanted to popularize political economy among common people. Her aim was to promote a free-market education for girls by following the economic thought of Smith, Ricardo, and Malthus. In 1816, Marcet published her *Conversations in Political Economy* (Marcet 1816), which became a bestseller, reaching 14 editions (Marcuzzo and Rosselli 2008). Ricardo appreciated her work and gave her some advice for a second edition; Macaulay, McCulloch, Say, and Malthus praised her book as well. In 1833, she wrote a collection of stories on economic issues intended to improve the working classes' conditions (Marcet 1833).

Like Marcet, Martineau was committed to an enlargement of economics education: she popularized economic knowledge through narrative. Between 1832 and 1834, Martineau published her *Illustrations of Political Economy* in nine volumes to promote liberal principles through an economic narrative. Martineau's publication gave her financial independence as well as enormous popularity. In Martineau's book, women played the role either of readers of the *Illustrations* or characters within the tales. They were depicted as fundamental elements of the economic process. Furthermore, they were considered potential economists: "till their day of emancipation arrives, till the customs of society shall allow them the natural rights of men and women, the power of social exertion, and the enjoyment of social independence" (Martineau 2018, 112). Martineau's works had been praised by James Mill, John Ramsay McCullogh, and John Stuart Mill.

Marcet and Martineau shared the ideal of making political economy accessible to the working class and to women. Although sometimes they preached rather than taught, their efforts represented the first attempt to embed political economy as a fundamental part of the ordinary educational system in order to promote economic knowledge among ordinary people (Polkinghorn 1995; Dalley 2010).

As it is well known, conditions of workers, either men or women, were particularly tough in Victorian England. In 1848, women's work hours were regulated at 10 hours per day. In the following decades, a wider discussion on factory legislation took place. Among economists involved in the debate, William Jevons made a distinction between married women and mothers and other women as well as between women working in factories and as domestics (Jevons 1883). Influenced by social Darwinism as developed by Herbert Spencer, Jevons claimed that work hours and workplaces should be differentiated according to class, race, and gender, recommending the complete exclusion of mothers from factories (Peart 1996). So he suggested decreasing the range of occupations for married women and mothers whose main duty was to take care of their families at home and eventually to help their husbands with an extramural job that would not affect their family duties (White 1994). Like Jevons, Alfred Marshall was hostile to the modern conception of women: he argued that women have different mental attitudes, which prevents them from theoretical works; thereafter, they cannot be valuable professionals. Furthermore, as he considered the traditional family a crucial factor in social development, women's role as wives and mothers was fundamentally much more important than their presence within the labor force (Groenewegen 1995).

Arguing against Jevons's and Marshall's attitudes, in his *Principles* (Mill 1848), John Stuart Mill blamed any factory legislation that limited women's work and regarded it to be the traditional idea of women as subject to men. In his *The Subjection of Women* (Mill 1869), Mill explored patriarchy and slavery as expressions of the collective self-interest of the dominant group in society, who used legal framework, political structures, and cultural pressure to institutionalize their power and to force gender inequality, women being compared to slaves (Folbre 2009). Mill insisted on the fact that women's individual liberty in workplaces as well as in the political arena should be granted and it would make society better off as a whole (Mill 1869). The divergence between Jevons, Marshall, and Mill about the sexual division of labor emerged in their different theories of negative externalities of married women's work: "while Mill rejects the laws on women's work as unfair and conflicting with [individual] utility, Jevons affirms that [social] utility justifies the sacrifice of women's liberty of work" (Gouverneur 2013, 771).

John Stuart Mill's works (1859; 1869) were fundamental for the women's parliamentary vote campaign in Britain.[1] His own campaign to be elected to Westminster in 1865 may be considered as the beginning of women's struggle for suffrage: votes for women were in fact a central point in his election address (Purvis 2016). The suffragettes' goal was reached only in 1918 (for married women over 30 years old) and finally in 1928 for every adult woman regardless of their marital status.

The publication of Mill's *The Subjection of Women* made the woman question central to the national and international debate. Reprinted in New York and Philadelphia and translated into many European languages, it represented a milestone for classical liberal feminism (Hekman 1992; Donner 1993; Szapuova 2006) and also paved the way for more radical forms of feminism (Nussbaum 2010).[2]

Deeply influenced by his life-partner and wife, Harriet Hardy Taylor Mill (1807–1858), Mill advocated freedom of individual choice as "the only thing that leads to the adoption of the best processes, and puts each operation into the hands of those who are best qualified for it" (Mill 1869, 11).[3] Harriet Taylor's contribution to Mill's *Principles* can be identified as a perfect mix of classical liberalism and utilitarianism: she adopted utilitarian principles to support a complete free access to the labor market for women and men. Firmly convinced that gender roles were socially determined, Harriet Taylor Mill supported women's access to the labor market because their presence would have broken the male monopoly in the labor market and would have increased the general level of competition within society. Taylor Mill had certainly influenced her husband when he affirmed that restrictions to women's employment and economic dependence were the results of patriarchy.

Although John Stuart Mill endorsed equality between sexes in labor market, he clearly claimed that, once married, a middle-class woman must choose to devote herself to being a wife and a mother. Mill's position was a typical case of the Victorian bias applied to gender roles within families. Diverging from her husband, Harriet Taylor Mill insisted on the importance of married women earning their own income. In her *The Enfranchisement of Women* (Taylor Mill 1851), she demanded: "*education* in primary and high schools, universities, medical, legal, and theological institutions; *partnership* in the labors and gains, risks and remunerations, of productive industry; and a *coequal share* in the formation and administration of laws – municipal, state, and national – through legislative assemblies, courts, and executive offices" (Taylor Mill [1851] 1994, 179, author's emphasis).

According to Taylor Mill, any social restriction on women, such as being segregated into motherhood, prevented them from maximizing their happiness. She applied classical philosophical liberalism in favor of women's economic equality and self-determination that is made possible by a proper education and training. A proper education included the necessity to get rid of the gender stereotypes, internalized by both men and women, upon which patriarchy was rooted. She insisted on the necessity to reduce any possible gender wage gap in order to raise the general level of productivity that would be increased by women's multitasking abilities (Pujol 1992, 2000).

Among women activists who were clearly influenced by Harriet Taylor Mill, Barbara Leigh Smith Bodichon (1827–1891) authored several pamphlets concerning women's suffrage as well as education, legal rights, and economic conditions of women. In her *Women and Work* (Bodichon 1857), she supported gender equal pay by introducing the principle that women and men share the same attitude and motivations when they choose to work. Their motivations include necessity, self-fulfillment, and greed. She denounced the gender–educational gap and men's monopoly over the most remunerative jobs as a determinant of job discrimination. Furthermore, Bodichon rejected the idea, according to which women workers would have stolen jobs from men by implementing the consequence of Say's law: "along with Mill, she developed the notion of overcrowding of women, arguing that the surplus of women workers drove down their wages, but only because of the laws, rules, and customs that restricted women's entry into the workforce" (Sockwell 2000, 55).

Bodichon fought against the Victorian bias according to which women are naturally weak and she challenged the patriarchal claim that married women did not need a job, being under their fathers' or husbands' protection and responsibility. Bodichon promoted her ideas by opening up her own school for girls and by getting involved in the Women's Employment Bureau (1858) which aimed to fight women's exclusion from trade unionism and factory legislation, such as the Factory Act (1870), and against any form of the gender wage gap (Pujol 1992).

Along with Matilda Mary Hays and Bessie Rayner Parkes, Bodichon founded the monthly periodical *English Women Journal* (1858–1864), to promote female employment. The journal had a major influence on many women activists interested in economic emancipation, such as Jessie Boucher-ett (1825–1905), who promoted a campaign for nontraditional occupations for women. Along with Adelaide Ann Procter (1825–1864), Boucherett was the founder of the Society for Promoting the Employment of Women (1859). The two pals joined the Langham Place Group, a circle led by Bodichon and aimed at improving women's education and employment across all classes (Fraser et al. 2003).

Among classical liberal early feminists who strongly supported women's education as a tool to prevent any form of exploitation, there was Josephine Grey Butler (1828–1906), the first British antiprostitution campaigner. In her book, *The Education and Employment of Women* (1868), Butler underlined the fact that women's economic and social repression was due to their lack of education. In the late 1860s, she started to observe lower-class women in Liverpool: they usually turned to prostitution mainly because of their difficulties feeding their children. In 1868, Butler started a campaign against the *Contagious Diseases Acts* (introduced some years earlier to permit police to put prostitutes in military towns, often for several weeks, to test them for venereal diseases). The *Acts* were repealed only in 1886 thanks to Butler's long-lasting efforts. She also introduced *the Criminal Law Amendment Act*, issued in 1885, which raised the age of consent in sexual acts for girls from 13 to 16 (Jordan and Sharp 2003).

Among classical liberal women economists, Helen Dendy Bosanquet (1860–1925) strongly stressed the importance of women's education and on access to labor as well as on the equal wage level between men and women (Akkerman 1998; Groenegewen 2000). Much more influenced by Thomas Green than by John Stuart Mill, she was an influential member of the Charity Organization Society,[4] an association devoted to launching liberal values and to the struggle for limitation of government intervention, against programs based on state charity. In her major book, she explained that the only way for poor people to get a higher standard of life is based on education and freedom, not on charity (Bosanquet 1902).

Following her classical liberal principles, Bosanquet put more emphasis on the subjective aspects rather than the objective of social phenomena to explain them. For example, she specifically rejected Charles Booth's theory, which refused the idea that the majority of the poor were immoral (Booth 1889), and she enumerated the lack of personality among the most significant causes of unemployment (Bosanquet 1909). According to Bosanquet, a weak personality is partially the effect of a lack of proper education, which especially damages growing-up girls. Hence her efforts were specifically driven by her concern about women's educations and economic conditions: she anticipated the theory of human and social capital by pointing out the fact that an increase of educated women will better not only women's conditions (by reducing the gender labor gap) but also the society as a whole.

However, Bosanquet was not immune from Victorianism. In fact, she promoted women's development only for unmarried women: in her book on family and household, she clearly stated that married women should consider their role of good wives as the most important contribution to the well-being of the society. Not by chance, Bosanquet approved women's suffrage only for unmarried women, married women being automatically represented by their husbands (Bosanquet 1906).

Contrary to Bosanquet, Millicent Garrett Fawcett (1847–1929), a nonacademic economist, was a major leader of the women's suffrage and she did not consider any difference between married and unmarried women (Pujol 1992; Pujol and Seitz 2000; Groenewegen 2000). In her essays on political economy, she dealt with the importance of women's education, arguing against the tendency of parents to consider investment in education as a valid and proper choice only for sons, and to avoid any investment in education for daughters bound not to work once they get married.

Against this commonly shared patriarchal attitude, Fawcett wrote several articles that dealt with gender labor gap and gender wage gap (Fawcett 1892, 1917, 1918a, 1918b) and she engaged a debate with Sidney Webb in *The Economic Journal*. Webb had claimed that the gender wage gap was the inevitable consequence of the general inferiority of women in terms of quantity and quality of labor provided by them (Webb S. 1891). Fawcett's reply was centered on the fact that women's lower performance in labor was due to the peculiar way the labor market had relegated women to low-wage jobs, by creating *de facto* an occupational segregation, as well as to some distorted trade unions' policy of exclusion (Fawcett 1892, 1917). The debate on equal pay went on in the pages of *The Economic Journal* and was dominated at the beginning by women economists: besides Fawcett, Heather-Bigg, Beatrice Webb, and Eleanor Rathbone were other major figures involved. In an article by Ada Heather-Bigg (1855–1944), she denounced men's attitude opposing women's employment as an attempt to protect their dominant status:

> It is clear that something else moves [men] than 'mere dread that maternal and household duties may be neglected. Analyzing carefully, we find that what they object to is the wage-earning not the work of wives. Homework enables a married woman to become joint earner with her husband, and they profess to fear that facilities in this direction may lead to the gradual substitution of the wife for the husband as breadwinner. ... It is indisputable that women of the working classes always have been joint earners with their husbands. At no time in the world's history has the man's labour alone sufficed for the maintenance of his wife and children. ... Though women did not earn wages for all the multifarious occupations which 'looking after the home' formerly involved, it is clear they did as much of the necessary work of the world as they do now. If, then, the fallacy that there is a limited amount of work to be obtained, and that the more the women take the less the men get, be supposed true, it is certain that female labour competed as much with male labour heretofore as now. The only difference was that each woman took an infinitesimal share of a great many different kinds of work ...

So long as the wife must contribute her quota to family maintenance, it is distinctly advisable that she should be allowed to do this in the way she herself finds least irksome.

(Heather-Bigg 1894, 55–58)

Heather-Bigg's explicit attack on patriarchy was the first feminist article ever published in an academic economic journal. Against Heather-Bigg's and Fawcett's voices for equal pay, Beatrice Webb and Eleanor Rathbone shared, for different reasons, a critical attitude towards equal pay. Eleanor Rathbone (1872–1946), much more influenced by family allowance issues than by the woman question, claimed that equal pay would have determined women's exclusion from skilled jobs; therefore, she supposed a differentiated wage system and a form of state subsidy for motherhood, which implicitly reinforced the stereotype of feminine role in society (Rathbone 1917). Beatrice Webb was convinced that equal pay was a threat to the standard of living of the working class and instead promoted state regulation of the sweating system (Webb 1896). Rathbone saw the formula as a 'trap' set by the trade union movement to decrease women's employment (Chassonnery-Zaïgouche 2019). Beatrice Webb never fully endorsed equal pay for equal work, it being irrelevant for the majority of women who were forced into separate jobs and were struggling for a minimum wage as well as for better working conditions. According to Beatrice Webb, the only possible condition to better women's status was to let them join trade unions and to put woman question in trade unions' general agenda of social reforms.

As Pujol rightly pointed out, the differences between Fawcett, Rathbone, and Webb depended on their political orientation: Fawcett belonged to classical liberal feminism's rooted on the principle of equal rights; Rathbone, "politically unaligned", switched from classical liberal positions towards "welfare socialism"; Webb, a founder of Fabianism, considered the woman question subordinate to the gradual socialism project (Pujol 1992, 91).

The debate on equal pay involved male economists as well, such as Alfred Marshall, Arthur Cecil Pigou, and Francis Edgeworth.

Alfred Marshall, who had dealt with the woman question in economic matters in his *Principles* (1890), was opposed to employment for married women and proposed a family wage paid to husbands by the state. Marshall also promoted a reform of the educational system able to improve the supply of the skilled male labor force. According to Marshall, women's employment was detrimental because it reduced the time they might spend in childbearing and, consequently, reduced the investment in human capital to better society. Marshall insisted on the fact that women should be educated not to be more competitive in the labor market, but to be more careful in contributing to the human capital investment of their children. Hence Marshall endorsed the gender wage gap, women's lower wages being an incentive to stay at home.

Later, Pigou (1920) presented a notion of wages based on marginal productivity and not on subsistence requirements. According to Pigou, the common idea that women are paid less than men because their salaries support only themselves while men's salaries support the whole family is fallacious. Nevertheless, Pigou justified lower pay for women ('unfair wages'): quoting Marshall, he developed a general national human capital investment policy restricted to men's skills because women are bound to nonmarket reproductive work.

In two articles published on *The Economic Journal*, Edgeworth (1922, 1923) seemed to promote an enlargement of the possibilities in the job market for women, but like Marshall and Pigou, he questioned women's abilities and justified unequal wage (Pujol 1992).

To sum up: enthusiastic followers of pure Victorianism, while promoting a wider education for everyone, and male economists, who coped with equal pay debate, exiled women to their domestic duties: women should be granted a better education for its own sake but not as a tool to achieve economic independence, as they are bounded to childbearing and eventually to domestic work. The position of Marshall's wife, Mary Paley Marshall (1850–1944), is emblematic. She was involved in economic education through her activity as a teacher of political economy at the extramural courses program for women at Oxford. She worked there since the early 1880s, until her retirement from public life 40 years later. Education for the Marshalls was not intended to be a tool for women's economic emancipation, but rather to be a part of the broader theory of human capital that relegated women to the role of good wives and mothers.

It is important to note that until the First World War, in Great Britain the urgency of education for girls was a complicated issue for several reasons. First, the debate was limited to middle-class girls, while lower class girls were not even intended to be subjected to any form of education. Second, schools and colleges functioned as conservative organizations, by nurturing conventional values about women's role in society. This complexity has been well explained by Clara Collet (1860–1948) in her book on educated working women (Collet 1902), reviewed by Mary Paley Marshall the same year it was published (Paley Marshall 1902). According to Collet, working-class girls were bounded to get married so needed to be trained only in domestic labor, while middle-class girls, who might face a much more uncertain future, need to be trained at higher educational institutions in order to get a chance to become economically independent. So Collet concluded that women's wages should be above a minimum standard and women's education should be raised in order to better women's standard of life as well as women workers' efficiency. Collet's conclusion was an application of Alfred Marshall's theory of salary efficiency to women workers (Groenewegen 1994).

1.1.2 The socialist tradition between Fabianism and Guildism

In the late 19th century, the woman question became popular among British socialists too. The socialist economist William Thompson and the feminist writer Anna Doyle Wheeler were forerunners of woman-question matters in the socialist tradition. In 1825, they jointly published *Appeal of One Half the Human Race, Women, Against the Pretension of the Other Half, Men, to Retain Them in Political, and thence in Civil and Domestic, Slavery*, the most powerful attack on the patriarchy since Wollstonecraft's (Thompson and Wheeler 1825). Thompson and Wheeler wrote the *Appeal* as a reply to James Mill's argument that women did not need political representation because their fathers or husbands represented their interests well enough (Mill 1820). In their *Appeal*, the authors presented motherhood as the primary cause of women's social inferiority. Even in a hypothetically equal society, motherhood would force women to perform unremunerated reproductive labor. Contrary to Wollstonecraft, who advocated emancipation in the name of motherhood, Thompson and Wheeler (1825) perceived that motherhood intrinsically disadvantaged women, at least under capitalism, since capitalists spoil women's free labor as mothers.

In Great Britain, socialist women economists belonged to a political tradition that was far away from Marxism and was much closer to a gradual form of socialism that was grounded on Robert Owen's socialism and traditional Christian socialism.

Among socialist women economists in Great Britain, Beatrice Potter Webb (1858–1943) gained a special place. Her political position was an authentic example of the British spirit mainly shaped and influenced by Owen's cooperativism. Webb wrote that during the initial stage of the first Industrial Revolution, two opposite philosophical tendencies spread: universal competition, supported by Adam Smith and his followers, and the cooperative system, led by Owen, "the Don Quixote of the cotton trade".[5] According to Webb, Owen's merit was to have underlined that the human natural principle upon which a prosperous society might be built is not competition but cooperation. Therefore, she decided to devote her first work to the cooperative movement in the United Kingdom that she regarded as the most important democratic element within British society (Webb 1891). During the 1890s, Beatrice Webb joined the Fabian Society, which had been founded in 1884 by Sidney Webb (Beatrice's husband), George Bernard Shaw, and Graham Walls. Far from continental socialism, and Marxism in particular, Fabians stood for a gradual set of reforms whose final aim was the socialist society, to be reached not by a revolution but through a self-transformation based upon a new ethics able to involve any single citizen and community member.[6]

Beatrice Webb's initial contributions between 1887 and 1892 were a series of articles on the sweating labor system in East London. Originated by the 'evil spirit' of capitalism, the sweating system had worsened women's conditions of life because women were forced to spend too much hours in factories, which made them unable to take care of their families at home[7] (Webb 1888). Webb proposed a more rigid regulation of working hours for women whose essential role was connected to their presence at home and promoted a minimum standard of economic comfort for women workers who were forced into a system that had terrible effects on their lives (Webb 1888). In Webb's vision of women's roles within families, the influence of Victorianism is evident. Women workers had to be protected by a special legislation against *sweating labor* (Webb 1891, 1901). According to Webb, when factory legislation in the cotton and mining industries was introduced in the 1830s, the conditions of workers were better off, profits increased, and a general improvement at national stage occurred. Beatrice Webb insisted that the same results would occur in case of regulation of women workers in other industrial sectors: similar to Marshall's formulation of efficiency–salary, Beatrice underlined that an improvement in women workers' conditions or a rise in women's wages would have been a benefit for the nation as a whole. In 1890s, Beatrice proposed to amend the Factory Act with some specific clauses to better women's working conditions; she claimed that evidence had proved that the extension of factory legislation as well as wage regulation had broadened the employment opportunities for women and an improvement of women's conditions had made the system more efficient (Webb and Webb 1897; Webb 1901, 1920).

A further and ineludible step toward a better regulation of the sweating system should have included the possibility for women workers to join the unions: Beatrice Webb pointed out that, in the 1890s, only 100,000 out of 3 million women workers had joined the unions and she denounced the weakness of unionism in the country (Webb and Webb 1894). According to Beatrice Webb, the combination of specific factory legislation for women workers and their membership in trade unions would gradually have led them to political emancipation, which was seen as a direct consequence of their economic and social emancipation.

Against Webb's battle to extend factory legislation, many classical liberal feminists, such as Millicent Fawcett, fought for so-called 'equal right' feminism, grounded on the classical liberal tradition, and explicitly endorsed gender neutrality as a major form of women's emancipation. Many classical liberal activists preferred to fight for the extension of suffrage to women as an ineludible priority. Regarding women's suffrage, in 1889, Beatrice Webb wrote an article against it. Things changed a few years later. In 1906, she publicly wrote to Fawcett to endorse women's suffrage, because she realized that "the state was failing to give women adequate support in those areas she considered the particular province of her sex – 'the rearing of children, the advancement of learning, and the promotion of spiritual life'" (Nyland and Ramia 1994, 129).

In 1908, along with some other women economists within the Fabian Society, Beatrice Webb founded the Fabian Women's Group "to further the principle of equal citizenship within and without the Society, and second to 'study women's economic independence in relation to socialism'" (Alexander 2013, 5).[8] They all converged in maintaining that, from an economic perspective, women, as family members, were subordinate to family male figures, and as workers, were relegated to unskilled and sweatshop laborers. In 1913, the Webbs founded a newspaper, *The New Statesman*, used by Beatrice as a tool for promoting women's emancipation, by hosting several articles by Fawcett and many more activists of both side of the political spectrum. Mabel Atkinson (1876–1958) summed up the conditions of women's emancipation movements in Great Britain in the late 19th century as follows:

> [On one hand there is] the movement of the middle class women who are revolting against their exclusion from human activity and insisting, firstly, on their right to education... secondly, on their right to earn a livelihood for themselves, ... and, thirdly, on their right to share in the control of Government, the point round which the fight is now most fiercely raging. These women are primarily rebelling against the sex-exclusiveness of men, and regard independence and the right to work as the most valuable privilege to be striven for. On the other hand, there are the women of the working classes, who have been faced with a total different problem, and who naturally react in a different way. ... What the woman of the proletariat feels as her grievance is that her work is too long and too monotonous, the burden laid upon her too heavy. Moreover, in her case that burden is due to the power of capitalistic exploitation resulting from the injustice of our social system. ... Therefore, among the working women there is less sex consciousness. ...) The working woman feels her solidarity with the men of her class rather than their antagonism to her.
>
> (Atkinson 2013, 270)

Fabian women belonged to the second group. First-generation Fabian women economists had focused their efforts on challenging the traditional view of women as wives and mothers. Following Mill's book, *The Subjection of Women*, Rosalind Nash (1862–1952) developed analogies between working-class women's marriages and slaves and servants: in both groups individual freedom of their members was constrained by the impossibility to negotiate conditions and this mechanism was reinforced by legislation and by social pressure (Madden and Persky 2019). Bessie Hutchins (1858–1935) wrote a systematic treatment of the subject of protective labor in order to influence public opinion on the conditions of home work legislation (Hutchins and Harrison 1903). In her pamphlet *Home Work and Sweating: The Causes and the Remedies* (Hutchins 1907), she promoted the introduction of a minimum wage and minimum income for unemployed people.

A generation later, Margaret Cole (1893–1980), who played a leading role in the history of British feminism within the Guild movement (a form of syndicalism founded by her husband G. D. H. Cole),[9] was deeply engaged in the reform of the educational system in order to eliminate the double system of public and state school. Her major efforts were devoted to the elimination of the gender gap in any field (Cole 1946). According to Cole, universal suffrage, which was gained in 1918, was not enough to build a fair society that would guarantee the same opportunities for everybody: without any legislation against sexual discrimination, inequality would persist, and among several forms of inequality, gender wage gap was the most dangerous and unfair.

The Women's Co-operative Guild for the advancement of women in society was founded in 1899 and led by its major member, Margaret Llewelyn Davies (1861–1944), until 1921. Its purpose was to prepare a reform program focused on several aims: the proposal of minimum wage for women employed in cooperatives; the introduction of some new forms of credit to reduce poverty among women; the establishment of women as owners of co-operatives; and the eradication of women's marginalization in the household. The Women's Co-operative Guild fought for the establishment of a minimum wage in the co-operative movement and for the extension of co-operative retailing to poorer communities. Against working class women's isolation and dependency, the Women's Co-operative Guild promoted state-supported maternity benefits. Both Virginia and Leonard Woolf had been active in the Women's Co-operative Guild; Virginia Woolf wrote the Preface to Davies' *Life as We Have Known It* (Davies 1931; Wood 2014).

A turning point in the history of the connection between women's emancipation and political economy was the introduction of women as faculty members at the London School of Economics (LSE). Founded in 1895 by the Fabian Society, LSE had always admitted women to college, unlike Oxford and Cambridge, which officially admitted women students in 1920 and 1948 respectively (Tullberg 1998). Founders of LSE were particularly interested in developing an economic knowledge oriented to social reform and economic history, which implied a historical reconstruction of women's economic and social conditions (Pomata 2004).

The first generation of women economists at LSE mainly worked in the research field of economic history. The first woman to work as adjunct professor at LSE was Gertrude Tuckwell (1861–1951), who gave six lectures on factory legislation in 1896. In 1905, Tuckwell became President of the Women's Trade Union League and was involved in the foundation of the British section of the League, along with Sidney Webb (Hunt 2013). Later, Eileen Power (1889–1940) and Eleanora Carus-Wilson (1897–1977) became professors of economic history, while Elizabeth Levett (1881–1932), after a time as a reader in economic history, became professor of history at the University of London. Eileen Power founded the Economic History Society in 1926 and the *Economic History Review* in 1927. Among faculty members at LSE, Lilian Knowles (1870–1926) was the first full-time lecturer, then professor of economic history (1920), and, finally, dean of the Department of Economics (1920–24). Knowles worked on the consequences of industrialization for women (Knowles 1921) and supervised many female young economists (Vera Anstey, Ivy Pinchberk, Mabel Buer, Julia Mann, Dorothy Marshall, M. G. Jones, Dorothy George, B. L. Hutchins, Amy Harrison, Mildred Bulkley, Alice Clarke, and Alice Murray).[10]

LSE's women economic historians were mainly engaged in a debate on the effects of industrialization from the first Industrial Revolution to First World War. This debate was influenced by their shared involvement to the women's suffrage campaign as well as by their commitment in the League of Nations. A major core of their economic research was also focused on social policy and women's employment (Berg 1992). Economic history as a major research field was common to academic women economists before and during the interwar period, not only in Great Britain but also in Austria and Germany, as will be shown in the next paragraph.

1.2 The woman question in Austria and Germany: Jewishness and political economy

Between the 19th century and early 20th century, the history of the interconnection between the woman question and political economy in German-speaking countries was very similar to the British situation: middle-class women, who traditionally had been excluded by higher education, fought for access to universities and to get enrolled in nontraditional educational fields, which included political economy. Contrary to the situation in Great Britain, several Austrian and German female students had been able to get their Ph.D. in Switzerland, which had opened the door of academia to women in the 1860s. When they got back to their countries, many of them were able to start their own careers. For example, the Viennese Gabriele Possanner von Ehrenthal (1869–1940) got her Ph.D. in medicine in Zurich (1894). Back in Vienna, however, she was not allowed to practice, as her Swiss Ph.D. was not valid in Austria. Hence, the Rector of the University of Vienna, Prof. Leo Reinisch, who was a fierce supporter of women's rights, organized for her a second examination before a Viennese committee in order to make her able to work in the country. She succeeded and in 1897 became the first woman to officially get a Ph.D. in medicine at the University of Vienna and the first female doctor in the Hapsburg Empire.

In this process of progressive education, many similarities and differences occurred between Austria (known the Hapsburg Empire up to the First World War and the Austrian Republic between 1918 and 1938) and Germany (known as the German Empire between 1871 and 1918, the Republic of Weimar between 1919 and 1933, and the Third Reich between 1933 and 1945). A common feature of women activists in both Austria and Germany was the fact that they belonged to the Jewish middle class.

Between the last phase of the Hapsburg Empire and the collapse of Austrian Republic under Nazis' annexation, the *Anschluss* (1938), Austrian women activists fought for their inclusion in public life. Initially, they were mainly involved in the cultural battle focused on equal access to the educational system at the highest level as well as on access to political economy and political science traditionally precluded to women. Like in Great Britain, the struggle for women suffrage came later and was pursued by classical liberal activists such as Ernestine Kisch von Fürth (1877–1946), who was one of the most influential activists of women's political rights among the assimilated Austrian Jewish middle class. In 1906, she founded the women's suffrage committee along with Leopoldine Glöckel (1871–1937). The establishment of a women's suffrage association initially was discouraged because of the persistence of a state law that prohibited women from joining any kind of associations. Fürth also was a leading participant in the convening of the first Austrian women's suffrage conference in Vienna, which was held in March 1912, and the leader of the *Frauenstimmrechtskomitee* (Committee for Women's Suffrage), which was active between 1906 and 1918. Jointly with Hertha Jäger (1879–1970) and Ludwig Wittgenstein's sister, Clara (1850–1935), Fürth was a member of the *Neuer Wiener Frauenclub*. Her son, the lawyer and economist Josef Herbert Fürth, was well acquainted with Ludwig von Mises and Friedrich August von Hayek. In 1938, mother and son fled in the United States because of racial laws against Jews.

Liberalism in both Austria and Germany went under attack at the end of the 19th century when pan-Germanism nationalism emerged in German-speaking countries' bourgeoisie. Spattered with anti-Semitism, the Austrian Christian Social Party, led by the populist and anti-elitist Karl Lueger, gained control to the City Hall of Vienna in 1897 and seized power to 1910. In Germany, Schönerer's nationalistic movement arose in the same period.

Although at least until 1919 remnants of the former liberal party persisted, either as unreconstructed liberals or as the progressive liberals, during the interwar period, Austrian and German liberalism suddenly split apart and left many Jews politically homeless and ready to diverge towards the political left (either in the Social-Democratic Party or in the Communist Party), or, alternatively, toward Hertz's Zionism. In fact, neither Lueger's Christian Party nor Schönerer's Pan-Germanism were proper options for Jews (Schorske 1981).

1.2.1 *The classical liberal tradition in Austria and the Austrian school women economists*

The connection between Jewishness and early Austrian women activists and economists was determinant within both the classical liberal tradition and socialist tradition; however, the first group was much more relevant at least until the First World War.

In 1812, the Emperor Franz I issued the Austrian General Civil Code, which granted women legal rights in property and inheritance. Later, the Constitution of 1861 granted wealthy women the right to vote in Lower Austria. Although Austrian women were granted some legal and political rights, they were not allowed to be admitted to universities as regular students at any level, including Ph.D. courses, nor, consequently, to be permitted to work in their field once graduated. Hence, the fight for education in Austria in the second half of the 19th century was seen as a crucial aim of women's emancipation in the Hapsburg Empire.

During the 19th century, the Austrian–Hungarian Empire's public-school system offered girls only the basic education provided by the eight classes of compulsory primary and secondary school (*Volksschule* and *Bürgerschule*). Thereafter, while boys might choose between *Gymnasium* and *Realschule*, which allowed them to get access to academia and to engineering studies respectively, girls were forced to enroll in very expensive private schools to extend their education beyond the basic level they had achieved at the compulsory school. Hence, several private institutions arose and a new type of school for girls, called *Mädchen-Lyzeum*, was established to provide six more years after basic education. However, those new private schools kept girls into the traditional educational pink ghetto. In fact, they did not entitle their female graduates to academic studies: they only allowed access to teaching and to health care professions such as pharmacy.

The first *Lyzeum* for girls in Vienna was founded in 1871 by the *Frauenerwerbsverein*; only in 1892, the *Verein für erweiterte Frauenbildung* established a *gymnasiale Mädchenschule*, a school aimed to prepare girls for their *Matura*, the university-entrance diploma, which students would receive after passing an exam at a public *Gymnasium*. Only in 1897, female students were admitted to the University of Vienna, but their access was limited to the school of philosophy, where they might study philosophy or classical literature. Elise Richter (1865–1943) was the first woman to get a Ph.D. in romance philology at the University of Vienna (1901); in 1907, she also got her *Habilitation*, that is, the *venia docendi*, which allowed her to teach and to officially join the university as a faculty member; however, she had to wait after the First World War, when in 1921 she was the first woman to be appointed associate professor at the University of Vienna. During the 1920s and 1930s, she chaired the Association of Austrian Academic Women. In 1938, because of Nuremberg laws, she was dismissed from her university position and deported to Theresienstadt, where she presumably was killed. The National Socialist regime interrupted the careers of many pioneering women: a gap of almost 50 years separates Richter's habilitation and the next academic appointment of a woman professor at the University of Vienna, which took place in 1956, when the physicist Berta Karlik (1904–1990) got her position as full professor.

In 1902, Marianne Hainisch (1839–1936) founded the *Bund österreichischer Frauenvereine* (*BÖFV*), an organization that unified all the women's liberal associations in the country. Hainisch led the association until 1918. The main focus of *BÖFV* was to secure an extended secondary education for female students. The admission of women students to any academic curriculum was granted only in 1919. Until then, Austrian women activists were not allowed to be enrolled in many curricula, such as political economy, which was taught at the school of law. Therefore, before 1919, women students interested in political economy had to attend specific economics programs, either in Germany, where political economy was taught in the school of philosophy and female students had been admitted since 1897, or in Switzerland, where a free access to any school had been allowed since the 1860s, as previously mentioned. In spite of those limitations and restrictions, an entire generation of Austrian women economists arose. They belonged either to the tradition of classical liberalism (such as the first generation of Austrian school women economists) or to the socialist tradition.

Before describing the story of both groups, it is necessary to better understand the role of Jewishness as a fundamental aspect of women's cultural emancipation in German-speaking countries: Jewishness was in fact a determinant factor in Austrian early feminism and was a relevant element in German early feminism.[11] The connection between Jewishness and the woman question is part of the story of the relationship between Jewishness and civil rights that occurred in the Hapsburg Empire.

The University of Vienna was founded on 1365, but (male) Jews only were allowed to enroll four centuries later, in 1782, when the Emperor Joseph II issued the *Toleranzpatent* (Edict of Tolerance), which allowed them access to the army and let them enter the school of medicine and the school of law (which included economic studies) as regular students. In 1867, the Emperor Franz Joseph granted (male) Jews citizens equal rights at any level, which had been denied for centuries. The immediate consequence was the willingness of Jews to get an education at any level, including academic degrees, with a strong preference for medicine and law.

As a massive literature had described, between the late 19th century and 1919, during the late phase of the Hapsburg Empire, Jews had been symbolized a supranational group embedded in a multiethnic state. Furthermore, any cultural avant-garde in *felix* Austria counted on many Jewish artists and scholars. Jewish bourgeoisies felt the urgency to get actually be involved in the national elite: middle-class Jews were, consciously or unconsciously, fighting for their emancipation from their isolationism, figuratively symbolized by the culture of shtetl. Escaping from the shtetl into a world ruled by Catholicism and anti-Semitism led to an identity crisis, which demanded a redefinition of Jewishness able to balance traditional culture and assimilation. The process of assimilation often was coupled with the rejection of Yiddish as official language and the adoption of Hebrew in classical studies as well as the rejection of Judaism as religion and the adoption of a status of irreligion (*Konfessionlosigkeit*).

For Jews, the university had always been a battleground to gain reputation as persons and citizens; the combination of being a Jew and being a woman made this process even more dramatic. In 1897, during the winter semester, the Faculty of Philosophy of the University of Vienna opened its doors to female students. The immediate effect was that 60% of women enrolled as regular students were Jewish. A similar situation occurred a few years later in the school of medicine and the school of law, where female students were allowed to enroll in 1900 and 1919 respectively.

One of the major reasons for the centrality of Jewishness within that process of emancipation had been recognized as the importance of education to Jews, either assimilated or religious. Literature had explained this phenomenon in many ways that can be collected in the fact that the enormous reputation of knowledge, study, reflections, and any other form of theoretical understanding able to build up a valid set of pragmatic rules had always been the quintessence of Jewish identity. As Stefan Zweig wrote in his *The World of Yesterday*: "the true desire of a Jew, his inbuilt ideal, is to rise to a higher social plane by becoming an intellectual". From a cultural perspective, Jewishness had been identified as the ability to merge a speculative attitude with a practical reasoning in order to define a specific conduct of life in conformity with the Torah and the Talmud. Regardless of their economic conditions, three-year-old Jewish kids were required to be enrolled to the *cheder* (a religious primary school for boys). The Singer brothers' novels as well as Peretz's, Sforim's, and Aleichem's novellas (to name only a few among Yiddish authors) had revealed that there were no exceptions: even the poorest kid in the most remote shtetl had to attend the local *cheder*. The importance of teaching and studying, as developed through millennia of Jewish history, was the categorical imperative for Jewish women too, especially within the Ashkenazi *milieu* (mostly in Germany and in the Hapsburg Empire). This aim directly derived from the concept of *Bildung*, a combination of personal self-fulfillment, education, and culture, which typically was related to the German-speaking cultural framework.

Hence, access to higher education was the most important aim for both Jews' emancipation and (Jewish) women's emancipation. In fact, since its beginning, the Austrian women's emancipatory movement was attacked as a 'Jewish invention', especially by right-wing associations and press (Kaplan 1991; Rose 2003; Freidenreich 2002; Malleier 2006).

Many associations for the improvement of women's education arose during the 19th century. Their members did not belong to any political movement or party, and their motivations were mainly cultural and socioeconomical as they considered the emancipation of women a cultural and economic – not political – matter (Anderson 1992). Although not politically involved in any specific party, Austrian women activists belonged to the Austrian middle class and were active in both the classical liberal and socialist emancipatory movements (Beller 1989; Brenner and Penslar 1999).

As Hyman claimed: "in such major European centers, as Paris, Berlin, and especially Vienna, Jews exerted a considerable influence as creators, critics, and consumers of high culture. ... The assimilation of Jews in Western societies in the past two centuries and the forging of a modern Jewish identity cannot be separated from the middle-class contexts in which these processes were embedded" (Hyman 1995, 18). Research on Viennese Modernism high-lighted that Jewish women played a leading role in this cultural and intellectual process. Embedded in the peculiar cultural *milieu* of *Finis Austriae* and inspired by their desire of emancipation, Jewish middle-class women in Vienna were very active in organizing welfare activities. Since the early 19th century, they played a fundamental and leading role building up an educational system for girls in Vienna. Either liberal or socialist, assimilated Jewish activists pursued the fight for women's emancipation by using a twofold strategy: to open up education at any level for girls and to promote social studies; in par-ticular, political economy, which had been an exclusive prerogative of men students and scholars. As Hirsch wrote: "[the] role of Jewish women in the fight for women's graduate education is not a coincidence but an unintended effect of the specific symbolic order of Judaism. In two respects, Jewish university women were part of Jewish tradition. First, they belonged to the culture of 'learning' that has been the central element of Jewish religious practice since the destruction of the second Temple. Second, they were a modern permutation of the cultural institution of women as family breadwinners that has its roots in Ashkenazic Judaism and is indirectly part of the cultural 'learning' as well" (Hirsch 2013, 5).

The interconnection between gender and Jewishness often has been used to explain the process of assimilation of both women and Jews that occurred in Vienna (Rozenblit 2001; Edelman 2010). The central role of Jewishness in the Austrian early feminism had been intended as a critical category to analyze the debate around Austrian modernity either in terms of interaction, by adopting the label 'Jewish Austrian', or in terms of contraposition, by adopting the label 'Jewish *versus* Austrian' (Beller 2001; Silverman 2009, 2012). A fundamental peculiarity of Austrian women's cultural emancipation came from the high percentage of Jewish women belonging to social and cultural movements engaged in the emancipation of Jews as a minority as well as of Jewish women as a minority within a minority.

As previously stated, education was an essential feature in Jews' emancipation and was a crucial point for building a Jewish feminist consciousness, which will be later developed in a broader attack to patriarchy. During the 19th century, Austrian Jewish women had confined themselves to household because of the double traditional patriarchal system (within Jewish communities and Hapsburg's Empire) with some significant exceptions (Rudavsky 1995). In 1816, the *Israelitische Frauenverein* was founded: members were women engaged in charity, although an important part of their activities was devoted to girls' education. After the revolution of 1848, the Viennese Democratic Women's Association requested access to higher education; the request was rejected by government and the press described the movement as unfeminine and impudent (Bader-Zaar 2016). In 1852, the *Israelitische Kultursgemeinde* was settled and soon became a powerful association for promoting Jewish life in Vienna. Its main focus was education: in contrast with some other major urban Jewries that reserved education to the private sphere, and in cooperation with state authorities, the *Israelitische Kultursgemeinde* organized children's religious education in public school. Religious education was mandatory by law and was organized under the supervision of the state, which delegated several religious associations, including the Catholic Church, to organize it. The inclusion of Judaism within public school programs made the Jewish community's leaders directly connected with state authorities and accelerated the process of assimilation (Yanowsky 2010).

In 1866, a group of middle-class women founded the *Verein für erweiterte Frauenbildung* (Viennese Professional Women's Association), whose main goal was the admission of women to secondary school, universities, and the labor market (Perloff 2003; Malleier 2006). Given that high school for girls had to be private, with the exception of training colleges, an entire generation of women cultural entrepreneurs emerged. Between 1860s and 1890s, Ottilie

Bondy (1839–1921) and Regine Ulmann (1847–1939), became active in promoting professional education for girls. In 1886, Ulmann cofounded the *Mädchen-Unterstützungs-Vereins* (Girls Support Club) to promote some welfare measures. In 1892, Bondy founded a private *Gymnasium* for girls, which offered a curriculum based not only on liberal arts, but also on mathematics and natural history. In 1907, Olga Steindler (1879–1933) and Olly Schwartz (1877–1960) established the first business school for preparing girls for a career in business (*Handelsakademie für Mädchen*).

At the same time, Salka Goldmann (1870–1942) founded a school for girls in the suburbs of Vienna to promote education among working-class girls. Among these cultural entrepreneurs, Eugenie Nussbaum Schwarzwald (1873–1940) emerged as a major figure. Eugenie Nussbaum had attended the University of Zurich, where she graduated in philosophy and literature in 1900. In the same year, she married Hermann Schwarzwald. The couple went back to Vienna and settled down. In Vienna, Eugenie was nicknamed 'Frau Dr. Phil.' She carried her title illegally, having refused to go to the Hapsburg authorities in order to get her Swiss title recognized in Austria as many others did. In 1901, Schwarzwald bought Eleonore Jeiteles' *Lyceum* and gradually transformed it into a school center, which comprised an elementary school, a junior high school, a high school, and some general training and professional courses. In 15 years, the number of female students grew from 200 in 1901 to more than 1,000 in 1915. Her school also provided extra curricula courses to prepare for the *Matura*, which allowed access to the University of Vienna. In opposition to traditional education, Schwarzwald's school curricula included modern foreign languages and science. Influenced by Maria Montessori, with whom Schwarzwald was in contact, Eugenie promoted girls' creativity as a basic educational idea.

Besides girls' schools, Schwarzwald founded and ran cooperative restaurants, daycare centers, and rural and holiday homes for children and adults. The money for both schools and cooperatives came from her activity of fundraising and from other business, such as a taxi company, a market garden, and a beauty parlor. In Josefstädterstraße 68, Schwazwald opened her saloon, where artists like Kokoschka, Schönberg, and Loos, and scholars like Kelsen and Popper, as well as writers like Kraus, Canetti, Musil, and Bettauer, along with many female artists, regularly attended and often showed up at the school.[12] Schwarzwald's school and salon were in fact strictly interconnected. On one side, Eugenie succeeded in obliging several well-known personalities among her attendees to give some classes at her school, and, on the other side, some of her best students often visited her salon to enjoy some informal conversations with intellectuals in a format that was similar to *Privat seminars* offered by university professors to their male students (Holmes 2012).[13]

The result of the hectic activity of these cultural entrepreneurs was that at the beginning of the 20th century, in Vienna, there were much more educated Jewish women than non-Jewish women (Rozenblit 1984; Rose 2008). In 1910, 46% of the female students at Lyceums, 30% at Gymnasium, and 68%

at the University in Vienna were Jewish. When the School of Law was opened to women in 1919, 50% of first-year enrollees were Jewish (Embacher 1998).

Jewish female students were not a homogeneous group, however: on average, most of them filled out their enrollment form by writing that their native language was German and around 20–25% declared that they spoke Polish and Yiddish at home; minorities spoke Hebrew and other languages from other parts of the empire. Like their male colleagues, Jewish female students were enrolled in the school of medicine and the school of law, where political economy was taught. During the interwar period, the number of Jewish students collapsed. Possible explanations include the impoverishment of the middle class, which affected Jewish families, as well as enrollment in other national universities (in Poland, Hungary, Italy, and so forth) as a consequence of the increasing anti-Semitism (Hanak-Lettner 2015).

Regarding other forms of women's emancipation, which were emerging in the late 19th century, historians agree on the fact that the theme of sexuality was another key point in Vienna. Writers, artists, and physicians opened the debate about sexuality, which became a broader field related to other fundamental issues of that time: the crisis of individual identity, and the conflicts between reason and emotion and between domination and subjection. The debate around sexuality brought many Viennese gentlemen into the women's movement, especially liberal thinkers influenced by John Stuart Mill, although some of them were ambiguous. For instance, Theodore Gomperz regarded higher education and professional life suitable only for exceptional women (Luft 2007).

In 1892, the *Allgemeiner Österreichischer Frauenverein* (Austrian Association of Austrian Women), a radical association, was founded and in 1899, its journal *Dokumente der Frauen* (*Documents for Women*), began to be published under the direction of Anitta Müller-Cohen (1890–1962). During the First World War, she organized the Jewish Relief Society in Bucovina and Galicia and in Vienna took care of the adoption of Jewish child victims of Russian pogroms. Engaged in the Zionist movement, Müller-Cohen later became a leading member of the Jewish National Party. She also worked as a journalist for *Neues Wiener Tagblatt*, *Wiener Morgenzeitung*, and *Jüdische Rundschau*. In her articles, she broadcasted a new image of women, no longer bound to be a perfect housewife and mother, but an educated and free member of her own society. In 1935, Müller-Cohen immigrated to Palestine and founded a special program for new immigrants, especially for refugees who were coming from Austria.

During the First World War, in Austria, as in many other European countries, women took the burden of saving the country from the economic and social collapse while men were drafted into the army: women served as nurses, public transportation drivers, postwomen, and factory workers; they stood in line in food queues; and they became an auxiliary labor force. After the war, when the solution to the Jewish question finally seemed to be solved in the form of total assimilation (which included the long-run effects of conversions and mixed marriages (Hertz 1988)), a new wave of anti-Semitism arose; it dramatically increased during the first years of the First Republic, a homogeneous nation-state that required an exclusive identity (being 'Austrian') that was alien to Jews. Eastern Jews in particular, having emigrated from Poland and Russia, became the target of many nationalist enemies of the First Republic. The creation of a new Jewish subculture in a nationalistic Austria was instrumental in the formation of the well-known Red Vienna (1918–1926) but simultaneously determined a loss of identity for secular Jews. Paradoxically, Jews' efforts to be secularized and embedded in Austrian culture had been 'rewarded' by an increased anti-Semitism that was institutionalized under Seipel, the leader of the Christian Party and Chancellor between 1926 and 1929 (Holmes and Silverman 2009).

Interwar dramatic dynamics converged toward the rise of the ultra-right-wing party and toward the final annexation to the Nazi Germany (1938).[14] These dynamics, plus the crisis of Austrian liberalism, brought many Jews, including activist women, to become aligned with social democracy (Embacher 1998). In 1923, the two Jewish sides – classical liberal and socialist – of Austrian women's emancipation movement converged into the World Conference of Jewish Women, held at the Hofburg Palace in Vienna and organized by Regine Ulmann and Anitta Müller-Cohen along with Marianne Hainisch.

Besides anti-Semitism, the financial crisis,[15] hyperinflation,[16] high unemployment rate,[17] and social riots[18] were the threatening dynamics that deeply changed the social situation of 'Red' Vienna, which soon became the capital of 'Black' Austria. Both classical liberal and socialist men and women were equally damaged: in 1933, restrictions of the press and denial of any form of assembly occurred. In 1934, the Social-Democratic party has been banned. Both liberal and socialist intellectuals were forced to exile or worse, being them mostly Jews, were arrested, deported and killed in the Nazi camps during the Second World War.

Faculty members and students at the University of Vienna shared the same fate. As Klausinger (2014) recalled, the three heaviest disadvantages in Viennese academia in the interwar period before the *Anschluss* (1938) were: to be a Jew, to be a classical liberal, and to be a woman. Although this process of total annihilation affected Austrian women economists of both sides – liberals and socialists – their personal stories, their theoretical contributions, and their engagement in women's emancipation had been a milestone in the story of women's studies and of Jewish studies as well as in the history of economic thought.

Classical-liberal women economists in Austria converged into the historical Austrian school of economics, a cohesive group of Viennese economists who worked in Vienna between the 1870s and 1938, either as professors at the university (Carl Menger, Eugene Bohm-Bawerk, Friedrich Wieser, and Hans Mayer) or as instructors in private economic institutions (Ludwig von Mises, Friedrich Hayek, and Oskar Morgenstern). Along with their male masters and colleagues, two generations of Austrian school women economists worked in Vienna between the late 19th century and the interwar period when they were forced to leave Vienna because of the Nazi racial ban. The contributions of Austrian school women economists has been often neglected and forgotten, and only recently it has been highlighted (Becchio 2019). Members of the first generation of Austrian school women economists, Else Cronbach, Louise Sommer, and Toni Kassowitz Stolper, had studied under the supervision of Bohm-Bawerk and Wieser. Members of the second generation of Austrian school women economists – Martha Braun, Elly Spiro Offenheimer, Marianne Herzfeld, Helene Lieser, Gertrud Lovasy, and Ilse Schüller Mintz – were Mises's students and attendees at his extramural meetings. Members of both generations belonged to the assimilated Jewish middle class and were fierce classical liberals: strong opponents of any form of interventionism in regulating international trade (Sommer, Braun, Lovasy, Schuller), enemies of socialist economic planning (Cronbach, Sommer, Braun), and critics of any monetary policy in favor of inflation to reduce unemployment (Stolper, Braun, Lovasy, Herzfeld, Lieser).

Else Cronbach (1879–1913), who had studied political economy with Bohm-Bawerk in Vienna, was the first Austrian woman who got a Ph.D. in political economy in Germany, since Austria yet did not allow women to be officially enrolled in the school of law at that time. Back in Vienna, she was involved in the foundation of the Austrian *Nationalökonomische Gesellschaft* along with her friends and ex-classmates: Ludwig von Mises, Emil Perels, and Karl Pribram (Pribram 1913).[19] Cronbach was active in several sociopolitical associations for the emancipation of women. Although she never got an official academic position, she earned her living by teaching at the Viennese *Handelsakademie*, a business-oriented secondary school for girls. Her publications, between 1907 and 1910, dealt especially with agricultural and industrial policy in German, as well as with the condition of workers in Austria.[20]

Antonie (Toni) Kassowitz Stolper (1890–1988) was the first and only female to attend the School of Law of the University of Vienna as a regular student, in 1911 before the official admission of female students to the School of Law. Because of the impossibility of getting a Ph.D. in Vienna, she moved to Berlin, where, in 1917, she got her degree in national economic policy. Her memories, recollected in an interview she gave to her grandson in 1982, are an emblematic description of the life of many Viennese girls belonging to an assimilated and wealthy Jewish family in Vienna (Stolper 1982). According to Toni's memories, Austrian anti-Semitism did not affect her happy childhood: Toni's father, Max, was a well-known physician and college professor, who founded the first children's public hospital, where Sigmund Freud had been working as a neurologist between 1886 and 1896. Kassowitz's family lived in an apartment above the hospital. Toni and her four siblings attended private schools: Tony attended the sisters Wertheim's girls' school where she was registered as *konfessionslos* (without religion), like many other Jewish Austrian children of that time. As Toni explained, in Austrian private schools, separate curricula were offered to boys who were supposed to become doctors and lawyers and to girls who might aspire to study *belles lettres* and eventually to become teachers. In the late 19th century, this gendered stereotype was refused by many Jewish families, including Toni's, who promoted a similar education for both sons and daughters. After her graduation at the Cottage Lyceum, founded by Salka Goldmann, Toni took private lessons in order to be prepared for admission to the University of Vienna. Deeply interested in Menger's economic thought and methodological individualism, she studied with Bohm-Bawerk; she attended lectures in art history and Karl Kraus' lectures. As a member of the newly founded Viennese women's club (*Neuer Wiener Frauenclub*), Toni was involved in several social activities to promote the emancipation of women and minorities in town. After her graduation, she wrote several economic articles that were mainly devoted to the side effects of inflation and monetary instability in Austria during the interwar period. In her articles, she strongly criticized any form of interventionism in monetary policy. In 1921, Toni married Gustav Stolper, editor of *Der Österreichische Volkswirt*, the most important liberal economic journal in Austria. When the couple immigrated to Germany, Gustav directed *Der Deutsche Volkswirt*, one of the most respected liberal economic journals in the Weimar Republic. She regularly wrote for both *Volkswirt* about the economic situation in the British Empire and in the Soviet Union as well as on other topics. The Stolpers left Berlin in 1933 to migrate in the United States, where Toni played a leading role in a program of emigrants' assistance (Balabkins 2011).

Louise Sommer (1889–1964) got her Ph.D. in political economy in 1919 at the University of Basel. She spent several years in Switzerland while teaching and working as a freelance journalist. In 1926, she got her *Habilitation* at the University in Geneva, where Karl Pribram (1877–1973), whom she knew from Vienna, had become the director of the Department of Statistics and Research at the International Labor Organization. Back in Vienna in late 1920s, she worked on public finance's department at the *Verein für Sozialpolitik* before its dissolution (1936). After the Second World War, Sommer became visiting professor at the New School for Social Research in New York City, at Aurora College in Illinois and, finally, and at American University in Washington, D.C. Friend of Mises, Sommer shared with him the concept of socialism as a liberticidal principle (Hülsmann 2007). She was mainly a historian of economic thought: she specifically worked on mercantilism and cameralism (the German version of mercantilism). Her major contributions were in the methodology of economics. She was interested in the definition of the nature of economics as a social science: like Menger, she insisted on the possibility to find regularities in economic phenomena and to formulate exact laws, against the historical approach, typical of the German Historical School, which considered economics as a merely descriptive discipline unable to produce any scientific knowledge.

After 1919, women students were finally allowed to register at the School of Law of the University of Vienna, to get a Ph.D. in *Staatswissenschaften*, a combination of law, statistics, sociology, public finance, and political economy. Many women students were officially enrolled, but paradoxically, they were much more involved with Mises' extramural circles than with official academic courses. After Wieser's retirement, courses of political economy were taught by

Hans Mayer and Othmar Spann. Mayer was a low-profile figure comparing with Mises, who never got an official academic position in Vienna, mainly because of his Jewish origins; Spann was a fanatic forerunner of Austrian fascism, who preached universalism and spiritualism. Members of the second generation of the Austrian school of economics, Braun, Spiro, Herzfeld, Lieser, and Lovasy were permanent members of Mises' private seminar, held from 1920 to 1934 in the Viennese Chamber of Commerce, where Mises had served from 1909 to 1938 (Craver 1986; Mises 2013 [1978]). Along with Johanna Morgenstern (Oskar Morgenstern's sister), Lovasy was also a member of the Austrian Institute for Business Cycle Research, founded by Mises and Hayek in 1927 (Hülsmann 2007; Klausinger 2016). Later, many of them pursued an academic position abroad in the countries to which they were forced to emigrate to escape from the application of racial laws against the Jewish population, which occurred in 1938.[21]

Martha Hermann Braun (1898–1990) belonged to a Viennese Jewish middle-class family. During the First World War, she was enrolled at the Faculty of Philosophy and at the Faculty of Law and Political Science (*Staatswissenschaften*) at the University of Vienna. Between 1918 and 1919, while she was still a student, she worked in the statistical and scientific department of the *Kriegs Getreide Anstalt* (War Grain Institution). In the 1920s, she started working at the Viennese Chamber of Commerce. She attended lectures and courses given by Wieser, Weber, and Mises. In 1921, she got her Ph.D. in political science, being one of the first women to graduate from the University of Vienna. Mainly influenced by Mises, Braun's first book on monetary economics and economic policy dealt with the inopportunity of any monetary policy (Braun 1929). In 1930, she coauthored a volume on Austrian feminism (Braun 1930), in which she specifically described the fundamental role of the Women Employment Association in the admission of women to university and to the job market.[22] In 1938 she was forced to emigrate: she went to London and to the United States, where she started working as an economic analyst at the State Department. Between 1947 and 1969, Braun taught at Brooklyn College in New York. After her retirement, she lectured at the New York University. In 1989, she was awarded an honorary doctorate in social and economic sciences at the University of Vienna (Leischko 2002).

Elly Spiro (1903–2001) obtained her Ph.D. in political economy in 1922 from the University of Vienna. Her dissertation dealt with the nature of credit in utopian socialist thinkers such as Owen, Proudhon, and Solvay. She reviewed several books for the *Zeitschrift für Nationalökonomie* and attended Mises' seminar until her marriage to Ernest Offenheimer. In 1929, the couple moved to Frankfurt, and in November 1938 they escaped from Germany to the United States. in 1941, they settled down in San Francisco, where Elly gave private classes for girls and women until 1992. She regularly exchanged letters with Mises, Machlup, and Hayek for many years (Nautz 2002).

Marianne Herzfeld (1893–1976) got her Ph.D. in history at the University of Vienna and worked as secretary in the Austrian Banker Association up to

1938, when she left Vienna for Scotland. Helene Lieser (1898–1962) got her Ph.D. in economic policy (*Staatswissenschaften*) in 1920 at the University of Vienna, with a dissertation on monetary policy of *Bankozettelperiode* (the period of bankruptcy in Austria). She was a permanent member of the *Nationaloekonomische Gesellschaft* until her expulsion in 1938, and she worked at the Austrian Bankers Association up to 1939, when she left Austria for France. In 1948, in Paris, she became the assistant to George MacDougall, the Director of the Economic Secretariat of the Organization for Economic Co-operation and Development. From 1949 on, she worked at the UNESCO (Nautz 2000a)

Gertrud Lovasy (1902–1974) was a member of Mises' seminars as well as a staff member at the Austrian Institute for Trade Cycle Research under the supervision of Oskar Morgenstern. In 1928, she got her Ph.D. at the University of Vienna, with a thesis on cartels in the Austrian iron industry. In 1938 she left Vienna, and in 1939 she reached the United States, where she worked mainly on international oligopoly and cartels at the International Monetary Fund (Feichtinger 2001; Nautz 2000b)

Ilse Schüller Mintz (1904–1978) was the daughter of Richard Schüller, one of the best students of Carl Menger's and a close friend of Hayek; he was an honorary professor at the University of Vienna and a high civil servant in the Ministry of Trade until 1938. Ilse got her Ph.D. in 1927, and then started working at the Institute under Hayek's supervision until the birth of her first child in 1931. Married to Maximilian Mintz, another regular member of the Mises's circle, she escaped with her family to the United States, where she studied statistics at Columbia University and got another Ph.D. in 1951. Between 1951 and 1973, Mintz was a staff member at the National Bureau of Economic Research and focused her work on business cycle theory and foreign trade policy (Perloff 2003; Nautz 2000c).

1.2.2 The socialist tradition in Austrian women economists

Along with classical liberal Austrian school women economists, a significant movement of Austrian socialist women activists and economists arose between the late 19th century and the interwar period. Although their movement's main goal was primarily political and related either to Austro-Marxism or Marxism, Austrian socialist women activists and economists considered both education and the introduction of the woman question within political economy to be central aims for women's emancipation. Similar to their liberal counterparts, a high percentage of Austrian socialist women economists were Jewish. Their movement arose under the auspice of the Social Democratic Labor Party, *Sozialdemokratische Arbeiterpartei* (SDAP). Charlotte Glas (1873–1944) was among the founders of the Party: she mainly fought for women's suffrage. It is important to remember that "her dilemma as a woman, Jew and socialist were captured in the character of Therese Golowski in Arthur Schitzel's *Der Weg ins Freie*" (Mattl 2016, 1). Among Viennese socialist activists, Auguste Fickert (1855–1910), Rosa Mayereder (1858–1938), Adelheid Dworschak

Popp (1869–1939), and Therese Schlesinger (1863–1940) had central roles in the battle for women's emancipation. Fickert and Mayereder were the editors of the *Dokumente der Frauen* (*Documents of Women*) and of *Neues Frauenleben* (*New Woman's Life*). In 1891, Adelheid Popp joined the *Arbeitrinnenbildungsverein* (Working Women's Education Association), whose main goal was to guide women to get involved into politics (Kölp 2006).

Connected to them, but not close to the Austrian Socialist Party, Marianne Hainisch (1839–1936) had an important role in women's emancipation movements. Along with her son, Michael Hainisch, Marianne belonged to the circle of the Social Policy Party (Eugen von Philippovich was one of its representatives), which upheld a progressive liberal approach, combining a general pro-market view with the advocacy of some measure of welfare. In 1888, Hainisch had founded the League for Extended Women's Education, whose aim was the enrollment of girls in higher education. She was mainly involved in the organization of a proletarian section of her association aimed to promote education and legal protection for working-class women, as well as to fight for women's suffrage in Austria (Bader-Zaar 2006). In 1893, Marianne Hainisch, Auguste Fickert (1855–1910), and Rosa Mayereder (1858–1938) co-founded the *Allgemeiner Österreichischer Frauenverein* (Austrian Women's Organizations). Although Fickert was mainly a political activist and spent her life as a teacher in different professional schools for girls, Mayereder was an active writer and published many articles especially related to art criticism; however, she was forced to use a male pseudonym, Franz Arnold, in order to get an audience (Flich 1990; Holmes 2012).

Therese Eckstein Schlesinger (1863–1940) came from a well-established Jewish family. Therese's younger sister, Emma, was a patient of Sigmund Freud's and became one of his most brilliant students. Her brother, Friedrich Eckstein, better known as Mac Eck, was well acquainted with the cream of the Viennese *intelligentsia* including Sigmund Freud, Arthur Schnitzler, and Karl Kraus, and he was a close friend of Victor Adler, one of the major leaders of the Social Democratic Party. Another brother of Therese's, Gustav, was a well-known member of the Social Democratic Party and a close friend of Kautsky, who became Therese's lifelong mentor and friend.

In the 1890s, Therese attended some classes at the University of Vienna, and she was particularly interested in Emil Reich's lectures on social ethics. In 1894, she was introduced to a radical feminist organization, the *Allgemeiner Österreichischer Frauenbund* (the Austrian Women's General Federation) by her close friend, Marie Lang (1858–1934). The Federation demanded an end to legal and social discrimination of minorities, including women. In 1896, Schlesinger attended the first women's international congress, held in Berlin, where she presented her research on female workers' situation in Vienna. During the fall of 1897, Schlesinger officially joined the Austrian Social Democratic Party and started her publishing activity for various socialist newspapers and magazines. Therese's position within the party was not simple: she was accused of female separatism. Furthermore, her Jewish origin and her bourgeois background were additional problems for the establishment within the party, which was oriented to promote members with a lower-class background. Nevertheless, she fervently devoted herself to the Social Democratic Party cause and ceaselessly worked for the party.

In her pamphlet, *What Women Want in Politics* (Schlesinger 1909), she pointed out the importance of educating women to political maturity. A few years later, in 1912, Schlesinger developed a project of communal housing that focused on envisioned central kitchens, laundry, kindergartens, and some recreational spaces for the youngest in order to relieve women's work at home. Furthermore, she proposed an innovative educational system, against the separation of boys and girls in educational terms: her program was based on same chores and same roles in the households for boys and girls in order to overcome gender stereotypes in society, to prevent adult men's chauvinism, and to promote a more equal division of labor within married couples (Raggam-Blesch 2009). The modernity of Schlesinger's thought on this specific point is impressive: she thought that social power's structures were founded on gender dynamics and were culturally determined by the artificial distinction between a male rational sphere and a feminine emotional sphere. Her reflections on the gendered nature of power anticipated the critique of feminist philosophy to the Western culture that occurred many decades later (see Chapter 3).

Although, until the First World War, Austrian socialist women economists were mostly influenced by Austro-Marxism, during the interwar period, many of them became much closer to Marxism and were much more focused on women's economic equality. During the interwar period, a consistent group of Austrian socialist women economists in Vienna gathered around Schlesinger. Among them, there were Helene Bauer, Marianne Pollak, Stella Klein-Low, Emmy Freundlich, and Käthe Pick Leichter. Like their liberal counterpart members, all of them belonged to the Jewish liberal middle class (Raggam-Blesch 2009; Hauch 2012).

Helene Gumplowicz Bauer (1871–1942) was he wife of Otto Bauer, the leader of the Austrian Social Democratic Party. She studied political science in Zurich and Vienna and got her Ph.D. in 1905. During the interwar period, Helene worked as editor-in-chief of *Der Kampf*, the Social Democratic Party's journal. In her articles, she criticized the Viennese establishment, including the reactionary atmosphere at the University of Vienna, which was well represented by Othmar Spann, professor of political economy, as previously mentioned. Strongly committed to several adult education projects, Helene Bauer taught a highly rated course on statistics at the party's Workers' University (*Arbeiterhochschule*) for many years. She also founded a student organization, the Socialist Working Group for Economics and Politics, to promote the study of political economy and political science (Gruber 1991).

Marianne Springer Pollak (1891–1963) attended the Civic and Business School in Vienna. Between 1923 and 1925, she worked as a secretary of Friedrich Adler, the co-editor of the magazine *Der Kampf* along with Otto Bauer, who was working to organize the Socialist Workers International Association.

Marianne Pollak herself was member of the Social Democratic Party of Austria (SDAP) since 1914. In 1925, she became co-editor and publisher of the Social Democratic Party magazine, *Das kleine Blatt*, along with Adler. She also wrote for the *Arbeiter-Zeitung*, whose editor-in-chief was her husband, Oscar Pollak, and was the editor of the magazine *Die Frau* (The Woman). Stella Herzig Klein-Low (1904–1986) studied German philology and psychology at the University of Vienna. After her graduation, and until 1933, she served as a teacher at a private Jewish secondary school, founded by Zwi Perez Chajes in Vienna's 2nd district (*Leopoldstadt*). A member of the Socialist Workers Youth, Stella Klein-Low became a member of the Social Democratic Party of Austria (SDAP) in 1922. In 1939 she had to flee to Britain, and in 1942 she joined the Social Democratic Labor Party.

Emma Kögler Freundlich (1878–1948) was one of the most important figures of Austrian social democracy. Influenced by Fabian socialism, she joined the social-democratic circle around Karl Renner (1870–1950), the organizer of the first consumers' cooperative in Vienna. Following Renner, Emma founded and led a women's cooperative organization, which was active especially during the war and that enabled women to develop some useful skills in order to improve their standard of living. Convinced that women's emancipation was mainly a matter of education, Freundlich organized several educational programs. During the early phase of the First World War, an urgent appeal to 'Austria's women' widely circulated in the national press. The appeal asked Austrian women to ignore their different class status, political positions, and religious differences, and to perform war service. The call for 'Austria's women' was mainly endorsed by the *Frauenhilfsaktion Wien*, an umbrella organization of a Viennese women's group that had been founded in 1914 as soon as the Austro-Hungarian army was mobilized (Maureen 2002). On that occasion, Freundlich claimed that the state should pay women for their work at home while their men were at the front. Hence she called for doubling the support subsidy (given only to married women) and for eliminating the differentiated pay for younger children. According to Freundlich, the support "replicated in the public sphere the dependent status of women within the family, so that women remained, in the eyes of the state, wives and mothers" (Maureen 2002, 33). Between 1907 and 1928, Freundlich wrote numerous articles for the social-democratic monthly review *Der Kampf*. Between 1917 and 1923, she served as secretary of the *Reichsverein der Kinderfreunde* and between 1921 and 1923 she served as president of the International Cooperative Women's Guild. She was also a member of the Vienna City Council from 1918 to 1923. Between March 1919 and November 1920, she was a member of the Constituent National Assembly. In 1929, Freundlich was the only female delegate in the Committee of the Economic Union of the League of Nations. After she immigrated to London in 1939, she founded the Austrian Committee for Relief and Reconstruction. After the Second World War, she moved to New York, where she worked in the newly formed United Nations (Michalitsch and Schalager 2007).

Käthe Pick Leichter (1895–1942) was the younger daughter of Josef Pick, a lawyer from a wealthy Bohemian Jewish family of textile manufacturers, and Lotte Rubinstein, who belonged to an affluent Romanian Jewish family of bankers. Käthe was briefly attracted to religious observance while she was a young teenager, but at 17 years of age, she rebelled against both Judaism and liberal middle-class values and became *konfessionslos*. She joined socialism by entering the Viennese youth movement, led by Siegfried Bernfeld. In 1914, she began studying political economy at the University of Vienna. In 1918, she got her Ph.D. in political economy in Heibelberg, with a thesis on foreign trade relations between the Austro-Hungarian Empire and Italy. Back in Vienna, she became a member of the Social Democratic Party and the director of women's affairs for the Viennese Chamber of Labor (*Arbeiterkammer*). While working as an official of the Social Democratic municipal government, Leichter systematically gathered material on women workers' critical conditions in Austria; she compiled statistical data and published a massive number of articles and reports. Her efforts were aimed at preparing a specific legislation to protect working women, including household servants, home workers, and agricultural workers, who were excluded from healthcare and unemployment insurance. Leichter was also concerned about the exclusion of educated women from professional opportunities and tried to promote quota for hiring women at any level of social administration. Finally, she demanded equal pay for equal work in order to eradicate gender wage gap in any public and private sector. Leichter spread her ideas not only through her publications, but also through lectures and courses she offered in several schools, in trade union meetings, and on radio broadcasts.

Before the First World War, Leichter moved left towards Marxism and was involved in the *Wiener Jugendbewegung* (Viennese Youth Movement), a radical left-wing organization. Therefore, she became a member of the *Parteischüler-Bildungsverein Karl Marx* (Karl Marx Association for Party Scholars and Education), the Marxist wing of the Austrian Social Democratic Party, whose members were strong opponents of the war. In 1918, she joined the *Reichswirtschaftskommission der Arbeiterräte* (State Economic Committee of the Workers' Councils), the *Sozialisierungskommission* (State Committee for the Socialization of Industry), and the *Zentralverband für Gemeinwirtschaft* (Central Organization for Public Goods and Corporations) and started to serve at the Federal Ministry of Finance.

Between 1925 and 1934, Leichter joined the *Frauenreferat der Wiener Arbeiterkammer* (the Women's Department of the Viennese Chamber of Labor). By the late 1920s, Käthe and her husband, Otto, a fellow socialist, had become leaders of the New Left faction within the Austrian Social Democratic Party. She was particularly active in numerous and often vigorous debates against the more conservative elements within the movement. In those years, she became an orthodox Marxist, and in 1932, she was elected to the *Betriebsrat der Wiener Arbeiterkammer* (Workers' Committee of the Viennese Chamber of Labor). When the Social Democratic Party was banned in Austria, in 1934, Leichter officially joined the *Revolutionäre Sozialisten* (Revolutionary Socialists), an underground socialist movement, and was elected at the Revolutionary Socialists' chair of education. She wrote antifascist pamphlets and published many articles under the pseudonyms Maria Mahler and Anna Gärtner. On May 30, 1938, she was arrested by the Gestapo in Vienna and, in 1940, was sent to Ravensbrück concentration camp where, in early 1942, she was killed at the Bernburg Euthanasia Centre (Freidenreich 2002, 2009).

The biographies of Austrian socialist women economists show their commitment to the woman question, and specifically to the economic conditions of women workers, which were scrutinized as a factor of social instability that affected the national economy. The same attitude may be recognized in women economists in Germany between the late 19th century and the interwar period, when Nazis seized power and annihilated any social reforms, which included women's emancipation.

1.2.3 Early feminism and political economy in Germany

Shifting from Austria to Germany, the history of the interconnection between the woman question and political economy is quite similar: it started with the fight for an equal education between the sexes, which shaped new educational programs from pre-K schools on; it involved a relevant percentage of Jewish women; and it was carried on by both classical liberal and socialist activists and economists. The most important difference between the two countries is that the role of orthodox Marxism in Germany was much more central than in Austria.

Louise Otto-Peters (1819–1895) was the pioneer of the woman question in Germany. Between 1849 and 1851, she promoted women's emancipation in her journal, the *Frauen-Zeitung* (*the Review of Women*) and in the activities of the society she had founded in 1865, the *Allgemeiner Deutscher Frauenverein* (General German Women's Association). Both the journal and the association adhered to the liberal and democratic movements of that time.

In 1887, the liberal thinker Helene Lange (1848–1930) stressed the centrality of education in her sharp critique of the Prussian government, which was accused of fomenting a separated educational system for boys and girls since the pre-K years. The critique against the German educational system may be dated back to Friedrich Froebel (1782–1852), who started an official protest against traditional daycare centers, which were led by clergy who applied a pedagogy based on the principle that children must be subjected to 'fatherly' discipline, rooted in the cult of authority and obedience. The same educational principle was applied in primary and secondary schools, where teachers were supposed to be men. According to Froebel, this masculine idea of education was bounded to destroy children's emotions as well as their creativity. He suggested hiring only female teachers for pre-K children, according to his idea that women have a special vocation for early childhood education. Hence, Froebel developed a new form of pedagogy for kindergartens, which aimed to emphasize the special connection between children and mothers and to develop creativity and to understand emotions. According to Froebel, his new educational project would have developed a more emphatic society. Inspired by Froebel, in 1850, Carl and Johanna Künster founded the first *Hochschule für das weibliche Geschlecht* (comprehensive school for girls) in Hamburg. The reform of the kindergarten educational principles reached its momentum when women activists adopted it to criticize traditional conventions in the private as well as the public dimension, and to promote the idea that a female ethics, intended as a sort of social motherhood, would be much more efficient and fair than the paternalistic welfare policy with its bureaucratic apparatus (Allen 1991). In this context, Helene Lange prepared a petition to abolish the traditional educational system and published a brochure, the *Gelben Broschüre* (*The Yellow Pamphlet*), to summarize her stance on education. Lange's proposal was focused on the idea that male teachers reinforced and perpetuated gendered stereotypes, therefore, women must be appointed as teachers, at least in girls' schools. Although the petition was rejected, it had much influence on public opinion and paved the way for Lange to open her own schools in Berlin. In 1889, she offered *Realkurse* (middle high school courses) for girls; in 1890, she founded and directed the *Allgemeinen Deutschen Lehrerinnenverein* (General German Women Teachers Association) to represent the interests of female instructors; and in 1893 she offered *Gymnasialkurse* (high school courses). In 1893, Lange became the director of the magazine *Die Frau* (*The Woman*), the most important magazine of the German women's civil rights movement, and in 1894, along with Gertrud Bäumer (1873–1957), Lange founded the *Bund Deutscher Frauenvereine* (Federation of German Women's Associations).

During the Second International Congress (1889), an official socialist feminist movement was founded by the Marxist thinker Clara Zetkin (1857–1933), who gave a memorable speech about the connection between socialism and the woman question that she regarded as indissoluble. Zetkin started her speech by presenting data about men and women employed in the German industrial sectors that testified the increasing number of female workers in any sector; she clarified that women workers had a massive role in the increase of Germany's GDP. Hence, Zetkin concluded, the inclusion of women's economic emancipation and the pursuit of equality between sexes may not be postponed as central points of any political agenda, especially within socialist programs. After Zetkin's speech, the number of socialist women activists in Germany increased enormously. They joined either its social-democratic wing or its more radical wing. Radical feminists, like Helen Stoctöcker, Minna Cauer, and Anita Auspurg, combined the question of women's suffrage; the international campaign for peace; and the pressure for 'sexual' reforms, which included a redefinition of legal rights within marriage, a regimentation of prostitution, and the stop of any discrimination against illegitimate motherhood and abortion. Both the social-democratic women activists and members of the more radical groups refused to join the newly founded *Bund Deutscher Frauenvereine* because it represented the expression of classical liberal principles they totally rejected. The divergence between classical liberal women activists and social-democratic women activists in Germany was mainly on the nature of women emancipation: the former considered it a cultural battle grounded on economic emancipation; the latter considered it a political issue grounded on revolution (Lefke 1997; Gerhard 2002).

Meanwhile, the rules for getting access to higher education had been changing in Germany.[23] As stated earlier, until 1895, no women were officially allowed to be enrolled at the university and were forced to get their academic degrees in Switzerland. The most famous case was Rosa Luxemburg, whose role in the story of the interconnection between the woman question and political economy will be described later in this paragraph. However, during the 1880s and early 1890s, the Prussian Administration had granted some female students special permission to attend some courses at Berlin University. Some faculty members, who specifically took care of women's access to university, made great efforts to promote woman's admission to college degrees. The economist Gustav Schmoller had a fundamental role in this story. He used to privately tutor many female students by allowing then to join his *Staatswissenschaftliches* seminar. Furthermore, he encouraged his female students to publish in his journal, *Schmollers Jahrbuch*, which was a high-quality journal and well-known in the country and abroad. Among his female students were Elisabeth Gnauck-Kühne, Gertrud Dyhrenfurth, and Helene Simon. Although they did not get any formal degrees, they became prominent figures in the German women's emancipation movement and may be regarded as the first generation of German women economists to deal specifically with the woman question, by focusing their research on women's access to labor work and on their economic conditions in factories and at home.

Elisabeth Gnauck-Kühne (1850–1917), who later became a leader of the German movement for the emancipation of women, *Frauenbewegung*, wrote a book on the educational system in Germany, which became very popular (Gnauck-Kühne 1909). Her major work in political economy, *Die Lage der Arbeiterinnen in der Berliner Papierwarenindustrie* (1895), dealt with the conditions of female workers in Berlin paper factories and appeared in *Schmollers Jahrbuch* as the first publication written by a woman in the journal. Gertrud Dyhrenfurth (1862–1945) authored several publications. She mainly focused on women workers and trade unions in Great Britain and on the economic conditions of female textile workers in Berlin. She published on a study on women farmers who were working on her own estate property near Wroclaw. Helene Simon (1862–1947) studied at the London School of Economics between 1895 and 1897. When in London, she focused her attention on English factory legislation and on the conditions of female workers, and she became a member of the Fabian Society. Back in Berlin, she translated and edited many of Webbs' books into German and published a large number of journal articles in trade union magazines such as *Die Gleichheit* and *Die neue Zeit*, as well as several books and book contributions. She authored the biographies of Robert Owen, William Godwin, Mary Wollstonecraft, and Elisabeth Gnauck-Kühne.

In 1904 at the International Women's Congress in Berlin, Simon gave a speech on worker protection laws. In 1911, she was a committee member of the Society for Social Reform. Member of the SPD since 1919, she got an honorary doctorate from the University of Heidelberg in 1922. In 1933, she was sentenced to speechlessness by Nazis, and after *Kristallnacht* (1936), was forced to immigrate to England.

The second generation of German women economists who specifically dedicated their work to the woman question came up after 1895, when they were admitted to the School of Philosophy at Berlin University and finally had a chance to get a degree in political economy, which was offered at the School of Philosophy. Among the many female students to get a Ph.D. in political economy in Berlin were Alice Salomon, Frieda Wunderlich, Charlotte Leubusher, Cora Berliner, Marguerite Steinfeld Kuczynski, and Cläre Tisch.[24]

Alice Salomon (1872–1948) was a Jewish middle-class socialist economist and got her Ph.D. in *Nationaloekonomie* at the Friedrich Wilhelm University in Berlin in 1908, with a dissertation on the gender wage gap among German workers (Lees 2004). In 1908 in Berlin, she founded the first women's school, which offered curricula in social education. For social education, she intended "not only a matter of teaching knowledge, but a question of the development of conscience, the care of the character traits" (Salomon 1908, 42). According to Salomon, a proper education, which included economic matters, would have been able to provide the rise of a new individual conscience based on sharing responsibilities at any level, which may improve the society as a whole. In Salomon's vision, this task required a deep reform of the educational system that included a more specific role for women, whose ability to handle emotions may helpful in creating this new form of social consciousness. In 1909, Salomon became secretary of the International Women's League and held that position until 1933, when she was forced to leave Germany and went to New York.

Frieda Wunderlich (1884–1965) got her Ph.D. in Berlin in 1919. She taught political economy and sociology at the *Staatliches Berufspädagogisches Institut*. After the First World War, she worked for the Brandenburg War Department of Labor and Welfare as a specialist in legislation on the protection of women in the industrial sector and as an employment counselor. Meanwhile she was active at the Central Board for Foreign Relief, responsible for the distribution of food and textiles that were arriving from abroad. Between 1923 and 1933, she edited the political journal *Soziale Praxis* and published numerous books and articles on social policy and political economy, especially on gender discrimination in the labor market. She regularly gave lectures at a variety of educational institutions, including the Women's School for Social Welfare and the Graduate School for Civil Administrators. She was an activist of the DPP, a left liberal German Party, and in 1930 was elected member of the German Reichstag. In 1933, being a Jew, she was dismissed from any position and was forced to leave Germany. In New York, where she emigrated to, she joined the New

School of Economic and Social Research and was appointed the first female member of the University on Exile (Meyer 1966).

Charlotte Leubuscher (1888–1961) got her Ph.D. in 1911 in Berlin. In 1929, she was the first woman to join the faculty as associate professor of political economy; four years later, when Nazis seized power, she was dismissed due to her Jewish origin. Leubuscher's work was mainly focused on development economics and on the international economic relationships between Germany and its colonies.

Cora Berliner (1890–1942) got her Ph.D. in 1916 in Heidelberg under the supervision of Emil Lederer, with a dissertation of the economic and social conditions of Jewish youth in Germany. After the First World War, she worked on the effects of monetary instability in the Weimar Republic. Between 1927 and 1933, she was professor of political economy at the Technical College. Fired in 1933 because of her Jewish origin, she continued to work in a freelance capacity, especially on the economic conditions of German Jews after the Nazis seized power, and she specifically emphasized the difficult situation of Jewish women. Head of the committee for Emigration, Information, Statistics, and Women's Emigration, she was very active in organizing emigration from Germany to many other European countries as well as to Palestine. Unfortunately, she never left Germany, and was deported and murdered, presumably in Minsk, Belarus (Maierhof 2002).

Marguerite Steinfeld Kuczynski (1904–1998), wife of the Communist economic historian Jürgen Kuczynski, went to the United States in the 1920s to attend the Brookings Institution as a graduate student. Thereafter, she started to work at National Bureau of Economic Research (NBER). During the 1930s, she settled down in London, where she gave several lectures on women's resistance in Germany (Kuczynski 1942). In 1943, she was elected to the executive committee of the Women's Co-operative Guild. After the Second World War, she went back to the German Democratic Republic (DDR), where she worked extensively on history of economic thought, by focusing mainly on Quesnay, Turgot, Marx, and Engels.

Cläre Tisch (1907–1941?) got her Ph.D. in Bonn in 1931. A former student of Schumpeter, she worked for two years as assistant at the same university, before she was expelled because of her Jewish origin. Her research mainly focused on the nature of cartels and on the business cycle. Although a classical liberal, she was in favor of cartels among small business as a sort of protection against big cartels, which would have improved the general level of competition in the market. Tisch's position on oligopoly was shared by the majority of economists of that time in Germany, where small-sized and medium sized firms were allowed to consolidate cartels in order to be protected by external competitors. Her Ph.D. thesis (Tisch 1932) on economic calculation was praised by Hayek, who was working on the same issue during the early 1930s: in her work, Tisch criticized Mises' argument of the theoretical impossibility of economic calculation and explained that the limit of the economic calculation system was mainly computational. Although she presented a static system to simulate a planned economy, her work gave Hayek (1935) the chance for a more structured critique to economic planning, not based on a theoretical impossibility, in Mises' terms, but rather on a practical difficulty in a simultaneous calculation of prizes (Vaughn 1980; Hagemann 2000). Tisch's contribute in this debate has been completely forgotten. She had no chance to keep working as presumably she was killed in Minsk, according to what is reported in a deportation list.

The role of Rosa Luxemburg (1871–1919) within the story of the connection between the woman question and political economy must be considered as a separate case, given her central role in the history of Marxist feminism. Luxemburg got her Ph.D. in political economy in 1897 at the School of Law of the University of Zurich, with a dissertation about the rise and development of industry in Poland (Luxemburg 1898). Her biography and works are well-known: since the publication of Nettl's two biographical volumes (Nettl 1966), a massive amount of literature around the most important women within the history of socialism has spread up and covered any single aspect of her life and contributions. Hence, in this context, Luxemburg's work is scrutinized only in relation to her attention to the woman question.

As previously stated, the woman question emerged within socialism much later than in the tradition of classical liberalism. Marx never dealt with it in a specific way, while Engels wrote his well-known book on the origin of family in 1884, in which he depicted the subjection of women as a consequence of the introduction of the private ownership system, which established social rules that were reinforced by the capitalistic system. These social rules included men's control on women's labor and sexual norms aimed to reinforce patriarchy. As previously mentioned, Clara Zetkin basically followed Engels' critique, which had great influence on the well-known Russian activist Alexandra Kollontai (1872–1952), who was very popular for having preached free love as a measure for women's emancipation (Kollontai 1918 [1971]). By adopting Engels and Zetkin's arguments, Kollontai explicitly criticized classical liberal feminism for prioritizing political goals, such as suffrage, in order to benefit middle-class bourgeois women and to reinforce the division between capitalists and proletarians (1909 [1977], 1916 [1977]).

Luxemburg's position on women's emancipation was peculiar. Although she was aware of the fact that a movement for women's emancipation was a necessary step towards the fulfilment of the proletarian revolution, she strongly fought for working class emancipation without a specific focus on the woman question. According to some secondary literature, unlike her mentor and friend Clara Zetkin, who was a fervent feminist, Luxemburg did not put the woman question on the top of the revolution's agenda. She was skeptical about feminism and considered it an "old ladies' nonsense", which was carried on by European classical liberal thinkers (Evans 2013, 161). Nevertheless, recent literature has pointed out the fact that Luxemburg was in fact engaged in women's emancipation: she was involved in the organization of some female workers' groups; and she expressed her support to the feminist movement in some private correspondence, for instance, in a letter to Luise Kautsky, Luxemburg wrote: "I have become a feminist!" (Čakardić 2018).

Luxemburg wrote several papers on woman question (Luxemburg [1902] 2004a, [1904] 2004b, [1907] 2004c, [1912] 2004d), and she dealt with it in her book *The Accumulation of Capital* ([1913] 2003) by criticizing classical liberal feminist programs. Luxemburg's criticism against classical liberal feminism was a direct consequence of her broader critique to bourgeoisie and capitalism: she never trusted the middle class, and middle-class feminists were not an exception. For instance, she often claimed that the battle for women suffrage, which was a priority in the classical liberal feminist agenda, would have been useless without a class revolution.

Luxemburg wrote: "most of those bourgeois women who act like lionesses in the struggle against 'male prerogatives' would trot like docile lambs in the camp of conservative and clerical reaction if they had suffrage" (Luxemburg 2004d, 240). According to Luxemburg, classical liberal feminism was a tool adopted by some clever capitalists to reinforce their power on proletariat by shifting the core of the problem from class to gender. According to Luxemburg, classical liberal feminism, which included the stance for women's suffrage, was grounded on an individualistic philosophy, which did not allow to develop a strategy for the proletarian revolution whose nature is classist and anti-individualistic. The woman question was important for Luxemburg but was subordinated to the proletarian question. She wrote: "women's suffrage is the goal. But the mass movement to bring it about is not a job for women alone, but it is common class concern for women and men of the proletariat" (Luxemburg 2004d, 239). Luxemburg wrote: "for the property-owning bourgeois women, her house is the world. *For the proletarian women the whole world is her own house*" (Luxemburg 2004b, 243, Luxemburg's emphasis); and later she added: "aside from the few who have jobs or professions, the women of the bourgeoisie do not take part in social production. They are nothing but co-consumers of the surplus value their men extort from the proletariat" (Luxemburg 2004d, 240). Moreover, she further criticized classical liberal feminism by emphasizing its reactionary nature that never denied the traditional role of women within household as well as the overemphasized role of motherhood.

As in Great Britain, the importance of economic studies was crucial in the story of early feminism in German-speaking countries, where women activists, mostly Jews like in Austria, were economists either within or outside academia. They played a fundamental role in the creation of what was supposed to be a new society, which was partially shaped after the First World War; however, their efforts were abruptly interrupted by Nazism.

1.3 The woman question in the United States: political economy between abolitionism and social reforms

The story of the connection between the woman question and political economy in the United States goes through two different levels. First, between the early and late 19th century, the woman question in the United States was deeply linked to the story of American abolitionism and activism for civil rights. Second, it was related to the admission of female students to womens colleges, which offered degrees in economics and the consequent emergence of women economists as faculty members within academia. This process gradually occurred between the late 19th century and the First World War, during the 'Progressive Era', when academia hired women economists who were predominantly focused on the woman question (Forget 1995, 2011).

1.3.1 The fight for civil rights

The biographies of American civil rights activists reveal that they fought for both women's emancipation and for the African American population's freedom. Both early feminism and abolitionism in the United States were inspired by the principles of individual freedom and of the equality among human beings that was rooted mainly in the Quakers tradition. The movement, which involved both black and white American activists, rapidly increased in the country and had an important international impact, which echoed the European audience. In Great Britain's colonies, slavery was still allowed; in 1831, Mary Prince (1788?–1833), a former slave born in Bermuda who had managed to escape, wrote a book to describe the horrors of the Caribbean slave trade (Prince 1831) and presented an antislavery petition to the Parliament in London. Although some black abolitionist women came from middle-class families, the majority belonged to the working class; some of them were freeborn and many others were former slaves. They mainly lectured in open debates and published in popular magazines in order to promote both the woman question and abolitionism (Yee 1992).

Predecessors of the movement in the United States were Judith Sargent Murray (1751–1820) and the Scottish-born socialist Frances Wright (1795–1852). In 1832, a free black domestic, Maria W. Stewart (1803–1879), was the first American woman to give a memorable speech addressing a public audience of both women and men. She spoke out against slavery and against chauvinism, which was an additional problem for female slaves. In 1833 in Philadelphia, supporters of the abolitionist movement, which included both black and white men and women, founded the American Anti-Slavery Society. A few days later, a group of women established the biracial Philadelphia Female Anti-Slavery Society (PFAS). The group included Sarah Mapp Douglass, Sarah Moore Grimké, Sarah Forten, Margaretta Forten, and Lucretia Mott (Rowbotham 2012). Like many European activists, the founders of PFAS insisted on the necessity to expand education for girls and to get rid of gender social roles. The freeborn Sarah Mapp Douglass (1806–1882) was a passionate educator: she taught human rights to black children and adults in New York and Philadelphia and worked for both the *Liberator* and the *Anglo-African Magazine* (Presley 2016). In 1837, Sarah Moore Grimké (1792–1873) published a series of letters in the *New England Spectator,* later collected under the title *Letters on the Equality of the Sexes* (1988). In her letter to her sister Angelina, she complained about the restrictions on the "miserably deficient" education imposed by the conservative American society to women "[who] are taught to regard marriage as the one thing needful, the only avenue to distinction and to spend their live investing in *fashionable* world" (Grimké 2010, 75). Grimké passionately requested a broader education for girls than the usual knowledge of household affairs, in order to improve the general condition of society as a whole. She also denounced persistent gender discrimination in the labor market as well as the gender wage gap as inevitable consequences of women's cultural subjection. Grimké was a pioneer figure of classical liberal feminism which emerged during the 19th century in the United States, which included Ezra Heywood and Sarah E. Holmes, both pioneers in the battle for sexual liberation of women. In 1872, inspired by Wollstonecraft, Ezra Heywood (1828–1893), founded the journal *The Word* to scrutinize woman question in a framework of sexual liberation against traditional marriage and in favor of economic independence of women. Sarah E. Holmes (1847–1929) often wrote about sexuality and marriage; her articles published on Benjamin Tucker's journal *Liberty* were aimed to promote the advantages of both partners sharing domestic duties.

Charlotte Forten, along with her three daughters Sarah, Margaretta, and Harriet and her granddaughter Charlotte (the five ladies were known as 'the Fortens'), organized informational fairs to promote their abolitionist agenda and were engaged in publishing and lecturing all over the country as well as in assisting runaway slaves (Sumler-Lewis 1981). Lucretia Coffin Mott (1793–1880) constantly fought to grant former male and female slaves the right to vote. Elizabeth Cady Stanton (1815–1902) was involved in the battle to increase parental rights for women, which included children's custody, divorce, and birth control, as well as in the fight against the gender labor gap. In 1890, she founded the National American Woman Suffrage Association and made major efforts to introduce the word 'female' in the Fourteenth and Fifteenth Amendments in order to extend suffrage to women.

In the 1840s, along with their husbands, Lucretia Mott and Elizabeth Cady Stanton attended the World's Anti-Slavery Convention in London as delegates from the United States. During that meeting, women were relegated to a separate section and were not allowed to speak. Hence, Mott and Stanton, forced to sit apart and to keep silent, started to think about the organization of a mass meeting to address women's rights. The project for a women's rights congress was presented by Coffin, Mott, and Lucretia's sister, Martha Coffin Wright (1806–1875), during the annual Quaker convention (1848) and became concrete on July 19–20, 1848, at the Seneca Falls Convention, organized by Mott, Coffin Wright, Elizabeth Cady Stanton, Mary Ann M'Clintock, Jane C. Hunt, Susan B. Anthony, and Amelia Bloomer. Meanwhile, Bloomer founded *The Lily*, the first newspaper devoted to women's rights. The Seneca Falls Convention was attended by about 200 women and 40 men. Among the male attendees, ex-slave, abolitionist, and newspaper owner Frederick Douglass (1818–1995) was the only African American man. The Women Rights Convention presented the *Declaration of Sentiments*, which was modeled on the Declaration of Independence (1776) and enumerated a list of women's grievances, and enlisted some resolutions that were aimed to propose women's suffrage. The documents were published by Douglass in his Rochester newspaper, *The North Star* (Armitage 2002).

Before the American Civil War, the number of black American activists in abolitionism increased and included many women. In 1851, Sojourner Truth (1797–1883) delivered the well-known speech "Ain't I a Woman" to strongly denounce the double discrimination she was facing as a woman and as an African American (Gage 1863). Between 1849 and 1860, Harriet Tubman (1820–1913), whose nickname was Moses, rescued dozens of slaves and worked constantly to provide crucial information in order to allow other slaves to make their own escape from Maryland (Oertel 2015).

Unfortunately, during the mid-19th century, a trade-off between African American civil rights and the woman question emerged within the civil rights movement. This trade-off highly damaged both white women and African American women. Some abolitionist leaders in the Republican Party, supported by Lucy Stone, wanted women to postpone their campaign for suffrage until after it had been achieved for male African Americans. In 1870, the Fifteenth Amendment to the Constitution of the United States gave the right to vote to men without regard to "race, color, or previous condition of servitude". Hence the Amendment excluded women, either white or African American. Only after the Civil War did the two stances begin to converge in the American Equal Rights Association (AERA), cofounded by Elizabeth Stanton and Susan Brownell Anthony (1820–1906). The major purpose of AERA was to campaign for equal civil rights and universal suffrage of all citizens by insisting that the female population and the African American population should be enfranchised at the same time. In November 1869, Lucy Stone (1818–1893), Julia Ward Howe (1819–1910), and many others, cofounded the American Woman Suffrage Association (AWSA) as a section of AERA. The internal division made AERA collapse in the same year: Anthony, Stanton, and others formed a third association, the National Woman Suffrage Association (NWSA). In 1890, AWSA and NWSA merged again into the National American Woman Suffrage Association (NAWSA). NAWSA pushed for a constitutional amendment to guarantee women's suffrage, which was instrumental in the ratification of the Nineteenth Amendment in 1920 (Dudden 2011; McConnaughy 2013). Besides the battle for suffrage, the fight to get higher education started to include African American women citizens. In 1870, Susan Smith McKinney Stewart (1847–1918) became the first African American woman to receive an M.D. from the New York Medical College and Hospital for Women.[25] A decade later, a new age of economic and social reforms changed American society. That period is known as the Progressive Era (1890–1918), the label used by historians to describe intellectuals and reformers who promoted the idea of a social welfare led by experts

(Leonard 2009). In those frantic decades, the American society changed: from an agrarian society, it became an urbanized society under a massive process of industrialization led by small, medium, and large corporations. That quick process of transformation pushed progressive leaders and scholars to formulate a program of socioeconomic reforms to better off working people's life conditions.

During the Progressive Era, both abolitionism and feminism set their own final agenda. Many economists, especially women economists, were involved in social reforms' agenda: they gathered around the American Association of Labor Legislation (AALL), founded in 1905, at the American Economic Association's (AEA's) annual meeting. As Leonard (2005, 2009) pointed out, members of AALL were not necessarily leftists: they devoted their efforts to the labor question without any specific political orientation. An emblematic example of their position was the debate on the role of women in society and specifically in the labor market: although members of AALL supported women's suffrage, they advocated for removing women from labor market in order to better off men's wages and to promote women to fulfill their natural role of mothers. Evidently, they did not carefully read John Stuart Mill.

During the Progressive Era, the national feminist movement emerged. Although it had always been identified as a white and upper-class movement, in 1896, a group of African American women, led by Mary Church Terrell (1863–1954), Harriet Tubman (1822–1913), and Ida Wells Barnett (1862–1931), joined the cause and created the National Association of Colored Women (Sklar and Stewart 2007). Under the influence of Social Darwinism, many feminist thinkers during the Progressive Era converged towards a sort of female "sovereignty", which implied not only a concept of self-determination of the body but also a racial supremacy. Women's economic, political, and sexual autonomy was defined, debated and justified through eugenic and imperialist discourse. The initial connection between the woman question and abolitionism converged into a white supremacist agenda grounded on a form of eugenics, which was not alien to many African American intellectuals, both men and women, who promoted the idea of a black race purity (Athney 2000).

1.3.2 Women's emancipation within economic departments and the role of female entrepreneurship

The woman question was a common issue in women economists' research and some efforts to recognize it as an official research field had been made by AEA. Since 1886, AEA had held an annual essay competition on the woman question within economics (Dimand and Black 2012). Claire de Graffenreid (1849–1921) was among the first winners of the competition. Graffenreid described the conditions of employment for women and children. Her prizewinning work was published in the *Publications of the American Economic Association* (Graffenreid 1890). Furthermore, since its foundation in 1885, AEA has had women economists as members. More precisely, there were seven women among the

182 members of the AEA in 1886 and 60 women among 1339 members in 1910 (May and Dimand 2016). Nevertheless, women economists in the United States experienced sex discrimination in employment, wages, upgrading, and tenure-ruled academia. As Hammond clarified (1993), academic gender segregation emerged immediately and was hierarchical (women were often employed in subordinate roles) and territorial (women were especially employed in so-called 'feminized' fields, such as home economics). Women participated in the annual meetings but were excluded from the first annual meeting reception and forced to join a separate reception set up at the last minute for the 15–20 women participants, which they boycotted. Discrimination was perpetuated from families to their peers within departments in which they were engaged in making their own careers. Social pressure on women economists came from instructors as well as future colleagues: even in institutions that allowed women, segregation by sex was the norm and women often did not have equal access to courses. During a year of study at the London School of Economics in the 1920s, Berkeley economist Emily Huntington recalled that Professor Frank W. Taussig segregated women economists in classrooms. Self-discrimination emerged as well, as it had in Victorian Great Britain, where economists like Mary Paley Marshall and Beatrice Potter Webb succumbed to the culturally prevailing notion that women do not share higher-order intellectual capability with men and never got academic positions (Dzuback 2006; 2019; Madden 2019). Furthermore, many women who pursued academic careers chose not to marry in order to avoid job-market discrimination: in fact, married women were systematically downgraded in job-market competition, being already able to count on their husbands' income. The situation worsened after the application of antinepotism rules beginning in the first half of the 20th century, with the intention of preventing political appointments based on patronage. This was the case of Dorothy Wolff Douglas (University of Chicago), Theresa McMahon (University of Washington), Margaret Gordon (University of Berkeley), and so forth, who were not allowed to get an academic position as their husbands were faculty members in their departments.

Between the late 19th century and early 20th century, the number of women economists in the United States increased, especially in some universities: Columbia University in New York City, the University of Chicago, Harvard University (Radcliffe), the University of Pennsylvania, Yale University, the University of Michigan, Wisconsin University, and the University of California, Berkeley. In the early 1920s, women with a Ph.D. in economics was more than 20% of the total number of Ph.Ds. in economics in the United States, before declining to a low of 10% in the middle 1950s (Dzuback 2006, 2019). Although many of them were invited to take teaching positions largely at women's colleges rather than in regular departments of economics, a significant group managed to developed economics programs in their institutions, to train young women in economics, and to influence economic policy at any level. They were usually hired at women's colleges, especially Wellesley, Vassar, Bryn Mawr, Smith,

Mount Holyoke, or Barnard. In 1874, Harvard University had opened its doors to women via creation of Radcliffe, a women's college (Libby 1984). Standards for being an economist included: a Ph.D.; a membership of AEA, which had been founded in 1885; a position as faculty member in a university; and publications in academic journals.

According to the *American Economic Review,* during the early 1900s, the number of graduate female students in economics rapidly increased. Their dissertations mainly dealt with social problems related with economic discrimination, the labor market, and economic history. In 1896, Helen Page Bates (1870–1933) was the first woman to earn a Ph.D. in economics in the United States. She was hired by Richard Ely as a lecturer in economics at the University of Wisconsin–Madison in order to teach undergraduate economics courses, the demand for which was rapidly increasing. She never got a permanent position as a faculty member and was forced to accept the position of librarian. Unlike women economists in Chicago, Columbia, or Harvard, mainly focused on home economics or household economics (see Chapter 2), Wisconsin women economists worked on labor economics: they were used to handle with statistical dataset without adopting any mathematical formulism, the use of which was dramatically increasing within the discipline at the time (Johnson 2019).

As mentioned earlier, during the Progressive Era, scholars were involved in social reforms. Women economists were not an exception: many of them were especially influenced by John R. Commons' institutionalism. In 1904, Commons was appointed head of the department of economics at the University of Wisconsin–Madison, an institution that was particularly committed to progressive reforms. Under Commons' direction, the University of Wisconsin–Madison became a niche for women economists interested in developing the institutionalism approach, which was based on empirical analyses of institutions and on the provision of some programs of social control. Women economists at the University of Wisconsin–Madison were involved in a nationwide agenda for labor reforms. In those years, the department of economics of University of Wisconsin–Madison ranked fourth in the number of women doctoral candidates, following Columbia, Chicago, and Harvard (Rutherford 2011, 2006).

Women economists who combined economic research on labor, the woman question, and social reforms included Katharine Bement Davis, Sophonisba Preston Breckinridge, Edith Abbott, Frances Kellor, Katharine Coman, Emily Green Balch, Helen Sumner, Elizabeth Butler, Elizabeth Faulkner Baker, Emily Hutchinson, Hanna Sewall, Elinor Pancoast, Jean Trepp McKelvey, Selma Mushkin, Phyllis Wallace, and Minnie Throop England (Fitzpatrick 1990; Dimand et al. 1995).

Davis, Breckinridge, Abbot, and Kellor were trained at the University of Chicago, the scientific community was affected dramatically by the rapid social changes of the urban environment and at which the role of minorities was emerging as a fundamental factor of social transformation. Katharine

Bement Davis (1860–1935) got her Ph.D. in Chicago in 1900, under the supervision of Thorsten Veblen. She spent the 1898–1899 academic year as a visiting fellow at the University of Vienna, where she worked on her dissertation about the living conditions of farmers as well as their wage level in the Hapsburg Empire. A part of her thesis became a specific article on wages in Austria (Davis 1899) and another part of her thesis was published as an article on agricultural labor market in Bohemia (Davis 1900). Back in the United States, Davis did not get an academic job and worked as a superintendent of the Reformatory for Women in New York where she started to do researches on female delinquency by using data collected at the new Laboratory for Social Hygiene. Her publication on prostitution in New York City, based on collected data aimed to test the causes for entering prostitution, made her one of the pioneering figures of the field, which is known today as economics and crime. Although she firmly asserted that education rather than enforcement was the way to reduce crimes which is rooted on social dysfunctionality, she accepted a position at the Committee on Eugenics of the United States' Advisory Council: she was influenced by the *Weltanschauung* of her time.

Sophonisba Preston Breckinridge (1866–1948) graduated from Wellesley College in 1888 and she studied law to join her father's office as a lawyer. Gender discrimination did not save her, and she was unable to practice. Therefore, she enrolled at the University of Chicago graduate school where, in 1901, she became the first American woman to receive a Ph.D. in political science; in 1904, she got another Ph.D. in law. The economist J. Laurence Laughlin was the supervisor of her dissertation on monetary history in the United States. Between 1904 and 1912, she taught in the Department of Household Administration. Since 1907, Breckinridge was involved in the Women's Trade Union League as well as in the project of Hull House settlement, where she lived between 1907 and 1920. Breckinridge promoted several welfare programs them through her books and courses and by publishing reports in the *Social Service Review*, which she cofounded in 1927 and edited until 1948. In 1904, Breckinridge was hired as a faculty member at the University of Chicago, when the new Department of Household Administration got approved under the direction of Marion Talbot (see Chapter 2). Along with Talbot, Breckinridge wrote *The Modern Household* (1912), an analysis of the social conditions of women who were forced to obey a double obligation as workers and as housekeepers. Along with her student Edith Abbott, Breckinridge authored *The Delinquent Child and the Home* (1912) to investigate the social influence of poverty and isolation in underage criminals. Breckinridge helped to organize the Woman's Peace Party and the Women's International League for Peace and Freedom. She was also popular for her activities with the National American Woman Suffrage Association, the Illinois Consumer's League, the U.S. Children's Bureau, Chicago's Immigrants' Protective League, and the National Association for the Advancement of Colored People.

Edith Abbott (1876–1957) got her Ph.D. at the University of Chicago in 1905, under Breckinridge's supervision. As a visiting fellow at the London School of Economics, Edith met Sidney and Beatrice Webb, who had a great influence on her vision of society and on her thesis on the history of the conditions of blue-collar women in the United States (Abbot 1910) as well as on her historical papers. In her thesis, she showed that:

> Contrary to contemporary popular opinion, women were not displacing men in factories: ongoing labor shifts and adjustments [were] not to sort of Gresham's law in which cheap women's labor drove out men's but instead ... [were determined by] immigration, workplace monopolization by men's union, and technological innovation.
>
> (Hammond 2000b, 2)

Furthermore, Abbott explained the gender wage gap as the result of unskilled labor by women because of educational and social restrictions. Back in Chicago, she started to collaborate with Breckinridge. They coauthored several articles on Chicago's tenement housing, which included black neighborhoods, and on juvenile crime, which massively affected the city. In their researches, they concluded that the role of urban environment was more detrimental than the role of families to explain the source of juvenile crime. Their results were often used to promote welfare initiatives. The collaboration between Breckinridge and Abbot was long-lasting: in 1927, they founded the journal *Social Service Review*, to promote social-work research in academic and to strengthen the welfare agenda in politics (Hammond 2000a).

Frances Kellor (1873–1952) graduated from Cornell in 1897. Thereafter she got a fellowship at the University of Chicago to work on her book on the role of social and economic deprivation in criminal behavior: against any biological explanation, Kellor claimed that crime was due to poor education and unemployment (Kellor 1901).

Katharine Coman (1875–1915) was appointed professor of history and economics at Wellesley College, a new private college for women. Deeply influenced by institutionalism, she introduced the first courses of political economy and statistics in her college and travelled for four years over the country to collect data to study the reasons for industrial development in the Western states. She concluded that development was the consequence of the legal battle over ownership of water rights as well as over land ownership (Coman 1912). She travelled in Europe to scrutinize the social reforms occurring in several European countries. She was the only woman among the cofounders of the American Economic Association (Fitzpatrick 1955, 1990; Vaughn 2016; Ponder 2017).

Emily Green Balch (1867–1961) studied economics and sociology at the University of Chicago in the 1890s. First recipient of the European Fellowship granted by her university, she spent the academic year 1895-1896 in Berlin, where she studied under Adolph Wagner and Gustav Schmoller. Back in the United States, she was invited by Katharine Coman (they had met during a journey from Europe to the United States) to join the department of economics at Wellesley, where she taught history of socialism, labor economics, and the economic role of women. She was a declared fervent socialist and very active in promoting pacifism during the First World War and interwar period. Nevertheless, some years later, in the 1930s, she discarded socialism, which had been converted into Marxism and Stalinism (Dimand 2000a). During a sabbatical year spent in the Balkans (1904–1905), Balch travelled around the Hapsburg Empire to get acquainted with the economic conditions of Slavic people. When she went back home, she worked on Slavic immigration in the United States. She fought strongly against any form of restriction of immigration, which had been proposed by Commons and Fisher (Balch 1912). In Balch's articles on the economic role of women (Balch 1910, 1914), her inquiry was centered on the importance of education for women in order to make them efficient professionals and workers as well as good wives and mothers. According to Balch, this kind of education would have fit the six types of modern women: single professionals (evidence of self-exclusion from marriage was common in medicine, law, architecture, art, and business); educated married professionals able to combine motherhood and a profession that was very elastic in terms of time; educated married professionals, who chose to quit their jobs for full-time motherhood but who had the chance to get back into the workforce when children were grown up; unmarried women of leisure, who "make the most disposable force in our society. Some of them, the spenders, live purely parasitic lives, absorbing the services of others and consuming social wealth without rendering any return"; married women who devoted themselves to family and housekeeping, no matter their education; and working-class women, no matter their marital status (Balch 1910, 64). Balch was the Nobel Peace Prize winner in 1946 for her activities with the Women's International Committee for Permanent Peace, later named the Women's International League for Peace and Freedom (Redmond 2016).

Helen Laura Sumner Woodbury (1876–1933) got her Ph. D. in 1908 with a thesis on *The Labor Movement in America, 1827–1837*, under Coman's supervision. Her work was later revised by Commons in his two volumes, *The History of Labor in the United States* (1918). Her previous research on the role of women workers in the American labor force was published in the U.S. Bureau of Labor Statistics (Sumner Woodbury 1910).

Elizabeth Beardsley Butler (1885–1911) graduated from Barnard College in 1905. Her research was focused on the conditions of women in the labor force in different ethnic groups. She showed that gender segregation was usual everywhere: Polish women workers were mainly hired in cracker factories; Hungarian and Croatian female workers usually got a job in cigars factories; Jewish girls were employed in garment factories; and American-born women workers were hired in less labor-intensive factories and stores, such as telephone companies, candy stores and factories, bookstores, and so forth. Butler explained the gender wage gap neither as a consequence of women's missing involvement in unionism nor as their presumed lower productivity, but as a lower self-investment on their own education. According to Butler, the high rate of prostitution among working-class women might be explained by both educational and wage gaps. Hence, Butler concluded, a specific agenda of welfare measures to increase women's education as well as some protective labor legislation would have reduced the gender wage gap and, consequently, increased their well-being and social well-being (Butler 1909, 1912).

Another group of women economists of the Progressive Era emerged at Columbia University. They were mainly influenced by Emilie Hutchinson's work on women's wage (Hutchinson 1919). Hutchinson (1877–1938) got her Ph.D. in economics at Columbia University in 1919 and therefore, was appointed associate professor of economics at Barnard. Later, Hutchinson served as head of the department of economics until her death in 1938. In her work on women's minimum wages, she denounced the limits of women's wage legislation and advocated for a wage legislation for all workers without any gender differentiation (Hutchinson 1919). Women economists at Columbia considered the minimum wage legislation as a general problem in labor market rather than a specific issue of women workers. Hence, they proposed a universal extension of labor legislation to improve society as a whole (Prash 1999; Mattei 2019). Elizabeth Faulkner Baker (1885–1973) got her Ph.D. at Columbia University in 1925.[26] Influenced by Hutchinson, Baker's doctoral thesis dealt with labor legislation for women workers in New York State (Baker 1925). Although she was not a fan of special legislations for minorities, she admitted that some progressive legislation was needed to protect the weakest workers, not specifically women, and she urged the advancement of women into more professional and skilled jobs. Baker's second book (1933) dealt with technological unemployment of manual press-feeders who had been displaced by mechanical feeders. In her book, she adopted the term 'techno cultural employment' and explained that improved pressroom technology had increased the demand for skilled labor as well as it had decreased the demand unskilled and semiskilled workers. Hence, she stressed the fact that unemployment that affected the industry was not simply the inevitable result of technological change, but rather was a cultural and sociological effect of technical improvement. In her major work (Baker 1964), Baker merged her concerns with the effects of technological changes and her interest in the conditions of women at home and women in industry by analyzing women's transition from homework to workplace and paid work. Baker was aware of the fact that, on one hand, many women were unable to divest themselves entirely of domestic and family responsibilities. On the other hand, many others had changed the nature of the traditional women's professions: from school-teaching, nursing, office work, sales assistants, and so forth (the so-called pink ghetto's occupations), they transitioned to high-skilled professions. The role of technology in this process was central: technology had opened up many jobs to anyone, including women and girls.

Although some new technological jobs might be repetitive and might require little or no training, many other new technological jobs, which required relatively high levels of education, training and skills, had emerged and they had broadened job occupations for everyone, including women. Furthermore, according to Baker, the Second World War had acted as a catalyst by accelerating the positive effect that technological development had played in improving the quality of women's work offer: properly educated women proved that they were as capable as men of doing 'men's jobs' in the office as well as in the factory.

The discussion around minimum wage legislation had started a few years earlier. In 1903, Oregon passed a law that said that women could work no more than 10 hours a day in factories and laundries, while men were allowed to negotiate their contract. It happened that a woman employed at Muller's laundry required to work more than 10 hours. In 1908, the case *Muller v. Oregon* went to the Supreme Court to establish whether women were free to negotiate a contract with an employer like men.[27] Muller, the owner of the laundry, was convicted of violating the law grounded on the necessity to protect the integrity of the home and the race by limiting female wage labor (Leonard 2005; 2016). A few years later, in 1912, the Commonwealth of Massachusetts passed the first act to provide a minimum wage for women and established a commission to set wage rates according to material conditions in workplaces. By 1919, minimum wage laws were applied in 15 states, including Washington, D.C. Nonetheless, after the First World War, things changed: in 1923, the minimum wage law was declared unconstitutional by a sentence issued in D.C. The final decision of the United States Supreme Court reinforced the unconstitutionality of the law, which made individual freedom subjected to social protection.

Many women activists like Hutchinson and Baker started to campaign for equal opportunities and to claim for the abolition of labor legislation, which made women workers weaker when entering the job market. Hutchinson's latest work (1929) was historical research. She analyzed the transition from the domestic industrial system to a highly technological industrial production which decreased workers' wages. The immediate effect was that many women joined the labor marker to support their husbands' lower incomes. Hence, in her perspective, the gender labor gap and wage gap were not actually a matter of gender but rather an issue of the evolving industrial system (Mattei 2019).

Hanna Sewall (1861–1926) got her Ph.D. in 1898 at the University of Minnesota. In 1901, AEA rewarded her dissertation on the theory of value in the pre-Classic age, which dealt with the economic thought of Aristotle, Thomas Aquinas, Grotius, Pufendorf, Steuart, and Quesnay (Sewall 1901). Sewall's work was enthusiastically praised by Mitchell in 1902 and, many years later, by Blaug (1978) and by Hutchinson (1988). She also authored the first investigation on child labor legislation in the United States (Sewall 1904).

Elinor Pancoast (1924–1960) got her Ph.D. in economics at the University of Chicago in 1927 and a faculty position at the Goucher College in

Baltimore. She worked on labor conditions in industry, on the impact of the economy on low-wage workers, especially women, and on adult education, whose aim was to help both working class women and educated women. She promoted the abolition of night work for women during their childbearing years (Pancoast 1921).

Jean Trepp McKelvey (1908–1998) received her M.A. and Ph.D. degrees from Radcliffe College in early 1930. Thereafter, she taught at Sarah Lawrence College until 1946, when she moved to Cornell University as the first faculty member in the School of International and Labor Relations. She wrote the curricula for the school and taught courses in arbitration, labor law, and labor practices. During her tenure, she instituted an arbitration training program for women. Selma Mushkin (1913–1979) got her Ph.D. at the New School Social Research, in 1956. Specializing in health economics, she worked on the economics of education during her career as research professor at George Washington University.

Phyllis Wallace (1921–1993) got her M.A. and Ph.D. from Yale in 1944 and in 1948. Appointed researcher at the National Bureau of Economic Research, while also teaching part-time at the College of the City of New York, she became chief of technical studies at the Equal Employment Opportunity Commission's Office of Research between 1966 and 1969. Wallace's works were instrumental in creating a precedent-setting legal decision in the federal case against American Telephone and Telegraph Co., which was the largest private employer in the United States. The case against Telephone and Telegraph Co. occurred in 1973: the company had perpetuated discrimination against women and minorities and agreed to pay millions in back wages as well as to make other pay adjustments. Wallace became the first woman to hold the rank of professor at the Massachusetts Institute of Technology (MIT), where she was also involved in promoting a serious campaign against sexual harassment on campus. In 1983, Mount Holyoke College conferred on her an honorary Doctor of Laws degree for having begun her "career at a time when neither blacks nor women had a fair chance, [she has] witnessed great progress toward equal employment opportunity-progress due, in no small measure, to [her] scholarship on the economics of discrimination in the labor market".[28]

Minnie Throop England (1875–1941) got her Ph.D. in economics from the University of Nebraska in 1906 and worked as assistant professor at the same university until 1921. Unlike her female colleagues, her focus was not specifically on the economic conditions of women workers but rather were directed to settle a possible social reform agenda which was able to take account of the origin and effect of business cycle. She was a macroeconomist who published important articles on crises (England 1915) and business cycles (England 1913) (Dimand 1999). Influenced by Schumpeter's theory on innovation, she dealt with monetary fluctuations by refusing Fisher's explanation. According to England, financial crises happen when "a larger number than usual of debtors are unable to meet their obligations, primarily because industry and finance have failed to yield returns as large as the estimates upon which borrowings or subsequent expenditures were based, and secondarily because of a contraction of credit" (England 1915, 749). As England wrote:

> An industrial crisis is a marked falling-off in the demand for goods. . . . Taking up the industrial cycle first, the prosperity of industry preceding the crisis is due to the enlarged demand for goods. This increased demand comes primarily from promotion, that is, from efforts to procure capital goods to enlarge industries and to establish new ones . . . Undoubtedly, there is great risk attached to every new enterprise, for there is no way to tell whether a new industry will pay except to try it; and then it is too late, if the enterprise proves to be a failure, to withdraw fun" (England 1913, 346–348). Against Fisher, England claimed that "there was no evidence for lagged adjustment of the nominal interest rate than for lagged adjustment of any other price.
> (Dimand 2000b, 153).

During the Progressive Era, other women scholars who were trained as economists emerged as key figures outside academia. Among them, Mary Abby Van Kleeck and Esther Peterson.

Mary Abby van Kleeck (1883–1972) received her bachelor's degree from Smith College in 1904. She began her career as a social researcher at the College Settlements Association, by working on women workers in factories and child labor in New York City. For decades, she served as director of the Russell Sage Foundation's department of industrial studies, where she focused her efforts on women's employment. During the First World War, van Kleeck set the standards for women working in the war industries by leading the War Labor Policies Board. In 1920, she was appointed head of the Women in Industry Service agency, established within the Department of Labor, which later became the United States Women's Bureau, a federal agency for the promotion of working women's rights and welfare.[29] At the Bureau, Esther Peterson (1906–1997), who had earned a master at Columbia University in 1930, worked as a consumer advocate, a position that included the analysis of the correctness of advertising, uniform packaging, unit pricing, and nutritional labeling (Cicarelli and Cicarelli 2003).

To conclude this partial and incomplete story of the connection between women economists as social reformers during the Progressive Era, Charlotte Perkins Gilman (1860–1935) must be mentioned. She was not a trained economist, but a prolific writer, and her main publications appeared in popular press. Nonetheless, her economic writings on women's economic issues were fundamental to the history of the relationship between the woman question and political economy. In *Women and Economics* (1898), Perkins Gilman argued that women had been subjugated in their role of wives and mothers and insisted on the necessity for women to become independent from a material point of view. Their financial autonomy would have improved not only their personal conditions but also their position within marriage. She advocated some social reforms to make women's financial independence possible. They included the professionalization of housework, as well as the building of communal living spaces with public kitchens in order to prevent isolation and frustration among housewives. Moreover, Perkins Gilman proposed some measure for an equal division of homework between men and women and insisted on the necessity to educate people to consider women's self-determination in their professions as a valid way to improve the society as a whole. One year after the publication of Perkins Gilman's book, in 1899, Thorsten Veblen used the same argument and insisted on the fact that women's work had become a tool for improving their own class status as well as their husband's class status.[30]

Perkins Gilman was certainly influenced by John Dewey and Jane Addams. More radical than John Dewey, Perkins Gilman hoped to end gender discrepancies within society by creating a fundamentally 'new woman' that aimed to challenge the traditional role of women in society as well as to change the traditional society developed around gender stereotypes rooted on an androcentric vision. According to Perkins Gilman, the 'new woman' was required to be well-informed, well-educated, assertive, confident, and influential as well as compassionate, nurturing, and sensitive. Perkins discussed education in terms of gender discrepancy based on the fact that sex relation is also an economic relation. In fact, the liberation of women went through education and economic independence. According to Perkins Gilman, education was the most effective way to transform society. She criticized the degree of competition in the schools, which perpetuated the patriarchal culture and reinforced the cult of domesticity for girls and insisted on considering social responsibility as a central issue in the education of both men and women. Perkins Gilman wrote several female utopian novels (Perkins Gilman and McLean 1907; Perkins Gilman 1915; 1916), based on the rejection of the existing androcentric society grounded on male-dominated culture and on a reevaluation of social values and attitudes towards women and their role within the economy and society. She underlined that society and education might be very different "if motherhood rather than manliness became the cultural ideal" (De Simone 1995, 16).

Perkins Gilman never stopped to question the traditional gender division of labor within household: in her later publication, she proposed to move household production to the market to benefit of a greater specialization and economies of scale. This shift would have enabled women to choose their own work without being forced to cover traditional roles within families (Perkins Gilman 1898). Finally, she insisted on the fact that institutions had been shaped around male dominance, which implied the subjection of women, constrained into houses, by perpetuating traditional gender roles.

Perkins Gilman's ideas were fundamental in the tradition of female authors who wrote in order to transform society by educating other women towards a more democratic system (Martin 1985; Lewis 1999; Allen 2009; May and Dimand 2016). In 1919, the Nineteenth Amendment passed and granted women their political rights. Nevertheless, during the interwar period, if we consider the market of academia for women, the number of Ph.D. female students collapsed as well as the number of women among faculty members. Causes have been traced by Forget as follows:

> First, social work started to emerge as an academic subject and drew to it women who saw economics as a way of addressing social injustice. Second, home economics began to grow in importance during this period and attracted a number of women interested in questions of labor and consumption economics away from economics towards this newly professionalizing discipline. Third, the expansion of federal government employment in areas of agriculture, home economics, consumer affairs and labor offered another, more-welcoming, employment opportunity for women.
>
> (Forget 2011, 23)

The nature of home economics will be scrutinized in the next chapter.

Besides academic careers and public engagement in social reformism, women's emancipation in the United States during the Progressive Era was promoted by the number of female entrepreneurs, which dramatically increased in that period. The phenomenon was common in Great Britain as well as in Austria, as previously seen. Businesswomen were limited by social barriers such as separate entrances and separated women's departments in brokerage firms and banks; they were recommended only for moderate credit and discouraged from making investments; the mainstream press devaluated and underestimated women's entrepreneurial ambitions. Furthermore, women's accumulation of wealth was barely recognized and often stigmatized. This led many women in business to wear a male face, by using their husbands or sons' names (Scott 1988).

Things gradually changed in the late 19th century. As Yohn (2006) rightly pointed out, the fervent process of women's emancipation as entrepreneurs allowed them to renegotiate and reconstruct gender ideology. Many examples that occurred in the United States may be remembered.

In 1870, sisters Victoria Claflin Woodhull (1838–1927) and Tennessee Claflin (1844–1923) opened a Wall Street brokerage firm. Two years later, Victoria ran for the presidency of the United States, although nobody took the candidacy seriously. Hetty Green (1834–1916), better known as the 'Witch of Wall Street', became the wealthiest woman in the country by combining her inheritance with conservative investments, substantial cash reserves to back up any movement, and an exceedingly cool head amidst turmoil. Miriam Folline Leslie (1836–1914) was forced to take her husband's full name (Frank Leslie) to keep their editorial and publishing business empire alive and productive after her husband's death. Harriet Ayer (1849–1903) started the first cosmetic company in the United States and was highly regarded as the author of articles about beauty, health, and etiquette. Ellen Demorest (1824–1898) launched a quarterly magazine, *Mme Demorest's Mirror of Fashions*, and opened a women's fashion emporium at 473 Broadway, where she employed both black and white female workers. Sarah Gammon Bickford (1852?–1931) was the first African American entrepreneur in the United States: a former slave, she owned the Virginia City Water Company in Montana since 1890 (Baumler 2014). Madame C. J. Walker (1867–1919), aka Sarah Breedlove, became the wealthiest African American woman in the country by developing and marketing a line of beauty cosmetics and hair products for black women through her 'Madame C.J. Walker Manufacturing Company', the cosmetic firm she founded in 1910 in Indianapolis (Chesler and Goodman 1976; Gamber 1998; Ginzberg 1992; Nenadic 1998; Kwolek-Folland 2002).

The interconnection between women in business and women engaged in social activism was twofold. On one side, because of the difficulties to participate in financial markets and traditional business, many women in the United States became social entrepreneurs. As already mentioned earlier in this chapter, this phenomenon was common in European countries too. The number of social reform organizations founded and led by women dramatically increased, as well as the amount of dollars they collected. On the other side, many businesswomen transformed their financial success into political strategies to advocate for women's rights (Yaeger 1999).

Notes

1 Active suffragists in Great Britain gathered around two groups: the National Union of Women's Suffrage Societies, founded on 1897 and led by Millicent Garrett Fawcett (1847–1929), and the Women's Social and Political Union, established in 1903 by Emmeline Pankhurst (1858–1928).
2 The debate on Mill's contribution to the history of feminism has been broadly analyzed (see Sommers 1994).
3 Their romance and reciprocal influence on the woman question has been the object of many scholars, among them Friedrich Hayek (1951).
4 Founded in 1869, the society was aimed to promote a serious inquiry about poverty. It attacked any form of charity being it a source of social parasitism for some citizens constantly dependent on it.
5 Owen's program, which converged into the so-called Factory Act (1819), included non-negotiable 10 working hours per day, the prohibition for children below 10 years old to be employed as workers; and only part-time work for children between 10 and 12 years old.
6 Fabians' doctrine was a tentative to combine social and economic emancipation of working class and Ricardo's concept of rent (Beer 1920).
7 The analysis of the sweating system was started by Charles Booth's investigation on the poverty level in London. Influenced by his wife, Mary Macauly, Booth mainly investigated women workers' conditions. Published in 17 volumes between 1886 and 1903 and organized in three sections (poverty, industry, and religion), his inquiry revealed the urgency to an active labor reform against the traditional charity system in Great Britain. Booth's results had a big impact on many women activists, such as Clara Collet, Clementina Black, and Beatrice Webb.
8 Among them: Maud Pember Reeves, Barbara Drake, Alice Clark, Lilian Dawson, Helen Blagg, Charlotte Wilson, Charlotte Payne-Townshend Shaw, Emma Brooke,

Constance Long, Ernestine Mills, Gasquoine Hartley; Millicent Murby, Ethel Bentham, Ruth Cavendish Bentinck, Mabel Atkinson, and Helena M. Swanwick.

9 Closely associated with unionism, cooperativism, and Owenism, Guildism reached its momentum especially after John Stuart Mill's endorsement of the cooperative system as a possible solution to solve the conflict between capitalism and socialism.

10 Vera Anstey was a lecturer in economic history and reader in commerce at the London School of Economics; Ivy Pinchbeck and Mabel Buer were readers in economic history at Bedford College and at the University of Reading, respectively. Julia Mann and M. G. Jones, after having served as college tutors in Oxford and Cambridge, respectively became principal and vice-principal of their colleges. Dorothy Marshall taught at Bedford College, and afterwards at University College in Cardiff. Dorothy George, B. L. Hutchins, Amy Harrison, and Mildred Bulkley were full-time researchers with high academic profiles. Alice Clark was an economic historian as well as a businesswoman and political activist. J. Dunlop was very active in organizing voluntarism to support women workers' conditions.

11 The relationship between the rise of a feminist consciousness and the high number of Jewish scholars and activists within feminist movements between the late 19th and early 20th century has been extensively studied, especially in relation to the contributions of German-speaking female writers and political activists (Freidenreich 2002), and within modern Jewish philosophy (Fricker and Hornsby 2000; Ross 2004, Rudavsky 2007).

12 Schwarzwald inspired several fictional characters, such as Kraus's Hofrätin Schwarz-Gelber, Musil's Diotima, Bettauer's Dr. Eugenia Harz (Holmes 2012). Another famous Viennese salon was hosted by a witty journalist, Bertha Zuckerkandl (1864–1945): her salon became the headquarter of the artistic movement, the Secession. Alma Schindler (1879–1964), a talented musician better known as the wife of Gustav Mahler, Walter Gropius, and Franz Werfel, run her own salon where many intellectuals converged.

13 In 1938, Schwarzwald decided not to return to Vienna from a lecture tour in Denmark and to emigrate to Switzerland. The National Socialists sold her entire property, the school was closed, and most of her students were expelled or forced to fly out.

14 Although during the Austro-fascist regime (1933–1938) the climate towards Jews was generally hostile, discrimination was restrained, while it was introduced by the Nurnberg laws in 1938 when Nazis seized power in Austria.

15 The Viennese stock market collapsed in 1924.

16 Between 1919 and 1923, Austria's money supply increased by 14,250%, and the cost-of-living index, which had risen to 1,640 by November 1918, had gone up to 1,183,600 4 by January 1923. As retrieved on May 21, 2019, at: https://fee.org/articles/the-great-austrian-inflation/.

17 Between 1929 and 1933, the unemployment rate increased from 6% to 16%.

18 The Palace of Justice was burnt in 1927.

19 The *Nationalökonomische Gesellschaft* (the Austrian Economic Society) was renewed in 1918 by Mises, Mayer, Schumpeter, and Pribram. The Society represented a place where it was possible to regularly discuss economic problems, besides Mises' *Privatseminar*, which were held on a regular schedule. The Society was revived in 1927 with the addition of Hayek, Machlup, Rosenstein-Rodan, and Strigl as new members. In 1932, Haberler, Morgenstern, Schlesinger and Strigl joined the board members. The Society was dismissed in 1938 because of the racial ban against Jews, who were the majority of its members (Mises [1978] (2013); Hülsmann 2007; Klausinger 2016; Dekker 2014, 2016).

20 As retrieved on July 21, 2018, at: www.fraueninbewegung.onb.ac.at/Pages/PersonDetail.aspx?p_iPersonenID=12538457

21 Their male colleagues and mentors followed the same destiny. Mises moved to Geneva in 1934, thereafter to New York in 1940; Schumpeter went to Harvard in 1932; Hayek

left Vienna for London in 1931, thereafter, left London for Chicago in 1950; Morgenstern went to Princeton in 1938.

22 The Association was founded in 1866 in Vienna (Albisetti 1996).

23 As retrieved on June 7, 2018, at: www3.wiso.uni-hamburg.de/en/professuren/geschichte-der-vwl/research/early-women-economists-infrom-german-speaking-countries/

24 To be added the names of Charlotte Engel-Reimers (1870–1930), Elisabeth Altmann-Gottheiner (1874–1930), Charlotte Reichenau (1890–1952), Charlotte Lorenz (1895–1975), Edith Hirsch (1899–2003), Elisabeth Liefmann-Keil (1908–1975), Ingeborg Esenwein-Rothe (1911–2002), Fanny Ginor (1911–), Wilhelmine Dreißig (1913–1977); however, they did not specifically work on the woman question. As retrieved on June 5, 2018, at: www3.wiso.uni-hamburg.de/en/professuren/geschichte-der-vwl/research/early-women-economists-infrom-german-speaking-countries/.

25 Biographical details about Susan Smith McKinney Stewart are available at: www.bklyn library.org/blog/2018/01/25/susan-smith-mckinney.

26 Before undertaking graduate studies, Baker was instructor in economics at Lewiston State Normal School in Idaho (1915–1917) and Dean of Women at Ellensberg State Normal School in Washington State (1917–1918). She left Ellensberg for Barnard College, where she worked as instructor in economics between 1919 and 1926. She was promoted to assistant professor of economics at Barnard College in 1926, and in 1939 became associate professor of economics. In 1948, Baker was appointed professor of economics at Barnard, where she remained until her retirement in 1952, serving as chair of the department of economics between 1940 and 1952 (Nyland and Rix 2000). Outside academia, she joined the Taylor Society for the diffusion and development of management principles as pioneered by Frederick Winslow Taylor. Between 1935 and 1946, Baker served as Director of its New York section. Baker was a member of AEA, the Industrial Relations Research Association, and the National Planning Association.

27 As retrieved on May 19, 2018, at: https://supreme.justia.com/cases/federal/us/208/412/.

28 As retrieved on February 24, 2019, at: http://iwer.mit.edu/about/iwer-pioneers/phyllis-a-wallace/.

29 The United States Women's Bureau's goals included the following: to make women aware of their rights in the workplace; to design laws and policies able to promote the interests of working women; to collect and analyze data related with women and work; and to report research results to the President, the Congress, and the nation. The Bureau had a major role in the inclusion of women's work under the terms of the Fair Labor Standards Act: issued in 1938, the act set minimum pay and maximum hours. It was also determinant in promoting the Equal Pay Act (1963) as well as in preparing many more contributions for a specific legislation able to guarantee equal employment opportunity, family and medical leave, and protection against discrimination in hiring due to age or pregnancy.

30 Veblen wrote: "Where the fighting class is in the position of dominance and prescriptive legitimacy, the canons of conduct are shaped chiefly by the common sense of the body of fighting men. . . . The discipline of predatory life makes for an attitude of mastery on the part of the able-bodied men in all their relations with the weaker members of the group, and especially in their relations with the women. . . . All the women in the group will share in the class repression and depreciation that belongs to them as women, but the status of women taken from hostile groups has an additional feature. Such a woman not only belongs to a subservient and low class, but she also stands in a special relation to her captor. She is a trophy of the raid, and therefore an evidence of exploit, and on this ground, it is to her captor's interest to maintain a peculiarly obvious relation of mastery toward her" (Veblen 1899, 506–507).

References

Abbott E. (1910) *Women in Industry: A Study in American Economic History*. New York: D. Appleton and Company.

Akkerman T. (1998) "Liberalism and Feminism in Late Nineteenth Century Britain". Akkerman T. and Stuurman S. (Eds.) *Perspectives on Feminist Political Thought in European History: From the Middle age to The Present*. London: Routledge, pp. 168–185.

Albisetti J. (1996) "Female Education in German Speaking Austria, Germany, and Switzerland". Good D., Grandner M., and Mayes M.J. (Eds.) *Austrian Women in the Nineteen and Twentieth Century*. Oxford: Berghahn Books, pp. 39–57.

Alexander S. (2013) "Introduction". Alexander S. (Ed.) *Women's Fabian Tracts*. London: Routledge, pp. 1–13.

Allen A. (1991) *Feminism and Motherhood in Germany, 1800–1914*. New Brunswick, NJ: Rutgers University Press.

Allen J. (2009) *The Feminism of Charlotte Perkins Gilman: Sexualities, Histories, Progressivism*. Chicago: The University of Chicago Press.

Anderson H. (1992) *Utopian Feminism: Women's Movements in 'fin-de-siècle' Vienna*. New Haven, CT: Yale University Press.

Armitage D. (2002) "The Declaration of Independence and the International Law". *The William and Mary Quarterly*. Vol. 59:1, pp. 39–64.

Athney S. (2000) "Eugenic Feminisms in Late Nineteenth-Century America: Reading Race in Victoria Woodhull, Frances Willard, Anna Julia Cooper and Ida B. Wells". *Genders*. Vol. 3:6. Electronic Journal: www.colorado.edu/gendersarchive1998-2013/2000/06/01/eugenic-feminisms-late-nineteenth-century-america-reading-race-victoria-woodhull-frances

Atkinson M. (2013) "The Economic Foundation of the Women's Movements". Alexander S. (Ed.) *Women's Fabian Tracts*. London: Routledge, pp. 256–282.

Bader-Zaar B. (2006) "Marianne Hainisch". De Haan F., Draskalova K., and Loutfi A. (Eds.) *A Biographical Dictionary of Women's Movements and Feminisms in Central, Eastern, and South Eastern Europe, 19th and 20th Centuries*. Budapest: Central European University Press, pp. 173–176.

Bader-Zaar B. (2016) "Liberalism and the Emancipation of Women in Austria in the 19th and Beginning of the 20th Century". *Bulgarian Historical Review*. Vol. 25:1, pp. 137–141.

Baker E. (1925) *Protective Labor Legislation With Special Reference to Women in the State of New York*. New York: Columbia University Press.

Baker E. (1933) *Displacement of Men by Machines*. New York: Columbia University Press.

Baker E. (1964) *Technology and Women's Work*. New York: Columbia University Press.

Balabkins N. (2011) "Gustav Stolper's Influence on U.S. Industrial Disarment Policy in West Germany, 1945–1946". Backhaus J. (Ed.) *The Beginning of Scholarly Economic Journalism. The Austrian Economist and the German Economist*. New York, Dordrecht, Heidelberg, London: Springer, pp. 147–162.

Balch E. (1910) "The Education and Efficiency of Women". *Annals of the Academy of Political Science*, Vol. 1:1, pp. 61–71.

Balch E. (1912) "Restriction of Immigration: Discussion". *American Economic Review*, Vol. 2:1, pp. 63–66.

Balch E. (1914) "The Economic Role of the Housewife". *Home Progress*. Vol. 4:(September), pp. 620–624.

Baumler E. (2014) "Celebrating Sarah Bickford". *Woman*. Vol. 406, pp. 72–73.

Becchio G. (2019) "Austrian School Women Economists". Madden K. and Dimand R. (Eds.) *Routledge Handbook of the History of Women's Economic Thought*. London: Routledge, pp. 309–324.

Beer M. (1920) *History of British Socialism*. London: G. Bells & Sons.

Beller S. (1989) *Vienna and the Jews, 1867–1938: A Cultural History*. Cambridge: Cambridge University Press.

Beller S. (2001) "Is There a Jewish Aspect to Modern Austrian Identity?". Mittelmann H. and Wallas A. (Eds.) *Österreich-Konzeptionen und jüdisches Selbtverständnis: Identität-Trasfigurationen um 19. und 20. Jahrhundert*. Tübingen: Max Niemeyer, pp. 43–52.

Berg M. (1992) "The First Women Economic Historians". *The Economic History Review*. Vol. 45:2, pp. 308–329.

Blaug M. (1978) *Economic Theory in Retrospect*. Cambridge: Cambridge University Press.

Bodichon B. (1857) *Women and Work*. London: Bosworth and Harrison.

Booth C. (1886–1903) *Life and Labour of the People*. 17 volumes. London: Macmillan.

Bosanquet H. (1902) *The Strength of the People. A Study on Women's Wage*. London: Macmillan.

Bosanquet H. (1906) *The Family*. London: Macmillan.

Bosanquet H. (1909) *Poor Law Report of 1909: A Summary*. London: Macmillan.

Botting E. (2016) *Wollstonecraft, Mill, and Women's Human Rights*. New Haven, CT: Yale University Press.

Braun M. (1929) *Theorie der staatlichen Wirtschaftspolitik*. Leipzig and Vienna: Franz Deuticke.

Braun M. et al. (Eds.) (1930) *Frauenbewegung, Frauenbildung und Frauenarbeit*. Vienna: Bund österreicischer Frauenverein.

Breckenridge S. and Abbot E. (1912) *The Delinquent Child and the Home*. New York: Russell Sage Foundation.

Breckinridge S. and Talbot M. (1912) *The Modern Household*. Boston: Whitcomb and Barrows.

Brenner M. and Penslar D. (Eds.) (1999) *In Search of Jewish Community: Jewish Identities in Germany and Austria, 1918–1933*. Bloomington, IN: Indiana University Press.

Brown L. (1973) "Jane Austen and the Feminist Tradition". *Nineteenth-Century Fiction*. Vol. 28:3, pp. 321–338.

Butler E. (1909) *Women and the Trades: 1907–1908*. New York: Charities Publication Committee.

Butler E. (1912) *Saleswomen in Mercantile Stores: Baltimore 1909*. New York: Charities Publication Committee.

Butler J. (1868) *The Education and Employment of Women*. Liverpool: Thomas Brackell.

Butler M. (1978) "Early Roots of Feminism: John Locke and the Attack on Patriarchy". *The American Political Science Review*. Vol. 72:1, pp. 135–150.

Čakardić A. (2018) "From Theory of Accumulation to Social-Reproduction Theory. A Case for Luxemburgian Feminism". *Historical Materialism*. Vol. 25:4, pp. 37–64.

Chassonnery-Zaïgouche C. (2019) "Is Equal Pay Worth It?". Madden K. and Dimand R. (Eds.) *Routledge Handbook of the History of Women's Economic Thought*. London: Routledge, pp. 129–149.

Chesler P. and Goodman E. (1976) *Women, Money, and the Power*. New York: William Morrow.

Cicarelli J. and Cicarelli J. (2003) *Distinguished Women Economists*. Westport, CT: Greenwood Press.

Cole M. (1946) *The Rate for the Job, a Pamphlet Prepared for the Fabian Women's Group and Based on the Evidence of the Group Before the Royal Commission on Equal Pay*. London: Gollancz.

Collet C. (1902) *Educated Working Women*. London: P.S. King and Sons.

Coman K. (1912) *Economic Beginnings of the Far West*. New York: MacMillan.

Combs M.B. (2006) *"Cui Bono?* The 1870 British Married Women's Property Act, Bargaining Power, and the Distribution of Resources within Marriages". *Feminist Economics.* Vol. 12:1–2, pp. 51–83.

Craver E. (1986) "The Emigration of the Austrian Economists". *History of Political Economy.* Vol. 18:1, pp. 1–32.

Dalley L. (2010) "Domesticating Political Economy: Language, Gender, and Economics in the *Illustrations of Political Economy*". Dzelzainis E. and Kaplan C. (Eds.) *Harriet Martineau: Authorship, Society and Empire.* Manchester: Manchester University Press, pp. 103–117.

Davies M. (Ed.) (1931) *Life as We Have Known It: By Co-operative Working Women.* London: Hogarth Publisher.

Davis K. (1899) "An Error in Austrian Wage Statistics". *Journal of Political Economy.* Vol. 8:1, pp. 102–106.

Davis K. (1900) "The Modern Condition of Agricultural Labor in Bohemia". *Journal of Political Economy.* Vol. 8:4, pp. 491–523.

De Grouchy S. ([1798] 2019). *Letters on Sympathy: A Critical Engagement with Adam Smith's The Theory of Moral Sentiments.* Oxford: Oxford University Press.

De Pizan C. (1999) *The Book of the City of Ladies.* London: Penguin.

De Simone D. (1995) "Charlotte Perkins Gilman and the Feminization of Education". *WILLA.* Vol. 4, pp. 13–17.

Dekker E. (2014) "The Vienna Circles: Cultivating Economic Knowledge Outside Academia". *Erasmus Journal for Philosophy and Economics.* Vol. 7:2, pp. 30–53.

Dekker E. (2016) *The Viennese Students of Civilization.* Cambridge: Cambridge University Press.

Dimand M.A., Dimand R., and Forget E. (Eds.) (1995) *Women of Value: Feminist Essays on the History of Women in Economics.* Aldershot: Edward Elgar.

Dimand R. (1999) "Minnie Throop England on Crises and Cycles: A Neglected Early Macroeconomist". *Feminist Economics.* Vol. 5:3, pp. 107–126.

Dimand R. (2000a) "Emily Green Balch". Dimand R., Dimand M.A., and Forget E. (Eds.) *A Biographical Dictionary of Women Economists.* Cheltenham: Edward Elgar, pp. 21–24.

Dimand R. (2000b) "Minnie Throop England". Dimand R., Dimand M.A., and Forget E. (Eds.) *A Biographical Dictionary of Women Economists.* Cheltenham: Edward Elgar, pp. 153–155.

Dimand R. (2003) "An Eighteenth-Century English Feminist Response to Political Economy: Priscilla Wakefield's *Reflections* (1798)". Dimand R. and Nyland C. (Eds.) *The Status of Women in Classical Economic Thought.* Cheltenham: Edward Elgar, pp. 194–205.

Dimand R. and Black G. (2012) "Clare de Graffenreid and the Art of Controversy: A Prizewinning Woman Economist in the First Decade of the American Economic Association". *Journal of the History of Economic Thought.* Vol. 34:3, pp. 339–353.

Donner W. (1993) "John Stuart Mill's Liberal Feminism". *Philosophical Studies.* Vol. 69:2–3, pp. 155–166.

Dubois E. and Gordon L. (1983) "Seeking Ecstasy on the Battlefield: Danger and Pleasure in Nineteenth-Century Feminist Sexual Thought". *Feminist Studies.* Vol. 9:1, pp. 7–25.

Dudden F. (2011) *Fighting Chance: The Struggle Over Woman Suffrage and Black Suffrage in Reconstruction America.* New York: Oxford University Press.

Dzuback M.A. (2006) "Berkeley Women Economists, Public Policy, and Civic Sensibility". Warren D., and Patrick J. (Eds.) *Civic and Moral Learning in America.* New York: Palgrave Macmillan, pp. 153–172.

Dzuback M.A. (2019) "Women Economists in the Academy. Struggles and Strategies, 1900–1940". Madden K. and Dimand R. (Eds.) *Routledge Handbook of the History of Women's Economic Thought.* London: Routledge, pp. 221–228

Edelman T. (2010) "Gender and Conversion Revised". Moore D. and Kaplan M. (Eds.) *Gender and Jewish History*. Bloomington, IN: Indiana University Press, pp. 170–188.

Edgeworth F.Y. (1922) "Equal Pay for Men and Women for Equal Work". *The Economic Journal*. Vol. 32:128, pp. 431–457.

Edgeworth F.Y. (1923) "Women's Wages in Relation to Economic Welfare". *The Economic Journal*. Vol. 33:132, pp. 487–495.

Elston M.A. (2017) "Elizabeth Garrett Anderson". *Oxford Dictionary of National Biography*. As retrieved on July 2, 2018 at: https://doi.org/10.1093/ref:odnb/30406

Embacher H. (1998) "Middle Class, Liberal, Intellectual, Female, and Jewish: The Expulsion of 'Female Rationality' from Austria". Bischof G., Pelinka A., and Thurner E. (Eds.) *Women in Austria*. London: Transaction Publisher, pp. 5–14.

England M.T. (1913) "Economic Crises". *Journal of Political Economy*. Vol. 21:4, pp. 345–354.

England M.T. (1915) "Promotion as the Cause of Crises". *The Quarterly Journal of Economics*. Vol. 29:4, pp. 748–767.

Evans R. (1977) *The Feminists: Women's Emancipation Movements in Europe, America and Australasia 1840–1920*. London: Croom Helm. Reprinted (2013) *The Feminists: Women's Emancipation Movements in Europe, America and Australasia 1840–1920*. London: Routledge.

Fawcett Garrett M. (1892) "Mr. Sidney Webb's Article on Women's Wage". *The Economic Journal*. Vol. 2:5, pp. 173–176.

Fawcett Garrett M. (1918a) "Equal Pay for Equal Work". *The Economic Journal*. Vol. 28:109, pp. 1–6.

Fawcett Garrett M. (1918b) "Equal Pay for Equal Value". *The Economic Journal*. Vol. 114:18, pp. 387–390.

Feichtinger J. (2001) *Wissenschaft zwischen den Kulturen. Österreichische Hochschullehrer in der Emigration 1933–1945*. Frankfurt am Main and New York: Campus Verlag.

Filmer R. ([1680] 1969) *Patriarcha or the Natural Power of King*. New York: Hafner.

Fitzpatrick E. (1990) *Endless Crusade: Women Social Scientists* and *Progressive Reform*. New York: Oxford University Press.

Fitzpatrick P. (1955) "The Early Teaching of Statistics in American Colleges and Universities". *The American Statistician*. Vol. 9:5, pp. 12–18.

Flich R. (1990) "Der Fall Auguste Flickert-eine Lehrerin macht Schlagzeilen". *Wiener Geschichtsblatter*. Vol. 45:1, pp. 1–24.

Folbre N. (2009) *Greed, Lust, and Gender*. Oxford: Oxford University Press.

Forget E. (1995) "American Women Economists, 1900–1940: Doctoral Dissertations and Research Specialization". Dimand M.A., Dimand R., and Forget E. (Eds.) *Women of Value*. Aldershot and Brookfield: Edward Elgar, pp. 25–38.

Forget E. (2003) "Cultivating Sympathy: Sophie Condorcet's Letters on Sympathy". Dimand R. and Nyland C. (Eds.) *The Status of Women in Classical Economic Thought*. Cheltenham and Northampton, MA: Edward Elgar, pp. 142–161.

Forget E. (2011) "American Women and the Economics Profession in the Twentieth Century". *Oeconomica*. Vol. 1:1, pp. 19–30.

Fraser H., Johnson J., and Green S. (2003) *Gender and the Victorian Periodical*. Cambridge and New York: Cambridge University Press.

Freidenreich H. (2002) *Female, Jewish, and Educated: The Lives of Central European University Women*. Bloomington, IN: Indiana University Press.

Freidenreich H. (2009) "Käthe Leichter". *Jewish Women: A Comprehensive Historical Encyclopedia*. As retrieved on June 13, 2018 at: https://jwa.org/encyclopedia/article/leichter-kaethe.

Fricker M. and Hornsby J. (2000) *The Cambridge Companion to Feminism in Philosophy*. Cambridge: Cambridge University Press.

Gage F. (1863) "Sojourner Truth". *Independent*: New York, 23 April.

Gamber W. (1998) "A Gendered Enterprise: Placing Nineteenth-Century Businesswomen in History". *Business History Review*. Vol. 72:2, pp. 188–241.

Gerhard U. (2002) "The Women's Movement in Germany". Griffin G. and Braidotti R. (Eds.) *Thinking Differently: A Reader in European Women's Studies*. London and New York: Zed Books, pp. 321–331.

Ginzberg L. (1992) *Women and the Work of Benevolence: Morality, Politics, and Class in Nineteenth-Century United States*. New Haven, CT: Yale University Press.

Gnauck-Kühne E. (1909) *Das soziale Gemeinschaftsleben im deutschen Reich. Leitfaden der Volkswirtschaftslehre und Bürgerkunde in sozialgeschichtlichem Aufbau für höhere Schulen und zum Selbstunterricht*. Mönchengldbach: Volksvereins Verlag.

Gournay (de) M. ([1622] 2002) *Egalité des Hommes et des Femmes*. Arnould J., Berriot-Salvadore E., Bichard-Thomine M., Blum C., Franchetti A., and Worth-Stylianou V. (Eds.) *Œuvres complètes*. Paris: Honoré Champion.

Gouverneur V. (2013) "Mill Versus Jevons on Traditional Sexual Division of Labour: Is Gender Equality Efficient?". *The European Journal of the History of Economic Thought*. Vol. 20:5, pp. 741–775.

Graffenreid (de) C. (1890) "Child Labor". *Publications of the American Economic Association*. Vol. 5:2, pp. 195–271.

Grimké S. (2010) "Letter VIII: On the Condition of Women in the United States". Barker D. and Kuiper E. (Eds.) *Feminist Economics: Critical Concepts in Economics*. London: Routledge, pp. 75–80.

Groenewegen P. (1994) "A Neglected Daughter of Adam Smith: Clara Elizabeth Collet (1860–1948)". Groenewegen P. (Ed.) *Feminism and Political Economy in Victorian England*. Aldershot and Brookfield: Edward Elgar, pp. 147–173.

Groenewegen P. (1995) *A Soaring Eagle: Alfred Marshall 1842–1924*. Aldershot and Brookfield: Edward Elgar.

Groenewegen P. (2000) "Helen Dendy Bosanquet". Dimand R., Dimand M.A., and Forget E. (Eds.) *A Biographical Dictionary of Women Economists*. Cheltenham: Edward Elgar, pp. 60–65.

Gruber H. (1991) *Red Vienna: Experiment in Working-Class Culture 1919–1934*. Oxford: Oxford University Press.

Hagemann H. (2000) "Cläre Tisch (1907–41)". Dimand R., Dimand M.A., and Forget E. (Eds.) *A Biographical Dictionary of Woman Economists*. Aldershot: Edward Elgar, pp. 426–429.

Hagemann H. (forthcoming). "Louise Sommer (1889–1964)". Dimand R. and Forget E. (Eds.) *A Biographical Dictionary of Woman Economists*. 2nd Enlarged Edition. Aldershot: Edward Elgar.

Halldenius L. (2016) *Mary Wollstonecraft and Feminist Republicanism*. London: Routledge.

Hammond C. (1993) "American Women and the Professionalization of Economics". *Review of Social Economy*. Vol. 51:3, pp. 347–370.

Hammond C. (2000a) "Sophonisba Breckinridge". Dimand R., Dimand M.A., and Forget E. (Eds.) *A Biographical Dictionary of Women Economists*. Cheltenham: Edward Elgar, pp. 81–87.

Hammond C. (2000b) "Edith Abbot". Dimand R., Dimand M.A., and Forget E. (Eds.) *A Biographical Dictionary of Women Economists*. Cheltenham: Edward Elgar, pp. 1–7.

Hanak-Lettner W. (2015) *Die Universität Eine Kampfzone: The University a Battleground*. Vienna: Picus Verlag.

Hauch G. (2012) "Against the Mock Battle of Words – Therese Schlesinger, nee' Eckstein (1863–1940)". Bishop G., Plasser F., and Maltschnig E. (Eds.) *Austrian Lives*. Innsbruck: Innsbruck University Press, pp. 71–91.

Hayek F.A. (1935) *Collectivist Economic Planning*. London: George Routledge & Sons.

Hayek F.A. (1951) *John Stuart Mill and Harriet Taylor: Their Correspondence and Subsequent Marriage*. Chicago: The University of Chicago Press.

Heather-Bigg A. (1894) "The Wife's Contribution to Family Income". *The Economic Journal*. Vol. 4:13, pp. 51–58.

Hekman S. (1992) "John Stuart Mill's the Subjection of Women: The Foundations of Liberal Feminism". *History of European Ideas*. Vol. 15:4–6, pp. 681–686.

Hertz D. (1988) *Jewish High Society in Old Regime Berlin*. New Haven, CT: Yale University Press.

Hirsch L. (2013) *From the Shtetl to the Lecture Hall: Jewish Women and Cultural Exchange*. Lanham, MD: University Press of America.

Holmes D. (2012) "Genia Schwarzwald and Her Viennese Salon". Bischof G., Plasser F., and Maltsching E. (Eds.) *Austrian Lives*. Innsbruck: Innsbruck University Press, pp. 190–211.

Holmes D. and Silverman L. (2009) "Beyond the Coffeehouse. Vienna as a Cultural Center between the World Wars". Holmes D., and Silverman L. (Eds.) *Interwar Vienna: Culture between Tradition and Modernity*. Rochester: Camden House, pp. 1–20.

Hülsmann G. (2007) *The Last Knight of Liberalism*. Auburn, AL: Ludwig von Mises Institute.

Hunt C. (2013) "Gertrude Tuckwell and the British Labour Movement, 1891–1921: A Study in Motives and Influences". *Women's History Review*. Vol. 22:3, pp. 478–496.

Hutchins B. (1907) "Home Work and Sweating, the Causes and Remedies". *Fabian Tract 130*. London: The Fabian Society.

Hutchins B. and Harrison A. (1903) *A History of Factory Legislation*. Westminster: P.S. King and Son.

Hutchinson E. (1919) *Women's Wages: A Study of Wages of Industrial Women and Measures Suggested to Increase Them*. New York: Columbia University Press.

Hutchinson E. (1929) "The Economic Problems of Women". *The Annals of the American Academy of Political and Social Science*. Vol. 143:1, pp. 132–136.

Hutchinson T. (1988) *Before Adam Smith: The Emergence of Political Economy, 1662–1776*. Oxford: Basic Blackwell.

Hyman P. (1995) *Gender and Assimilation in Modern Jewish History: The Roles and Representation of Women*. Seattle: University of Washington Press.

Jevons W.S. (1883) "Married Women in Factories". Jevons W.S. (Ed.) *Methods of Social Reform and Other Papers*. London: Macmillan and Co.

Johnson M. (2019) "Daughters of Commons. Wisconsin Women and Institutionalism". Madden K. and Dimand R. (Eds.) *Routledge Handbook of the History of Women's Economic Thought*. London: Routledge, pp. 299–249.

Jordan J. and Sharp I. (2003) *Josephine Butler and the Prostitution Campaigns: Diseases of the Body Politic*. London: Routledge.

Kaplan M. (1991) *The Making of the Jewish Middle Class: Women, Family and Identity in Imperial Germany*. New York: Oxford University Press.

Kellor F. (1901) *Experimental Sociology: Descriptive and Analytical*. London: McMillan and Company Limited.

Klausinger H. (2014) "Academic Anti-Semitism and the Austrian School: Vienna, 1918–1945". *Atlantic Economic Journal*. Vol. 42:2, pp. 1–14.

Klausinger H. (2016) "The Nationalökonomische Gesellschaft (Austrian Economic Association) in the Interwar Period and Beyond". Fiorito L., Scheall S. and Suprinyak E. (Eds.) *Research in the History of Economic Thought and Methodology*. Vol. 34A. Bingley: Emerald, pp. 5–44.

Knowles L. (1921) *The Industrial and Commercial Revolutions in Great Britain During the Nineteenth Century*. London: Routledge.

Knox J. (1558) *First Blast of the Trumpet Against the Monstrous Regiment of Women*. Geneva: J. Poullain and A. Rebul.

Kollontai A. ([1918] 1971) "New Woman". *The Autobiography of a Sexually Emancipated Communist Woman*. As retrieved on April 14, 2019 at: www.marxists.org/archive/kollonta/1918/new-morality.htm

Kollontai A. ([1909] 1977) "The Social Basis of the Woman Question". *Selected Writings of Alexandra Kollontai*. Allison & Busby. As retrieved on April 14, 2019 at: www.marxists.org/archive/kollonta/1909/social-basis.htm

Kollontai A. ([1916] 1977) "Working Woman and Mother". *Selected Writings of Alexandra Kollontai*. As retrieved on April 14, 2019 at: www.marxists.org/archive/kollonta/1916/working-mother.htm

Kölp R. (2006) "Adelheid Popp". De Haan F., Draskalova K., and Loutfi A. (Eds.) *A Biographical Dictionary of Women's Movements and Feminisms in Central, Eastern, and South Eastern Europe, 19th and 20th Centuries*. Budapest: Central European University Press, pp. 447–449.

Kuczynski M. (Ed.) (1942) *Women under the Swastika*. London: Free German League of Culture in Great Britain.

Kwolek-Folland A. (2002) *Incorporating Women: A History of Women and Business in the United States*. New York: Palgrave MacMillan.

Lees A. (2004) *Character Is Destiny: The Autobiography of Alice Solomon*. Ann Arbor, MI: The University of Michigan Press.

Lefke S. (1997) "'Truly Womanly' and 'Truly German'. Women's Rights and National Identity in *Die Frau*". Herminghouse P. and Mueller M. (Eds.) *Gender and Germanness: Cultural Productions of Nation*. New York and Oxford: Berghahn Books, pp. 129–144.

Leischko H. (2002) "Braun Martha Stephanie". Keintzel B. and Korotin I. (Eds.) *Wissenschafterinnen in und aus Österreich. Leben – Werk – Wirken*. Vienna: Böhlau Verlag, pp. 92–95.

Leonard T. (2005) "Protecting Family and Race: The Progressive Case for Regulating Women's Work". *American Journal of Economics and Sociology*. Vol. 64:3, pp. 757–791.

Leonard T. (2009) "American Economic Reform in the Progressive Era: Its Foundational Beliefs and Their Relation to Eugenics". *History of Political Economy*. Vol. 41:1, pp. 109–141.

Leonard T. (2016) *Illiberal Reformers*. Princeton, NJ: Princeton University Press.

Lewis M. (1999) "History of Economic Thought". Peterson J. and Lewis M. (Eds.) *The Elgar Companion to Feminist Economics*. Cheltenham: Edward Elgar, pp. 433–441.

Libby B. (1984) "Women in Economics Before 1940". Perkins E. (Ed.) *Essays in Economic and Business History*. Los Angeles, CA: Economic and Business Historical Society, University of Southern California, pp. 273–290.

Locke J. (1693) *Some Thoughts Concerning Education*. London: A. & J. Churchill.

Luft D. (2007) "Thinking About Sexuality and Gender in Vienna". Bischof G., Pelinka A., and Herzog D. (Eds.) *Sexuality in Austria: Contemporary Austrian Studies*. Vol. 15. New Brunswick, NJ: Transaction Publishers, pp. 21–30.

Luxemburg R. (1898) *Die industrielle Entwicklung Polens*. Leipzig: Duncker und Humblot.

Luxemburg R. ([1913] 2003) *The Accumulation of Capital: A Contribution to an Economic Explanation of Imperialism*. London: Routledge.

Luxemburg R. ([1902] 2004a) "A Tactical Question". Hudis P. and Anderson K. (Eds.) *The Rosa Luxemburg Reader*. New York: Monthly Review Press, pp. 233–236.

Luxemburg R. ([1904] 2004b) "The Proletarian Woman". Hudis P. and Anderson K. (Eds.) *The Rosa Luxemburg Reader*. New York: Monthly Review Press, pp. 242–245.

Luxemburg R. ([1907] 2004c) "Address to the International Socialist Women's Conference". Hudis P. and Anderson K. (Eds.) *The Rosa Luxemburg Reader*. New York: Monthly Review Press, pp. 236–237.

Luxemburg R. ([1912] 2004d) "Women's Suffrage and Class Struggle". Hudis P. and Anderson K. (Eds.) *The Rosa Luxemburg Reader*. New York: Monthly Review Press, 237–242.

Madden K. (2019) "Anecdotes of Discrimination: Barrieres to Women's Participationin Economic Thuoght During the Late Nineteenth and Early Twentieth Centuries". Madden K. and Dimand R. (Eds.) *Routledge Handbook of the History of Women's Economic Thought*. London: Routledge, pp. 169–190.

Madden K. and Persky J. (2019) "The Economic Thought of the Women's Co-operative Guild". Madden K. and Dimand R. (Eds.) *Routledge Handbook of the History of Women's Economic Thought*. London: Routledge, pp. 150–168.

Maierhof G. (2002) *Elbstbehauptung im Chaos. Frauen in der jüdischen Selbsthilfe 1933–1943*. Frankfurt and New York: Campus.

Malleier E. (2006) "Making the World a Better Place. Welfare and Politics, Welfare as Politics? Activities of Jewish Women in Vienna Before 1938". *Aschkenas – Zeitschrift für Geschichte und Kultur der Juden*. Vol. 16:1, pp. 261–268.

Mallett P. (2016a) *Women, Marriage and the Law in Victorian Society*. As retrieved on June 15, 2018 at: www.routledgehistoricalresources.com/feminism/essays/women-marriage-and-the-law-in-victorian-society.

Mallett P. (2016b) *Victorian Education and the Women's Movement*. As retrieved on June 15, 2018 at: www.routledgehistoricalresources.com/feminism/essays/victorian-education-and-the-womens-movement.

Marcet J. (1816) *Conversation on Political Economy*. London: Longman.

Marcet J. (1833) *John Hopkins' Notion on Political Economy*. London: Longman.

Marcuzzo C. and Rosselli A. (2008) "The History of Economic Thought through Gender Lenses". Bettio F. and Verashchagina A. (Eds.) *Frontiers in the Economics of Gender*. London: Routledge, pp. 3–20.

Marshall A. (1890) *Principles of Economics*. London: Macmillan.

Martin J. (1985) *Reclaiming a Conversation: The Ideal of the Educated Woman*. New Haven, CT: Yale University Press.

Martineau H. ([1983] 2018) *Illustrations of Political Economy*. As retrieved on April 5, 2018 at: http://oll.libertyfund.org/titles/martineau-illustrations-of-political-economy-9-vols.

Mattei C. (2019) "Early Women Economists at Columbia University". Madden K. and Dimand R. (Eds.) *Routledge Handbook of the History of Women's Economic Thought*. London: Routledge, pp. 272–289.

Mattl S. (2016) "Between Socialism and Feminism: Charlotte Glas (1873–1934)". *Religions*. Vol. 7:8, pp. 1–10.

Maureen H. (2002) "Becoming Austrian: Women, the State, and Citizenship in World War I". *Central European History*. Vol. 35:1, pp. 1–35.

May A.M. and Dimand R. (2016) "Women in the First Sixty Years of the American Economic Association, 1885–1945". Paper presented to the AEA Committee on the Status of Women in the Economic Profession and the History of Economics Society, San Francisco, CA.

McConnaughy C. (2013) *The Woman Suffrage Movement in America: A Reassessment*. New York: Cambridge University Press.

Meyer J. (1966) "In Memoriam: Frieda Wunderlich, 1884–1965". *Social Research*. Vol. 33:1, pp. 1–3.

Michalitsch G. and Schalager C. (2007) "Lost Generation – Austrian Female Pioneers of Economics". *European Journal of Economics and Economic Policies: Intervention*. Vol. 4:1, pp. 67–73.

Mill J.S. (1820) *Essays on Government*. London: J. Innes.

Mill J.S. (1848) *Principles of Political Economy*. London: Parker.

Mill J.S. (1859) *On Liberty*. London: Parker.

Mill J.S. (1869) *The Subjection of Women*. London: Longmans, Green, Reader, and Dyer.

Mises L. ([1978] 2013) *Notes and Recollection*. Indianapolis, IN: Liberty Fund.

Mitchell W. (1902) "Review of Hannah Sewall's *The Theory of Value Before Adam Smith*". *Journal of Political Economy*. Vol. 11:1, pp. 144–145.

Nautz J. (2000a) "Helene Lieser". Dimand R., Dimand M.A., and Forget E. (Eds.) *A Biographical Dictionary of Women Economists*. Cheltenham: Edward Elgar, pp. 259–260.

Nautz J. (2000b) "Gertrud von Lovasy". Dimand R., Dimand M.A., and Forget E. (Eds.) *A Biographical Dictionary of Women Economists*. Cheltenham: Edward Elgar, pp. 260–261.

Nautz J. (2000c) "Ilse Schüller Mintz". Dimand R., Dimand M.A., and Forget E. (Eds.) *A Biographical Dictionary of Women Economists*. Cheltenham: Edward Elgar, pp. 311–312.

Nautz J. (2002) "Offen(heimer) Elly". Keintzel B. and Korotin I. (Eds.) *Wissenschafterinnen in und aus Österreich. Leben – Werk – Wirken*. Vienna: Böhlau Verlag, pp. 540–541.

Nenadic S. (1998) "The Social Shaping of Business Behavior in Nineteenth-Century Women's Garment Trades". *Journal of Social History*. Vol. 31:3, pp. 625–645.

Nettl J.P. (1966) *Rosa Luxemburg*. London: Oxford University Press.

Nussbaum M. (2010) "Mill's Feminism: Liberal, Radical, and Queer". Varouxakis G. and Kelly P. (Eds.) *John Stuart Mill: Thought and Influence. The Saint of Rationalism*. London: Routledge, pp. 130–145.

Nyland C. (1993) "John Locke and the Social Position of Women". *History of Political Economy*. Vol. 25:1, pp. 39–63.

Nyland C. and Ramia G. (1994) "The Webbs and the Rights of Women". Groenewegen P. (Ed.) *Feminism and Political Economy in Victorian England*. Aldershot and Brookfield: Edward Elgar, pp. 110–146.

Nyland C. and Rix M. (2000) "Elizabeth Faulkner Baker". Dimand R., Dimand M.A., and Forget E. (Eds.) *A Biographical Dictionary of Women Economists*. Cheltenham: Edward Elgar, pp. 16–21.

Oertel K. (2015) *Harriet Tubman Slavery, the Civil War, and Civil Rights in the Nineteenth Century*. London: Routledge.

Paley Marshall M. (1902) "Review of *Educated Working Women* by Clara Elizabeth Collet". *The Economic Journal*. Vol. 12:46, pp. 252–257.

Pancoast E. (1921) "The Prohibition of Night Work for Women". *Studies Leaflet Series*. Vol. 7. Washington, DC: National League of Women Voters, Committee on Women in Industry.

Peart S. (1996) *The Economics of W.S. Jevons*. London: Routledge.

Perkins Gilman C. (1898) *Women and Economics*. Boston: Small, Maynard and Co.

Perkins Gilman C. ([1915] 1979) *Herland*. New York: Pantheon Book.

Perkins Gilman C. ([1916] 1997) *With Her in Our Land*. Santa Barbara, CA: Greenwood Press.

Perkins Gilman C. and McLean F. (1907) "The Extent of Child Labor in the United States: Discussion". *Publications of the American Economic Association*, third series, Vol. 8:1, pp. 260–267.

Perloff M. (2003) *The Vienna Paradox: A Memoir*. New York: New Directions Book.

Pigou A.C. (1920) *The Economics of Welfare*. London: Macmillan.

Polkinghorn B. (1995) "Jane Marcet and Harriet Martineau: Motive, Market Experience and Reception of Their Works Popularizing Classical Political Economy". Dimand R., Dimand M.A., and Forget E. (Eds.) *Women of Value: Feminist Essays on the History of Women in Economics*. Aldershot: Edward Elgar, pp. 71–81.

Pomata G. (2004) "Rejoinder to Pygmalion. The Origins of Women's History at the London School of Economics". *Storia della Storiografia*. Vol. 46:2, pp. 79–104.

Ponder M. (2017) *From Sea to Shining Sea: Katharine Lee Bates*. Chicago: Windy City.

Poullain de la Barre F. (1673) *De l'Égalité des deux sexes, discours physique et moral où l'on voit l'importance de se défaire des préjugés*. Paris: Chez Jean du Puis.

Prash R. (1999) "Retrospectives: American Economists in the Progressive Era on the Minimum Wage". *The Journal of Economic Perspectives*. Vol. 13:2, pp. 221–230.

Presley S. (2016) *Black Women Abolitionists and the Fight for Freedom in the 19th Century*. As retrieved on February 24, 2018 at: www.libertarianism.org/columns/black-women-abolitionists-fight-freedom-19th-century.

Pribram K. (1913) "Dr. Else Cronbach". *Neues Frauenleben*. Vol. 15:5, pp. 3–4.

Prince M. (1831) *The History of Mary Prince, a West Indian Slave. Related by Herself. With a Supplement by the Editor. To Which Is Added, the Narrative of Asa-Asa, a Captured African*. Electronic Edition. As retrieved on February 24, 2019 at: https://docsouth.unc.edu/neh/prince/prince.html.

Pujol M. (1992) *Feminism and Anti-Feminism in Early Economic Thought*. Cheltenham: Edward Elgar.

Pujol M. (2000) "Harriet Hardy Taylor Mill". Dimand R., Dimand M.A., and Forget E. (Eds.) *A Biographical Dictionary of Women Economists*. Cheltenham: Edward Elgar, pp. 307–311.

Pujol M. and Seitz J. (2000) "Millicent Garrett Fawcett". Dimand R., Dimand M.A., and Forget E. (Eds.) *A Biographical Dictionary of Women Economists*. Cheltenham: Edward Elgar, pp. 156–161.

Purvis J. (2016) "The Campaign for Women's Suffrage in Britain". *Routledge Historical Resources: History of Feminism*. As retrieved on February 7, 2018 at: http://dx.doi.org/10.4324/9781138641839-HOF9-1

Raggam-Blesch M. (2009) "Therese Schlesinger-Eckstein". *Jewish Women: A Comprehensive Historical Encyclopedia*. As retrieved on May 8, 2018 at: https://jwa.org/encyclopedia/article/schlesinger-eckstein-therese.

Rathbone E. (1917) "The Remuneration of Women's Services". *The Economic Journal*. Vol. 27:105, pp. 55–68.

Redmond J. (2016) "Journeys Toward a Gentleman's Education: 1900–1930". Panayotidis L. and Stortz P. (Eds.) *Women in Higher Education, 1850–1970: International Perspective*. London: Routledge, pp. 145–163.

Robb G. (1992) *White-Collar Crime in Modern England: Financial Fraud and Business Morality: 1845–1929*. Cambridge: Cambridge University Press.

Rose A. (2003) "Gender and Anti-Semitism: Christian Social Women and the Jewish Response in Turn-of-the Century Vienna". *Austrian History Yearbook*. Vol. 34, pp. 173–189.

Rose A. (2008) *Jewish Women in Fin de Siècle Vienna*. Austin, TX: University of Texas Press.

Ross S.G. (2009) *The Birth of Feminism: Woman as Intellect in Renaissance Italy and England*. Cambridge, MA: Harvard University Press.

Ross T. (2004) *Expanding the Palace of Torah: Orthodoxy and Feminism*. Waltham: Brandeis University Press.

Rostek J. (2014) "Female Authority and Political Economy: Jane Marcet and Harriet Martineau's Contradictory Strategy in Disseminating Economic Knowledge". Nischik R. and Mergenthal S. (Eds.) *Anglistentag 2013: Proceedings*. Trier: WVT, pp. 21–33.

Rostek J. (2019) "English Women's Economic Thought in the 1970s". Madden K. and Dimand R. (Eds.) *Routledge Handbook of the History of Women's Economic Thought*. London: Routledge, pp. 33–52.

Rowbotham S. (2012) Women in Movement *Feminism and Social Action*. London: Routledge.

Rozenblit M. (1984) *The Jews of Vienna (1867–1914): Assimilation and Identity*. Albany, NY: State University of New York Press.

Rozenblit M. (2001) *Reconstructing a National Identity. The Jews of Habsburg Austria during World War I*. Oxford: Oxford University Press.

Rudavsky T. (1995) *Gender and Judaism: Tradition and Transformation*. New York: New York University Press.

Rudavsky T. (2007) "Feminism and Modern Jewish Philosophy". Morgan M. and Gordon P. (Eds.) *A Cambridge History of Modern Jewish Philosophy*. Cambridge: Cambridge University Press, pp. 324–348.

Rutherford M. (2006) "Wisconsin Institutionalism: John R. Commons and His Students". *Labor History*. Vol. 47:2, pp. 161–188.

Rutherford M. (2011) *The Institutional Movement in American Economics, 1918–1947*. New York: Cambridge University Press.

Rutterford J. and Maltby J. (2006) "The Widow, the Clergyman, and the Reckless: Women Investors in England: 1830–1914". *Feminist Economics*. Vol. 12:1, pp. 111–138.

Salomon A. (1908) *Soziale Frauenbildung*. Berlin: B.G. Teubner.

Schorske C. (1981) *Fin de siècle Vienna*. Chicago: The University of Chicago Press.

Schwartz L. (2011) "Feminist Thinking on Education in Victorian England". *Oxford Review of Education*. Vol. 37:5, pp. 669–682.

Scott J. (1988) *Gender and the Politics of History*. New York: Columbia University Press.

Seiz J. (2000) "Eleanor Rathbone". Dimand R., Dimand M.A., and Forget E. (Eds.) *A Biographical Dictionary of Women Economists*. Cheltenham: Edward Elgar, pp. 350–356.

Sewall H. (1901) *The Theory of Value before Adam Smith*. New York: The MacMillan Company for the American Economic Association.

Sewall H. (1904) "Child Labor in the U.S.". *U.S. Bureau of Labor Bulletin*. Vol. 52:(May), pp. 485–637.

Silverman L. (2009) "Reconsidering the Margins: Jewishness as an Analytical Framework". *Journal of Modern Jewish Studies*. Vol. 8:1, pp. 103–120.

Silverman L. (2012) *Becoming Austrians: Jews and Culture Between the World Wars*. Oxford: Oxford University Press.

Sklar K. and Stewart J. (Eds.) (2007) *Women's Rights and Transatlantic Antislavery in the Era of Emancipation*. New Haven, CT: Yale University Press.

Sockwell W. (2000) "Barbara Bodichon". Dimand R., Dimand M.A., and Forget E. (Eds.) *A Biographical Dictionary of Women Economists*. Cheltenham: Edward Elgar, pp. 53–56.

Sommers C.H. (1994) *How Stole Feminism? How Women Have Betrayed Women*. New York: Simon and Schuster.

Stolper T. (1982) *Recorded Memories*. Taped and transcribed by A. Campbell. Vienna, Berlin, and New York, Microfilm Collection: Leo Baeck Institute, MM 134, Roll 176.

Sumler-Lewis J. (1981) "The Forten-Purvis Women of Philadelphia and the American Anti-Slavery Crusade". *The Journal of Negro History*. Vol. 66:4, pp. 281–288.

Sumner Woodbury H. (1910) *History of Women in the Industry in the United States*. Washington, DC: Government Printing Office.

Sumner Woodbury H. (1918) *History of the Labor in the United States*. New York: MacMillan Company.

Szapuova M. (2006) "Mill's Liberal Feminism: Its Legacy and Current Criticism". *Prolegomena*. Vol. 5:2, pp. 179–191.

Taylor Mill H. ([1851] 1994) "Enfranchisement of Women". Robson A. and Robson J. (Eds.) *Sexual Equality: Writings by John Stuart Mill, Harriet Taylor Mill, and Helen Taylor*. Toronto: University of Toronto Press, pp. 178–203.

Thompson W. and Wheeler A. (1825) *Appeal of One Half the Human Race, Women, Against the Pretension of the Other Half, Men, to Retain Them in Political, and Thence in Civil and Domestic, Slavery*. London: Longman, Hurst, Rees, Orme, Brown and Green.

Tisch C. (1932) *Wirtschaftsrechnung und Verteilung im zentralistisch organisieren sozialistischen Gemeinwesen*. Wuppertal-Elberfeld: Scheschinski.

Todd J. (2014) *Mary Wollstonecraft: A Revolutionary Life*. London: Bloomsbury Reader.

Tullberg R. (1998) *Women at Cambridge*. Cambridge: Cambridge University Press.

Vaughn G.F. (2016) "Katharine Coman: America's First Woman Institutional Economist and a Champion of Education for Citizenship". *Journal of Economic Issues*. Vol. 38:4, pp. 989–1002.

Vaughn K. (1980) "Economic Calculation Under Socialism. The Austrian Contribution". *Economic Inquiry*. Vol. 18:4, pp. 535–554.

Veblen T. (1899) "The Barbarian Status of Women". *American Journal of Sociology*. Vol. 4:4, pp. 503–514.

Wakefield P. ([1798] 2015) *Reflections on the Present Condition of the Female Sex, With Suggestions for Its Improvement*. Cambridge, MA: Cambridge University Press.

Webb B. (1888) "The Sweating System". *Charity Organization Review*. Vol. 37, p. 15.

Webb B. (1891) *The Co-operative Movement in Great Britain*. London: Swan Somanschein.

Webb B. (1901) *The Case for the Factory Act*. London: Grant Richards.

Webb B. (1920) *Men's and Women's Wages: Should They be Equal?* London: The Fabian Society.

Webb B. and Webb S. (1894) *History of Trade Unionism*. London: Longmans and Co.

Webb B. and Webb S. (1897) *Industrial Democracy*. London: Longmans.

Webb S. (1891) "Alleged Differences in Wages Paid to Women and Men for Similar Work". *The Economic Journal*. Vol. 1:4, pp. 369–358.

White M. (1994) "Following Strange Gods: Women's in Jevons' Political Economy". Groenewegen P. (Ed.) *Feminism and Political Economy in Victorian England*. Aldershot and Brookfield: Edward Elgar, pp. 46–78.

Wollstonecraft M. ([1792] 1994) *A Vindication of the Rights of Woman*. London: Penguin.

Wood A. (2014) "Facing Life as We Know It: Virginia Woolf and the Co-operative Guild". *Literature and History*. Vol. 23:2, pp. 18–34.

Yaeger M. (1999) "Will There Ever Be a Feminist History?". Yaeger M. (Ed.) *Women in Business*. Vol. I. Cheltenham: Edward Elgar Press pp. 3–43.

Yanowsky S. (2010) "Jewish Education in Interwar Vienna: Cooperation, Compromise and Conflict between the Austrian State and the Viennese Jewish Community". Berger P., Bishop G., and Plasser F. (Eds.) *From Empire to Republic*. Innsbruck: Innsbruck University Press, pp. 316–335.

Yee S. (1992) *Black Women Abolitionists: A Study in Activism*. Knoxville, TN: University of Tennessee Press.

Yohn S. (2006) "Crippled Capitalists: The Inscription of Economic Dependence and the Challenge of Female Entrepreneurship in Nineteenth-Century America". *Feminist Economics*. Vol. 12:1–2, pp. 85–109.

2 Home economics, household economics, and new home economics in the United States

Between the early 20th century and the interwar period in the United States, the relationship between the woman question and political economy started to become better defined into a determined research field: home economics. Home economics was focused on the scientific management of the house, which was traditionally led by women. Home economics' central element was a strong expertise in economic matters, which should have been taught to girls, who were bound to become good wives and excellent mothers, in order to shape families as ideal consumers. Somehow, home economics' attention to better management of the household was related to the shared desire to promote social reforms aimed at increasing social well-being. Nevertheless, the nature of home economics may seem problematic in relation to the battle for women's emancipation from traditional gendered stereotypes. On one side, the nature of home economics reinforced the gender stereotype of women's main role as housekeepers. Nonetheless, on the other side, home economics gave women the opportunity to excel in a more specific set of expertise which would improve families' performance and, consequently, the performance of society as a whole. Furthermore, although the emergence of home economics departments allowed many women to get hired in academia, it pushed many women economists to devote themselves to home economics and to abandon economics *tout cour*, which was a too-competitive research field (see Paragraph 1). As Folbre rightly pointed out, home economics allowed "economists to accommodate new concerns while resisting the 'feminization of their own profession'" (Folbre 1998, 40).

Strictly interconnected with home economics, household economics emerged as an independent research field in academia. The development of household economics took place mainly between New York and Chicago, and more precisely at Columbia University and the University of Chicago. Founders of household economics were Hazel Kyrk, Margaret Reid, and Elizabeth Hoyt, who mentored an entire generation of women home economists. The nature of household economics was twofold. On one side, it can be regarded as a development of home economics because of the centrality of families as economic actors or representative agents. In fact, household economics covered the economic analysis of all decision makers within a family concerning consumption, savings, and allocation of time in labor or leisure. On the other side, household economics diverged from home economics because it stressed the centrality of household production function as a possible substitute for the market. After the Second World War, the divergence between home economics and household economics in terms of scientific contributions as well as of academic departments became more visible (see Paragraph 2).

In the 1960s, Theodore Schultz, Gary Becker, and Jacob Mincer introduced the new home economics in academia. Although they presented their new home economics as a relatively new research field, it was in fact a development of household economics. More precisely, it can be considered an application of the neoclassical economics to household economics. Not by chance, between 1960s and 1970s, the department of economics at the University of Chicago became the stronghold of both neoclassical economics[1] and new home economics.[2] New home economics developed such microeconomic topics as fertility, marriage (including mate selection), divorce, childhood support, intra-house risk-sharing, and macroeconomic policy related to these topics (see paragraph 3). The connection between neoclassical economics and the new home economics would have a tremendous influence on what later would have been labeled 'gender economics', also labeled 'economics of gender' (see Chapter 4). According to many historians of economic thought, the spread of the new home economics during the following decades (1970s–1990s) redefined the woman question within economics "in a blatantly anti-feminist fashion" (Pujol 1992, 2) (see Chapter 3).

2.1 The birthing of home economics

The birthing of home economics as a separate research field in academia must be analyzed in connection with two phenomena that emerged between the late 19th and early 20th century: the debate on women's access to the labor force and the rise of the 'cult of domesticity'. As previously seen in Chapter 1, the idea that the access of women to the labor force would have decreased men's wages was explicitly introduced by many activists, including several economists. Although they encouraged women to get a higher education, they prevented them from competing with their husbands in the job market. As Folbre specified, this attitude was common within economists of the classical school: with the exception of John Stuart Mill, they depicted women as "economic unproductive but morally crucial, [and their] conventional economic theory provided an explicit rationale for discrimination, which discouraged the kinds of research that could effectively challenge theoretical assumptions, which in turn reinforced discrimination" (Folbre 1998, 36–37). Meanwhile, almost paradoxically, the ideal of the virtuous housewife was gradually substituted for the concept of the unproductive housewife: housewives became 'dependents', like children, seniors, and any other subject unable to be part of the workforce.

This conundrum was partially solved by the emerging of the 'cult of domesticity' that was intended as a reaction to the effects of the Industrial Revolution, which was leading the society towards a form of dehumanization. Home was described in feminine terms, while the market was described in masculine terms, and "those few scholars who remained interested in household production stepped outside the traditions of political economy to found the new discipline of home economics. In that sphere, the productive housewife lived on, in theory as well as in practice" (Folbre 1991, 483).

Sisters Catherine Beecher (1800–1878) and Harriet Beecher (1811–1896) had been pioneers of home economics, albeit the term 'home economics' was not coined yet when they were promoting their agenda of home economics education, which relied entirely on the central role of mothers within families. The Beechers devoted themselves to promoting the introduction of home economics as an autonomous educational field in primary and secondary schools. They described the ideal woman as a woman educated in domestic economy and able to teach it. Therefore, an investment in women's education would have been a determinant for the well-being of the society as a whole (Beecher 1841; Beecher and Beecher 1870; Sklar 1973).

Home economics dealt with the connections among family members in material terms, as well as with the economic dynamics between families and communities. The aim of home economics was to create a 'domestic science'; that is, a system of formal education in domestic matters. The role of a home economics education, either at a primary school or at higher-level school, was intended as a powerful expression of women's emancipation: educated women would form solid families, which would build up cohesive communities and a strong and healthy society (Apple 2006; 2015). The number of home economics graduates rapidly increased in early 20th century. They mainly entered the job market being hired by marketing sections in several industry sectors. A relevant percentage of home economics graduates worked in hospitals as dietitians. In academia, newly formed departments of home economics were required to test new products to get the 'woman's perspective' on products. In 1873, the first home economics department was established at Kansas State University as a part of the Morrill Land-Grant Acts (1862–1890), a set of legislative acts intended to create land-grant colleges in the United States by using the proceeds of federal land sales. In many other land-grant colleges, home economics departments were opened (Ehrenreich and English 1978).

Although home economics was intended as a tool to form good housewives, home economics' main assumption was that everything related to the management of house and family was neither intuitive nor strictly feminine and was addressed to anyone interested in social responsibility, including institution managers and social workers. Furthermore, many home economists handled social problems, such as immigration and the integration of minorities, especially in urban environments. Home economics was in fact one of the best expressions of the ideals of the Progressive Era. Based on the concept of social responsibility in an age of rapid and dramatic social and economic changes related to urbanization, industrialization, and migration, home economics considered education the only tool to handle the complexity of those dynamics. Embedded in that cultural atmosphere, home economics emerged as a way to learn social responsibility. The home economists and activists involved in the home economics agenda who were especially concerned with social responsibility within an urban context included Helen Stuart Campbell, Jane Addams, Caroline Hunt, and Alice Norton.

Helen Stuart Campbell (1839–1918) wrote one of the earliest textbooks in the field of home economics. She wrote weekly in the *New York Tribune* about women's conditions in workplaces such as department stores, where they were paid three dollars per week – much less than their male colleagues (Stuart Campbell 1887; 1889). In the 1880s, she analyzed the effects of poverty in New York City with a particular emphasis on women's low wages: her book on the gender wage gap (Stuart Campbell 1893) was honored by AEA and was largely endorsed by Richard Ely, who invited her to deliver two lectures on household economics at the University of Wisconsin–Madison in 1895. In 1896, Stuart Campbell joined the University of Wisconsin–Madison faculty as untenured professor. One year later, Stuart Campbell was appointed professor of home economics at Kansas State Agricultural College. In 1898, she resigned her position to work as a freelancer (Davis 2000).

Although not a trained economist, 1931 Nobel Peace Laureate Jane Addams (1860–1935) was one of the most prominent social activists of that time. She grounded her social activism on the principles of home economics. Addams cofounded Hull House with Ellen Starr (1859–1940). Located in the Near West Side of Chicago and named after the original house's first owner, Charles Jerald Hull (1820–1889), Hull House was opened in 1889 and soon hosted massive communities of immigrants from Europe. In 1892, Addams described 'the three Rs' of Hull House: residence, research, and reform. Its mission was to provide social and educational opportunities as well as free lectures on current economic issues to working-class women. Furthermore, Hull House operated clubs for both children and adults regardless of gender, and, in 1893, established the city's first public playground, bathhouse, and gymnasium (Wade 1967).[3]

Hull House attracted many female residents who later became prominent and influential reformers at various levels. They worked on educational and political reforms and investigated housing, working, and sanitation issues. Caroline Hunt (1865–1927) attended the University of Chicago and lived at Hull House. She worked for the U.S. Department of Agriculture preparing statistics on the dietary histories of immigrants and taught domestic economy at the Lewis Institute of Chicago, until 1903, when she was appointed professor of home economics at the University of Wisconsin–Madison. According to Hunt, the final aims of home economics were freedom and social justice, which should be taught under the form of social 'maternalism' or municipal housekeeping (Apple 2015). Alice Norton (1860–1928) joined the University of Chicago Institute as an adjunct faculty member in 1900. One year later, when the

Institute merged with the University of Chicago and became the School of Education, she was promoted to assistant professor of home economics. She authored several publications and was amongst the founder of the home economics department at the Woman's College in Istanbul (1921–23).[4]

Another important figure in the early home economics movement was Maria Parloa (1843–1909), a culinary instructor who became very popular after having opened several cooking schools in Boston and New York. Although in her work the distinction between home economics, domestic economics, and household economics was not yet clear cut, she defined home economics as the "management of the home" (Parloa 1898, V). In 1898, she authored a handbook on how mothers could transform a house into a real home, which was a popularization of the cult of domesticity. The book's topics spanned from the size of the house and rooms to the number and size of facilities; from furniture to daily routine; from cleaning duties to food provision and preparation. Parloa's book remarked on the centrality of mothers as the "most precious thing[s]" in a home (Parloa 1898, 352). In 1899, Parloa attended the founding meeting for professionalizing home economics in Lake Placid, New York State; later in 1908, she also attended the founding meeting of the American Home Economics Association (AHEA).

The first Lake Placid Conference took place in 1873 and was organized by Ellen Swallow Richards (1842–1911), an American chemist who was the first woman admitted to MIT. In 1876, Richards invited the Woman's Education Association of Boston to fund a Woman's Laboratory at MIT in order to encourage women to get enrolled in scientific and technological curricula.[5] In the 1890s, Richards lobbied for the introduction of courses in domestic science into the public schools of Boston.

Lake Placid conferences took place regularly every year. As Forget recalls (2011), the term 'home economics' was introduced at the Lake Placid Conference in 1899, after that some alternatives, which included 'oekology' and 'euthenics'; that is, 'the science of right living', had been discarded. The label 'home economics' survived until 1994, when it was substituted by the new label 'family and consumer science', which was adopted to underline that the field covers other aspects besides of home life and wellness.

In 1908, Lake Placid conferees founded AHEA to promote home economics in primary, junior, and high school curricula and to fundraise the expansion of the discipline.[6] Richards was elected president. During the same meeting, the *Journal of Home Economics* was established. Its first issue revealed that the aim and scope of the association was "the improvement of living condition in the home, the institutional household and the community". The Association welcomed anyone who was "in sympathy in bringing science and art into the service of the home", as they were specifically explained in the program of Lake Placid Conference. Home economics' principles included:

A classification of household economics as a working basis; provision for the higher education of some selected young women who shall be fitted by the best training for a higher leadership; an intensive promotion of domestic economy, including the foundation of home economics' department within universities.

(p. 2)[7]

The choice of the label 'home economics' was explained as follows:

A general name, simply yet comprehensive enough to cover sanitation, cookery and kindred household arts, and instruction in the art or science of living from the kindergarten to the college was not an easy thing to find . . . a title preferable for the whole general subject of economics; so that it should find a logical place in the college and university.

(p. 4)[8]

In 1913, the Committee on Nomenclature and Syllabus of AHEA published a new syllabus of home economics, which gave emphasis to the interconnection between families and communities. During the first two decades of the 20th century, home economics spread within universities and colleges in the United States. Nevertheless, most women's colleges on the East Coast refused to introduced home economics, given the special emphasis given to women's curricula, which were regarded a form of educational ghettoization, perpetuating an unequal education for men and women (Nerad 1987). Things were different in Midwest and on the West Coast. For instance, Isabel Bevier (1860–1942), who had previously worked in chemistry with Ellen Richards at MIT, promoted home economics at the University of Illinois at Urbana–Champaign, where she taught between 1900 and 1921. A strong supporter of women's education in home economics, she emphasized the use of science to solve problems that involved the everyday life of millions of women at home: Bevier regarded chemistry as instrumental to food preparation and preservation as well as to clothing conservation, especially in situations of shortages of any basic necessity.

In 1916, the department of home economics was officially founded at the University of California, Berkeley, where a course labeled "The Household as Economic Agent" was offered in 1909: 92 students, all women, were enrolled in the courses offered by the new department. Jessica Peixotto (1864–1941) had been a forerunner of home economics at Berkeley, where she got her Ph.D. in 1900 with a thesis on the relationship between French Revolution and French socialism (Peixotto 1901). In 1904, she joined the faculty, and, in 1918, was the first woman to become full professor in social economics. Her research was focused on household expenditure among different income groups in California, especially among professionals and skilled workers (Peixotto 1927, 1928). According to Peixotto, home economics was a specific area of economic research able to give women economists an open space to develop their works and to eventually get a position within academia. In 1928, she served as vice president of AEA.

During the interwar period, home economics gained a central place as a prominent research field in some economic departments. In 1927, the Bureau of Home Economics Act passed and home economic education was promoted and funded in many cities around the country.[9] Ten years later, in 1937, the George–Dean Act further increased funds for the discipline. As Whitcomb (a specialist of home economics education at the Bureau) reported, progress in home economics education had increased business opportunities for women trained in home economics who were especially involved in health system within public schools and communities, in children's education, in editorial departments of women's magazines, in department stores and banks, and in advertising agencies. The home economics program for children's education was based on fixed parameters aimed to develop "pupils' appreciation for home and family life" (Whitcomb 1929, 5), which have been targeted for boys and men too. Furthermore, all the departments of home economics in junior and high schools offered a specific program in social relationships among family members, which included questionnaires about affectivity and responsibility, money management, investments, and savings.

The home economics movement created a formidable chance for many women economists who worked on labor and social issues to pursue an academic career. They seized the new opportunity offered by home economics and chose to devote themselves to statistics at a time when the economics profession was itself moving towards applied work. Women economists' dilemma was centered on the choice to enter as faculty members either in well-established universities, where they could teach economic theory while facing some relevant gender discrimination (mainly the 'glass ceiling' phenomenon; that is, the difficulty to get a promotion), or in new home economics departments at land-grant institutions, high schools, or primary schools, where they could easily get extra funds for independent research projects. As Forget (2011) claimed, many women chose to get involved in home economics, which became a niche for women economists who wanted to have a real chance at getting an academic position.

The massive presence of women economists in home economics departments had an important side effect: it led towards the so-called doctrine of separate spheres, according to which men and women should kept their abilities separated. As Rowles pointed out, the separate doctrine was grounded on the idea that a formal education in homemaking was necessary:

> Because women felt that homes were in danger. Girls, as they grew up, were spending years in school, instead of learning housekeeping from their own mother all day long, every day of the week. Young women were becoming factory workers, stenographers, teachers, or doing all sorts of other jobs outside the home until they were married and then they did not know how to keep house.
>
> (Rowles 1965, 35)

In the 1960s and 1970s, the doctrine of separate spheres as well as home economics' feminine model were deeply challenged by the rise of the second wave of feminism that requested a radical revision of the model of woman as a perfect wife and mother totally devoted to a rational planning of household. Principles of home economics, in fact, were extremely connected with the status quo: the centrality of motherhood; the possibility for married women to get a job outside the home only for financial reasons, without any consideration of personal fulfillment; the idea that family life may be monotonous and dull but is a necessary step for the well-being of society as a whole. Home economics was rejected by the second wave of feminist activists as a form of reinforcement of gender roles, in spite of the fact that home economics had officially opened its audience to boys and men both in educational curricula and in professional activities.

Another element that may explain the crisis of home economics may be recognized in the fact that the field had gone through many transformations and lost its original intent to be linked with social responsibility, which had characterized the birthing and the development of home economics, disappeared over the decades. Although during the interwar period, home economics' main aim continued to be the education of girls and women, the initial emphasis on social justice was lost, substituted with a sort of knowledge that was limited and reduced to receipts and commercials, useful for family members, and the focus on the education of girls and women was oriented in a form of consumerism *per se*, rather than a form of social education. Furthermore, around the mid-1950s and 1960s, when the first generation of professors of home economics reached retirement age, they were not replaced in a majority of cases, and many home economics departments were eliminated or merged into other departments, renamed 'family and consumer science' without converging into homogeneous curricula (Stage and Vincenti 1997; Elias 2008).

Historians agree that home economics has developed three different dilemmas. First, it dealt with human needs both in academic programs and in professional practice but often took for granted the complex interaction between individual needs and social phenomena without scrutinizing the origin and the nature of social norms and gender roles. Second, home economics advanced educational programs aimed to provide employment opportunities for everyone, but was never able to involve men as professionals in the field and remained a kind of niche for women by reinforcing the gendered stereotype that children's education and family matters are under the domain of women. Third, although home economics was a multidisciplinary field that included hard sciences, social sciences, arts, and humanities, these fields never gave credit to home economics (Kay and Nickols 2015).

Summing up, the rise of home economics as a discipline had a double and somehow paradoxical effect. On one side, it was a powerful tool to confine female students at a time when their admission to universities and colleges was inevitable. On the other side, it was a great occasion to promote women's emancipation. The label 'home economics' revealed its ambiguous nature: home economics recognized domestic work as a specific skill to improve the efficiency of households, but did not raise questions about patriarchy as the dominant status quo. Only more recently have home economics and some feminism rejoined because of an internal transformation of both movements.

Today, the International Federation for Home Economics (IFHE) has officers in five continents and a partnership with the institutions of the United Nations. It carries out many different projects that involve the traditional issues of home economics – education and parenting – as well as new ones, such as women's empowerment through entrepreneurship in sustainable development.[10]

2.2 Household economics at the University of Chicago

During the interwar period, household economics emerged as a partially new research field at the University of Chicago. The "Chicago case" has been considered a peculiar result of "unusual circumstances, exceptional faculty, and carefully planned collective action" (Folbre 1998, 37). Founders of household economics were the women economists Marion Talbot, Hazel Kyrk, Margaret Reid, and Elizabeth Hoyt, who worked at the department of economics at the University of Chicago. Although often forgotten, their contributions had a central role in the history of the interconnection between the woman question and political economy as well as in the history of women economists within academia. Their works represented the link between home economics and the new home economics, which arose later, between the 1960s and 1970s. They shared with home economics a vision based on the idea that a proper consumers' education would improve the national economy, but they extended the economic analysis to household production intended as the production of goods and services (accommodation, meals, clean clothes, and child care) provided by the members of the household, for their own consumption, by using their own capital and their own unpaid labor.[11] Marion Talbot (1858–1948), as mentioned earlier in Chapter 1, was an influential leader in the movement to promote the access to higher education for women in the United States. In 1880, Talbot received her B.A. from Boston University, where her father, Israel Tisdale Talbot, was dean of the medical school. In 1888, she was granted a B.S. from MIT, and began serving as the president of the Massachusetts Society for the University Education of Women as well as the secretary of the Association of Collegiate Alumnae. Both organizations had been founded by her mother, Emily, to promote higher education among women. In 1892, after having worked as an instructor at Wellesley College, Talbot resigned to join the newly opened University of Chicago. In Chicago, Talbot became assistant professor of sanitary science, then professor of household administration, and between 1895 and 1925 she served as dean of the newly created Department of Household Administration. During her tenure with the University of Chicago, Talbot, along with Alice Freeman Palmer (1855–1902), organized the women's dormitories and promoted several events to improve the social life of the women who were employed at the University of Chicago. Palmer covered the position of on-resident dean and helped female students plan their educational careers. During the partnership between Talbot and Palmer, the percentage of the female students at the school doubled, from 24% to 48%.

In her book on higher education for women, Talbot asserted that education is fundamentally a social issue that must be studied in relation to the economic and social conditions of people (Talbot 1910). She resolutely fought to increase the number of female students, to reduce gender discrimination within faculty members, and to overcome any restriction that prevented or discouraged an equal access to higher education.

Influenced by home economics, Talbot felt the urgency to ground it in a more theoretical and technical base. She was partially motivated by her concern that the field might become an academic pink ghetto if standards of rigor were not upheld. Talbot's concern was deeply forward-looking, but it remained silent: home economics actually became an academic pink ghetto, as previously seen. After her retirement, the Department of Household Admin-istration was merged with the Department of Home Economics in the School of Education, while household economics merged with the Department of Economics (Gillen 1990).

Although Talbot's work was fundamental in preparing the emergence of household economics in Chicago, the founders of household economics *strictu sensu* were Hazel Kyrk, Margaret Reid, and Elizabeth Hoyt, as previously mentioned. Kyrk was mentor to an entire generation of women economists that included Reid and Hoyt. Most of her students moved between the disciplines of economics and home economics and between government employment and academic appointments when opportunities arose. Like Kyrk, Reid and Hoyt mentored the following generation of women economists at the University of Chicago as well as at the Iowa State University (Thorne 1995).

Kyrk, Reid, and Hoyt shared the necessity to free home economics from the cult of domestic skills and to transform it into household economics, intended as a specific subfield of microeconomics, which deals with the house-hold's function of production and with unpaid domestic labor as an input which stands behind the demand curve.

Hazel Kyrk (1886–1957) got her B.A. in economics in 1910 at the University of Chicago. During the First World War, she was enrolled as a graduate student under the supervision of James Field with whom, in early 1918, she joined a mission at the War Shipping Board to London. During that mission, she worked as a statistician for the American Division of the Allied Maritime Trans-port Council. In 1920, she earned her Ph.D. in economics from the University of Chicago with a thesis on possible waste in the welfare system (Kyrk 1923). Thereafter, she got a position as a faculty member in both the economics and home economics departments at the University of Chicago up to her retirement in 1952. Although her Ph.D. was in economics, Kyrk went into the field of home economics for two reasons. First, she was interested in household's dynamics as well as in social reforms to better women's economic and social conditions. Second, home economic departments were the most secure way to get an academic position (Beller and Kiss 2001).

Kyrk was influenced by Veblen's institutionalism[12] and by Dewey's pragmatism.[13] Based on the principle of education, moral responsibility, and personal enrichment intended as the final goals of individuals' life, Dewey's pragmatism inspired the moral vision behind Kyrk's theory of the welfare system (Trentmann 2012). Kyrk's first book (1923) dealt with the notion of waste from an economic as well as an ethical perspective. She presented waste from an economic point of view as the result of an inefficient use of productive resources, while from an ethical perspective waste was a misplaced distribution of resources. Kyrk insisted on the necessity for welfare economics to take account of the relation between economic and ethical waste in order to prevent either inefficiency (by providing unnecessary goods) or unfairness (by giving away benefits to people who do not need them and vice versa). According to Kyrk, marginal utility theory was useless to simultaneously handle with these two concerns because it was only focused in the economic aspect. As Kyrk stated: "marginal utility theory's emphasis upon utility, or desirability, or desiredness, as a causal factor in the phenomena of market value, does not in itself involve an understanding, or even an interest, in the consumer's attitudes which lie back of choice" (Kyrk 1923, 17).

Kyrk underlined that decision-making is a physiological and psychological process of forecasting future satisfaction, which is influenced by social factors; waste is the result of social costs that are due to the use of productive resources for luxury and to an unfair distribution. Although Kyrk did not provide any prescription to avoid waste, she insisted on the role of education, which would have directed consumers to a more equilibratory method of consumption. The influence of home economics may be recognized in Kyrk's vision of an equilibratory consumption.

Kyrk's book was reviewed in *The Quarterly Journal of Economics* by Clara Dickinson (1924), who criticized Kyrk's thesis by labeling it as institutional economics, unable to go beyond consumption economics: an example of "sociological economics" based more on a "psychological theory of value" rather than on an "experimental psychology, applied to inductions on concrete quantitative data" (Dickinson 1924, 343–344).

In 1929 and in 1933, Kyrk published two other books to better explain the double role of households in production and consumption of American families' standard life (Kyrk 1929, 1933). The two books merged in Kyrk's last publication (1953). Meanwhile, Kyrk regularly published in the *Journal of Home Economics*. In her numerous articles, she tried to explain the nature of home economics as a scientific research field focused on family's well-being, especially against critics who considered home economics simply as a matter of specialized knowledge about food, clothing, and the management of the house.

Kyrk's work aimed to transform home economics into household economics. She overcame her home economics' view, which was focused on developing an educational program suitable for girls and women bound to be perfect wives, by reinforcing the stereotype of female consumers who need to be educated towards a more rational choice, because their behavior was essentially driven by emotions. Kyrk adopted a theory of endogenous preferences and extended it to a broader consumers' decision theory which took account of both psychological and cultural factors. As earlier mentioned, she criticized the model of rationality behind the marginal utility theory of consumption, which gives no room for not-rational behavior. According to Kyrk, the theory of maximizing behavior was a good assumption for a firm, but not for a household. Furthermore, the theory of maximizing behavior ignored the connection between ethics and economics by forgetting that the decision-making process is influenced by both ethical motivations and utility, and that a coherent welfare economics must take account of both. Hirschfeld (1997) and Velzen (2003) pointed out that, on these specific objections, Kyrk's work anticipated today's feminist economics, which deeply criticized the neoclassical assumption of maximization of an expected utility in a value-free framework.

Margaret G. Reid (1896–1991) got her B.A. in home economics in 1921 in Manitoba. After her graduation, she moved to Chicago, where, in 1931, she got her Ph.D. in economics under Kyrk's supervision. Reid published her dissertation three years later (Reid 1934). The same year, she became full professor at the Iowa State University, where she met Elizabeth Hoyt. Later she joined the University of Illinois at Urbana–Champaign as a faculty member at the department of economics. Between 1951 and 1961, she went back to the University of Chicago until her retirement. Reid played a significant role in the development of household economics' curricula. The focus of her research was household production as well as the fundamental role of women in market labor and in the national economy (Reid 1934, 1938). Although criticized by her colleagues, Ruth Allen (1934) (see later in this chapter) and Hildegarde Kneeland[14] (1934), who were reluctant to give emphasis on home production, the importance of Reid's books allowed her to get a position at the department of economics at the University of Chicago, where she began working as a statistical expert along with Modigliani and Friedman. As emerita, she kept on working on a never-ending book that would deal with the relationship between health conditions and individuals' average income (Forget 1996, 2000; Folbre 2009).

Reid's definition of household economics centered on the notion of the provision of goods and services produced by the household, which are able to substitute goods and service produced by the market (Forget 1996, 2010; Yi 1996). In her major publications, Reid described household production in detail, with a special view on the conditions of women who are burdened by the unpaid labor within households. Reid clarified that household production is the total unpaid activities within a household and she tried to measure the economic value of women's housework as follows:

> Household production ... consists of those unpaid activities which are carried on, by and for the members, which activities might be replaced by market goods, or paid service, if circumstances such as income,

market conditions, and personal inclinations permit the service being delegated to someone outside the household group.

(Reid 1934, 11)

Like Perkins Gilman previously did, Reid considered the increasing costs of raising children as a potential factor able to reduce the number of births and as one of the most significant elements to increasing women's presence in the labor force. Reid considered four alternative methods of valuing household activities: opportunity cost (a measure of the value of the potential earnings foregone because of time spent on household production); retail price (an attempt to estimate value added by household production by subtracting the cost of purchased inputs from the prices of market substitutes); working costs of hiring someone for household production; and the boarding service cost provided in a boarding house (Reid 1943b). According to Reid, women's role in the household production assumes a less relevant position when considering their opportunity costs. In fact, many tasks provided by women within the household might be delegated to paid workers, without forcing wives and mothers to give up any chance to get a better-paid job by working outside the household (Reid 1943a).

Some literature (Yi 1996; Forget 2000) considers Reid's research consistent with the neoclassical economics that was becoming dominant within the discipline in that period, especially in the University of Chicago, making Reid's household analysis a forerunner of the new home economics, which was developed later. Her works directly inspired Theodore Schultz, Milton Friedman, Franco Modigliani, and Gary Becker. More specifically, Reid's empirical work on income and consumption was instrumental in prompting Friedman's development of the permanent income hypothesis (Friedman 1957; Forget 2000; Grossbard 2001; Rutherford 2010). Friedman paid homage to Reid (Friedman 1957) and Modigliani cited Reid in his Nobel lecture (Modigliani 1985). Unlike his colleagues, Becker never explicitly paid homage to Reid's research, in spite of the fact that he used her theory of opportunity cost in analyzing household production and in dealing with the trade-off between the unpaid activities within household and employment in the job market.

Some other literature considers Reid's critical perspective of unpaid labor closer to a feminist economics critique to neoclassical approach applied to gender issues (Hara 2016).

Regardless of the way Reid might be considered – a neoclassical or a protofeminist economist – her role has been central in the history of gender issues within the discipline as well as in the history of women's contribution to economics. As Folbre wrote:

Her classic *Economics of Household Production*, first published in 1934, was initially marginalized by a profession that considered 'home economic' a distinctly feminine distraction. Not until the 1980s were Reid's conceptual insights heralded as a major contribution to economic theory and widely cited in a growing field of applied research.

(Folbre 1996, xi)

Elizabeth Hoyt (1893–1980) graduated in 1913 from Boston College. Between 1917 and 1921, she spent worked on the Cost of Living Index for the National Industrial Conference Board,[15] where she did some research on household budgeting and consumption. Thereafter, between 1921 and 1923, Hoyt worked as instructor of economics at Wellesley College. In 1924, she got her M.A. and, in 1925, her Ph.D. from Radcliffe College at Harvard (Thorne 2000). Her doctoral thesis dealt with trade and exchange based on trust rather than on profits and included some anthropology and ethnography (Hoyt 1926). After her graduation, Hoyt joined the Iowa State College as associate professor, being the only women among the faculty members.[16] When in 1928 she got her full professorship, she was jointly appointed to the department of economics and the department of home economics. Furthermore, she was partly engaged in the department of sociology, which had been led by Theodor Schultz since 1934. Schultz played an important role in transforming household production from a subject studied by a small number of women into the new home economics (Jefferson and King 2001; Beller and Kiss 2001).

In the 1930s, at Iowa State College, Reid and Hoyt became friends. Under Schultz's suggestion, they started a proficient collaboration by combining their two different approaches (Reid was much more interested in empirical research, while Hoyt had a broader cultural vision) which merged in their book (Hoyt and Reid 1954). Influenced by her research pursued in the late 1940s, which converged in an introductory economics textbook (Hoyt 1950), Hoyt focused her attention on the connections between economics and society and wrote a chapter on the ethics of consumption; Reid, who was much more focused on isolating economic theory from any extra-economic factor, wrote a chapter on the distribution of income and consumption (Thorne 2000).

Along with Kyrk's work (1939) and Reid's research (1934), Hoyt pioneered the so-called consumption economics field (Hoyt 1928, 1938), which introduced the dimension of rational calculation applied to the allocation of intra-house time and resources within the household economics. In Hoyt's terms, consumption theory included present goods and services, as well as the future use of economic resources in the service of consumption. Furthermore, she emphasized the importance of desires, as opposed to merely needs in guiding the household production system, by introducing the role of fashion and taste (Parson 2013).[17]

Hoyt's view of consumption choice was influenced by her concern with the distribution of economic resources in a welfare system. Under Kyrk's influence, Hoyt was particularly interested in the careful use of resources: although she did not directly deal with the moral or environmental consequences of consumption, her focus on 'economic awareness and economic planning' revealed a specific concern for the use of resources in the future. In her works, Hoyt often used anthropological examples to explain consumption's wider role within the exchange system, to measure the maximization of satisfaction, and to explain not only exchange but also other forms of economic relations such as integration. According to Hoyt, all these economics relations, not only exchange, are useful for understanding the nature of economic systems, especially in other cultures (Hoyt 1961).

Although not involved in household economics, the previously mentioned Ruth Alice Allen (1889–1979) was a leading figure among women economists who got their Ph.D. in Chicago and devoted their efforts to the woman question. Allen received her Ph.D. in Chicago in late 1920s, with a dissertation on women workers' conditions in cotton farms (Allen 1933). She spent her professional life at the University of Texas, where she taught until her retirement in 1959. Devoted to education and concerned with racial equality, she helped many women economists to follow the academic profession. She offered the first courses on women's economic role in the country. In her course, she adopted an institutionalist approach to labor studies as had been pioneered by John R. Commons (Bernasek and Kinnear 2000).

Allen prepared several surveys that were addressed to hundreds of women who were working in farm households in Texas, and personally conducted many interviews. In her reports, which included economic as well as sociological insights, Allen concluded that women's work in farms was influenced more by tradition and custom than by real economic costs and benefits. In fact, it emerged that, in local farms, women were underpaid and cotton was overproduced. The overproduction of cotton kept its price artificially low, and perpetuated depressed wages of farm workers.

2.3 From household economics to the new home economics

After the Second World War, new opportunities emerged for women economists, especially in those universities that had welcomed home economists and household economists during the interwar period. At the University of Chicago, Kyrk, Reid, and Hoyt introduced household economics as a scientific field and strengthened it by combining a theoretical approach and empirical technique. Their efforts converged later in the 1960s and the 1970s into the new home economics. As Grossbard (2001) explained, Jacob Mincer and Gary Becker who were the founders of the new home economics, were directly inspired by Kyrk and Reid. More specifically, around Reid, an intellectual circle of women economists grew up. The circle included Rose Friedman[18] and Dorothy Brady,[19] and a generation later, Charlotte Phelps[20] and Shoshanna Grossbard.[21] Both Phelps and Grossbard specifically focused their work on the theory of marriage. Arleen Leibowitz also played an important role during the early 1970s in the passage from household economics to the new home economics.

In 1971, classical liberal feminist economist Barbara Bergmann (see Chapter 3) invited Phelps to join a symposium on women in the labor force, which was held at the Allied Social Sciences Association meetings in New Orleans. On that occasion, Phelps wrote an article about the nature of household economics. In her article, Phelps wondered whether household economics has become obsolete due to the rapid development of the new home economics (Phelps 1972).[22] As Grossbard (2001) pointed out, although household economics "as an academic specialty has been defined principally as economic research on consumption and on value of time devoted to household production, the new home economics transformed household economics by widening its application in the areas of labor economics, demographic economics, health economics, transportation economics, and public economics" (Grossbard 2001, 104).

The emergence and the success of the new home economics between the 1960s and 1970s was principally related with the works of Mincer and Becker at Columbia University, and of Becker at the University of Chicago. While working together at Columbia University in 1960s, Becker and Mincer made a great effort to set up a permanent workshop that attracted many Ph.D. students who were trained in labor economics. Mincer and Becker considered labor economics a branch of human capital theory. During the permanent workshop on labor economics, which was reinforced by their commitment with the National Bureau of Economic Research (located in New York City), Mincer and Becker introduced their new home economics. When Becker left Columbia in 1968, "mostly because of the way the faculty – not Jacob [Mincer]! – dealt with the student unrest of the late 1960s" (Becker 2006, 27), he got a position at the University of Chicago, where he managed transforming the long tradition of home economics and household economics into the new home economics, much more targeted around neoclassical economics. As Grossbard pointed out: "what Mincer and Becker did was to import the tools of microeconomic and econometric analysis, which had been developed in the context of firms, in order to model home-based decisions" (Grossbard 2001, 105).

Mincer's specific research dealt with women's labor supply (Mincer 1962) and fertility, seen as a negative function of parents' wages related to the opportunity cost of their time (Mincer 1963). In general terms, Mincer's works emphasized human capital as the core of labor economics. This affected the consideration of the role of women when they enter the labor market and of their role in accumulating human capital for preschool kids (Mincer 1962, 1963). Mincer stated that an analysis of married women's labor force behavior in terms of the demand for leisure was incomplete, work at home being an activity to which women, on average, devoted the largest part of their married life. While analyzing family's consumption behavior based on the distribution of consumption among family's members, which depended on their tastes, Mincer elaborated that the theory based on the trade-off between work and leisure was too simplistic and insisted on the necessity to pay a deeper attention to the alternative uses of time. According to Mincer, a family's income has a positive effect on the demand for leisure and a negative effect on the total amount of work: if husbands' wages remain constant, an increase in the wage rate of married women would lead to an increase in their labor force rate and to a reduction of the number of children. In fact, a reduction of fertility is a tool for women to rise their opportunity cost of time in home production.

In some following publications (Mincer 1974; Mincer and Polachek 1974), Mincer showed that higher levels of education and training are relevant in determining higher wages. Mincer and Polacheck showed that the differential allocation of time and of investments in human capital is generally sex determinate (Ferber and Birnbaum 1977a, 1977b; Grossbard M. 2006; Leibowitz 2006).

As a student at the University of Chicago, Becker had been exposed to the ideas of Margaret Reid on household production and consumption. Furthermore, working along with Mincer at Columbia, Becker's interest in studying family behavior, including women's role in the labor force, as well as his attention to the fertility model increased.

In Becker's new home economics, the household was regarded as a productive agent and household activities were modeled as a series of industries. His model postulates that households "combine time and market goods to produce more basic commodities that directly enter their utility functions" (Becker 1965). Any change in incomes and prices would have led households to modify expenditure, as in the classical household production theory. However, in the new home economic theory, households adjust their behavior as soon as they discover new commodities which may be useful for the household production process.

The simplicity of Becker's model of the household production depends on accepting the right combination of two auxiliary assumptions: the assumed absence of a joint production, and the assumed observability and measurability of commodities. The essential insights of the household production model – that incentives matter as well as the fact that changes in incentives may plausibly change behavior in predictable directions – remain valid.

As Pollak and Wachter (1975) pointed out:

> Households with different tastes [and the same technology] will select different commodity bundles ... and the commodity bundles they select will imply different commodity prices. The unwary economist might attribute some part of the difference in the [commodity] consumption pattern of our two households to these differences in commodity prices, but such an interpretation would be highly misleading; the differences in commodity prices are reflections of differences in tastes, not differences in opportunities.
>
> (Pollak and Wachter1975, 265)

In the traditional consumer theory of choice, consumer behavior maximizes a utility function, given income, tastes, and prices. The weakness of this model is its scarce range of applicability. Hence, Becker proposed an alternative theory, that is, the household production function approach that would have opened the gate of economic approach to noneconomic fields. Like Mincer, Becker pointed out that the relation between labor markets and family roles was crucial to determine household production behavior. His unitary model of household assumed that household members agree by consensus to maximize a single utility function, subjected to a budget constraint, and composed of the sum of all family members' income. If total income is constant, the individual contributions to the household budget as well as any change in those contributions are independent of each person's influence over the allocation of the budget (Becker 1974, 1981).

In his model, Becker posed a benevolent head of the family (the husband/father) who considered fairly the preferences of all household members but also adjusted allocations in response to family members' behavior. In case a family member (a rotten kid) would try to raise his own consumption by lowering the consumption of others, the head of the household may reduce transfers in order to induce the rotten kid to behave properly (Vermeulen 2002; Wax 2018).

Becker's new theory of consumer was rooted in his theory of allocation of time between different activities and its empirical applications: when earnings, income, prices, and the productivity of working and consuming change, time is reallocated as well as demanded goods and supplied commodities (Becker 1965). The household production function:

> Systematically and symmetrically incorporates numerous constraints on the household's behavior, strengthens the reliance on changes in income and prices as explanations of observed behavior, and correspondingly reduces the reliance on differences in tastes and preferences ... the new approach *expands the applicability of the economist's theory of choice into the non-market sector* and hence makes the theory more useful in analyzing household behavior in its many dimensions. [emphasis added]
>
> (Michael and Becker 1973, 394)[23]

Becker's *Treatise on the Family* (Becker [1981] 1991) was an application of his previous works on household economics (Becker 1965; Michael and Becker 1973) and on human capital (Becker 1964)[24] to family "not in the sense of an emphasis on the material aspects of family life, but in the sense of a choice-theoretic framework for analyzing many aspects of family life" (Becker 1991, ix).[25] Becker's *Treatise* was grounded on his efforts to define "economic approach [as a way] to understand *all human behavior* in a variety of contexts and situations" [emphasis added] (Becker 1976, 1).[26] Becker scrutinized family behavior in rational choice terms and he applied the economic approach to family matters such as the division of labor in households,[27] marriage,[28] fertility,[29] the demand for children,[30] and divorce.[31]

Becker was influenced by Schultz's work on education as human capital: Schultz had ignored the role of families into the development of children's capabilities, being much more oriented in interpreting human capital as investments by mature students or adult individuals without paying much attention to its cost (Schultz 1963). Becker initially followed Schultz by emphasizing that human capital accumulation is a result of adult people's self-investment (Becker 1975); therefore, following Mincer's human capital model, he shifted his attention from individuals to families. Becker cited Mincer's works on the central role of married women in the labor force and on the conditions of women's participation in the labor force, which are determined not only by their potential wages but also by their husbands' earnings and by the number of children they have to raise. According to Becker, parental present expenditure on their children's education should be regarded as an investment in the future productivity of children. The role of parents' expenditure of money and time in children's education was later scrutinized by Arleen Leibowitz (1974a) in a book edited by Schultz.

According to Becker, both Mincer and Schultz had introduced pivotal studies and research able to build up his own work on the economic approach to the family, which also may help in understanding the degree of inequality among families, the effects of inequality specifically on women, and the consequence of some welfare policies on women (Folbre 2009). The following long quotation by Becker (1991) better explains the nature and the consequence of inequality within families. He wrote:

> Inequality clearly depends on the relation between fertility and family income; on the extent of underinvestment by poorer families in their children's human capital; on the degree of assortative mating by education, family background, and other characteristics; on divorce rates and the amount of child support to divorced women; and on any inequity in the distribution of bequests among children. Inequality also depends on government efforts to redistribute income through subsidies to education, social security programs, and other techniques, although the net effect on inequality of these programs depends crucially on how families respond. For example, a welfare program may widen rather than narrow inequality if women on welfare raise their fertility and reduce their time and effort spent on each child.
>
> (Becker 1991, 19)

Following the Chicago tradition of household production, Becker assumed that time and goods are inputs within household production function whose utility is supposed to be maximized by family behavior. As previously stated, human capital investment is central to Becker's definition of the specialization of household: an optimal decision should take into account skills of different members as well as of conflicts in their incentives. In his model, neoclassical assumptions are implicit: knowledge is perfect; everyone is intrinsically identical and perfectly able to maximize the commodity output of their household. Therefore, he continued analyzing the division of labor within households that specifically affects married women, who are traditionally burdened with childbearing and unpaid domestic work because of a combination of biological effects, cultural models, and different investments in human capital.

Becker's definition of marriage was a long-term commitment to assure that women would not be abandoned and to protect them from life's troubles. Becker explained the sexual division of labor in families as a partial consequence of the intrinsic differences between the sexes as well as a major component of household production: women have a "heavy biological commitment" to the production, feeding, and caring of children, and they "want their heavy biological investment in production to be worthwhile" (Becker 1991, 38). Given that there are evident biological differences between sexes, the time of men and of women are not perfect substitutes, but are complementary. Hence, it is much more rational to allocate the time of women mainly to the household sector and the time of men mainly to the market sector. In fact, "household with only men or only women are less efficient because they are unable to profit from the sexual difference in comparative advantage" (Becker 1991, 39).

According to Becker, biological differences are reinforced by specialized investments on boys (oriented to the market) and girls (oriented to the household): "the optimal strategy would be to invest mainly household capital in *all* girls and mainly market capital in *all* boys until any deviation from this norm is established" (Becker 1991, 40). Any deviation from this model, in Becker's terms, conflicts with biology: "investments in children with 'normal' orientations reinforce their biology, and they become specialized to the usual sexual division of labor. Investments in 'deviant' children conflict with their biology, and the net outcome for them is not certain" (*ibid*).

As previously mentioned, not only biology but also specialized investments in comparative advantages reinforced the division of labor between men in the market and women in the household sector. This specialization justifies an overall gender labor gap as well as a significant wage gap between married and unmarried women, in favor of the latter. According to Becker, human capital theory well explains the gender wage gap: the incentive to invest in human capital is positively related to the time spent in that activity. If less women, and especially married women, join the labor force (as traditionally happened), they are inevitably bound to earn less than men. This rationale led Becker to conclude that sexual differences in comparative advantage are independent of the exploitation of women. Both the institution of marriage, as a long-term contract to produce commodities in the household, and the institution of divorce, as a form of reimbursement for abandonment, had emphasized the peculiarity of the model.

Becker's work had a deep influence on his colleagues and students, including women economists at the University of Chicago. Charlotte Phelps, mentioned earlier, was a pioneer in modeling household production based on the coordination of an individual decision with other household members' decisions. Her work aimed to bridge the gap between the old household economics and the new home economics approach. Following the traditional household economics, she focused her attention on three main conditions for economic equality between men and women: the elimination of gender labor gap, the elimination of gender wage gap, and a more balanced redistribution of unpaid work at home between the sexes.

Phelps' contribution to the economic modeling of marriage implied two assumptions. First, that women's choice to become housewives did not necessarily hurt them. Second, that an in-couple negotiation about the management of the household is crucial. In dealing with this topic, Phelps used the new home economics analysis by providing a theory of household's formation, which was based on three assumptions. First, the ability to give and to receive love is a static condition that determines the level of self-respect. Second, household equilibrium is intended as the assumption, according to which no family member will leave. Third, if each person wants to maximize his/her own happiness, which depends on given and received love, he/she must consider that happiness is greater in a not-single household.

Recently, Grossbard (2019) has compared Phelps (1972), Becker (1973), and her own model of the economic theory of marriage (Grossbard 1984). According to Grossbard, Phelps preceded Becker in adopting the following ideas: married women's utility function and single women's utility function must be compared; individuals' utility depends on private consumption; allocation of time to household production and individual in-couple consumption are relevant factors; marriage should been seen as a bilateral form of contract; the concept of equilibrium must be regarded as the final stage of the model; and the unmeasurable individual utility is a function of something else that is unmeasurable (which may be identified with self-respect in Phelps' terms and with individual access to commodities in Becker's terms).

Grossbard (2019) pointed out that, contrary to Phelps, Becker had included formal models and testable predictions grounded on the following assumptions: the household is a unit; couples make time-allocation decisions; and time constraint is intended as the total time available to both partners. Becker's (1973, 1991) theory of marriage had emphasized the implication that a traditional division of labor is optimal.[32] Although Becker did not explain how households actually organize production, both Phelps (1972) and Grossbard (1984; 2015) considered the role of negotiations within the process of distribution and consumption between partners as well as the cost of negotiations by assuming that families, like firms, emerged in order to reduce negotiation costs. The formation of a family depends mainly on gender-role norms, which can be traditional or egalitarian. Although traditional households play an important role in Phelps' model, she never used her theory to offer a foundation for housewives' specialization in household production (Ben-Porath 1980; Pollak 1985; Lamanna et al. 2014).

During the 1970s, many other economists in Chicago contributed to develop the new home economics approach. Among them, DeTray (1973), Gronau (1973), Michael (1973), Willis (1973), and Heckman (1974)[33] had a central role, along with Arleen Leibowitz (Ph.D. 1972 from Columbia University, now emerita at the University of California, Los Angeles Luskin School of

Public Affairs), and Shoshana Grossbard (Ph.D. 1978 from the University of Chicago, now emerita at San Diego State University). As mentioned earlier, Grossbard focused her attention mainly on the economics of marriage (early papers included Grossbard 1978, 1981, 1984),[34] while Leibowitz focused her attention on education (Leibowitz 1974a, 1974b, 1975, 1976, 1977, 2006) and later devoted herself to health economics.

According to Leibowitz, education is likely to have a large allocative effect in the household. Leibowitz (1974a) insisted on the idea that home investments increase measured stocks of childhood human capital and claimed that the process of acquiring preschool human capital is analogous to the acquisition of human capital through schooling or on-the-job training. In another article, Leibowitz (1974b) highlighted the reasons that led more-educated women to enter the labor force, especially if they belong to families with constant income. In fact, education has the non-neutral effect of raising the productivity of labor-market time more than that of time spent in home production. In her paper on schooling investments, Leibowitz (1976) demonstrated that the rate of return on schooling investments cannot be identified from the linear regression of years of schooling, and that the greater intensity of schooling investments may allow high-ability students to enter the labor force earlier than their peers of average ability. Leibowitz (1977) dealt with the influence of family environment, such as parental education, occupation, and income on children's future earnings. She explained that the mechanism of parents' influence on children is twofold. On one side, family-background variables are supposed to be related to the quantities of time and goods devoted by parents to increasing the human-capital stock of their children. On the other side, family income may also be related to time devoted to children by married women who are less likely to enter the labor force, if their husbands' incomes are high. Hence, maternal education is positively related to the quantity of time devoted to children, either because more-educated mothers have fewer children or because they spend more time with each child.

Grossbard's first paper (1978) was an effort to cope with the analysis of marriage by unifying studies in anthropology and in economics. She noted that a certain convergence between the two disciplines was occurring: on one side, formal anthropology started to be concerned about the possibility of introducing quantitative measurement; on the other side, economics started to consider the role of qualitative factors in determining some economic phenomena. Marriage, according to Grossbard, was a possible issue for a combination of economic and anthropological inquiries. She described marriage by using the neoclassical approach of the new home economics, according to which people are rational maximizers of an expected utility function. Grossbard wrote: "this new brand of 'human economics' can contribute to the analysis of all human behavior that potentially involves use of reason and rational decision making" (Grossbard 1978, 37). Simultaneously, she became aware of the fact that anthropology may help to more deeply understand cultural factors that are relevant when dealing with marriage.

A few years later, in 1984, Grossbard explicitly adopted a model not "necessarily descriptive of actual behavior or attitudes in any particular society", which allowed her to consider marriage markets and labor markets as mutually related (Grossbard 1984, 864). By assuming marriage to be an exchange of household labor between spouses, she presented the new home economics as a research field that, on one side, gave emphasis to household structure and, on the other side, paved the way for labor economists to deal with the specificity of married women's time and their marital status within the economic analyses of consumption. Grossbard based the interrelation between labor markets and marriage markets on the theory of the allocation of time and on the assumption that individuals can either enter marriage contracts or exit them. Her study aimed to show that the labor force participation of married women depends on the sex ratio of those eligible for marriage; and the variations of income have a major influence on married women's labor supply and a minor impact on married men's labor supply.

In the 1970s some criticism against the new home economics emerged. In 1974, a long article by Nerlove (1974) appeared in the *Journal of Political Economy*. It summarized that criticism. Nerlove was mainly concerned about the fact that the model was too simple to rightly cope with the complexity of its issues. He identified four main problems within the new home economics.

The first problematic element in the new home economics was that it merely applied the mechanism of maximization of an expected utility function to the families. Nerlove wrote: "the Chicago utility function does not involve nonmarket goods or physical commodities, but abstract goods composed of a number of attributes which must themselves be produced within the household" (Nerlove 1972, S202). Furthermore, in the so-called Chicago utility function, children's well-being and other family members' well-being were embedded in the utility function of a single decision maker; that is, the husband or father figure. This happened in Becker's model and had happened earlier in Samuelson's model (Samuelson 1956), which assumed a fixed family membership, which is problematic because children's utility function was not included. Although the problem had been partially solved by Schultz (1972), Nerlove pointed out that casual observations suggested that each individual's concern for others diminishes when distance in both time and space increases.

According to Nerlove, Morishima (1970) had presented a more dynamic utility function as well as the conditions under which such function can be reduced to the sum of discounted utilities of each future generation, regardless of the situation of the generation that is actually involved. Nonetheless, as Koopmans (1967) had earlier pointed out, that kind of concern, which involved an intertemporal distribution problem; that is, the intergenerational transfers of material wealth and human capital as it was described by Knight (1921), may be considered an ethical issue not an economic issue.

The second problematic aspect of the new home economics was related to the household production technology model described by a production function, as Becker did (1965): in its simplest form, the economic theory of fertility assumed that there are two inputs (husband's time and wife's time), which are used to produce three household goods (children numbers, children quality, and a general commodity called 'other satisfactions') (Willis 1973; DeTray 1973). Both Willis and DeTray had assumed that children numbers and children quality are mothers' time-intensive effort and they neglected the sequential and dynamic character of investments in children quality. Again, according to Nerlove, casual observation suggested that in many societies and families, the eldest son often is the beneficiary of the bulk of the investment in the human capital that takes place in the second generation.

A third problematic element in the new home economics was a set of assumptions about the way in which household resources, principally time, can transform commodities to be used in the household production process: the lack of any dynamism within the new home economics' model had important implications, especially for fertility and female labor force participation.

The fourth problematic element in the new home economics focused on resource constraints in the process of household production and optimization decisions: these constraints are divided into partners' time (assuming that the husband devotes himself full-time to the market and the wife devotes herself full-time to the household) and unpaid income. Aside from Leibowitz's study, which had showed how much human capital is transferred from one generation to another, insufficient attention had been paid to the quality of the time resources and of other family resources passed over generations.

Summing up, in Nerlove' own words:

> The four main elements of the theoretical structure of the new home economics – (1) a utility function with arguments which are not physical commodities but home-produced bundles of attributes; (2) a household production technology; (3) an external labor-market environment providing the means for transforming household resources into market commodities; and (4) a set of household resource constraints- are incapable of yielding a series of well-defined implications about the main problems of household behavior with which we are concerned.
>
> (Nerlove 1974, S210)

Nerlove's critique was not an isolated case. Detractors of the new home economics stated that it predicted the obvious: the composition of a woman's family is supposed to be strongly associated with her labor-force participation; highly educated married women participate in the labor force to a greater extent and work more hours than less-educated married women; and married women tend to withdraw from the labor force when they have children, children being more female time-intensive than other commodities produced within the home. Furthermore, Nerlove and Schultz (1970) and Hall (1973) emphasized that educational investments, labor-force participation, and fertility must be viewed, at least partly, as simultaneously determined choices against the static model proposed by the new home economics.

Major critiques of the new home economics were based mainly on the rejection of neoclassical assumptions, according to which households are able to make rational decisions while allocating resources and time. Furthermore, the new home economics was accused of being grounded on traditional gendered stereotypes, which systematically ignored the separate and autonomous identities of the family members (Ferber and Nicosia 1972). Another main concern about the new home economics was that it underestimated noneconomic factors that had always played a fundamental role in influencing the formation and the dissolution of families: economic factors are important, but they are not the only determinants of household decisions. For instance, in a paper by Ferber and Sander (1989), the relation between religion and divorce has been analyzed in order to show an inverse relation and to support the view that individual behavior is heavily influenced by social norms.

In 1977, a lively debate on the nature of the new home economics took place and was hosted in *The Journal of Consumer Research*. The debate involved Marianne Ferber and Bonnie Birnbaum, Margaret Reid, and the sociologist John P. Robinson. Ferber and Birnbaum (1977a; 1977b) recognized that the new research field might be regarded as an interesting application of "sophisticated theory and econometric models" to the "long-neglected area of nonmarket activities in the household sector". Nevertheless, they criticized the new home economics because it adopted unrealistic assumptions that did not take into account the "complex reality of the world" (Ferber and Birnbaum 1977a, 19). They suggested the urgency to scrutinize a totally different image of the household. In fact, according to Ferber and Birnbaum, household should be regarded "no longer [as] necessarily rational, no longer [as] an indivisible unit, no longer static" (ibid). Moreover, they pointed out the discrepancies between the real world and the model of a family as a maximizing agent. According to the new home economics, any increase in the husband's wage should lead his wife to spend less time in the labor market and more time at home, but empirical evidence in time series had shown that when the husbands' wage increases, the opposite situation occurs. Furthermore, according to the new home economics, husbands are expected to take a broader part in household production when their wives' comparative advantage at home is not high enough to keep them out of the labor market. Yet, data present extensive evidence that, on average, husbands of women working outside the home spend very little more time working at home than those whose wives are at home full time.

In response to Ferber and Birnbaum (1977a), Margaret Reid wrote an article on the nature of the new home economics (Reid 1977) in which she claimed that the new home economics, as developed by Becker, was not new from a theoretical point of view. In fact, it was a development of household economics, rather than of home economics, as the label might suggest. According to Reid, what was really new in the new home economics approach was the formal technique adopted to scrutinize such phenomena as allocation of family time to pursue activities in nonmarket production as well as conditions affecting joint decisions of spouses between market and nonmarket production and between production and consumption. Unfortunately, Reid continued, this new technique seemed to be very problematic. For instance, according to Reid, Stigler and Becker's model (1977) presented some faults that may be summarized as follows: the model is unrealistic; the assumption of perfect rationality is at least problematic; status quo of social gender dynamics is accepted; and it does not question traditions and conventions. Furthermore, in spite of what they claimed, their model was far from being value-free: by considering the family as a maximizing unit able to provide an optimal outcome, they provided a definition of rational behavior which "deals with *ex ante* behavior not the *ex post* appraisal of its outcome" (Reid 1977, 182). Finally, Reid pointed out that Stigler and Becker's static model was failed to recognize any possible path dependence effects on household demand and on labor force participation.

Even more critical than Reid, John P. Robinson followed Ferber and Birnbaum's critique by claiming that the formal development adopted by the new home economics' model opened up a serious set of problems, especially related to their initial assumptions "usually treated as trivial matters" (Robinson 1977, 178). Problematic methodological assumptions included: the role of wives as the only partner to perform household tasks; the failure to contemplate lifetime in earning potentials; and "the unrealism and fuzziness of joint preference functions" (ibid). Robinson followed some previous critiques, such as Berk and Berk's article ([1976] 1978), which had listed several other problems related to the fact that the new home economics did not capture the presence of conflicts among family members as well as the effects of power control within families. These faults made the new home economics model irrelevant in terms of policy, and may reinforce the status quo.

In a previous publication, Robinson and Converse (1972) had claimed that the new home economics' model oversimplified the nature of household work, which can be rated at the bottom of the list of activities that make people happy or satisfied. According to the authors, the failure of husbands to share burdens of household activities with their partners may seem rational rather than irrational, as preached by the new home economics model. A further problem related to the new home economics model is the fact that it failed to take account of differences across social class and income groups.

In their rejoinder, Ferber and Birnbaum (1977b) underlined that both Reid and Robinson raised three specific and pertinent issues: 1) family is not a rational maximizer; 2) family is not an indivisible unit; and 3) the model neglected uncertainty. Ferber and Birnbaum replied that they shared the same concerns and wished that these commonly shared critiques would have helped to enrich the new home economics and to push it towards a "more interdisciplinary interaction", in order to develop "more realistic economic models" (Ferber and Birnbaum 1977b, 183). In Chapter 4 we will see whether Ferber and Birnbaum's wish had been realized or instead it had been disappointed.

Further critiques to the new home economic model were raised later by feminist economists, such as Nancy Folbre (1986), who criticized the assumption of exogenous preferences as constant over time,[35] and Julie Nelson (1995), who noticed that the model assumed a 'benevolent dictator' as head of the family to overcome the problem of aggregating preferences, and that the model did not consider the heterogeneity of the members nor the predominant position of the household's head.

Notes

1 Among the major contributions of neoclassical economics from a methodological perspective are Samuelson's comparative statics (Samuelson 1947) and Friedman's definition of economics as a positive science (Friedman 1953). Both Samuelson's and Friedman's methodological positions were grounded on the notion of economics as it was previously defined by Lord Robbins: "the science which studies human behavior as a relationship between ends and scarce means which have alternative uses" (Robbins 1932, 16). Economics intended in these terms is grounded on rational choice theory; that is, the methodological assumption of individuals regarded as rational economic agents able to rank their preferences and, given budget constraints, able to choose an optimal solution (Becchio and Leghissa 2017).

2 Gary Becker gave the ultimate definition of neoclassical economics as "maximizing behavior, market equilibrium, and stable preferences" (Becker 1976, 7). It is worthwhile to remember that, in 1992, Becker was the recipient of the Nobel Prize in Economics "for having extended the domain of microeconomic analysis to a wide range of human behavior and interaction, including nonmarket behavior" (Becker 1992). As Becker stated: "now everyone more or less agrees that rational behavior simply implies consistent maximization of a well-ordered function, such as a utility or profit function" (Becker 1962, 1) and, given some incentives, even irrational agents often react in a rational way.

3 In mid-1960s, most of the Hull House buildings were demolished to build the University of Illinois Circle Campus. (Johnson et al. 2004).

4 As retrieved on June 7, 2018, at: https://digital.janeaddams.ramapo.edu/items/show/5903.

5 Richards published several books and pamphlets that reported her work at the Woman's Laboratory. They included *The Chemistry of Cooking and Cleaning* (Richards 1882), and *Food Materials and Their Adulterations* (Richards 1885).

6 In 1994, AHEA changed its name to the current American Association of Family and Consumer Sciences.

7 Quotations are retrieved on June, 7, 2018, at: http://hearth.library.cornell.edu.

8 Quotations are retrieved on June, 7, 2018, at: http://hearth.library.cornell.edu.

9 Among them: South Bend, Ind.; Kansas City, Mo.; Baltimore, Md.; Washington, D.C.; Chicago, Ill.; Long Beach and San Francisco, Calif.; Milwaukee, Wis.; Grand Rapids, Ann Arbor, Kalamazoo, and Flint, Mich. The states that revised their home-economics courses in the same biennium were Alabama, Connecticut, Florida, Georgia, Illinois, Kentucky, Massachusetts, Michigan, Mississippi, Missouri, Montana, New Hampshire, Oklahoma, Texas, Utah, and Wisconsin (Whitcomb 1929).

10 A list of the projects supported by IFHE is available at: https://he.ifhe.org/915/.

11 The total economic value added by household production function has been named Gross Household Product. It has been intended to be necessary even in an industrialized country (Eisner 1989; Ironmonger 1996). Today, economic textbooks, with a few exceptions, cope with households as consumer units and fail to discuss them as producer agents.

12 Thorsten Veblen left the department in 1906, two years before Kyrk arrived. Kyrk completed her undergraduate degree under the supervision of James Alfred Field,

another institutionalist economist. Along with Kyrk, another graduate student, Helen R. Wright (Ph.D. 1922), was influenced by institutionalism.

13 John Dewey was the most prominent public intellectual leader in the United States during the interwar period.

14 Hildegarde Kneeland (1889–1944) was professor and the head of the department of household economics, at Kansas State Agriculture College, and, since 1919, she was the principal economist in the Division of Economics at the U.S. Department of Agriculture.

15 In the 1920s, surveys were used to understand and profile the average consumer. The Cost of Living Index was a precursor to the large-scale social surveys that became very popular in the United States during the 1930s depression, when surveys provided raw data to set potential policy measures (Ward 2009).

16 Hoyt spent the rest of her career at Iowa State University. She tried to combine economics and anthropology. In early 1950s, she received a Fulbright fellowship to spend a sabbatical in Africa at Makerere College (Kampala, Uganda), in order to conduct her research on women's social conditions in Uganda (Parson 2013).

17 According to Hoyt, there are six basic human interests: two primary interests (sensory and social) and four secondary interests (intellectual, technological, aesthetic, and empathetic). Although these interests are shared by all cultures, in any culture there is a single secondary interest that usually dominates and prevails over other interests. For instance, technological interests prevail in Western society.

18 Rose Friedman (1910–2009) wrote some important articles on consumer behavior before becoming involved in writing books that were associated with her husband, Milton Friedman.

19 Dorothy Brady (1903–1977), Ph.D. in mathematics (1933), worked as a statistician and economist. In 1956, she joined the economics department at the University of Chicago. Two years later, she left Chicago for the Wharton School.

20 Charlotte D. Phelps was educated at Radcliffe College, Harvard University (B.A. and M.A., 1955) and Yale University (Ph.D. in economics, 1961). Before joining Temple University as a faculty member, she taught economics at Connecticut College for Women and was a member of the research staff at the Cowles Foundation for Economics Research at Yale University. She is now emerita at Temple University.

21 Shoshanna Grossbard got her Ph.D. in economics at the University of Chicago, in 1978, under Becker's supervision. She is currently emerita at the University of San Diego.

22 A formalized version of Phelps' article is presented by Grossbard (2019).

23 After having discarded the definition of economics in terms of the allocation of material good and welfare as useless and vague, Becker recognized in Robbins' definition of economics (Robbins 1932) the most general and valid definition of economics, although it often excluded nonmarket behavior. Hence, Becker modified Robbins' definition by considering "the combined assumptions of maximizing behavior, market equilibrium, and stable preferences" as "the heart of economic approach" to be applied to both market and nonmarket phenomena (Becker 1976, 5).

24 Becker's definition of human capital was focused on the idea that individuals' education may be regarded as an investment incentive, similar to firms' investments on input and machinery: human capital corresponds to any stock of knowledge and skills achieved by individuals during their lifetime. Like inputs are determinant in firms' productivity, human capital investments massively influence individuals' productivity (Becker 1971). The interest in human capital was not alien to economists at the University of Chicago: for instance, Knight (1941) had mentioned it during a discussion on economic freedom and human capital (Teixeira 2014), and Friedman used the human capital theory in two different papers (Friedman 1943, 1953). In the 1950s, Schultz introduced the topic in the economic curricula offered by his department, and, in 1960, his Presidential Speech to the American Economic Association was focused on human capital (Schultz 1961).

25 According to Becker, the rational economic approach can be applied to any human decision and to any human behavior, and it should not be restricted to monetary transactions. Furthermore, in his model, there are no differences between decision taken under emotional factors and decisions taken under material factors.

26 In spelling out the main attributes of the economic approach, Becker firmly wanted to present its "uniquely" power to "integrate a wide range of human behavior", which included health, education, discrimination, democracy, and legislation. Health can be economically rationalized as "the economic approach implies that there is an 'optimal' expected length of life, where the value in utility of an additional year is less than the utility foregone by using time and other resources to obtain that year" (Becker 1976, 9). Education can be economically rationalized as people's choice "to follow scholarly or other intellectual or artistic pursuits if they expect the benefits, both monetary and physic, to exceed those available in alternative occupations" (Becker 1976, 11). Discrimination is economically rational when "discrimination by any group W[hites] reduces own incomes as well as N[egroes]' (sic.), and thus retaliation by N makes it worse for N rather than better" (Becker 1976, 17). Regarding democracy, according to Becker, given the differences between an ideal democracy and the actual one, as well as the imperfection of government behavior, it is preferable not to regulate economic imperfections (that is, monopolies) "rather than to regulate them and suffer the effects of political imperfections" (Becker 1976, 38). Legislation was defined by Becker as "the method used formulates a measure of the social loss from offenses and finds those expenditures of resources and punishments that minimize this loss" (Becker 1976, 40).

27 Becker wrote: "A household assigns its members to investments and activities that maximize the household's output of commodities without regards to incentives" (Becker 1991, 48).

28 Becker wrote: "A person decides to marry when the utility expected from marriage exceeds that expected from remaining single or from additional search for a more suitable mate" (Becker 1974, 10).

29 Becker wrote: "Children are viewed as durable good, primarily a consumer's durable, which yields income, primarily psychic income, to parents. Fertility is determined by income, child costs, knowledge, uncertainty, and tastes. An increase in income and a decline in price would increase the demand for children, although it is necessary to distinguish between the quantity and quality of children demanded. The quality of children is directly related to the amount sent on them" (Becker 1976, 193). In the *Treatise*, Becker specified: "By relating the utility of children to their own consumption and to the utility of their children, we obtain a *dynastic* utility function that depends on the consumption and number of descendants in all generations" (Becker 1991, 156).

30 Becker wrote: "The demand for children would depend on the relative price of children and full income" (Becker 1991, 138).

31 Becker described divorce as a "special case of Coase theorem (1960) and is a natural extension of the argument that persons marry each other if, and only if, they both expect to be better off compared to their best alternatives" (Becker 1991, 331).

32 Bergmann (1995) and Woolley (1996) specifically criticized Becker's approach on this point (see Chapter III).

33 DeTray (1973) claimed that households can raise their production of child services either by increasing the numbers of children or by making further investments in existing children. Gronau (1973) attempted a general formulation of the intra-family allocation of time according to the members of a family comparative advantage in the production of market and home goods. Michael (1973) considered the way a couple's level of education might affect their fertility. Heckman J. (1974) presented a method able to directly estimate consumer indifference surfaces between money income and nonmarket time, which can be used to compare a variety of alternative programs and to investigate whether or not there is a Pareto-optimal redistribution

of income transfers and time, able to improve the general level of welfare of the community at large without reducing the welfare of individuals receiving income transfers. Willis (1973) assumed that husbands' time in household production is entirely unproductive.

34 Grossbard kept on publishing on the theory of marriage for decades. Her earlier contributions were significant for the story of the emerging of the new home economics.

35 The problem of aggregating individual preferences within the household had earlier been pointed out by neoclassical economists such as McElroy and Horney (1981) and was later analyzed by McElroy (1990) and Bourgignon and Chiappori (1992).

References

Allen R. (1933) *The Labor of Women in the Production of Cotton.* New York: Arno Press.

Allen R. (1934) "Review of Economics of Household Production". *American Economic Review.* Vol. 24:4, pp. 761–762.

Apple R. (2006) *Perfect Motherhood: Science and Childrearing in America.* New Brunswick, NJ: Rutgers University Press.

Apple R. (2015) "Home Economics in the Twentieth Century. A Case of Lost Identity?". Nickols S. and Kay G. (Eds.) *Remaking Home Economics: Resourcefulness and Innovation in Changing Times.* Athens, GA: The University of Georgia Press, pp. 54–70.

Becchio G. and Leghissa G. (2017) *The Origins of Neoliberalism: Insights from Economics and Philosophy.* London: Routledge.

Becker G. (1962) "Irrational Behavior and Economic Theory". *Journal of Political Economy.* Vol. 70:1, pp. 1–13.

Becker G. (1964) *Human Capital: A Theoretical and Empirical Analysis, with Special Reference to Education.* Chicago: The University of Chicago Press.

Becker G. (1965) "A Theory of the Allocation of Time". *The Economic Journal.* Vol. 75:299, pp. 493–515.

Becker G. (1971) *The Economics of Discrimination.* Chicago: The University of Chicago Press.

Becker G. (1973) "A Theory of Marriage: Part I". *Journal of Political Economy.* Vol. 81:4, pp. 813–846.

Becker G. (1974) "A Theory of Marriage". Schultz T. (Ed.) *Economics of the Family: Marriage, Children, and Human Capital.* Chicago: The University of Chicago Press, pp. 299–351.

Becker G. (1975) *Human Capital.* 2nd Edition. Chicago: The University of Chicago Press.

Becker G. (1976) *The Economic Approach to Human Behavior.* Chicago: The Chicago University Press.

Becker G. (1991) *A Treatise on the Family.* Enlarged Edition. Cambridge, MA: Harvard University Press.

Becker G. (1992) "The Economic Way of Looking at Life". Nobel Prize in Economics Documents: Nobel Prize Committee.

Becker G. (2006) "Working with Jacob Mincer: Reminiscences of Columbia's Labor Workshop". Grossbard S. (Ed.) *Jacob Mincer: A Pioneer of Modern Labor Economics.* Dordrecht, Heidelberg, London, and New York: Springer, pp. 19–27.

Beecher C. (1841) *A Treatise on Domestic Economy: For the Use of Young Ladies at Home, and at School.* Boston: Thomas Webb & Co.

Beecher C. and Beecher H. (1870) *Principles of Domestic Science as Applied to the Duties and Pleasures of Home: A Text-Book for the Use of Young Ladies in Schools, Seminaries and Colleges.* New York: J.B. Ford.

Beller A.H. and Kiss D.E. (2001) "Hazel Kyrk". Lunin Schultz R. and Hast A. (Eds.) *Women Building Chicago 1790–1990: A Biographical Dictionary.* Bloomington, IN: Indiana University Press, pp. 482–485.

Ben-Porath Y. (1980) "The F-Connection: Families, Friends, and Firms and the Organization of Exchange". *Population and Development Review.* Vol. 6:1, pp. 1–30.

Bergmann B. (1995) "Becker's Theory of the Family: Preposterous Conclusions". *Feminist Economics.* Vol. 1:1, pp. 141–150.

Berk R. and Berk S. ([1976] 1978) "A Simultaneous Equation Model for the Division of Household Labor". *Sociological Methods & Research.* Vol. 6:4, pp. 431–468.

Bernasek A. and Kinnear D. (2000) "Ruth Alice Allen". Dimand R., Dimand M.A., and Forget E. (Eds.) *A Biographical Dictionary of Women Economists.* Cheltenham: Edward Elgar, pp. 8–10.

Bourguignon F. and Chiappori P. (1992) "Collective Models of Household Behavior: An Introduction". *European Economic Review.* Vol. 36:2/3, pp, 355–364.

Coase R. (1960) "The Problem of Social Cost". *The Journal of Law and Economics.* Vol. 3, pp. 1–44.

Davis J. (2000) "Helen Stuart Campbell". Dimand R., Dimand M.A., and Forget E. (Eds.) *A Biographical Dictionary of Women Economists.* Cheltenham: Edward Elgar, pp. 101–103.

DeTray D. (1973) "Child Quality and the Demand for Children". *Journal of Political Economy.* Vol. 81:2, pp. 570–595.

Dickinson C. (1924) "A Theory of Consumption by Hazel Kyrk". *The Quarterly Journal of Economics.* Vol. 38:2, pp. 343–346.

Ehrenreich B. and English D. (1978) *For Her Own Good: Two Centuries of the Experts Advice to Women.* New York: Anchor Book.

Eisner R. (1989) *The Total Incomes System of Accounts.* Chicago: The University of Chicago Press.

Elias M. (2008) *Stir It Up: Home Economics in American Culture.* Philadelphia, PA: University of Pennsylvania Press.

Ferber M. and Birnbaum B. (1977a) "The 'New Home Economics': Retrospects and Prospects". *Journal of Consumer Research.* Vol. 4:1, pp. 19–28.

Ferber M. and Birnbaum B. (1977b) "How New Is the 'New Home Economics'?: Rejoinder". *Journal of Consumer Research.* Vol. 4:3, pp. 183–184.

Ferber M. and Sanders W. (1989) "On Women, Men, and Divorce: Not By Economics Alone". *Review of Social Economy.* Vol. 47:1, pp. 15–26.

Ferber R. and Nicosia F. (1972) "Newly Married Couples and their Asset Accumulation Decisions". Strümpbel B., Morgan J., and Zahn E. (Eds.) *Human Behavior in Economic Affairs.* Amsterdam: Elsevier, pp. 161–187.

Folbre N. (1986) "Cleaning House: New Perspectives on Households and Economic Development". *Journal of Development Economics.* Vol. 22:1, pp. 5–40.

Folbre N. (1991) "The Unproductive Housewife: Her Evolution in Nineteenth-Century Economic Thought". *Signs: Journal of Women in Culture and Society.* Vol. 16:3, pp. 463–484.

Folbre N. (1996) "For Margaret, With Thanks". *Feminist Economics.* Vol. 2:3, pp. xi–xii.

Folbre N. (1998) "The Sphere of Women in Early Twentieth Century Economics". Silverberg H. (Ed.) *Gender and American Social Science: The Formative Years.* Princeton, NJ: Princeton University Press, pp. 35–60.

Folbre N. (2009) *Greed, Lust, and Gender*. Oxford: Oxford University Press.

Forget E. (1996) "Margaret Gilpin Reid: A Manitoba Home Economist Goes to Chicago". *Feminist Economics*. Vol. 2:3, pp. 1–16.

Forget E. (2000) "Margaret Gilpin Reid". Dimand R., Dimand M.A., and Forget E. (Eds.) *A Biographical Dictionary of Women Economists*. Cheltenham: Edward Elgar, pp. 357–362.

Forget E. (2010) "Margaret Gilpin Reid". Emmett R. (Ed.) *The Elgar Companion to the Chicago School of Economics*. Cheltenham: Edward Elgar, pp. 315–317.

Forget E. (2011) "American Women and the Economics Profession in the Twentieth Century". *Oeconomica*. Vol. 1:1, pp. 19–30.

Friedman M. (1943) "The Spending Tax as a Wartime Fiscal Measure". *American Economic Review*. Vol. 33:1, pp. 50–62.

Friedman M. (1953) *Essays in Positive Economics*. Chicago: The University of Chicago Press.

Friedman M. (1957) *A Theory of the Consumption Function*. Princeton, NJ: Princeton University Press.

Gillen A. (1990) "Talbot, Marion". Lunin Schulz R. and Hast A. (Eds.) *Women Building Chicago, 1790–1990*. Indianapolis, IN: Indiana University Press, pp. 865–868.

Gronau R. (1973) "The Intrafamily Allocation of Time: The Value of Housewives' Times". *American Economic Review*. Vol. 63:4, pp. 634–651.

Grossbard M. (2006) "Household Production and Health". Grossbard S. (Ed.) *Jacob Mincer: A Pioneer of Modern Labor Economics*. Dordrecht, Heidelberg, London, and New York: Springer, pp. 161–172.

Grossbard S. (1978) "Towards a Marriage Between Economics and Anthropology and a General Theory of Marriage". *American Economic Review*. Vol. 68:2, pp. 33–37.

Grossbard S. (1981) "Gary Becker's Theory of the Family – Some Interdisciplinary Considerations". *Sociology and Social Research*. Vol. 66:1, pp. 1–11.

Grossbard S. (1984) "A Theory of Allocation of Time in Markets for Labor and Marriage". *The Economic Journal*. Vol. 94:376, pp. 863–882.

Grossbard S. (2001) "The New Home Economics at Columbia and Chicago". *Feminist Economics*. Vol. 7:3, pp. 103–130.

Grossbard S. (2015) *The Marriage Motive*. Dordrecht, Heidelberg, London, and New York: Springer.

Grossbard S. (2019) "Women's Neoclassical Models of Marriage, 1972–2015". Madden K. and Dimand R. (Eds.) *Routledge Handbook of the History of Women's Economic Thought*. London: Routledge, pp. 442–454.

Hall R. (1973) "Wages, Income, and Hours of Work in the U.S. Labor Force". Cain G. and Watts H. (Eds.) *Income Maintenance and Labor Supply*. New York: Academic Press, pp. 102–162.

Hara N. (2016) "Unpaid Labor and the Critique of Political Economy in Home Economics and the New Household Economics: From the Feminist Economics Perspective". *The History of Economic Thought*. Vol. 58:1, pp. 1–20.

Heckman J. (1974) "Effects of Child-Care Programs on Women's Work Effort". *Journal of Political Economy*. Vol. 82:2, pp. S136–S163.

Hirschfeld M. (1997) "Methodological Stance and Consumption Theory: A Lesson in Feminist Methodology". Davis J.B. (Ed.) *New Economics and Its History*. Durham, NC: Duke University Press, pp. 191–211.

Hoyt E. (1926) *Primitive Trade: Its Psychology and Economics*. London: Kegan Paul, Trench, Trubner and Co. Ltd.

Hoyt E. (1928) *The Consumption of Wealth*. New York: Macmillan.

Hoyt E. (1938) *Consumption in Our Society*. New York and London: McGraw-Hill.

Hoyt E. (1950) *The Income of Society: An Introduction to Economics*. New York: Ronald Press.

Hoyt E. (1961) "Integration of Culture: A Review of Concepts". *Current Anthropology*. Vol. 2:5, pp. 407–426.

Hoyt E. and Reid M. (Eds.) (1954) *American Income and Its Use*. New York: Harper and Brothers.

Ironmonger D. (1996) "Conting Outputs, Capital Inputs and Caring Labor: Estimating Gross Household Product". *Feminist Economics*. Vol. 2:3, pp. 37–64.

Jefferson T. and King J.E. (2001) "Never Intended to Be a Theory of Everything: Domestic Labor in Neoclassical and Marxian Economics". *Feminist Economics*. Vol. 7:3, pp. 1–32.

Johnson M. (2004) "Hull House". Johnson M., Grossman J., Keating A., and Reiff J. (Eds.) *The Encyclopedia of Chicago*. Chicago Historical Society. As retrieved on May 9, 2018 at: www.encyclopedia.chicagohistory.org/pages/615.html.

Kay G. and Nickols S. (2015) "Introduction". Nicklos S. and G. Kay (Eds.) *Remaking Home Economics: Resourcefulness and Innovation in Changing Times*. Athens, GA: The University of Georgia Press, pp. 1–8.

Kneeland H. (1934) "Review of *Economics of the Household Production* by Margaret Reid". *Journal of Home Economics*. Vol. 26:8, p. 525.

Knight F. (1921) *Risk, Uncertainty and Profit*. Boston and New York: Houghton Mifflin Company.

Knight F. (1941) "The Role of the Individual in the Economic World of the Future". *Journal of Political Economy*. Vol. 49:6, pp. 817–832.

Koopmans T. (1967) "Intertemporal Distribution and 'Optimal' Aggregate Economic Growth". *Cowles Foundation Discussion Papers* 228. New Haven, CT: Yale University Press.

Kyrk H. (1923) *A Theory of Consumption*. London: Sir Isaac Pitman and Sons, Ltd.

Kyrk H. (1929) "The Place of the Economic and Social Studies in the Home Economics Curriculum". *Journal of Home Economics*. Vol. 21:6, pp. 488–494.

Kyrk H. (1933) *Economic Problems of the Family*. New York: Harper & Brothers Publishers.

Kyrk H. (1939) "The Development of the Field of Consumption". *Journal of Marketing*. Vol. 4:1, pp. 16–19.

Kyrk H. (1953) *The Family in the American Economy*. Chicago: The University of Chicago Press.

Lamanna M.A., Riedmann A., and Stewart S. (2014) *Marriages, Families, and Relationships: Making Choices in a Diverse Society*. 12th Edition. Stanford, CT: Cengage Learning.

Leibowitz A. (1974a) "Home Investments in Children". Schultz T. (Ed.) *Economics of the Family, Marriage, Children, and Human Capital*. Chicago: The University of Chicago Press, pp. 432–452.

Leibowitz A. (1974b) "Education and Home Production". *American Economic Review*. Vol. 64:2, pp. 243–250.

Leibowitz A. (1975) "Education and the Allocation of Women's Time". Juster F. (Ed.) *Education, Income, and Human Behavior*. New York: National Bureau of Economic Research and Carnegie Commission, pp. 171–197.

Leibowitz A. (1976) "Years and Intensity of Schooling Investment". *American Economic Review*. Vol. 55:3, pp. 321–334.

Leibowitz A. (1977) "Parental Inputs and Children's Achievements". *Journal of Human Resources*. Vol. 12:2, pp. 242–249.

Leibowitz A. (2006) "Household Production and Children". Grossbard S. (Ed.) *Jacob Mincer: A Pioneer of Modern Labor Economics*. Dordrecht, Heidelberg, London, and New York: Springer, pp. 173–185.

McElroy M. (1990) "The Empirical Content of Nash-Bargained Household Behavior". *Journal of Human Resources*. Vol. 25:4, pp. 559–583.

McElroy M. and Horney M. (1981) "Nash-Bargained Household Decisions: Toward a Generalization of the Theory of Demand". *International Economic Review*. Vol. 22:2, pp. 333–349.

Michael R. (1973) "Education and the Derived Demand for Children". *Journal of Political Economy*. Vol. 81:2, pp. S128–S164.

Michael R. and Becker G. (1973) "On the New Theory of Consumer Behavior". *The Swedish Journal of Economics*. Vol. 75:4, pp. 378–396.

Mincer J. (1962) "Labor Force Participation of Married Women: A Study of Labor Supply". Lewis G.H. (Ed.) *Aspects of Labor Economics*. Princeton, NJ: Princeton University Press, pp. 63–105.

Mincer J. (1963) "Market Prices, Opportunity Costs, and Income Effects". Christ C. (Ed.) *Measurement in Economics*. Stanford, CA: Stanford University Press, pp. 66–82.

Mincer J. (1974) *Schooling, Experience and Earnings*. New York: Columbia University Press.

Mincer J. and Polachek S. (1974) "Family Investments in Human Capital: Earnings of Women". *Journal of Political Economy*. Vol. 82:2, pp. S76–S108.

Modigliani F. (1985) *Life Cycle, Individual Thrift and the Wealth of Nations*. Stockholm: Nobel Foundation.

Morishima M. (1970) "A Generalization of the Gross Substitute System". *Review of Economic Studies*. Vol. 37:2, pp. 177–186.

Nelson J. (1995) "Economic Theory and Feminist Theory: Comments on Chapters by Polacheck, Ott, and Levin". Kuiper E. and Sap J. (Eds.) *Out of the Margin: Feminist Perspectives on Economics*. London: Routledge, pp. 120–125.

Nerad M. (1987) *The Academic Kitchen: A Social History of Gender Stratification at the University of California, Berkeley*. Albany, NY: State University of New York.

Nerlove M. (1972) "On Tuition and the Cost of Higher Education: Prolegomena to a Conceptual Framework". *Journal of Political Economy*. Vol. 80:3, pp. S179–S218.

Nerlove M. (1974) "Household and Economy: Toward a New Theory of Population and Economic Growth". *Journal of Political Economy*. Vol. 82:2, pp. S200–S218.

Nerlove M. and Schultz T. (1970) *Love and Life Between the Census: A Model of Family Decision Making in Puerto Rico, 1950–1960*. Santa Monica, CA: Rand Corporation.

Parloa M. (1898) *Home Economics: A Guide to Household Management, Including the Proper Treatment of the Materials Entering into the Construction and Furnishing of the House*. New York: Century Co.

Parsons E. (2013) "Pioneering Consumer Economist: Elizabeth Ellis Hoyt (1893–1980)". *Journal of Historical Research in Marketing*. Vol. 5:3, pp. 334–350.

Peixotto J. (1901) *The French Revolution and Modern French Socialism: A Comprehensive Study of the Principles of the French Revolution and the Doctrines of Modern French Socialism*. New York: T.Y. Crowell and Company.

Peixotto J. (1927) "Family Budgets". *American Economic Review*. Vol. 17:1, pp. 132–140.

Peixotto J. (1928) "Family Budgets of University Faculty Members". *Science*. Vol. 68, pp. 497–201.

Perkins Gilman C. (1898) *Women and Economics*. Boston: Small. Maynard and Co.

Phelps C. (1972) "Is the Household Obsolete?". *The American Economic Review*. Vol. 62:1/2, pp. 167–174.

Pollak R. (1985) "A Transaction Cost Approach to Families and Households". *Journal of Economic Literature*. Vol. 23:2, pp. 581–608.

Pollak R. and Wachter M. (1975) "The Relevance of the Household Production Function and Its Implications for the Allocation of Time". *The Journal of Political Economy*. Vol. 83:2, pp. 255–277.

Pujol M. (1992) *Feminism and Anti-Feminism in Early Economic Thought*. Cheltenham: Edward Elgar.

Reid M. (1934) *The Economics of Household Production*. New York: John Wiley and Sons.

Reid M. (1938) *Consumers and the Market*. New York: F. S. Crofts.

Reid M. (1943a) "Trends in the Work of Married Women". *Marriage and Family Living*. Vol. 5:1, pp. 80–83.

Reid M. (1943b) *Food for People*. New York: John Wiley and Sons.

Reid M. (1977) "How New Is the 'New Home Economics'?". *Journal of Consumer Research*. Vol. 4:3, pp. 181–183.

Richards E. (1882) *The Chemistry of Cooking and Cleaning. A Manual for Housekeepers*. Boston: Estes & Lauriat.

Richards E. (1885) *Food Materials and Their Adulterations*. Boston: Whitcomb & Barrows.

Robbins L. (1932) *Essay on the Nature and Significance of Economic Science*. London: Macmillan.

Robinson J. (1977) "The 'New Home Economics': Sexist, Unrealistic, or Simply Irrelevant?". *Journal of Consumer Research*. Vol. 4:3, pp. 178–181.

Robinson J. and Converse P. (1972) "Social Changes as Reflected in the Use of Time". Campbell A. and Converse P. (Eds.) *The Human Meaning of Social Change*. New York: Russell Sage, pp. 17–86.

Rowles E. (1965) "Home Economics – A Basic Discipline". *THESA Journal*. Vol. 3:1, pp. 35–39.

Rutherford M. (2010) "Chicago Economics and Institutionalism". In Emmett R. (Ed.) *The Elgar Companion to the Chicago School of Economics*. Cheltenham: Edward Elgar, pp. 25–39.

Samuelson P. (1947) *Foundations of Economic Analysis*. Cambridge, MA: Harvard University Press.

Samuelson P. (1956) "Social Indifference Curve". *Quarterly Journal of Economics*. Vol. 70:1, pp. 1–22.

Schultz T. (1961) "Investment in Human Capital". *American Economic Review*. Vol. 51:1, pp. 1–17.

Schultz T. (1963) *The Economic Value of Education*. New York: Columbia University Press.

Schultz T. (1972) "Optimal Investment in College Instruction: Equity and Efficiency". *Journal of Political Economy*. Vol. 80:3, pp. S2–S30.

Sklar K. (1973) *Catharine Beecher: A Study in American Domesticity*. New Haven, CT: Yale University Press.

Stage S. and Vincenti V. (Eds.) (1997) *Rethinking Home Economics*. Ithaca, NY: Cornell University Press.

Stigler G. and Becker G. (1977) "De Gustibus Non Est Disputandum". *American Economic Review*. Vol. 67:2, pp. 76–115.

Stuart Campbell H. (1887) *Prisoners of Poverty: Women Wage Workers, Their Trades and Their Lives*. Boston: Robert Bros.

Stuart Campbell H. (1889) *Prisoners of Poverty Abroad*. Boston: Robert Bros.

Stuart Campbell H. (1893) *American Girl's Home Book. Work and Play*. New York and London: G. P. Putnam's Sons.

Talbot M. (1910) *The Education of Women*. Chicago: The University of Chicago Press.

Teixeira P. (2014) "Gary Becker's Early Work on Human Capital – Collaborations and Distinctiveness". *IZA Journal of Labor Economics*. Vol. 3:12, pp. 1–20.

Thorne A. (1995) "Women Mentoring Women in Economics in the 1930s". Dimand R., Dimand M.A, and Forget E. (Eds.) *Women of Value: Feminist Essays on the History of Women in Economics*. Aldershot: Edward Elgar, pp. 60–70.

Thorne A. (2000) "Elizabeth Ellis Hoyt (18–1900)". Dimand R., Dimand M.A, and Forget E. (Eds.) *A Biographical Dictionary of Women Economists*. Cheltenham: Edward Elgar, pp. 215–219.

Trentmann F. (2012) "Consumer Society Revised: Affluence, Choice, and Diversity". Jessen R. and Lange L. (Eds.) *Transformations of Retailing in Europe after 1945*. London: Routledge, pp. 19–33.

Velzen S. (2003) "Hazel Kyrk and the Ethics of Consumption". Barker D. and Kuiper E. (Eds.) *Toward a Feminist Philosophy of Economics*. London: Routledge, pp. 38–55.

Vermeulen F. (2002) "Collective Household Models: Principles and Main Results". *Journal of Economic Survey*. Vol. 16:4, pp. 533–564.

Wade L. (1967) "The Heritage From Chicago's Early Settlement Houses". *Journal of the Illinois Historical Society*. Vol. 60:4, pp. 411–441.

Ward D.B. (2009) "Capitalism, Early Market Research, and the Creation of the American Consumer". *Journal of Historical Research in Marketing*. Vol. 1:2, pp. 200–223.

Wax A. (2018) "Family and the Household Economics". Parisi F. (Ed.) *The Oxford Handbook of Law and Economics: Volume 2: Private and Commercial Law*. Oxford: Oxford University Press. As retrieved on May 5, 2018 at: www.oxfordhandbooks.com/view/10.1093/oxfordhb/9780199684205.001.0001/oxfordhb-9780199684205-e-010.

Whitcomb E. (1929) *Trends in Home Economics Education, 1926–1928: Bulletin n. 25*. Washington, DC: Department of Interior Bureau of Education.

Willis R. (1973) "A New Approach to the Economic Theory of Fertility Behavior". *Journal of Political Economy*. Vol. 81:2, pp. S14–S64.

Woolley F. (1996) "Getting the Better of Becker". *Feminist Economics*. Vol. 2:1, pp. 114–120.

Yi Y. (1996) "Margaret G. Reid: Life and Achievements". *Feminist Economics*. Vol. 2:3, pp. 17–36.

3 The genesis and development of feminist economics within academia

The genesis of feminist economics within academia was strictly connected with two phenomena: the introduction of women's studies in academic departments, which was a consequence of the so-called second-wave feminism; and the need to find an alternative to neoclassical economics as a whole and to propose an alternative to the new home economics' approach to gender issues.

In the late 1960s, second-wave feminism emerged as an effect of a broader cultural revolution that involved social and political norms and traditions that included the traditional role of women in society. Second-wave feminism focused on the demand for sexual liberation and on a request to realize that women had always been subjected to patriarchy, which had reinforced gendered norms. Second-wave feminism's requests affected universities and colleges everywhere in the Western countries. One of the major effects of the introduction of the principles of second wave feminism in academia was the emergence of a new research field: women's studies, which were introduced into social science departments in the early 1970s. Women's studies aimed to criticize the traditional way of considering gender relations within arts, literature, and science (see Paragraph 1).

Women's studies' challenging attitude for a radical rethinking and reorganization of traditional knowledge affected political economy too. Since the late 1970s, economists who were disappointed by the neoclassical treatment of gender issues within the new home economics founded feminist economics, which was structurally organized in the early 1990s around the International Association of Feminist Economics (IAFFE) and its academic journal (*Feminist Economics*). Feminist economics' main purpose was to radically change the nature of economic theory itself and the way gender issues were scrutinized within the discipline. Feminist economics emerged as the application of a new (feminist) philosophy and a new epistemology to political economy in order to analyze gender biases in economic models. Feminist economics' general aim was to eradicate androcentric bias from conventional economics by employing several paradigms, which went from a redefinition of neoclassical economics to a more radical challenge to it. As Figart and Mutari summed up: "the concepts of patriarchy, reproduction and gender, as well as the identification of the household as an economic realm, are among the major contributions that feminist economics have made to the discipline" (Figart and Mutari 1999, 337) (see Paragraph 2).

The development of feminist economics led feminist economists to establish the International Association of Feminist Economics (IAFFE) in 1992 and to found IAFFE's official journal, *Feminist Economics*, in 1995. Nevertheless, feminist economics was officially recognized as an autonomous research field only in 2006, when AEA finally assigned a JEL code to feminist economics (JEL code is the official label to classify scholarly literature in an autonomous field within the discipline). The purpose of the founders of IAFFE contained a more radical challenge to what they considered a masculine bias in neoclassical economics and the initial intention of the editorial board of *Feminist Economics* was to find a new paradigm able to reformulate the discipline as a whole in a theoretical perspective, as well as to propose some policies to reduce gender inequalities in a practical dimension (see Paragraph 3).

Since its foundation, feminist economics was a heterodox economic approach based on feminist ideas against neoclassical economics and the new home economics. As Strassmann wrote in the editorial that opened the 10th anniversary of *Feminist Economics*: "Unlike most heterodox journals, *Feminist Economics* does not define a particular perspective of any sort as an essential requirement for inclusion. ... The only requirement has always been that articles engage with feminist ideas" (Strassmann 2004, 2). Nonetheless, feminist economics shares some similarities with other heterodox approaches, along with some relevant differences. Paragraph 4 deals with convergences and divergences between feminist economics and Marxian political economy, post-Keynesian economics, Austrian economics, social ontology, Sen's approach of capabilities, behavioral economics, and economic comparative systems.

3.1 The role of women's studies in the emergence of feminist economics

After the Second World War, a vast literature about the woman question emerged. Virginia Woolf's novels *A Room of One's Own* (1929) and *Three Guineas* (1938) had been emblematic in revealing the genesis of social and cultural barriers to women's emancipation and had become classical books within the feminist literature. In Woolf's vision, women have been deprived of basic instruments to get their own independence: only when this state of subjection is ended would they finally prove their ability to get success in any field. In 1946, historian Mary Beard published a fundamental book, *Woman as Force in History*. She pointed out that, besides the central role of many great women in the history of humankind, it had been proven that women were able to influence civil society at any level because of their agency in the private sphere. In Beard's vision, historical figures of women scholars, queens, and saints had been overestimated compared to the role of common women in shaping society, culture, customs, habits, and so forth. In 1949, Simone de Beauvoir published her well-known book, *Le Deuxième Sexe*, which was translated into English in 1953 and became a milestone in feminist literature, along with Betty Friedan's *The Feminine Mystique* (1963). Both de Beauvoir and Friedan promoted the liberation from patriarchy and underlined the oppression of women in their role of mothers and wives. Both de Beauvoir's and Friedan's books were deeply influential at the beginning of the second wave of feminism, which spread up in late 1960s and was focused on an inquiry about the nature of women's subjection as a result of men's traditional dominance in the sexual sphere.

Second-wave feminism was divided into two major groups, classical liberal and socialists, which included several subgroups, from conservatives to radicals. Although second wave feminist groups and subgroups differed in many aspects, they shared two pillars: 1) men's dominance had perpetually ruled society in any cultural, economic, and political sphere; and 2) sexual differences had generated strict gender social roles within both private and public life.[1]

A glance at some feminist movements that spread up in the United States during the 1960s and 1970s must be provided to understand the connection between the second wave of feminism and political economy and the subsequent development of feminist economics. In 1966, 28 women gathered around Betty Friedan and organized the National Organization for Women (NOW) at the Third National Conference of Commissions on the Status of Women in Washington, D.C. Members of NOW wanted to enforce Title VII of the Civil Rights Act (1964), especially by pointing out the persistence of the discrimination of women in pay and employment (Schneir 1994). In 1967, Robin Morgan, Carol Hanisch, Shulamith Firestone, and Kate Millett founded the New York Radical Women (NYRW) in New York. The nature and purpose of NYRW had been explained by Millett in her well-known book, *Sexual Politics* (1970). The group was active up to 1969, when some dissenters complained about the fact that NOW had lost its radicalism and founded The Feminists, which was active in New York City between 1968 and 1973.[2] According to The Feminists, women's subordination was the effect of the unconscious manifestation of internalized sex roles grounded on men's dominance.[3]

In 1969, Anne Koedt left The Feminists to co-found the New York Radical Feminists (NYRF) along with Vivian Gornick and Shulamith Firestone, who meanwhile had left the NYRW.[4] According to NYRF's members, the subjection of women was a psychological construct consciously directed by men who deliberately had kept their power on women, making them subject to it (Elchos 1990) while, according to members of another radical group – the Redstockings' Pro-Woman Line – women's submission to male supremacy was a conscious adaptation to their lack of power under patriarchy rather than an internalized brainwashing of them pursued by men (Willis 1984).

In that fervent and lively atmosphere, women's studies emerged as an interdisciplinary program to scrutinize the nature of women's subjection. Based on the premise that traditional education is biased by sexism, women's studies may be defined as the studies of the role of women in every possible context, which includes history, society, economy, politics, arts, literature, and science. Although there was no homogeneity in women's studies, they were mainly conceived as a way to explore sexuality as well as social norms associated with gender, which directly involved class and race, in order to investigate the origin of social inequalities, and women's studies aimed to propose different policies to overcome those social inequalities (Kennedy 2008). As Boxer claimed, the aim of women's studies "was not merely to study women's position in the world but to change it" (Boxer 1988, 13). Women's studies methodology started from the acceptance of standard results in any discipline, to proceed towards a critical look that was able to challenge the nature of the discipline itself. As Smith wrote:

> Woman's studies method can be said to involve a re-examination of old truth from a feminist or women-oriented perspective as opposed to the male perspective on which disciplinary methods were traditionally based ... The idea was to evaluate 'male' truth that was actually made on the exclusion of women. The devaluing of their achievement, and their erasure from important theories, analyses, and the accounts of events.
>
> (Smith 2013, 25)

Women's studies were interconnected with feminist theories either in the classical liberal version (which promoted the integration of women into traditional institutions) or in the more radical version (which pointed out the differences between men and women in order to radically change the traditional institutions based on masculine systems). Socialist feminism, which emerged between the 1960s and 1970s and was directly influenced by Engels' *The Origin of the Family, Private Property, and the State* (1884), can be obviously included in the latter group that was aimed to radically transform the traditional society to overcome both patriarchy and capitalism. Unlike socialist movements related to early feminism that were much more focused on class struggle regardless of gender identity, feminism became a central issue in the socialist movements that emerged during second-wave feminism, which were able to combine class struggle and women's emancipation.[5]

During the early 1970s, women's studies gradually gained a position within academia. Historians agree that the emergence of women's studies as academic fields was a further phase in women's fight to get access to higher education (Solomon 1985; Howe 1987; Boxer 2002). Forerunners of women's studies were Margaret Mead and Gerda Lerner.

Margaret Mead (1901–1978) got her B.A. at Barnard College in 1923 and attended graduate studies at Columbia University, where in 1924 she got her M.A., and in 1929 she got her Ph.D. in anthropology, under the supervision of Franz Boas, one of the founders of anthropology in the United States. Unlike earlier anthropologists, who imagined that civilization had gone from 'barbarism' to 'civilization', Boas argued that any separate culture had had its own specificities that did not follow a regular pattern. Influenced by Boas, Mead's research was mainly focused on the interconnection between individual personality and social culture. In her book, *Sex and Temperament in Three Primitive Societies* (Mead 1935), she scrutinized the stereotype of peaceful women versus warrior men. Mead showed that although the female dominance in many Western Pacific islands had led the local population to a relatively peaceful equilibrium amongst them, in some other geographical areas, tribes led by women are as aggressive as tribes led by men. In her *Male and Female: A Study of the Sexes in a Changing World* (Mead 1949), she demonstrated that gender roles may be differed if different societies are considered, and they depend as much on culture as on biology. According to Mead, it was neither sex nor race, but cultural norms and social expectations that had been slowly developed for centuries, to shape individual's psychological attitude to follow specific gendered stereotypes.

Born and educated in Vienna, Gerda Lerner (1920–2013) was forced to leave Austria in 1938 because of the racial law against the Jewish population, and she arrived in the United States. In New York, Lerner organized the Congress of American Women and, along with her husband Carl, was involved in various activities promoted by some leftist movements. In late 1940s, she took some courses at the New School, and got her M.A. and Ph.D. from Columbia University, where she persuaded her supervisors to allow her do some research on women's history for her thesis, which dealt with the biography of Grimkè sisters (see Chapter 1). Later, she introduced one of the first graduate program in women's studies at Sarah Lawrence College, and in 1980 was appointed professor at the University of Wisconsin–Madison. Lerner traveled around the country to promote her approach to women's studies and authored several classic volumes in the field, among them *Black Women in White America* (1972); *The Majority Finds Its Past* (1979); and her two-volume magnum opus, *The Creation of Patriarchy* (1987) and *The Creation of Feminist Consciousness* (1994). In her works, Lerner considered male dominance over women to be the result of a patriarchal system of organizing society, which began in the culture that had emerged since the second millennium B.C. in the ancient Near East, where the major gender stereotypes of the Western civilization are rooted (Gordon et al. 2013).

The first women's studies course was officially introduced in Australia in 1956, by Madge Dawson (1910–2003). Lecturer at the Department of Adult Education at Sydney University, Dawson started to research and to teach a course, 'Women in a Changing World', on the economic and political status of women in Western Europe, which was able to gather many students and is regarded as the starting point of the Australian feminist movement. Along with her research team, Dawson published *Graduate and Married* (Dawson 1965), a book on the situation of educated Australian women in the mid-20th century in order to show that education, and not marriage, was the only way for women to get any social improvement. Aware of the fact that academia was not immune from gender stereotypes, Dawson led another research project, authored by her student Bettina Cass (Cass et al. 1983), on the gender gap within the three major universities located in Sydney that revealed persistent forms of gender inequalities in wages and in promotions among their faculty members (Kaplan 2003).

In 1965, Muriel Johnson introduced the first modern women's studies course in the United States, 'Women in Contemporary Culture', at Kansas University. In 1969, at Cornell University, Sheila Tobias organized a conference on the exclusion of women from traditional academic disciplines. The conference drew the attention of approximately 2,000 attendees. As a direct consequence of the success of the conference, the first course of women's studies, 'The Evolution of Female Personality', was introduced at Cornell during the spring semester in the same academic year (1969–1970). Two hundred and fifty undergraduates and 150 auditors gathered. The course dealt with economic and psychological dynamics of consumer society, cross-cultural studies of marriage and child rearing, images of women in literature and media, and the sociology of race and sex (Ju 2009). In the fall semester of the academic year 1970–1971, at the Sir George Williams University (later renamed Concordia University) in Montreal, Greta Hoffman Nemirof (a faculty member at the department of English studies), along with Christine Allen (a faculty member at the department of philosophy), offered the first women's studies course in Canada. The course started as a critique of patriarchal knowledge and it proceeded in formulating the necessity to converge on a specific feminist knowledge.

In 1969, the first program of women's studies was established at San Diego State University (SDSU) and offered 11 different courses. The program was the result of the efforts of the Committee for Women's Studies, formed by many students, who were members of SDSU's Women's Liberation Group in cooperation with faculty and community members. They collected signatures from more than 600 students in support of the establishment of a Women's Studies Program at SDSU. The program actually started in the spring semester of the following academic year (1969–1970).[6] The second women's studies program in the United States was established in 1971 at the Wichita State University, Kansas. Harvard University followed through.

In 1971, a group of feminist activists approached the president of the Ford Motor Company, McGeorge Bundy, to involve the Ford Foundation in the feminist movement. Previously, the Ford Foundation had been very supportive of the American Civil Rights Movement, so feminists hoped to be helped in the same way. The project proposed to the Ford Foundation was focused on the expansion of women's studies within academia. McGeorge Bundy decided to endorse and fund it, and in 1972, he announced the first $1 million national fellowship program for faculty members and doctoral dissertation research to develop research projects on women's studies.

The first instructors of women's studies programs were part-time or assistant professors without any influence in their department: they taught women's studies courses in addition to their teaching loads and usually without any additional payment (Buhle 2000). Despite this situation, the number of women's studies courses increased from 600 courses taught in 1971 to 300 full-fledged programs a few years later in 1978; women's studies have been developing everywhere in world during the past three decades.[7] The first Ph.D. program in women's studies was established at Emory University in Atlanta, Georgia, in 1990 (Crouch 2012; Becchio 2015)

Scholarly journals in women's studies started to be published in the United States in the early 1970s. *Feminist Studies* was founded in 1972, after more than three years of discussions and planning, and *Signs: A Journal of Women in Culture and Society* started to be published in 1975.

Feminist Studies was a joint project led by a feminist network composed of a women's liberation group active at the Columbia University, several students of women's studies courses at Sarah Lawrence College, and feminist activists from New York City. The title of the journal was chosen specifically to indicate that it had a twofold nature: scholarly and political.[8] The first issue of *Feminist Studies* hosted a paper on sex discrimination in employment, which also dealt with gender wage gap and the consequences of maternity leave either in private employment or in governmental positions (Eastwood 1972).

Signs was a project of Jean Sacks, manager of the journal division at the University of Chicago Press. In 1974, she approached Catharine R. Stimpson, professor of literature at Barnard College, while both were attending a conference. Sacks proposed that Stimpson become the editor of a new feminist journal and Stimpson accepted. In her inaugural editorial, she presented *Signs* as a tool for interdisciplinary works and knowledge production which aimed to host multiple – and often contradictory – voices in order to give the reader the broadest perspective possible on the woman question.[9]

In 1977, the National Women's Studies Association was founded to enlarge the women's studies agenda, which was grounded on the necessity to free society from sexism, national chauvinism, racism, anti-Semitism, and ageism. The educational strategy of the Association was based on a strict refusal to accept any sterile division between academy and society. The Association promoted the development of many women's studies programs across the country. During the 1970s and the 1980s, women's studies spread and were introduced in any discipline: arts, literature, political philosophy, and political economy. In 1980, at Harvard, a special committee was established to promote women's studies. Many other Ivy League institutions followed through (Nussbaum 1997). In 1979, the first women's studies courses were officially introduced in Great Britain by the Bristol Women's Study Group; the course was labeled 'Half the Sky' (Eichler 2014).

Women's studies curricula were shaped around an interdisciplinary effort: typical issues such as reproduction, family, fertility, and so forth were scrutinized through different perspectives, which involved different fields. Psychology, anthropology, sociology, literature, and, later, economics clustered around women's studies topics, which included the introduction of contributions by women often neglected in their discipline. For instance, Sappho has been introduced in the program of classical literature at the University of Nevada at Reno, casting new light on everyday life in Ancient Greece (Pomeroy 1994). Susan Moller Okin tried to explain political justice starting from the specificity of institutions like families in which the role of women was central (Moller Okin 1979). At Harvard, Amartya Sen introduced a course on economic distribution by considering the role of families, which is not only a potential source of love but also can be a place where women are physically and psychologically oppressed. Later, Sen pointed out the consequences of calculating GDP by ignoring the specific contributions of women (Sen 1989). At Brown University, for the first time, Anne Fausto Sterling introduced experiments to show that cultural norms linked to sex have been determinant in shaping different gender roles (Fausto-Sterling 1985).

In a recent publication, Phyllis Chesler summed up the nature of women's studies and the impact they had on the Western culture.[10] Chesler pointed out that women's studies were a direct consequence of the rise of second-wave feminism in the United States (Chesler 2018). Chesler insisted on claiming that women's ignorance has always been a tactic used by the patriarchy to perpetuate itself and she highlighted that a sort of horizontal lack of communication among women had persisted and reinforced patriarchy. According to Chesler, consciousness and communications were the key tenets of second-wave feminism and these two features had led the movement to implement feminist ideas within many professions and academia.

The evolution of women's studies had played a crucial role in the passage from the second wave of feminism (1960s–1970s) to the third wave of feminism (1990s) as well as in the development of feminism outside Western society. Intellectually rooted in the work of Kimberlé Crenshaw and Judith Butler, the third wave of feminism emerged in the mid-1990s. In 1992, the Third Wave Foundation was settled and, in 2000, the *Manifesta: Young Women, Feminism, and the Future* was published (Baumgardner and Richards 2000).[11] Crenshaw coined the term 'intersectionality' to describe the ways in which different forms of oppression, based on gender and race, intersect (Crenshaw 1989). Butler explained the constructed nature of gender; she also pointed out that conventional notions of gender had helped to perpetuate patriarchy and to justify the oppression of homosexual and transgender persons (Butler 1990, 1993). The debate about the real and effective differences between the second wave of feminism and the third wave of feminism is still open. Some third-wave feminists labeled themselves as postfeminist, while many others argued that there are no differences between the earlier and the newer generation of feminists: the analysis of gender norms, the fight against gender discrimination, and the battle for women empowerment are common aims for both groups.

At the end of 20th century, feminist movements arose in developing countries too and some relevant internal tensions between Western feminists and feminists from Asia, Africa, and Latin America emerged. During the World Conference of the United Nations Decade for Women: Equality, Development, and Peace, held in Copenhagen in 1980, women from less-developed nations complained that the veil and infibulation had been chosen as conference priorities without consulting them. During the International Conference on Population and Development, held in Cairo in 1994, women from developing countries protested because organizers chose to focus on contraception and abortion rather than on the health condition of women and children in their countries. A year later in Beijing, at the Fourth World Conference on Women, women from developing countries wanted to focus on international debt, while Western women's priority was the interconnection between reproductive rights and sexual discrimination.

Along with the fast development of women's studies in early 1980s and the emergence of third-wave feminism, the use of the label 'women's studies' became problematic: women's studies were accused of being 'hegemonic narrow' because they did not consider transgender or lesbian identities. Hence, many institutions adopted the more neutral label 'gender studies' to avoid that specific critique. The notion of gender was used to explain social constructions that reflected and determined differences in power and opportunity, while the notion of sex was adopted as a physiological difference between male and female (see Chapter 4).

3.2 Feminist economics: from CSWEP to IAFFE

The emergence of feminist economics may be considered to be an effect of women's studies' influence on economists – mainly women economists, who felt the urgency for a real emancipation of women in the economic sphere and were disappointed by neoclassical economics' way of dealing with gender issues (Moller Okin 1979, 1989; Sen 1990a, 2005; Nussbaum 1997, 2000). For instance, unlike the new home economics, feminist economics refused to adopt the theory of comparative advantage in order to explain the division of labor between spouses and the discrimination against women in the marketplace. Barbara Bergmann underlined the neoclassical aura of the new home economists in her famous sentence "to say that the 'new home economists' are not feminist in their orientation would be as much of an understatement as to say that Bengal tigers are not vegetarians" (Bergmann 1990, 72). According to Bergmann, likewise the predominance of neoclassical economics had constrained the emerging of alternative approaches in economics, the development of the new home economics had delayed the rise of feminist economics.[12]

In the early 1970s, the economist Ester Boserup (1910–1999) harshly criticized the neoclassical economics approach, which was heavily affected by the stereotypical model of the Western family, built up on the combination of a male 'breadwinner', a female 'homemaker', and their dependent children. Boserup pointed out that the typical household's model was a myth that did not adhere to reality. In fact, the division of labor deeply varied across world's regions. Hence, she replaced the traditional model of household used by the new home economics with an alternative model. Her alternative model presented two advantages: it was able to acknowledge differences in preferences and priorities among household members; and it was able to pay a greater attention to the incentives aimed to promote cooperation and to avoid conflicts among family members (Boserup 1970).

Meanwhile, in the early 1970s, many women economists in the United States protested their underrepresentation in academia. During a meeting of the AEA, which took place in New Orleans on December 1971, Barbara Bergmann chaired a session on 'What Economic Equality for Women Requires'. On that occasion, a group of women economists formed the Women's Caucus and formally invited the Executive Committee of AEA to recognize that the economic profession should be more open to women than it had been until then. Carolyn Shaw Bell, who led the group, worked overnight on a set of resolutions to be presented to president John Kenneth Galbraith, president-elect Kenneth Arrow, and the executive committee. AEA board members reacted favorably to their requests by establishing CSWEP, which aimed to monitor the progress of women economists within academic departments and to reduce the gender gap in the profession (Barlett 1999).

A year later, in 1972, CSWEP's first official document was published and signed by Walter Adams, Kenneth Arrow, Francine Blau, Martha Blaxall, Kenneth Boulding, Carolyn Shaw Bell, John K. Galbraith, Collette Moser, Barbara Reagan, Myra Strober, and Phyllis Wallace. The document admitted that the origin of women' discrimination within the discipline was "a special case of a much larger process of role learning and role acceptance, which begins almost from the moment of birth" (Bell et al. 1973, 1049). The Committee recognized in information,[13] persuasion,[14] rewards,[15] and punishments[16] the four inputs that had a high negative impact on women's representation within the discipline.

Several resolutions were established. Among them, Resolution I declared that AEA recognized "that economics is not exclusively a man's field" (Bell et al. 1973, 1053), and that no gender discrimination will be tolerated in admission, recruitment, salary, or financial aid. Resolution II established a permanent CSWEP to monitor the real situation:

> The recommended actions are only symbolic of needed changes in policy and attitude, if we are to correct the bizarre and irrational underrepresentation of women in the economics profession. The unemployment and underemployment of currently available talent, as well as the loss of potential talent, require positive, broad-gauged action to correct some structural imperfections in the professional labor market. To help eliminate these imperfections, one mini mum step is continuing analytical study of the problem and regular, detailed reports to the Association and its members ... This implies a continuing obligation of the Association and its members to consider alternative mechanisms, consistent with professional standards and ethics, to promote genuine equality of opportunity and meaningfully free access for all scholars and practitioners in the discipline of economics.
>
> (Bell et al. 1973, 1961)

The Caucus also requested a formal commitment to promote equal opportunities, from early career encouragement to tenured positions, which led to the formation of 'Job Openings for Economists' (JOE) in 1974. Today, JOE still is the major platform for access to open positions in economics departments. In 1972, members of CSWEP, chaired by Carolyn Bell, published CSWEP's first annual survey. On that occasion, for the first time, gender imbalance in the economic academic profession was formulated as a form of discrimination.

As we have seen in the previous two chapters, up until the early 1930s the number of women economists who worked on specific topics, such as consumption theory, distribution, and home economics, had increased. Furthermore, many women economists had been able to publish in top journals. Since the 1930s, things had changed and the number of women economics dramatically decreased. The marginalization of women within academia occurred at least for two reasons. First, social work and home economics became separate academic fields, as seen in Chapter 2. Second, women economists who were systematically denied tenure positions in departments of economics diverged towards other institutions, including governmental positions (Forget 2011).

The first survey compiled by CSWEP revealed that women were 6% of faculty members and graduate students in economics departments and that there were no women economists in the AEA Executive Committee (Bell 1998; Forget 2011). Many years later, in 1995, Marianne Ferber published a paper on the minimal representation of women and minorities among students of economics and economics faculties.[17] According to Ferber, several reasons led to that situation, among them the narrow approach of neoclassical economics as well as the fact that some economic topics that are important for women, such as gender gap in labor market and the role of household and families as institutions, were systematically ignored in economic textbooks (Ferber 1995).[18] In a more recent debate, Cherrier (2017a) assumed that the rise of applied economics, which occurred in the 1970s, enabled more women to become tenure-track economists. In 2017, *The Economist* pointed out that the profession's problem strictly related to women in economics departments could be a problem with economics itself.[19]

The rise of feminist economics is part of this story, which combined underrepresentation of women economists within the discipline and a specific critique of the nature of the discipline. As seen in the previous paragraph, the rise of women's studies had brought new stimulus to economics too, especially if we consider the centrality of the debate around rationality, which affected the emergence of feminist economics in particular. The chronology of the classification system (JEL codes), used by AEA to list economic literature, allows us to understand the transformation the place of feminist economics, household economics, and gender economics as specific subfields within the discipline as a whole. As clearly reported on the JEL website, major revisions of JEL codes were undertaken in 1938–1944, in 1955–1956, in 1966, and in 1988–1990; further changes were undertaken more recently (Cherrier 2017b; Kosnik 2018). When feminist economics officially arose in the 1990s, it was embedded in gender economics' JEL code (J16, today labeled as 'economics of gender'). Only in 2006, a specific JEL code, B54, was created to label feminist economics as a different and independent research field, which was recognized as a heterodox approach.[20] In fact, B54 is as a subcategory of B,[21] and category B stands for 'History of Economic Thought, Methodology, and Heterodox Approaches'. AEA adopted category B to represent a niche for a non-neoclassical or anti-neoclassical approach to the discipline. Feminist economics (B54) is part of this niche, along with Socialist, Marxist, and Sraffian (B51); Historical, Institutionalist, and Evolutionary (B52); Austrian (B53); Others, which includes Econophysics, Green Economics, Islamic Economics, Pluralist Economics, and Real World Economics (B59) (Becchio 2015, 2018). The AEA website specified that:

> The categories for B5 were created to accommodate the recent substantial developments in non-mainstream (non-neoclassical) economic approaches to contemporary economic problems. Studies about an economic subject (or subjects) adopting a given heterodox approach should be cross-classified under the appropriate B5 category and also under the appropriate subject category (or categories).[22]

According to the official formulation on the JEL website, feminist economics deals with "studies about issues related to Feminist approaches to economics as well as studies about economic subjects, using these approaches. Studies may deal with either (applied) microeconomics or (applied) macroeconomics or both and may be either theoretical or empirical".[23] At the present time, the code J (Labor and Demographic Economics), under which feminist economics belonged until 2006, includes economics of gender, which "covers studies about economic issues related to gender, except for labor market discrimination, which is classified under J71 or J78".[24]

JEL codes are provided for household economics as well. Household economics belongs to D, which stands for Microeconomics and "covers studies about general issues related to household (consumer) behavior, including survey articles, textbooks, and data"; more specifically, D11 "covers studies about theoretical issues related to consumer economics"; D12 "covers empirical studies about issues related to non-financial household or consumer behavior, in particular empirical demand analysis"; D13 is dedicated to the new home economics: "it covers empirical or theoretical Beckerian studies. In particular, studies on the division of labor within a household"; D14 and D15 cover intertemporal consumer choice respectively; and D18 covers government policies for consumer protection. Both the D and J classification were in the initial version of the current JEL Classification System, which was instituted in 1990.[25]

Although the official recognition of feminist economists within the general classification of AEA is relatively recent (2006), the institutionalization of feminist economics within the discipline started earlier, in the early 1990s, when

IAFFE was founded. IAFFE was conceived as a result of small group discussions at the American Economic Association Conference, held in Washington, D.C., in 1990. On that occasion, in a session entitled 'Can Feminism Find a Home in Economics?', which attracted an overflow crowd, many women economists discussed the difficulties they were facing in doing feminist work within the discipline. A follow-up survey of that discussion was published in February 1991. A few months later, in August 1991, the first 'Feminist Economists Network Update' newsletter was printed. Between September and November 1991, Iona Thraen, Barbara Bergmann, April Aerni, and Jane Shackelford combined their energy to settle on an official organization: an e-mail network, *femecon-1*, which was aimed to give instant communication of any initiative or working paper related to feminist economics to feminist economists worldwide.

In January 1992, IAFFE was officially founded at the ASSA meetings held in New Orleans. The first IAFFE newsletter was published under the supervision of Nancy Folbre. In July 1992, Jean Shackelford was elected to serve as the first President of IAFFE. IAFFE had several purposes: to foster dialogue and resource sharing among economists and scholars of other disciplines from all over the world who take feminist viewpoints; to advance feminist inquiry into economic issues; to rethink economics from a feminist perspective; to expand opportunities for women within economic departments; and to encourage the inclusion of feminist perspectives in teaching economics to students in all levels (Shackelford 1999a, 1999b). As Ferber specified in an interview, although CSWEP was performing well in its function promoting women economists, founding members of IAFFE believed that an independent and institutionalized group in the field of feminist economics was necessary in order to promote progress of women in the profession and to expand feminist theory within the discipline (King and Saunders 1999).

In the following years, IAFFE set up many activities and organized an impressive network of scholars devoted to the field. Under the leadership of Margaret Lewis and KimMarie McGoldrick, IAFFE established its 'Teaching and Pedagogy Committee' to provide annual pedagogy workshops, online syllabi, and sessions of feminist pedagogy. In 1995, Bina Agarwal and Janet Seitz compiled a program of eight panels for the Fourth World Conference on Women, held in Beijing, which led to IAFFE's designation as a nongovernmental organization within the Economic and Social Council of the United Nations (Shackelford 1999a; Shackelford 1999b).

Classical liberal feminism, radical feminism tradition, and socialist feminism, along with some other nuances, were well represented in IAFFE. As Shackelford wrote: "IAFFE faces the challenge . . . to achieve the integral feminist traditions found in other social science discipline" (Shackelford 1999a, 487). Randy Albelda, Drucilla Barker, Barbara Bergmann, Susan Feiner, Marianne Ferber, Nancy Folbre, Ulla Grapard, Julie Nelson, Jean Shackleford, and Myra Strober were among its founding members.

Randy Albelda focused her work on economic policies which affected low-income women and their families. In her book *Economics and Feminism* (Albelda

1997), she examined the theoretical barriers built up by neoclassical economics to prevent dissension within the discipline and noticed that feminism had been especially unwelcome because neoclassical economics explicitly rejected any approach to economic matters that was grounded on gender bias.

Drucilla Barker's work investigated the nature of caring labor, which was traditionally intended as a specific women's responsibility. According to Barker, caring labor had been crystalized in forms that had reinforced the hierarchical social structure of gender relations as well as race discriminations and class subjections. According to Barker, the traditional and hierarchic Western society had shaped gender discrimination; more specifically, the gender labor gap and gender wage gap, which had become more evident in the highly unequal distribution of income and wealth that persist in the current phase of global capitalism (Barker and Feiner 2004: Barker 2005).

Barbara Bergmann (1927–2015) belonged to the classical liberal tradition of feminist economics, which insisted on the idea of making equal opportunity effective for women and men in the labor market.[26] As she remembered in an interview in 2000, she had been always considering Marxism and feminism in opposition, the former being too much focused on class revolution without taking any account of gender issues (Saunders and King 2000). In 1948, Bergmann got her first degree from Cornell, where she majored in mathematics, thereafter, in 1959, she got her Ph.D. in economics from Harvard, where she developed a strong interest in applied research, which privileged the direct observation of the subject (Bergmann 1987). Bergmann always had been focused on racial and gender discrimination in labor markets. She explained racial discrimination in unemployment, which affects minorities' income as an effect of the institutionalized racism in the United States, which had decreased the investment of human capital over the black population (Bergmann and Lyle 1971). The same process occurred in the investment of human capital over the female population and its effects were doubled on female black population. In her 'sex-role caste system', she described gender relations as social constructs rooted within families, which penalized not only women, but also the society as a whole, which resulted in being built on bad-performing models of knowledge. Moreover, policies were set up in a way that usually reinforced the initial penalization. A clear example of this vicious circle is embedded in the neoclassical economic methodology, which draws conclusions from a set of unrealistic and gender-biased assumptions, based respectively on perfect rationality and women's choice conditioned by their role within the household (Bergmann 1974; Bergmann and Adelman 1983).

In her major work, *The Economic Emergence of Women* (Bergmann 1986), Bergmann reinforced her idea that gender segregation in the labor force is grounded on misogyny, and explained the process as follows. Industrial revolution and technological improvements raised wages and made women's time too valuable to be entirely spent at home. This led to lower birthrates, a higher number of educated women, and an increasing number of divorces, as well as to other changes in social norms, which had previously constrained women to an overcrowded number of specific job markets (the pink ghetto sectors). Overcrowding women in pink ghetto jobs had lowered women's pay within those markets as well as within mixed-sex job markets. Moreover, it had decreased investments on human capital for women and it had strengthened gender-biased beliefs about women's capabilities, including their 'natural tendency' or preference to work at home. Against the new home economics, which used the theory of comparative advantages to explain the role of women as housewives, Bergmann affirmed that comparative advantages had been the result of employment discrimination (Olson 2007).

Susan Feiner adopted a Marxian approach to criticize neoclassical economics by highlighting the permanent and perverse relationship between class and gender that had historically forged social inequalities (Feiner 1990). Social inequalities forged by the relationship between class and gender had been completely neglected by neoclassical economics and had been completely ignored in any introductory economics textbooks (Barlett and Feiner 1992).

Marianne Ferber (1923–2013) got her Ph.D. in 1946 from the University of Chicago, where she was a student of Jacob Mincer and Oskar Lange. Her work, coauthored with Francine Blau, became a fundamental textbook for the inclusion of gender issues in the discipline (Blau and Ferber 1986). The book had gone through several editions, which lately converged towards a more neoclassical approach. In a recent interview, Ferber denied that they ever identified themselves as neoclassical economists: "we present the neoclassical story, which I still think is the thing to do, for a variety of reasons, and then we make an effort also to present alternative approaches" (King and Saunders 1999, 92). However, in the last edition of the book (Blau et al. 2010), although the attention to gender inequality in the labor market and in the household is still central, authors persist in emphasizing that "economics is still about opportunity costs and rationality ... and it is probably more realistic to assume that people tend to try to maximize their well-being rather than they are indifferent to it" (Blau et al. 2010, 3).

Ferber's book, *Women and Work, Paid and Unpaid*, was a comprehensive catalogue of economic research on women's work before feminist economics emerged (Ferber 1987). A few years later, she published a detailed report on the situation of women in the workplace and suggested the necessity to adjust the balance between family care and market jobs among spouses in order to get a more equal and fair situation (Ferber and O'Farrell 1991). Ferber's anthology, coauthored with Nelson, has been one of the first books done by economists who label themselves feminist (Ferber and Nelson 1993).

Nancy Folbre focused her research on the economics of care. Caring labor can be paid or unpaid, but it had been traditionally covered by women's underpaid work. Ignored by neoclassical economics, care work does not obey to the trade-off labor between leisure because it embeds some responsibility intrinsically related with femininity (Folbre 1994b). According to Folbre, the fight for an equal division of market work and care work between sexes pursued by the classical liberal tradition led to a paradox: given that women are no longer pressed to provide their care work, a reduction in the overall supply of caring within the home and in the market occurred. Therefore, standard neoclassical economists thought that care work would become scarce and its price would have arisen, while feminist economists, who considered care work outside the logic of market, preferred to find a way to ensure a greater supply and a better quality of caring labor provided by social institutions (Folbre 1994a).

In Folbre and Nelson (2000), the shift of caring activities from families to markets was presented as an important social change that led to some externalities concerning the quality of care work provided by the market. Folbre used the metaphor of 'the invisible heart' to represent family values of love and economic reciprocity (Folbre 2001). She challenged the new home economics' interpretation of child-raising as a process of consumption and she argued that new home economics ignored the fact that children are bound to become the workers and taxpayers of the next generation. Folbre also argued that, being part of the nonmarket sector, care work cannot be valued simply by utilizing its replacement cost (Folbre 2008). In *Greed, Lust and Gender: A History of Economic Idea* (Folbre 2009), Folbre showed that, in the Western culture, men had been more legitimate than women in the pursuit of both economic and sexual self-interest. According to Folbre, while demanding more freedom for women to act like men, like liberal feminists usually did, feminists should insist on balancing self-interest and care work in a less gendered way.

Ulla Grapard got her Ph. D. in 1978 at Cornell University. She focused her research in finding an alternative methodology to neoclassical economics (Grapard 1995). According to Grapard, economic knowledge depends on

> Who gets to define the domain of economic inquiry, how it is decided which activities will be the subject of economic inquiry, which variables will be considered important economic variables, and which assumptions about the world and the nature of scientific analysis economists will adhere to.
>
> (Grapard 1999, 545)

Julie Nelson received her Ph.D. in economics in 1986 from the University of Wisconsin–Madison. She argued that the neoclassical economics assumption, according to which people are insatiable, autonomous, self-interested agents, is an evidence of a peculiar gender bias, based on the notions of insatiability, autonomy, and selfishness, which have traditionally been regarded as masculine traits (Nelson 1993c). In her book *Feminism, Objectivity, and Economics* (Nelson 1996) Nelson envisioned individuals' cognition and social knowledge in terms of gender. According to Nelson, neoclassical economics is gender-biased because it is perceived as a masculine discipline rooted on a rational and competitive *homo oeconomicus* and as a male field from a professional perspective. A feminist approach to economics may make the discipline more realistic. Nelson considered feminist economics to be the result of the combination between

feminism and more-realistic economics. Against detractors of feminist economics, who insisted on the idea that a feminist approach to economics would have
made the discipline less objective, she insisted on explaining that feminist economics, focused on gender biases and social norms, would make the discipline
more objective.

Jean Shackleford was IAFFE's first president. Her work had been particularly focused on the relationship between feminist pedagogy and feminist economics' education: the aim of the former, based on a notion of constructive
knowledge rather than memorized notions, is to understand the emergence
of social dynamics that led to patriarchy, while the aim of the latter is to
analyze how patriarchy had established an underrepresentation of women's
social dimension in constructing knowledge (Shackelford 1992).

Like Shackleford, Myra Strober has been deeply focused on the relation
between economics and education. She urged to challenge the assumptions
underlying neoclassical economics; that is, full rationality, maximization, and
efficiency, which reflected a very narrow set of values, in order to include nonmarket sector as well as theories of discrimination (Strober 1984, 1987, 2003).
Strober outlined that the examination of the motivations behind some choices,
such as marriage and divorce, had been wrongly explained by Becker's model.
She proposed to overcome "reasoned judgement economics to make critical
evaluations of personal, familial, occupational, and societal economic alternatives" (Strober 1987, 145). Hence, according to Strober, the goal of economic
education was twofold: to teach that economic issues are more complex than
the model presented by the neoclassical economics system of equations and
to combine qualitative aspects with quantitative data, like other social sciences
usually do (Strober and Cook 1992).

Following Shackleford and Strober's concerns about education, feminist
economics pointed out some problems about the way economics had been
taught. Starting from an analysis of the *Voluntary Economics Content Standards
for Pre-College Economics Education* (1997), composed by the U.S. National
Council of Economic Education to improve the understanding of economics
at elementary and secondary schools, Ferber (1999) pointed out that neoclassical economists' goals in teaching economics at junior high and high schools
were very different from feminist economics' goals, and that teaching a single,
conventional, and coherent view is not a valid instrument in any educational
project. Rather, it is a sort of brainwashing which avoids handling the complexity of the world. Lewis and McGoldrick (2001) reinforced Ferber's argument by remarking on the lack of consensus among economists on the nature
of the discipline and by insisting on the urgency to develop "an economics
that more accurately captures real economies" (Lewis and McGoldrick
2001, 97). Along with feminist pedagogics, feminist economics had emphasized the importance of cooperation in learning (Aerni and McGoldrick
1999; Aerni et al. 1999) and the necessity to enlarge economic textbook by
including minority views of economic process (Ferber 1999; Schneider and
Shackelford 2001). As Strober (2003) later summed up, feminist economics'

pedagogy was operating on two levels: the revision of the contents of econom-ics' courses, which should include race and gender; and the introduction of some new syllabi able to present alternative models against neoclassical eco-nomics in order to offer a more interdisciplinary approach.

More radical members, such as Ritu Dewan and Michel Pujol, joined IAFFE. Dewan criticized human capital theory, which had assumed that men and women are free in choosing their education as well as their jobs, without taking account of social restrictions on both men and women, which are more dramatic in underdeveloped countries. Unlike the human capital approach, which had explained the gender wage gap and gender labor gap as the results of qualitative, biological, and psychological differences between men and women, feminist economics had considered gender eco-nomic gaps to be effects of a perpetuated system of power relationships in favor of men (Dewan 1995). Michèle Pujol (1951–1997) got her Ph.D. at Simon Fraser University in Vancouver and became professor of women's studies in Manitoba, and later at Victoria University. In her book *Feminism and Anti-Feminism in Early Economic Thought* (Pujol 1992), she strongly sup-ported the idea that the woman question did not figure in the work of classical and neoclassical economists, and this exclusion had led to the neoclassical par-adigm "which excluded women from the sphere of economic rationality [being them] constructed as not belonging in the market sphere and as unmo-tivated by self-interest" (Pujol 1992, 198). According to Pujol, the conver-gence between liberal tradition and neoclassical economics has been made possible by the combination of patriarchy, sexism, and misogyny that are indis-solubly connected with and committed to capitalism.

After the foundation of IAFFE, *History of Political Economy* hosted a mini-symposium to consider a possible convergence among historians of economics and feminist economists. Roy Weintraub, *History of Political Economy*'s editor at that time, opened up the discussion by quoting Scott's book on the connection between gender issues and historical studies, in which the author had defined gender issues as the social organization of sexual differences, which did not nec-essarily reflect natural differences (Scott 1988). Weintraub pointed out the necessity to understand how much history of economic ideas are gendered and invited some economists to answer the following question: "what differ-ence would serious attention to feminist theory make in our understanding, and reconstructing, the history of economic thought?" (Weintraub 1993, 118). Folbre (1993a), Nelson (1993a), Seitz (1993), and Strassmann (1993) accepted the invitation to answer.

Folbre (1993a) insisted on the theoretical nature of feminism, which too often had been relegated exclusively to a political sphere, and analyzed feminist economics' epistemology by scrutinizing Kuhn's notion of the scientific para-digm, Marx's notion of ideology, and "postmodern paranoias" on deconstruc-tion, against the notion of positive economics à la Friedman (1953). According to Folbre, feminist economics were able to deeply challenge standard economic methodology by exploring gender bias, in order to make economists able to "hew to conventional standards of consistency" (Folbre 1993a, 180). Nelson (1993a) pointed out that the necessity to build up a 'value-free' science – which was a *leitmotiv* in standard neoclassical economics – had hidden a sort of indifference and detachment (typically regarded as masculine), which had been considered a virtue able to lead towards objectivity. However, according to Nelson, this detachment was much more ideological than objective. A true objectivity may be pursued by including gender issues in economics and in the history of economic thought in order to reach a broader examination of the nature of economic phenomena as well as of the contribution of single economists. Seitz (1993) emphasized the benefits of eliminating androcentrism and other social biases from economics, by enlarging possible perspectives within the community of economists. Finally, Strassmann (1993) considered the relationship between power, interest, and rhetoric among economists. She underlined that "storytellers of economics" had been influenced by gender and social norms, and invited them to challenge "the rhetoric of the discipline" in order to tell "dissonant stories" able to enlarge it in a proficient way (Strassmann 1993, 161).

In 1993, Ferber and Nelson coedited the book *Beyond Economic Man: Feminist Theory and Economics* to collect essays that explored connections between feminism and economics. The book was considered the manifesto of feminist economics (Ferber and Nelson 2003a). Paula England opened up the book with a chapter on the 'separative self' that emerged from neoclassical economics: based on the presumption that humans are indifferent to social norms and have independent utilities, the separative self does not take any account of assumptions related to gender (England 1993). *Beyond Economic Man* was followed by another landmark book, *Out of the Margin: Feminist Perspectives on Economics*, edited by Kuiper and Sap (1995), aimed to criticize the narrow conception of rationality of neoclassical economics.

In 1999, a *Companion to Feminist Economics* was published, edited by Peterson and Lewis (1999). The book hosted 99 entries and aimed to introduce readers "to the extensive and evolving literature of feminist economics" which had finally become relevant both in feminism and in political economy (Peterson and Lewis 1999, xv).[27] Strassmann wrote the entry 'feminist economics' and remarked the distance between neoclassical economics and feminist economics: neoclassical economics required a deep revision of its accepted paradigm which was unable to handle a wide variety of economic phenomena, including familial and sexual relationships, reproductive life, and the role of institutions and cultural norms, while feminist economics was a field "which had begun to construct an economics that serves the interests of a broader and more representative group pf people" (Strassmann 1999, 370).

In 2003, 10 years after the first edition of *Beyond Economic Man*, Felber and Nelson published a new edition, *Beyond Economic Man: Feminist Economics Today*, to update readers on the developments of the field since the publication of the first edition. The authors recognized that neoclassical economics had remained silent or indifferent to the instances and goals of feminist economics which nonetheless had been growing up in the number of contributions and new contributors.[28] England opened up the volume again by proposing a new version of her previous article. She developed the concept of the 'soluble conception of self', which affected neoclassical models (especially Becker's new home economics): the soluble conception of self was based on a too-simplistic vision of family in which empathy and connectivity among members was overemphasized and it ignored the fact that men often are not altruistic to their partners and children. England pointed out that in the time-span between the first and the second edition of their book, efforts to correct the dichotomy of 'separative/soluble self' had been made by some neoclassical economists, who introduced new bargaining marriage models able to bring individual self-interest back in the family as well as models of endogenous preferences which finally considered the role of gender, race and class. Nonetheless, neoclassical economics had not yet provided a model able to include both altruism and selfishness in markets and families. The introduction of the economics of care in feminist economics had gone to that specific direction: "modeling behavior when selfishness and empathy are variables and when preferences can change in response to the environment" (England 2003, 53).

In late 1990s, the role of IAFFE within and outside the discipline grew. In 1997, IAFFE gained NGO in special consultative status with the Economic and Social Council of the United Nations. Since 2007, IAFFE has organized an annual conference and regular sessions and panels at annual AEA/ASSA meetings. Furthermore, it has provided a newsletter to keep members posted about reports on activities, opportunities, and resources of interest for feminist economists, including compilation of bibliographies, course syllabi, and a list of working papers on feminist economics.[29] An international forum (IAFFE-L) has been created to connect a broad international audience. To facilitate networking, IAFFE has established thematic groups which include care economy and unpaid work, environment, the labor market, rural development, LGBTQIA economic issues, income, poverty, and capability approach, macroeconomics policies, gender mainstreaming, and many more. In 2019, IAFFE has approximately 600 members including economists, students, policy makers, and scholars of other disciplines in 64 countries.

As Ferber and Nelson specified:

> IAFFE's objectives include the more radical aim of challenging the masculinist biases in the now well-enriched neoclassical economics. Feminist economists have questioned such fundamental neoclassical assumptions in economics as the 'separative self', the ubiquity of self-interest, the primacy of efficiency concerns for equity. They have tended to define economics in terms of real-world issues of concern to women, men, and children, rather than as merely the examination of choice under conditions of scarcity.
>
> (Ferber and Nelson 2003b, 7–8)

As Beneria (1995) suggested, the foundation of IAFFE and of *Feminist Economics* was a turning point in the history of feminist economics; conversely, the institutionalization of feminist economics had raised consciousness in two fundamental areas: the visibility of women in the labor market and national accountability as well as the role of gender in the policy agenda.

3.3 Feminist economics' analytical and methodological core

Feminist economics was shaped some years earlier than the official foundation of IAFFE, when many feminist social scholars scrutinized the origin and causes of gender discrimination in the economy by pointing out the fact that women's work had always been underestimated and subordinated to men's work (Beneria 1982). In the 1980s, sociologist Paula England focused her attention on sex segregation in the labor market. According to England, sex segregation in the economy must be intended not simply to be forms of the gender wage gap or gender discrimination during the hiring process, but mainly as a general cultural devaluation of women and social roles associated with them. In fact, in sectors in which occupations were feminized and the number of employed women increased, wages of both men and women workers usually decreased. The reason of this phenomenon was twofold: on one side, the more balanced sex composition of jobs influenced employers' vision on the quality of the sector, as if the quality of a male-dominated sector were much higher than the quality of a mixed-sex sector; on the other side, the institutional inertia reinforced this bias, which became commonly accepted (England and Farkas 1986; England et al. 1988; England 1992).

Before going into a more detailed description of the methodological and theoretical core of feminist economics, it is necessary to underline that feminist economics has been deeply influenced by feminist philosophy, which emerged in the second half of the 20th century. Since its foundation, feminist economists adopted a normative methodology, based on the inclusion of feminism into economic theory, in order to provide a theoretical approach for their instances, which were presented as alternatives to neoclassical economics. More precisely, feminist economics had been introduced into the discipline in order to challenge the *malestream* approach to economics provided by standard economics. As Nelson pointed out, neoclassical economics has been constructed in a "heavily gendered way" (Nelson 1993b, 291), because of the predominance of male economists in academia and of the relegation of women's issues and gender issues to a specific niche like home economics/household economics and the new home economics. Based on fully rational agents, social interconnections within standard economics had discarded "the terms 'responsibility' and 'dependence', indispensable to the prescription of the pattern of economic provisioning within families and in relation to the natural environment, are simply not a part of the standard neoclassical modeling kit" (Nelson 1993b, 294). Furthermore, neoclassical models based do not take account of gender inequalities. For instance, the measure of GDP had systematically neglected and ignored the unpaid domestic work and care work which are mainly carried out by women.

Differently from neoclassical economics based only on market relations, feminist economics considered the influence of social norms, love, power, and obligation on the economy. The assertion that gender relations had affected the economy as a whole does not mean that feminist economics should be intended simply as "economics for women"; rather, it should be intended as better economics *tout court*. Bergmann (1990) had suggested that feminist economics aimed to emphasize the institutional constraints that had burdened personal and interpersonal choices, customs, habits, and peer pressure, which had shaped social conventions as well as social sanctions applied to unconventional choices. Feminist economics were focused on the critique of male supremacy as well as on the struggle for women's emancipation in any field, including science and academic disciplines and, more recently, on the fundamental role of gender connotations to explain social dynamics. Nelson defined feminist economics as "a field that includes both studies of gender roles in the economy from a liberatory perspective and critical work directed at biases in the content and methodology of the economics discipline" (Nelson 2005, 1). As Strassmann wrote: "feminist economists call for a broadening of economic methods, with tools chosen for their usefulness in providing insight, rather than for their coherence with a specific methodological definition of economics" (Strassmann 1999, 369).

In several publications, feminist economists argued that neoclassical economics had been set on masculine values such as autonomy, separation, and abstraction, against a set of values that are considered culturally feminine-associated (interdependence, connection, and concreteness). This way to deal with the complexity of economic relations, used by neoclassical economists, weakened the discipline's capacity to understand real economic phenomena (Nelson 1992; Ferber and Nelson 1993; Kuiper and Sap 1995).

As Nelson pointed out:

> Feminist economics is not female economics, to be practiced only by women, nor feminine economics that uses only soft technique and cooperative models. Feminist scholarship suggests that economics has been made less useful by implicitly reflecting a distorted ideal of masculinity in its models, methods, topics, and pedagogy. Feminist scholars argue that the use of a fuller range of tools to study and teach about a wider territory of economic activity would make economics a more productive discipline for both male and female practitioners.
>
> (Nelson 1995, 146)

Feminist economics' most important critique of neoclassical economics was the rejection of the economic agent (*homo oeconomicus*), intended as a 'maximizer individual' who is able to make an optimal (or suboptimal) choice, in a context of scarcity, given a budget constraint. The neoclassical economic agent is supposed to be endowed by full (or bounded) knowledge and by complete information, and he is able to always rank his individual preferences. Quoting Nelson:

> While feminists' dissatisfaction with mainstream economic scholarship was originally rooted in its neglect and distortion of women's experiences, by the late 1980s feminists were also raising a more thoroughgoing critique. Many feminist economists were finding that traditional formal choice-theoretic modeling and a narrow focus on mathematical and econometric methods were a Procrustean bed when it came to analyzing phenomena fraught with connection to others, tradition, and relations of domination. Feminists began to raise questions about the mainstream definition of economics, its central image of 'economic man,' and the exclusive use of a particular set of methodological tools".
>
> (Nelson 2005, 1)

Some feminist economists had claimed provocatively that the rational behavior of neoclassical *homo oeconomicus* should be substituted by a more emotional behavior of *femina oeconomica* (McCloskey 1993; Nelson 1995; Burggraf 1998). The debate around the maleness of a representative agent, whose behavior had been used as a model to describe the economic decision-making process, was not an exclusive prerequisite of standard economics. In fact, maleness had affected several disciplines, which had shaped the Western *Weltanschauung* over the centuries. Masculinity and male values have been considered universal standards by which to assess the paradigms upon which arts and sciences were grounded. The genesis and development of modern science reinforced a male sociability model, which originated and perpetuated the mechanism of women's subjection. More specifically, metaphors of masculinity had been able to build up the ideals of rationality and objectivity in modern philosophy.

The founder of this supposed masculine notion of rationality, which soon became dominant, was the French philosopher René Descartes, who was able to construct a paradigm that was commonly shared by scholars in both natural and social sciences. Many feminist philosophers considered Descartes' dualism between mind (male) and body (female), which implied a supremacy of the former on the latter, as a primary source of patriarchy (Lloyd 1984; Bordo 1987; Jaggar 2002). Descartes' notion of rationality appeared masculine, or male-oriented, because it overemphasized the role of pure speculation and detachment, against a 'sympathetic thinking', which is much closer to a feminine approach. In fact, Descartes' notion of rationality was based on the purification from everything that derived from sensitive perception (including feelings and emotions), in order to achieve the theoretical purity of logical inference (Bordo 1987; Nelson 1996).

The idea that women are more emotional and less rational than men, grounded on Descartes' notion of rationality, had justified a secular tradition of discrimination against women and girls in a male-dominated society. The critique of a masculine notion of rationality was introduced by psychologists and philosophers. They underlined that the notion of rationality as the logical and objective faculty of thinking was gender-biased and related to the stereotype of masculinity against the feminine stereotype based on emotions, feelings, and instincts. This procedure had generated a gendered notion of rationality that had systematically ignored that gender differentiation was a part of a process of learning, and had ignored that both objectivity and emotionality are acquired, not innate. Furthermore, although some cognitive faculties might be innate, the ability to use them is learnt and depends on the social framework (Keller 1985; Oliver 1991). Hoppe (2002) described the emerging of Cartesian dualism as a cultural transformation from an organic worldview to a mechanistic one. Philosophical positivism, which emerged in the 18th century, was the final stage of this new paradigm, and was incorporated into economics a century later, when marginalism and formalism merged into neoclassical economics.

Feminist economics rejected the Cartesian notion of rationality embedded in neoclassical economics. Harding (1986), Feiner (1995), and Schönpflug (2008) analyzed the way gender relations had been affected by Renaissance utopias as well. For instance, although Tommaso Campanella's utopian model had described a community of solidarity in an egalitarian framework in which the integration of women was possible, women's care and reproductive work remained forfeited and domestic work remained the exclusive burden of women. Francis Bacon's utopian work was the perfect application of Cartesian rationality: it well represented a new mechanistic world in which (male) expertise was able to subjugate the chaotic (female) nature. As Nelson pointed out: "In the Cartesian view, the abstract, general, separated, detached, emotionless, 'masculine' approach taken to represent scientific thinking, is radically removed from, and clearly seen as superior to, the concrete, particular, connected, embodied, passionate, 'feminine' reality of material life" (Nelson 1996, 40).

In response to Cartesian dualism, many feminist philosophers proposed a more complex concept of rationality able to embed either the notion of "connectedness to others", by following Husserl's terms (Soloveitchik 1992), or the dimension of "ethics of care and responsibility", as intended in Kant's terms (Friedman 2000). Both connectedness to others and ethics of care and responsibility had considered the complex nature of relations among individuals and between humans and the environment. They had recognized the presence of a moral side in any interpersonal relation as well as moral implications behind any possible choice that may impact the lives of the others and may lead to ethical dilemmas.

A matter of controversy for the ethics of care was the autonomy of the other, which was a central assumption in Kant, Mill, and Rawls. Following Rorty (1988), Slote described the rationality of the ethic of care as a form of practical rationality and defined autonomy as the capacity to think and to act for oneself, by arguing that caring and autonomy are complementary when the role of empathy is regarded as central (Slote 2007). According to Hawk (2011), an ethic of care begins with the recognition that we are all embedded in a complicated scenario made of complex relationships, which implies a deep understanding of the specific context and a constant application of responsibility. Therefore, an ethics of care assumes that the notion of otherness is much more central than the notion of autonomy.

More recently, feminist scholars have converged around four commitments able to define a notion of science in a non-sexist way otherwise consistent with feminist ideals. It included relevance, experiential grounding, accountability, and reflexivity (Wylie 2007). Relevance means the act of addressing questions that are relevant to individuals oppressed by gender-based forms of inequality. Experiential grounding means that feminists should cope with dynamics constrained by sex/gender structures, and that women's everyday lives should become the starting point of their research agenda. Accountability means that feminists should do all they can to counteract the traditional hierarchical structures when designing a research project (Longino 2002). Reflexivity is intended as the capacity to uncover androcentric assumptions by reaching out a "strong objectivity, which requires that the subject of knowledge be placed on the same critical plane as the objects of knowledge" (Harding 2004, 136).

In economics, the concept of "otherness" was adopted by household economics,[30] while the concept of care related with individual responsibility was introduced by feminist economics. According to feminist economists, the notion of a gendered and masculine-oriented reason had influenced norms, which had considerably influenced individuals' lives and well-being. The hierarchical nature of gender-biased norms had determined and perpetuated patriarchy; that is, a system in which men have a primary role in any field and women are subjugated (MacKinnon 1987; Barker and Schumm 2009), but in some societies, strong patriarchy had been replaced with a form of soft paternalism that did not change the nature of men's domination over women (Pearse and Connell 2016).

Scientific professions and professional practices were not immune from patriarchy: they had been completely controlled by men through academies and circles in which women were excluded (as seen in Chapter 1). The battle of many early feminist activists to get women into male-dominated scientific professions may be seen as an act of self-awareness of the gendered nature of scientific knowledge. Feminist epistemologists constantly noted that scientists in any field were remarkably homogeneous with respect to sex (male), race (white), and sexual orientation (heterosexual), and they argued that the standards for credibility in scientific research are rooted in social constructions that reinforced the status quo. Hence many feminist scholars carried on the project of the elimination of masculine stances in the content of scientific inquiry, in order to realize an emancipatory movement within science able to include a feminine perspective and to reduce the role of patriarchy (Code 1981;

Harding 1982; Harding and Hintikka 1983; Longino 1990; Barker and Kuiper 2003; Grasswick 2011).

In feminist philosophy, the debate on the gendered nature of rationality was begun by Sandra Harding, who claimed the necessity "to understand the distribution by gender of *conceptions of rationality*" [author's emphasis] (Harding 1982, 227). After having rejected any distinction between a female knowledge and a male knowledge, feminist scholars – and, later, feminist economists – proposed to investigate how "to do science as a feminist" (Longino 1987, 53). As previously stated, although the standard paradigm of rationality had been accepted within neoclassical economics, feminist economics criticized it and considered it to be male-oriented, as it as based on a concept of rationality shaped around a male stereotype, grounded on a kind of rationality that is able to pledge efficiency through a simple mechanism of maximization.[31] Harding (1987) proposed to incorporate relationality and subjectivity within rationality to build up a more efficient process of problem-solving than thw standard economics problem-solving process. According to Harding, in fact, the most adaptive solutions to many situations are not always logical, because individuals are much more complex than rational agents, and the act of choosing often requires creativity along with logics.

Feminist economics conceived the notion of gendered-biased norms as a constraint on both women's voice and gender equality. Hence, feminist economics developed an alternative model of rationality able to overcome the masculine notions of objectivity, logic, and abstraction that led to social inequalities that had especially involved women's conditions in life. Feminist economics rejected the neoclassical model of the rational economic man, who was constructed as a self-sufficient adult.

As Jones (2004) summarized, there were three different ways of considering the relationship between rationality and gender within economics: 1. the classical vision (women are able to follow ideals of standard rationality); 2. the different voice (standard rationality is incomplete and has to be modified by a feminist approach in a way that is able to include emotions); and 3. the strong critical stance (standard rationality has to be reformed because of its fallacies) (Becchio 2019). Feminist economics followed the third approach, based on a notion of economics in terms of real-world issues concerning women, men, and children, rather than on a mere examination of a decision process under conditions of scarcity (Ferber and Nelson 2003a).

The contraposition between feminist economics and the new home economics had covered a broad spectrum. As Harding claims: "one cannot simply 'add women' as objects of knowledge to the existing bodies of our social and natural knowledge" (Harding 1982, 215) as the new home economics did. Feminist economics had always rejected the explanation of economic phenomena in terms of efficiency adopted by the new home economics. For instance, the new home economics had considered gender inequality as a market failure, which can inhibit institutions to respond to economic incentives.[32] As Folbre (1986) had highlighted, Becker's new home economics assumed exogenous preferences, which implied constancy over time and are based on "a Victorian-era model of the heteronormative family, ignoring the massive diversity of real households and families" (Pearse and Connell 2016, 32). England directly attacked the neoclassical theory of household and the new home economics (England 1993), while Nelson considered neoclassical economics "to be represented by its male 'head,' whose preferences, it was assumed, determined household labor supply and consumption decisions" (Nelson 2005, 1).

According to feminist economics, the main fault of new home economics' approach was that it did not consider the role of nonmarket institutions in the emergence of gender inequality. Patriarchy, property rights, and social norms against women had been powerful nonmarket institutions that perpetuated and reinforced men's dominance over resources: "social norms like the sexual division of labor are not simply solutions to the problem of coordinating family production, but rather a way to organize family labor in terms that benefit men" (Braunstein 2008, 967). According to feminist economists, neoclassical models had internalized gender inequality as a natural outcome of the specialization in reproductive labor. Consequently, standard economics had perpetuated patriarchy. Moreover, the adoption of neoclassical models showed that men had had incentives to force women to prolong the patriarchal system that had led to inefficiency (Hartmann 1981; McCrate 1988; Braunstein and Folbre 2001).

Folbre (1994a, 1994b) clarified the dynamic of social norms in an inefficient institutional framework by presenting the dynamic of parental investments on children's education that are fundamental for economic growth. According to Folbre, although women's labor in child-raising and caring had usually been much more relevant than fathers' engagement, women's efforts had been less appreciated than women's work in the labor market.

Seguino (2000) adopted a feminist economics' view in analyzing gender inequality in order to propose an endogenous growth theory. She worked on the economic situation in some developing countries, where women are isolated into manufacturing and export-oriented sectors, and where their lower wages allow a significant increase in foreign and national investments and consequently in overall GDP. According to Seguino, things may change in the long run if the gender educational gap is reduced, as feminist economics strongly supports. An increase in the number of more-educated women will decrease the productivity of unskilled women's labor and will make high-skilled women's wages higher. The immediate consequence will be a lack of investment opportunities in sectors rooted in low-cost labor, which will lead to a reduction of economic growth. Hence, feminist economics seems to suggest that gender equality (in this case, a reduction of the gender educational gap) should be promoted even when it will lead to inefficient outcome, because gender equality is just and fair. It is a matter of ethics, not simply of efficiency. The integration of ethics within economics had always been a fundamental topic in feminist economics. Against the indifference about ethical issues in the standard economics, which actually had entailed a constitutive rejection of ethics and values, feminist economics strongly supported a re-introduction of ethical issues within economics. England's battle against the neoclassical 'separative self' was an example of that effort to embed ethics in economics (England 1993).

The discarding of ethics from economics was a direct consequence of the logic behind neoclassical economics that had radically changed the meaning of freedom for individuals, who were gradually reduced to rational agents. In conventional economics, individual freedom was no longer the direct effect of natural justice, which included material progress, equality, and solidarity and which was generated by affections like empathy, compassion, and mutual understanding. In conventional economics, individual freedom became the logical consequence of a rational behavior, which cut off any moral premise and implied maximization as the unique efficient decision-making process.[33]

Nelson (2004) used the metaphor of a 'machine' to scrutinize the phenomenon as described above. Economy as a machine was depicted by Nelson as follows: in the neoclassical view, mechanisms and forces drive economy, like Newtonian physics rules the natural world. In a physics-like world, markets are independent from ethics and values; neoclassical economics hides "any social, other-regarding, interdependent, emotional, or habitual characteristics that may be important for explaining economic behaviour and everyone else, like women, who does not fit the autonomy of the neoclassical agent" (Nelson 2004, 391). As a possible alternative to the 'economy as a machine', Nelson proposed a notion of economy as 'a creative process', or as 'an organism', which is able to integrate ethical issues within economic process, because the endless evolution of organic systems implies different models of decision-making besides the neoclassical model of maximization under constraint.

Summing up, the rise of feminist economics was shaped around the following key tenets: the rejection of a masculine notion of rationality adopted by neoclassical economics; the demystification of social norms that had perpetuated and reinforced patriarchy; the recognition of traditional women's subjection in stereotyped roles that had justified gender inequalities in economic matters such as market labor, wage, access to finance, and so forth. Feminist economics had offered different strands which have been summed up by Power (2004) as follows:

> Incorporation of caring and unpaid labor as fundamental economic activities; use of well-being as a measure of economic success; analysis of economic, political, and social processes and power relations; inclusion of ethical goals and values as an intrinsic part of the analysis; and interrogation of differences by class, race-ethnicity, and other factors.
>
> (Power 2004, 3)

Furthermore, feminist economics can suggest a policy-related feature able to explain major factors affecting gender gap without any specifically political connotation as gender neoclassical economics does (Blau 2013), or it can be much more political oriented by demanding for a radical change in the discipline.

3.4 *Feminist Economics*: the academic journal

IAFFE's founders were aware of the necessity to publish an academic journal in order to provide a proper tool to develop feminist economics, and, in 1995, they began publishing *Feminist Economics*, based at Rice University in Houston, Texas. The journal aimed to challenge the discipline in order to change the status quo andfind a new paradigm to reduce gender inequalities. This paragraph provides a sort of thematic and chronological narration of the contents of *Feminist Economics*, in order to show the evolution of the journal, which mirrored the evolution of the field.

Strassmann wrote the editorial of the first volume of *Feminist Economics* (Strassman 1995); she specified that *Feminist Economics'* main intent was to promote an open debate on the urgency to create "a more intellectually resilient economics". An open debate occurred in the first issue of the first volume of *Feminist Economics*: Strober versus Grossman, about marriage market's conditions and their influence on women's participation in the labor force. Grossbard (1995) supported the idea that marriage and employment are substitutes for women and Strober (1995) denied it.

Editors of *Feminist Economics* converged on the idea that feminist economics would have highlighted contributions in research fields previously neglected, which included 1) the history of economic thought to explore the historical construction of the economic categories and the often-ignored contributions of women;[34] 2) the economic methodology to question the masculine nature of neoclassical economics; and 3) economic education to shed new light on the "relegation of home economics as a separated discipline" (Strassman 1995, 2).[35]

As Pollak (2003) pointed out, a strong attack on neoclassical economics has been shaped around a deep critique to Becker's model (Harding 1995; Bergmann 1995; Agarwal 1997) which included Woolley's invitation to provide a valid alternative (Woolley 1996). Along with its theoretical intent, *Feminist Economics* aimed to promote economic policies oriented to "challenge an economic practice that for too long has served the interests of a restricted and unrepresentative group of people" (Strassmann 1995, 4).

During the first 10 years of its publication (1995–2005), *Feminist Economics* hosted many articles that illustrated the twofold theoretical and practical nature of feminist economics. Harding's article (1995), which opened the first volume of *Feminist Economics*, was an inquiry into the possibility for feminist economics to increase objectivity in the discipline. Against the idea that the inclusion of gender relations would have reduced objectivity, Harding underlined that the integration of gender relations within economics actually improves its objectivity because gender relations have the merit to introduce more realistic elements in economic models. Conversely, standard economics' denial of the role of gender relations had made economic models less objective. Furthermore, conventional economists rejected gender relations as a matter of values, which spoiled the scientific nature of economics, which was supposed to be value-free. Against this attitude, Harding argued that economics is not a natural science but a social science, and it cannot achieve any value-neutrality.

Harding's arguments recalled the discussion around the androcentric nature of the Western notion of scientific knowledge and led to further reflections about the conventional notion of objectivity in the process of maximizing an expected utility function that had completely ignored culture, values, and interests and had made neoclassical economics "not just unachievable but incoherent" (Harding 1995, 27). Grapard's article criticized the androcentric nature of neoclassical economics, which had depicted Robinson Crusoe as the modern man who exercised simple optimization in a framework of free choice without paying any attention to inequality (Grapard 1995).

In response to Harding, two different papers by Seitz (1995) and McCloskey (1995) appeared in *Feminist Economics*. Seitz's central task was to show that, in the current epistemological debate on objectivity and relativism, feminist economics should reject both, while McCloskey reinforced the idea that neoclassical economics is *malestream* – but against Harding, who "argues in an old leftist way modernized with feminism that an androcentric ideology is immanent in economics" (McCloskey 1995, 119), McCloskey regarded the centrality of bourgeois virtues to be the only way to overcome the traditional and stereotyped gender categories persistent in standard economics.

The battle against neoclassical economics was further conducted in *Feminist Economics* by Barker (1995), Bergmann (1995), Grapard (1995), and Seguino et al. (1996). Barker (1995), who analyzed the gendered nature of neoclassical models in a historical perspective: started in the 1930s with the development of Pareto optimality as the sole scientific criterion of economic welfare, neoclassical economics had been enlarged by Coase's essay on social costs (Coase 1960). According to Barker, in the timespan between Pareto's writings and Coase's contribution, both Hicks and Kaldor had worked to give economics "the aura of science and certainty" rooted on the notion of efficiency that was built up as "a rationalization for the existing distributions of power and wealth, distributions that are often tied to race, class, and gender" (Barker 1995, 35–36). In Barker's terms, the notion of economic efficiency had gained much credit with neoclassical economists for two reasons. First, it was able to simultaneously combine efficiency and liberty by using the mechanism of revealed preferences: individual preferences, if well-ranked, may assure an efficient solution in a context of free choice. Second, it was able to show that, under certain conditions, the market may reach optimal decisions about economic policy. Bergmann (1995) directly attacked Becker's new home economics, which was accused to have failed in understanding family's dynamics as well as in providing a proper policy to better off family's conditions (Bergmann 1995). Phipps and Burton (1995) reinforced Bergmann's argument by showing that Becker's model of household behavior was based on the

Victorian ideal of family in which women were constrained in their roles
of mothers/wives. Moreover, Becker's model did not consider social and institutional factors, even though they had dramatically influenced household
members' behavior – especially married women's decision to join the labor
force. Becker's model was further criticized by Duggan, who reinforced Bergmann's argument by writing: "wages and prices are given in the market, and
households respond to these signals [without considering] the effect of power
differentials among family members" (Duggan 1995, 178).

Besides the critique of standard economics and Becker's new home economics, the first volume of *Feminist Economics* hosted an article on caring labor
authored by Folbre (1995) in which she distinguished between pro-market
and anti-market. Pro-market feminist economists discouraged a demand of
more public support for caring, because they wanted to encourage women
to be more ambitious in the marketplace. Their position reflects "not only
the masculine tradition of liberal individualism, but also a certain [over]-
confidence that women will not and cannot become too individualistic". Conversely, anti-market feminist economists, either within the socialist or the
liberal tradition, gave the right emphasis on the necessity to valuate caring
labor with some public economic incentives (Folbre 1995).

A year later, in the second volume of *Feminist Economics*, Nelson (1996) identified another example of the masculine perspective in Barten's model of the
demographic scaling method (Barten 1964), which had assumed that the
household utility function simply was the equivalent of the male adult consumption of commodities. Seguino et al. (1996) used the category of gender
to investigate the dynamic of altruism versus self-interest. Authors insisted on
the role of social norms as "structures of constraint" by assuming that neoclassical assumptions about human motivations behind individuals' behavior were
too narrow.

The battle against neoclassical economics to widen the debate on the nature
of the discipline went further in the third volume of *Feminist Economics*. Its
first issue was completely devoted to arguing the necessity of broadening economic theory by including heterodox approaches. An article by Katz (1997)
explained that the main failure of Becker's approach was its lack of recognition
of gender-based power relations within the process of household resource allocation, especially when considering intra-household voice and exit. Katz
considered the dynamics of households' bargain by following Hirschman's definitions of voice and exit. Voice was an attempt to improve the relationship
through communication within a group, while exit was an irreversible form
of withdrawal from a group (Hirschman 1970). According to Katz, in the
household bargain, voice is intended as the right and the ability to enter
into the household, while exit is intended as the social and economic alternative to withdraw from household when there is no cooperation within its
members. Katz suggested that the dynamics of voice and exit within households would be better explained by adopting an interdisciplinary feminist-
institutional approach, able to combine quantitative and qualitative methods,
than by the standard cooperative bargain.

In the same volume, Agarwal (1997) insisted on the complexity of gender relations and the necessity to include ideology and culture, which had had an enormous influence on power relations. According to Agarwal, formal models used by neoclassic economists never considered this complexity, because they had expressed intrahouse dynamics as forms of bargaining, containing elements of both cooperation and conflict without assigning any specific role to qualitative factors and extra-household parameters. Furthermore, formal models used by neoclassic economists had ignored the fact that gender interactions are relevant outside household too, especially in the market, in communities, and in the state. Colander and Woos (1997) directly criticized the human capital theory, which had considered the gender wage gap merely as a result of supply-side factors and had ignored discrimination in favor of insiders embedded in the demand-side.

The second issue of the third volume of *Feminist Economics* (1997) dealt with the methodological boundaries of economics and proposed some alternative forms to collect data and to build up a more representative theory of all humans, able to overcome the neoclassical agent. Meagher proposed to include unpaid work in the GDP (Meagher 1997); Duncan and Edwards (1997) suggested to use the concept of 'gendered moral rationalities' to properly describe individuals' economic decision-making.

Another topic that played a fundamental role in feminist economics was the economics of other gender identities or of other sexual-orientated agents. Since the beginning of its publication, *Feminist Economics* hosted several articles that accounted for other minorities such as gays, lesbians, and bisexuals. More specifically, an article by Badgett (1995) invited feminist economists to go much deeper in the analysis of how sexual orientation had influenced economics theory, policy, and economics profession. The article was focused on the differences between gender and sexuality and it argued that the two categories are "complementary and interdependent rather than mutually exclusive" (Badgett 1995, 136). The author also invited feminist economists to investigate lesbian and gay family structures in order to develop comparative methods. In response to Badgett, Lamos (1995) acknowledged that gendered biases may persist in same-sex families. One year later, the second issue of the fourth volume of *Feminist Economics* was completely devoted to gay, lesbian, and bisexual economics. As Strassmann wrote in the editorial: "incorporating insights of gay, lesbian, and bisexual economics can only strengthen the analytical power and usefulness of economics" (Strassmann 1998, viii). By analyzing the case of U.S. low-income bi- and heterosexual black women fatally affected by AIDS, Christensen's article (1998) criticized neoclassical models that had systematically ignored the influence of cultural inequalities and prejudices on market negotiations, including negotiations in the area of epidemiology. A special issue of *Feminist Economics* on AIDS, sexuality, and economic development would be published later, in 2008, and included many contributions that shared the idea that epidemiology, especially the HIV–AIDS epidemic, can be scrutinized by analyzing the influence of gender stereotypes in building up cultural prejudices (Conrad and Doss 2008).

Feminist Economics' focus on minorities included many articles on racial groups. Connections between race and gender in determining the condition of minorities had always been a key issue in feminist economics. Besides several articles which appeared throughout the journal's volumes, in 2001, a special issue on the relationship between race and gender appeared and was dedicated to Rhonda Williams (1957–2000).[36] Williams got her Ph.D. in economics from MIT (1983); she had served as associate editor of *Feminist Economics* between 1994 and 1998. Williams authored several studies on racial inequality in the United States, refusing to adopt both human capital theory and cultural diversity as plausible explanations of the phenomenon (Williams 1993; Williams and Kenison 1996). She argued that white male workers accept employers' discriminatory practices to get higher-wage and more stable jobs; she also urged creation of a racialized understanding of sexuality (Figart 2001; Dymski and Nembhard 2002).

Research papers on new insights into real economic phenomena by using specific datasets had been hosted since the first issues of *Feminist Economics*, and their number increased relevantly in the following years. For instance, the first issue of the sixth volume of *Feminist Economics* (2000) was devoted to childcare and family policy in a comparative perspective, by analyzing the situations in Sweden, Spain, Ireland, France, Germany, the United States, and the United Kingdom. The final result suggested a "common denominator: the pressure placed on women to maintain their traditional care responsibilities while also increasing their hours of paidwork" (Folbre and Himmelweit 2000, 1).

The third issue of the sixth volume of *Feminist Economics* was entirely dedicated to the effects of globalization on women in developing countries where the Monetary Fund had implemented international loans, by promoting financial liberalization and market deregulation. Beneria et al. (2000) considered the effects of this process and pointed out the influential role of preexisting gender dynamics in East Asia, India, and Mexico, especially in relation to gender division of labor and with gender division of control over economic resources. Authors concluded that globalization had lowered the quality of life of some groups, especially those of women living in low-income households, even though a decrease in the gender educational gap had raised economic growth.

The second issue of the 10th volume of *Feminist Economics* (2004) was devoted to investigating the condition of lone motherhood and to propose some possible policies that might improve the economic and social well-being of lone mothers: a comparative view on the situation in the United States, Russia, Norway, the United Kingdom, and Sri Lanka was provided to capture dilemmas faced by lone mothers, either heterosexuals or lesbians. A final section of the volume summed up reflections and proposals, which included policy that was oriented to enable all lone mothers to get involved in the job market as well as policy aimed to let mothers choose between employment and childcare. Other policies suggested different ways to support caregiving and to provide a set of incomes for childcare (Himmelweit et al. 2004).

On year later, in 2005, a special issue of *Feminist Economics* was published that dealt with gender and aging. Eldercare systems in the United States, Arabic countries, Australia, South Africa, and South Korea were compared in order to provide an overview of their public policy initiatives, welfare programs, and provisions for eldercare, a burden regularly carried by women. Articles showed that in wealthy countries, the responsibility for the economic support of the elderly had shifted from the public to the private sector and that this had become a serious problem for women, who tend to live longer and earn less than men (Folbre et al. 2005).

In 2005, 10 years after the publication of the first volume of *Feminist Economics*, Barker summed up the progress of the field in such terms:

> A knowledge project that works toward a feminist transformation of economics. Using gender as an analytical category, feminist economists have shown that unquestioned and unexamined masculinist values are deeply embedded in the theoretical and empirical aspects of economics. Absent feminist analyses, economics rationalizes and naturalizes existing social hierarchies based on gender, race, class, and nations.
>
> (Barker 2005, 189)

Barker went further, by remarking on the importance to fight against the hegemony of neoclassical economics and by describing "the instability of women as a category, the challenging posed by intersectionality and the positionality of the researcher" (*ibid.*) as dilemmas within feminist economics. She suggested that a methodological pluralism must be regarded as the best way to deal with gender issues within feminist economics.

On the same occasion, Wolley wrote a survey on the impact of the journal within the broader panorama of economic studies by showing that the greatest impact of the journal was "in interdisciplinary economics (for example, "economics, planning and development", "in health and medicine (broadly defined) and in environmental studies and geography) ... and outside economics" (Woolley 2005, 96). She continued:

> The journal has an impact on the mainstream economics profession when feminist economists swim with the current by publishing in mainstream journals, teaching and working in mainstream departments and institutions, and talking to mainstream people. It has an impact when people from the mainstream decide to explore another tributary, to Google 'feminist economics' and see what comes up.
>
> (Woolley 2005, 97)

Articles published on *Feminist Economics* after 2005 have been more technically oriented: recurrent subjects included gender and women disparity, child marriage, divorce, race, and ethnicity. Articles have been usually presented through specific cases in both developed and developing countries.[37] In 2005, *Feminist*

Economics started to host articles which revealed that its initial battle against neo-classical economics has gradually evolved into a milder critique. In a conversation I had with Nancy Folbre, she told me that the journal *Feminist Economics* explicitly tried to create a 'big umbrella' in order to host submissions from a variety of different theoretical perspectives, including neoclassical economics, and to deflect attention from theoretical differences. Along with this partial convergence between feminist economics and gender neoclassical economics, the traditional criticism of neoclassical economics by feminist economists persisted. For instance, in 2008, *Feminist Economics* inaugurated a new article series on feminist economic methodology aimed to explore human behavior and well-being, which are influenced by nonmarket aspects of life (that is, phenomena that are not measured by money). Among them, Miller and Meulen (2008) presented some insights to "improve the communication of empirical research findings beyond the narrow statistical meaning of "significant" to a broader definition of what is economically important" (Miller and Meulen 2008, 145).

Since late 2000s, *Feminist Economics* hosted special issues by using comparative approaches as well as empirical studies. As Strassmann pointed out in an editorial (Strassmann 2010), *Feminist Economics* has always welcomed contributions from scholars from many other fields and from all regions of the world. The commitment to inclusivity became more concrete starting from 2010, when two special issues (*Inequality, Development, and Growth*, Volume 15:3; and *Gender, China, and the World Trade Organization*, Volume 13:3/4) were hosted under the supervision of Günseli Berik. The aim of this new challenge was to intensify the participation of scholars from developing countries.

In 2016, nineteen years later Katz's article on 'voice and exit' (described earlier), *Feminist Economics* hosted a special issue to explore voice (the act of remaining in an organization by individuals dissatisfied with the performance of that organization, but attempting to improve its performance by 'voicing' their discontent) and agency (the capacity of individuals to act independently and to make their own free choices) of women and girls using bargaining theory, as well as behavioral and experimental economics, in order to understand inequalities within households in different countries (Gammage et al. 2016; Pearse and Connell 2016; Austen and Mavisakalayan 2016; Goez and Jenkins 2016; Hanmer and Klugman 2016; Kabeer 2016). The aim of that volume was manifold: to promote investments in girls' education, to scrutinize the ability of legal instruments and the quota system to increase women's role as policymakers, to end child marriage, to support cooperatives able to improve the conditions of women's employment and entrepreneurship, and to act on social norms to promote women's agency.

The new debate on exit and voice hosted in *Feminist Economics* involved Gammage et al. (2016), Pearse and Connell (2016), Austen and Mavisakalayan (2016), Goetz and Jenkins (2016), Hanmer and Klugman (2016), and Kabeer (2016).[38]

Gammage et al. (2016) focused their attention on structure and agency as tools of power, and they provided a survey of the feminist economics' literature, which included earlier contributions by Giddens (1984),[39] Sen (1987, 1990a, 1999),[40] Folbre (1994a),[41] Agarwal (1997),[42] and Kabeer (1999, 2008).[43] Gammage et al. (2016) asserted that the gap between rules and norms implies at least two scenarios: on one side, even if a specific legislation to reduce gender gaps is approved, it becomes effective only when social norms change as well; on the other side, legislation may become effective later than the emerging of norms, which may be more prone to gender equality than actual rules.

Pearse and Connell (2016) had focused their attention on individual and collective agency in the renegotiation of gender norms, which they considered social structures that are usually challenged by women, given that status quo largely privileges men who have no incentive to change them. Austen and Mavisakalyan (2016) had considered the role of formal legal institutions in enhancing women's agency through parliamentary representation. They pointed out that constitutional protection from gender-based discrimination can bolster women's exercise of agency and can make them able to exercise their voice. Goetz and Jenkins (2016) had analyzed agency within institutions. Although authors refused the conventional judgement that views women as natural peacemakers, they stated that women's participation and agency in peacebuilding depends not only on their own efforts and capabilities, but also on their actual access to resources and opportunities within peace-building agendas. Hanmer and Klugman (2016) pointed out the need to measure women's agency in terms of their ability to facilitate reproductive choices, child marriage, freedom of movement, freedom from violence, and control over resources. Kabeer (2016) explored the relation between gender equality and economic growth. As Kabeer and Natali (2013) had previously showed, although gender equality in education and labor force participation may increase economic growth, the reverse relationship is much less evident. Kabeer (2016) had identified the following possible explanations for this phenomenon in the fact that the patterns of growth determine the gender distribution of new economic opportunities, the state plays a greater role in redistribution, and structures of patriarchy persist in preventing gender equality.

Summing up, in more than 20 years of publication, *Feminist Economics* had covered a large spectrum of arguments connected with gender issues and women empowerment in a theoretical framework, which implied a strong criticism of neoclassical economics and the new home economics. As a matter of fact, feminist economics is a heterodox economic approach.

3.5 Possible interconnections between feminist economics and other major heterodox approaches

Under the label of 'heterodox economics' there is a massive number of economic approaches that adopt different methodological and theoretical models. They share a significant critique to the methodological assumptions of neoclassical economics. Feminist economics had often been related to some other heterodox economic approaches, such as Marxian political economy, post-Keynesian economics, Austrian economics, social ontology, Sen's approach of capabilities, American institutionalism, behavioral economics, and economic comparative systems.

The connection between feminist economics and Marxist political economy may be recognized in the emphasis on collective identity rather than on individuals (Hartmann 1981; Ferguson 1994; Matthaei 1992, 1996). Furthermore, in the 1970s, many feminists of the second wave labeled themselves socialists: their political identities created a sort of identification between feminism and socialism which had involved feminist economics by neglecting the central role of the classical liberal tradition within feminist economics. The main problematic feature in the identification of feminist economics with Marxist political economy is the fact that women are not a class, while in the Marxist approach class is the sole economic agent and political subject. According to Marx, a class is set of people who have historically achieved the material conditions to be exploiters (capitalists) or exploited (workers). This distinction cannot be applied to women in the same terms, even if we consider men exploiters and women exploited, for the following four reasons: first, the simultaneous presence of women among capitalists and workers, which had led today's Marxian feminist economists to reject a class-centric approach in favor of a broader emphasis on collective identity and action; second, the Marxist focus on inequality is exclusively determined by the material conditions of life, while in feminist economics the role of cultural constraints is independent from the material conditions of life and is not a superstructure as it was in Marxism; third, the pillar of Marxist political economy, that is, the theory of labor–value, is only partially adopted by feminist economics when coping with the intra-house sexual division of labor; and finally, as Hartmann suggested (1981), capitalism and patriarchy are the two faces of the same coin, even if they both are regarded as a process of oppression.

Some other scholars had considered it possible to find a consistent relationship between feminist economics and post-Keynesian economics, based on the inclusion of the category of gender into the post-Keynesian explanation of economic growth in terms of cultural development, in contrast to Becker's model (Lavoie 1992; Jennings 1994; Levin 1995; Fuller 1996; Staveren 2010; Alessandrini 2013). Another possible convergence between post-Keynesian economics and feminist economics was the role of uncertainty and sentiments (as in Minsky and Keynes), which are considered central in any decision-making process. The main problem with building up a feminist post-Keynesian economics is the fact that, even though gender issues can be determinant for policies, it is hard to find a relevant place for gender within macroeconomic dynamics as they are explained in post-Keynesian terms. In fact, feminist economics efforts have been driven by the urgency to reformulate the microfoundation of the discipline in a way that allowed the inclusion of feminist economics' concerns in microeconomics rather than the analysis of macroeconomics in feminist terms. Nonetheless, some tentative moves in that direction were made by Charusheela (2010) and Fukuda-Parr et al. (2013). Charusheela (2010), who analyzed the gendered nature of the consumption function "not by looking at 'male' versus 'female' consumption function [but as] the entire function is itself theorized as a 'bearer of gender'" (Charusheela 2010, 1155). Fukuda-Parr et al. tried to specifically focus their attention on distributional dynamics in order to yield a more robust analysis of crises, which is a burden of subordinate groups, including women. As Danby (2004) pointed out, much of the post-Keynesians had adopted some assumptions "which limit its capacity to think about gender: an undersocialized entrepreneur as the maker of investment decisions; a market/nonmarket divide that ignores and devalues household activity; A neutral, powerful state and law of contract" (Danby 2004, 56–57).

Some other economists had tried to find a connection between feminist economics and Austrian economics: in the 1990s, Vaughn (1994), Walker (1994), Horwitz (1995), and Waller (1999), and more recently, Galindo and Ribero (2012), Becchio (2015, 2018), and Hammond (2016). Besides a strong critique to neoclassical methodological assumptions as well as to the (ab)use of formalism into economics, Austrian economics and feminist economics shared some relevant points. First, both approaches commonly share the idea that competition and cooperation may be the two faces of the same coin: both Austrians and feminists agree on considering the fascination of the opposition between competition and cooperation as useless, sexist, and wrong. They also agree about the role of emotions in human decision process as decisive, as well as the fact that emotions do not bring any irrational motivation into the decision process, being a natural part of the decision-process dynamics, as many neuro-economists had recently revealed (Longino 1990; Haack 1996; Walker et al. 2004; Nelson 2011). Furthermore, both Austrian economics and feminist economics had strongly criticized Cartesian rationality: according to Garnett (2015), criticism to Cartesian rationality had led both Austrian economists and feminist economists to conceive and to promote another educational system and a new pedagogical model. This new pedagogy is based on a twofold pillar: unlike in the expert-center model, rooted on an expert teacher preaching to passive students, students are knowledge producers; and unlike the top-down learning process, education is intended to be a dynamic process of connected learning in top-down and down-top directions (Hayek 1948; Bordo 1987; Nelson 1996).

Another point of convergence between Austrian economics and feminist economics may be depicted in the attitude of entrepreneurs when they introduce innovation into the market. Emphasized by Austrians as the core of economic development, creativity embedded in entrepreneurship is similar to women's attitudes in problem solving. Furthermore, both Austrian economics and feminist economics consider creativity as a tool to create and improve social capital. Horwitz (1995) had first suggested that the role of the creative entrepreneur in a competitive market, which is central in an Austrian perspective and might be familiar with some feminist economics' glance. Hammond

(2016) had considered Schumpeter's description of the entrepreneur as a dreamer who fights for the joy of creating in similar terms as economic agents' identity in feminist economics. Furthermore, he reminds that, according to Schumpeter, the rise of feminism, with its stance of emancipation, had been possible within the capitalistic framework where entrepreneurial forces had been able to operate. Some other authors compared Kirzner's emphasis on the role of entrepreneurs to learn from the past (alertness) to women's role in the process of creations (Aaltio et al. 2008; Galindo and Ribero 2012; Mohsen et al. 2012).

Other scholars considered a possible convergence between feminist economics and social ontology (Lawson 1999, 2003; Harding 1999; Barker 2003; Nelson 2003; Peter 2003a). In 1999, a lively debate occurred in *Feminist Economics* between Tony Lawson and Sandra Harding. Lawson urged feminist economists to engage in a broad ontological analysis to include the specific topic of scientific realism, and Harding replied that feminist economics should be engaged with ontological arguments only if they had a strategic value for feminist issues. A few years later, in 2003, *Feminist Economics* hosted a new debate on how feminist economics had envisioned the nature of reality. In response to both Lawson and Harding, Peter (2003a) highlighted that Lawson's attempt to push feminist economics towards a new notion of scientific inquiry was an attempt to strengthen the foundations of heterodox economics against the imperialistic position of neoclassical economics rather than an attempt to incorporate feminist economics into social ontology. Unfortunately, according to Peter, Lawson's critical realism, which combined ontological realism and epistemological relativism, never provided an emancipatory notion – in the feminist sense –of scientific inquiry. According to Barker (2003), Lawson's approach had given too much emphasis on a humanist conception of human agency, which had been questioned by some feminists, while Nelson's reply to Lawson was focused on the fact that feminist economics is much more oriented towards the operation of incorporating feeling, emotions, and values within their model rather towards the building of a new ontology (Nelson 2003).[44]

A much more proficient way to find a connection between feminist economics and another possible heterodox approach was focused on similarities between feminist economics and Sen's capability approach (Qizilbash 2005; Gasper 2007; Addabbo et al. 2010; Nussbaum 2013; Robeyns 2017). Recently, Robeyns had summed up the definition of capability approach as a conceptual framework which includes "the assessment of individual levels of achieved wellbeing and wellbeing freedom; the evaluation and assessment of social arrangements or institutions; and the design of policies and other forms of social change in society" (Robeyns 2017, 21). In 2000, *Feminist Economics* hosted a call for papers to solicit papers about any possible theoretical and empirical connections between capability approach and feminist economics. The main results converged in the sixth volume of *Feminist Economics* (2003). The volume included contributions by Agarwal et al. (2003), Anderson (2003), Fukuda-Parr (2003), Gasper and Van Staveren (2003), Hill (2003),

Klasen and Wink (2003) Koggel (2003), Iversen (2003), Nussbaum (2003), Peter (2003b), Robeyns (2003). The last article was a contribution by Sen et al. (2003).

As Agarwal et al. claimed (2003), Sen had always been regarded as a feminist economist especially "for his humanitarian approach to economics" (Agarwal et al. 2003, 3). Anderson (2003) claimed that Sen and feminist economics shared the idea that gender issues should be considered as an epistemological resource to increase the degree of objectivity in the discipline. Furthermore, the capability approach as well as feminist economics may provide valid tools to transform gender differences from biases into resources.

Fukuda-Parr (2003) recalled that Sen's approach was determinant in the composition of the Human Development Reports, which, in an earlier stage, emphasized some general measures, such as the provision of public services for minorities and lower-income groups; more recently, it had been focused on a new agency-driven paradigm based on gender analysis.[45]

Starting from Sen's conception of freedom (Sen 1999) as the most important value in judging individual well-being as well as social development, Gasper and Van Staveren (2003) suggested to make a clear distinction between individual freedom and social values and to consider the latter more important than the former, while Sen had overemphasized the former. According to the authors, values are intended not simply in relation to individual autonomy and freedom of choice, but mainly in relation to fairness and connections among individuals.

Hill (2003) examined the effect of social institutions on human capabilities in order to achieve a new policy that may be useful to women's empowerment, while Klasen and Wink (2003) presented some topics introduced by Sen as fundamentals of feminist economics. For instance, Sen's work on gender bias in mortality, which had led him to formulate the concept of 'missing women', that is, women killed by unequal treatment in the allocation of survival-related goods (Sen 1990c, 1992), was without a doubt a feminist economics' subject.

Koggel (2003) added further layers of complexity to Sen's notion of freedom in order to include both negative and positive impacts of globalization on women's freedom and agency. Iversen's paper dealt with the application of Sen's capability approach in considering intra-household inequality when evaluating people's well-being: in a domestic relationship, an individual's well-being will depend not only on her own capabilities but also on those of her significant other. The analysis of the capability approach from a feminist perspective had drawn a special attention to domestic power imbalances, which had been ignored either by new home economists or by welfare economists who never took account of intra-house inequality (Iversen 2003).

Nussbaum (2003) argued that a possible convergence between the capability approach and feminist economics should begin with a normative scheme of the capability approach aimed to actually lead society towards gender justice. Hence, Nussbaum provided her list, which included life; body health and integrity; freedom of expression, thought, and emotions; and effective participation in political and material life. Directly influenced by Nussbaum, Robeyns (2003) proposed a method for selecting the most relevant capabilities to be applied to the analysis of gender inequality in affluent societies. She outlined that, unlike welfare economics, the capability approach can explain gender inequality. The capability approach, in fact, has an ethical and social nature, while welfare economics has an ontological and individualistic nature. The capability approach rejected the idea that women's well-being can be included under wider entities such as the household or the community. Furthermore, the capability approach gave major credit to the impact of care and interdependence among family members and community members. Moreover, the capability approach had included nonmarket scenarios, which are extremely relevant to feminist economics. Finally, the capability approach explicitly refused the assumption that any individual has the same utility function and acknowledged gender as a fundamental source of differences. Hence, Robeyns (2003) enlarged Nussbaum's list of valuable capabilities by including education, leisure activities, time autonomy, shelter, and environment.[46] In fact, according to Robeyns, the capability approach had not taken account of the fact that an androcentric social framework, which had led to gender discrimination, may reinforce discrimination and may be able to reduce women's capability.

Peter (2003b) examined the relation between gender studies and social choice, and he insisted on the fact that both Sen and feminist economics had converged in the rejection of a notion of social choice purely based on subjective assessments of individual welfare as well as they had emphasized the role of people's agency and participation in democratic institutions.

Further developments that deal with a possible connection between feminist economics and Sen's capability approach had recently been introduced by Addabbo et al. (2010), who adopted a macroeconomic perspective to make the capability approach operational within a specific feminist economics' context. They pointed out the central role of gender budgets, especially women's unpaid work, social and individual well-being, and considered the importance of gender budgets not only in determining the use of public resources to promote gender equity, but also in defining the multidimensional notion of well-being that is able to provide "a less ambiguous account of the gender-equity effects of public policies" (Addabbo et al. 2010, 497).

Connections between feminist economics and behavioral economics also had been scrutinized: Nelson (2003, 2006, 2009) as well as Austen (2017) found in Kahneman's framing effect a possible convergence with feminist economics.[47] Nelson (2014, 2016) used behavioral research to explore the consequences of stereotyping and confirmation biases within the connection between gender and risk aversion. Nelson (2014) showed that the mainstream literature on gender and risk aversion, according to which women are more risk-averse than men, is faulted by an "essentialist *a priori* belief". Nelson (2015) reinforced her argument by showing that the supposed strong evidence of fundamental gender differences in risk preferences between men and women usually does not provide any clear distinction between individual level and aggregate level.

Becchio (2019) had considered that a convergence between feminist economics and behavioral economics would be possible only if behavioral economics rejected the normative concept of rationality in neoclassical terms in order to adopt an ecological rationality, as feminist economics does.[48] Inspired by Nelson (2014, 2016) among others, Sent and Van Staveren (2019) tried to extend the behavioral approach in feminist economics' terms not only to risk appetite, but also to overconfidence, altruism, and trust. By reviewing 208 behavioral studies, authors found a few evidences of gender stereotypes and no consistent average gender differences in any of the four behavioral attitudes they analyzed. In response to Sent and Van Staveren's article, Nelson (2019) pointed out that, lately, behavioral economics literature on gender has become distorted for several reasons, which include some relevant methodological mistakes such as the confusion about statistical and substantive significance; the lack of recognition that collected data that are consistent with gender stereotypes are much more likely to be published than other data which are inconsistent; the fact that data are mainly collected in Western countries alone.

Other authors tried to find a compatibility between feminist economics and American institutionalism. Although institutionalism research on gender is limited, both approaches had considered knowledge as a cultural process socially constructed. Furthermore, both feminist economics and American institutionalism were engaged in embedding ethical issues into decision-making process, based on a dialectical reasoning which implies uncertainty, against a demonstrative reasoning, which implied full rationality as it has adopted in the neoclassical model (Waller and Jennings 1990). England and Folbre (2003) tried to find connections between feminist economics and the new institutionalist economics: both approaches emphasized how values, norms, and references help to coordinate individual choices. Furthermore, new institutionalists often deal with nonmarket institutions and with the impact of care work in order to explain contractual relationship between men and women in an alternative to Becker's model (Braunstein and Folbre 2001; England and Folbre 2003).

Some scholars had proposed that feminist economics should be integrated into the field of comparative economic systems, "a body of literature [that] examines and compares the working of different sets of economic institutions as well as ways in which institutions can be combined to achieve various goals, such as growth, efficiency, and equity" (Hopkins and Duggan 2011, 36). The advantage to combining comparative economics studies and feminist economics would stand in the possibility of understanding which institutions may have traditionally reinforced gender stereotypes and which institutions may contribute to the reduction of gender inequality at a present stage.

Notes

1 According to Fraser (2009), the second wave of feminism was mainly dominated and ruled by the anti-imperialist movement of the New Left, which aimed to challenge the capitalist society that appeared to be pervasively male-dominated. Fraser compared

the critique to capitalism that had emerged in the second wave of feminism with the present attack of the so-called third wave feminism to the neoliberal society. Following Fraser, Wilson (2015) more recently had described a complex trajectory from liberal to neoliberal feminism, in order to show that neoliberal feminism had deepened gender differences and inequalities rather than reduced them. Both Fraser and Wilson considered the battle against gender inequalities an exclusive result of radical feminism. Against their approach, Funk (2013) pointed out that only a minority of second-wave feminists was against the capitalistic system as well as the majority of third wave feminists are attacking neither neoliberalism nor capitalism.

2 Ti-Grace Atkinson was a central figure and the informal leader of The Feminists until 1971. Other prominent members included Anne Koedt, Sheila Michaels, Barbara Mehrhof, Pamela Kearon, and Sheila Cronan.

3 In September 1969, The Feminists organized a manifesto to protest the marriage contract at the New York City Marriage License Bureau (Love and Cott 2006).

4 In 1969, Gornick wrote an article in the *Village Voice* to promote the group and to invite women to join it.

5 Sheila Rowbotham (1972), Mitchell (1971), and Eisenstein (1979) were well-known socialist feminists (McFadden 2018).

6 As retrieved on September 22, 2018, at: https://womensstudies.sdsu.edu/history.htm.

7 Today, there are more than 800 women's studies programs colleges and universities in the United States. Hundreds of schools offer a Bachelor of Arts degree in women's studies. Close to 30 offer a master's degree and many schools have created a Ph.D. program.

8 The journal found its current home at the University of Maryland at College Park under the guidance of Claire G. Moses as Editorial Director. As retrieved on September 24, 2018, at: www.feministstudies.org/aboutfs/history.html.

9 As retrieved on September 24, 2018, at: http://signsjournal.org/about-signs/history/.

10 Born in 1940 to an Orthodox Jewish family in Brooklyn, Phyllis Chesler got her BA at Bard and her Ph.D. in psychology at the New School for Social Research. She pioneered women's studies courses in early 1970s. Like many other activists, Chesler combined feminist activism with scholarship: she was the cofounder of the National Organization for Women as well as of the Association for Women in Psychology in 1969.

11 The beginning of the third wave of feminism is also related with the Anita Hill case, and the emerging of the *riot grrrl* groups in the music scene. In 1991, Anita Hill testified before the Senate Judiciary Committee that Supreme Court nominee, Clarence Thomas, had sexually harassed her at work. Thomas was appointed anyway. Nonetheless, his appointment led to a national discussion about the overrepresentation of men in leadership roles. Similarities with the recent Kavanaugh case, which occurred in 2018 are evident. Differently from second-wave feminists who had rejected girls' aesthetics, such as makeup, high heels, fashionable clothes and accessories, and so forth, as tools of gender stereotyping, these musical groups emphasized them. Against the stereotypical images of women as passive or domineering, third-wave feminists redefined women and girls as assertive and empowered. They intended sexual liberation as a process of becoming conscious of how gender identities have been intentionally shaped by social norms.

12 In this passage, Bergmann anticipated the discussion around the economic imperialism of neoclassical economics, that is, the capacity to become mainstream within the discipline as well as to colonize other social sciences (Fine 2000; Laezar 2000). Laezar described economic imperialism well in such terms: "economics is not only a social science, it is a genuine science. Like the physical sciences, economics uses a methodology that produces refutable implications and tests these implications using solid statistical techniques. In particular, economics stresses three factors that distinguish it from other social sciences. Economists use the construct of rational individuals who engage in maximizing behavior. Economic models adhere strictly to the importance of equilibrium as part of any theory. Finally, a focus on efficiency leads economists to ask questions that other social sciences ignore. These ingredients have allowed economics to invade

intellectual territory that was previously deemed to be outside the discipline's realm" (Laezar 2000, 99).

13 Signers wrote: "Information properly organized changes the images of the world of people who receive it and consequently changes their behavior" (Bell et al. 1973, 1051).

14 Signers wrote: "Persuasion plays a particularly important role in the change of values, and without getting into the ancient controversy about the truth of values one has to recognize that change in our image of the world inevitably changes our values about it. As scientists, we have to guard against the information filter which our values create. We cannot pretend, however, that information is value free. . . . The relations between the sexes are often characterized by high levels of emotion, and hence are particularly subject to the distortions which arise from unconscious or irrelevant sources. It is one of the functions of ethical persuasion to raise our awareness and to set up defenses against attitudes and prejudices which arise from this source" (Bell et al. 1973, 1051).

15 Signers wrote: "It is by constructing a reward structure that society is most likely to achieve change. These rewards may be either internal or external ... A suggestion, for instance, that dues paid by members of the American Economic Association should be scaled down if the organization or department to which they belong had a high pro portion of women might be hard to legitimate, even though it might be effective" (Bell et al. 1973, 1051–1052).

16 Signers wrote: "There is one extreme good reason for the use of sanctions. In the case of public goods and public bads it is well recognized by economists that legitimated threat of some kind is essential if we are to avoid some 'tragedy of the commons'" (Bell et al. 1973, 1052).

17 Between 1993 and 2017, women have more than tripled their representation among new Ph.D.s, to 32.9%; they have tripled their representation among assistant professors to 28.8 and they have increased their representation at the associate level to 23%. They also have increased their representation at the full professor level more than five-fold. to 13.9%. Almost a third of the fulltime female faculty in Top 20 economics departments are in non-tenure track teaching positions (Lundberg 2018).

18 Today things have changed. Nevertheless, in the recent American Economic Association Annual Meeting, held in Philadelphia in 2018, Wu presented a paper on gender stereotypes in academia and revealed that conversations about women in the forum 'Econ Job Market Rumors' are mostly linked to words of abusive and sexist nature, while men tend to be paired with much more proper and work-related vocabulary (Wu 2017). Furthermore, Wu revealed that if a woman is mentioned on a thread, the probability is 2.1–2.3 percentage points higher that the conversation will deviate from the academic focus and shift towards some form of chauvinism. An article on *The New York Times* by Wolfers (2017) summarized Wu's results: "The 30 words most uniquely associated with discussions of women [are] definitely not related with profession. They include: hotter, lesbian, bb (internet speak for "baby"), sexism, tits, anal, marrying, feminazi, slut, hot, vagina, boobs, pregnant, pregnancy, cute, marry, levy, gorgeous, horny, crush, beautiful, secretary, dump, shopping, date, nonprofit, intentions, sexy, dated and prostitute. A parallel list of words associated with discussions about men ... includes words that are relevant to economics: adviser, Austrian, mathematician, pricing, textbook ... goals, greatest and Nobel". As retrieved on September 17, 2018, at: www.nytimes.com/2017/08/18/upshot/evidence-of-a-toxic-environment-for-women-in-economics.html. Quite impressed by Wolfers' article, the well-known macroeconomist Olivier Blanchard called for a civilized discussion between economists in order to stop this trend (Blanchard 2017).

19 As retrieved on September 25, 2018, at: www.economist.com/christmas-specials/2017/12/19/women-and-economics.

20 As retrieved on September 28, 2018, at: www.aeaweb.org/jel/guide/jel.php.

21 There are nineteen primary JEL categories; each JEL primary category has secondary and tertiary subcategories, which are defined by the JEL classification codes guide.

22 All definitions of JEL codes have been retrieved on September, 28, 2018 at: www.aeaweb.org/jel/guide/jel.php.

23 As retrieved on May 15, 2019, at: www.aeaweb.org/econlit/jelCodes.php?view=jel#B.

24 As retrieved on May 15, 2019, at: www.aeaweb.org/econlit/jelCodes.php?view=jel#B.

25 The D1x classes were previously under numeric JEL Classes 022, 841, and 921; while J16 was previously encompassed by the numeric JEL Classes 826 and 917 (JEL 1991).

26 *Feminist Economics*' Vol. 4:3, issued in 1998, was entirely devoted to Barbara Bergmann's contributions to economics.

27 Entries in the volume deal with theoretical and methodological issues within feminist economics.

28 Looking at the *Social Sciences Citation Index*, authors revealed that the journal *Feminist Economics* had registered a good score among heterodox literature. For instance, the *Journal of Economic Perspectives* (which is an official publication of AEA) devoted its winter 2000 issue to the last developments within the discipline as well as to the future of economics. Ferber and Nelson brought into attention the fact that on that occasion feminist economics was completely ignored.

29 As retrieved on June 4, 2018, at: www.iaffe.org/pages/resources/syllabus/.

30 As Horodecka (2015) rightly reminded, feminist economics' focus on household steps back to Aristotle's concept of *oekonomia* (the science of governing a household) against *chrematistics* (the theory of wealth as measured in money).

31 According to Nelson (1993c, 1996), the notion of provisioning should replace the notion of optimization in order to explain economic decision-making. Nelson's dichotomy between the notion of provisioning and the notion of optimization recalls Karl Polanyi's double meaning of 'economic' (Polanyi 1968). According to Polanyi, 'economic' may be intended either as the way of providing material subsistence (the substantive approach) or as related with the concept of scarcity (the formalist approach): although the former is a general concept that can be applied to different economic forms of interaction (redistribution, reciprocity, and exchange), the latter is a specific concept that can be exclusively applied to exchange dynamics within a market economy. Waller and Jenning (1991) considered a possible connection between Karl Polanyi's work and feminist economics. The authors claimed that Polanyi's substantive approach allows the inclusion of gender in economics. More recently, Beneria (1999, 2003) had adopted Polanyi's categories in his book, *The Great Transformation* (Polanyi 1944) to scrutinize the gender dimension within the overall process of globalization.

32 For example, some neoclassical economists studied the phenomenon of rent-seeking behavior in market institutions (Krueger 1974; Tollison and Congleton 1995).

33 From Robbins to Samuelson and Friedman, moral principles were discarded by economics. As Robbins wrote: "It is not because we believe that our science is exact that we wish to exclude ethics from our analysis, but because we wish to confine our investigations to a subject about which positive statement of any kind is conceivable" (Robbins 1927, 176). Both Samuelson (1947) and Friedman (1953) explicitly claimed the need to go from physics to economics to found economic analysis as a science; Friedman clearly stated the urgency to free economics from any ethics in order to make it a positive science (Becchio and Leghissa 2017).

34 During the first years of its publication, *Feminist Economics* hosted many articles which dealt with contribution by women economists in the history of economic thought. A special tribute was given to Margaret Reid (*Feminist Economics*' Vol 2:3 was entirely devoted to her life and work). Other articles dealt with classical economists, who scrutinized the role of women in society, such as J.B. Say (Forget 1997), Saint-Simon (Forget 2001), and women's agency in Smith, Taylor Mill, and Mill (Bodkin 1999).

35 For instance, Hill and King published an empirical research paper on the relationship among female education, gender differences, and economic development, and they showed that a reduction of the gender education gap would have improved the well-being of the society as a whole (Hill and King 1995).

36 In memory of Rhonda Williams, IAFFE has established a prize to help scholars from underrepresented groups work on feminist economics.

37 The Scimago Journal & Country Rank (SJR) provides bibliometric indicators embedded in a database of scientific journals in any field. The SJR indicator measures a journal's impact and influence by counting the number of citations in a determined time span. The SJR report, which collected data available between 1999 and 2015, revealed that the number of journals related to gender studies had been dramatically increased in any social sciences' research field, and indicated *Gender and Society* as the top journal in the field, with a SJR equals 2.461. *Feminist Economics* covered the 31st position with an SJR equals 0.548. If we disaggregate the data according to quartiles (art and humanities, business and management, economics, and gender studies), the quartiles for economics is Q2 and sometimes Q3 (in 1999, 2004, and 2008).

38 The debate recalled previous interpretations of Hirschman's seminal book *Exit, Voice, and Loyalty* (Katz 1997; Chubb and Moe 1988; Witte 2001; Gershuny et al. 2005). The model has been formalized as a simple game-theoretic model by Gelbach (2006) by assuming a conflict of interest between the leadership and other members within an organization. Authors previously involved in the debate had intended voice as an aspect of agency which must become a real way to change women's status quo within households, the state, and market.

39 Giddens (1984) pointed out the vicious circle between agency and social structures: although structures usually shape individuals' and groups' agency, individuals' and groups' agency usually shapes social structures. This situation makes it hard to challenge the status quo in order to improve minorities' empowerment.

40 In his work on well-being and capabilities in relation to social justice, Sen underlined that either an apparent consent with or silence about the status quo depended on the fact that oppressive structures had traditionally led to adaptation of those who occupied an inferior position in the household hierarchy (Sen 1987, 1990a, 1999).

41 Folbre (1994a) described social structures as social constraints in terms of a trade-off between official rules and implicit norms, which influenced individuals' positions within the social hierarchy.

42 Agarwal (1997) considered the power of social norms in shaping household members' roles, and she questioned the direct relation between the absence of protest and adaptation as suggested by Sen.

43 Kabeer (1999, 2008) regarded resources, agency, and achievements as a three-dimensional model of empowerment and she distinguished between agency that reinforces the status quo, and those that challenge it.

44 In the same volume, *Feminist Economics* hosted one more article by Lawson (2003a) in response to Peter, Barker, and Nelson as well as another article by Harding (2003) in response to Lawson 2003a, along with a final article by Lawson (2003b).

45 The report was first launched in 1990 by the Pakistani economist Mahbub ul Hag and by Sen himself.

46 See also Robeyns (2017) on the application of the capability approach to well-being, freedom and social justice.

47 Kahneman made a distinction between System 1 and System 2 in order to explain the decision-making process. System 1 is the intuitive and feelings-based system; System 2 is the analytical and reason-based system. According to Kahneman, although System 1 has been considered irrational, it is often logical and useful, while System 2, usually regarded as rational, may often produce irrational outcome. Although Kahneman never specifically analyzed the gender dimension, both social pressure and framing effect play a fundamental role in his model, as they do in feminist economic.

48 A possible connection between behavioral economics and feminist economics requires an introductory clarification about the twofold nature of behavioral economics. If behavioral economics adopts a neoclassical *normative* model of rationality and explains bias and mistakes as deviations from that model, it is not compatible with feminist

economics. If behavioral economics adopts an alternative model of rationality, that is, an ecological rationality to explain that simple strategies, when adapted to the environment, will produce clever decisions, it becomes consistent with feminist economics (Becchio 2019).

References

Aaltio I., Kyrö P., and Sundin E. (Eds.) (2008) *Women Entrepreneurship and Social Capital: A Dialogue and Construction.* Copenhagen: Copenhagen Business School Press.

Addabbo T., Lanzi D., and Picchio A. (2010) "Gender Budget: A Capability Approach". *Journal of Human Development and Capabilities.* Vol. 11:4, pp. 479–501.

Aerni A. and McGoldrick K. (1999) *Valuing Us All: Feminist Pedagogy and Economics.* Ann Arbor, MI: University of Michigan Press.

Aerni A., Barlett R., Lewis M., McGoldrick K., and Shackelford J. (1999) "Toward a Feminist Pedagogy in Economics". *Feminist Economics.* Vol. 5:1, pp. 29–44.

Agarwal B. (1997) "Bargaining and Gender Relations: Within and Beyond the Household". *Feminist Economics.* Vol. 3:1, pp. 1–51.

Agarwal B., Humphries J., and Robeyns I. (2003) "Exploring the Challenges of Amartya Sen: An Introduction". *Feminist Economics.* Vol. 6:2–3, pp. 3–12.

Albelda R. (1997) *Economics and Feminism: Disturbances in the Field.* New York: Twayne Publishers.

Alessandrini D. (2013) "A Social Provisioning Employer of Last Resort: Post-Keynesianism Meets Feminist Economics". *World Review of Political Economy.* Vol. 4:2, pp. 230–254.

Anderson E. (2003) "Sen, Ethics, and Democracy". *Feminist Economics.* Vol. 9:2–3, pp. 239–261.

Austen S. (2017) "Feminist Economics for Smart Behavioral Economics". Altman M. (Ed.) *Handbook of Behavioral Economics and Smart Decision-Making.* Cheltenham: Edward Elgar, pp. 173–187.

Austen S. and Mavisakalyan A. (2016) "Constitutions and the Political Agency of Women: A Cross-Country Study". *Feminist Economics.* Vol. 22:1, pp. 183–210.

Badgett M. (1995) "The Last of the Modernists?". *Feminist Economics.* Vol. 1:2, pp. 63–65.

Barker D. (1995) "Economists, Social Reformers, and Prophets: A Feminist Critique of Economic Efficiency". *Feminist Economics.* Vol. 1:3, pp. 26–39.

Barker D. (2003) "Emancipatory for Whom? A Comment on Critical Realism". *Feminist Economics.* Vol. 9:1, pp. 103–108.

Barker D. (2005) "Beyond Women and Economics: Reading 'Women's Work'". *Signs: Journal of Women in Culture and Society.* Vol. 30:4, pp. 2189–2209.

Barker D. and Feiner S. (2004) *Liberating Economics: Feminist Perspectives on Families, Work and Globalization.* Ann Arbor, MI: The University of Michigan Press.

Barker D. and Kuiper E. (2003) *Toward a Feminist Philosophy of Economics.* London: Routledge.

Barker D. and Schumm D. (2009) "Feminism". Pell J. and Van Staveren I. (Eds.) *Handbook of Economics and Ethics.* Cheltenham: Edward Elgar, pp. 159–165.

Barlett R. (1999) "Committee on the Status of Women in the Economics Profession (CSWEP)". Peterson J. and Lewis M. (Eds.) *The Elgar Companion to Feminist Economics.* Cheltenham: Edward Elgar, pp. 64–70.

Barlett R. and Feiner S. (1992) "Balancing the Economics Curriculum: Content, Method, and Pedagogy". *American Economic Review.* Vol. 82:2, pp. 559–564.

Barten A.P. (1964) "Family Composition, Prices and Expenditure Patterns". Hart P., Mills G., and Whitacker J. (Eds.) *Econometric Analysis for National Economic Planning: 16th Symposium of the Colston Society*. London: Butterworth, pp. 277–292.

Baumgardner J. and Richards A. (2000) *Manifesta: Young Women, Feminism, and the Future*. New York: Farrar, Straus and Giroux.

Beard M. (1946) *Woman as Force in History*. New York: MacMillan.

Beauvoir (de) S. (1949) *Le Deuxième Sex*. Paris: Gallimard.

Becchio G. (2015) "A Note on the History of Gender Economics and Feminist Economics: Not the Same Story". Moore S. (Ed.) *Global Perspectives in Contemporary Gender Economics*. Hershey, PA: IGI Global, pp. 28–38.

Becchio G. (2018) "Gender, Feminist, and Heterodox Economics: Interconnections and Differences in a Historical Perspective". *Economic Alternatives*. Vol. 12:1, pp. 5–24.

Becchio G. (2019) "Behavioral Economics, Gender Economics, and Feminist Economics: Friends or Foes?". *Journal of Economic Methodology*. Vol. 26:3, pp. 259–271.

Becchio G. and Leghissa G. (2017) *The Origins of Neoliberalism: Insights from Economics and Philosophy*. London: Routledge.

Bell C. (1998) "The Reasons for CSWEP". *Journal of Economic Perspectives*. Vol. 12:4, pp. 191–195.

Bell et al. (1973) "Findings of the American Economic Association Committee on the Status of Women in the Economics Profession". *The American Economic Review*. Vol. 63:5, pp. 1049–1061.

Beneria L. (1982) "Accounting for Women's Work". Beneria L. (Ed.) *Women and Development: The Sexual Division of Labor in Rural Societies*. New York: Praeger, pp. 119–147.

Beneria L. (1995) "Toward a Greater Integration of Gender in Economics". *World Development*. Vol. 23:11, pp. 1839–1850.

Beneria L. (1999) "Globalization, Gender and the Davos Man". *Feminist Economics*. Vol. 5:3, pp. 61–83.

Beneria L. (2003) "Economic Rationality and Globalization: A Feminist Perspective". Ferber M. and Nelson J. (Eds.) *Feminist Economics Today: Beyond Economic Man*. Chicago: The University of Chicago Press, pp. 115–133.

Beneria L., Floro M., Grown C., and MacDonald M. (2000) "Introduction: Globalization and Gender". *Feminist Economics*. Vol. 6:3, pp. vii–xviii.

Bergmann B. (1974) "Occupational Segregation, Wages, and Profits When Employers Discriminate by Race and Sex". *Eastern Economic Journal*. Vol. 1:2/3, pp. 103–110.

Bergmann B. (1986) *The Economic Emergence of Women*. New York: Basic Books.

Bergmann B. (1987) "'Measurement' or Finding Things out in Economics". *Journal of Economic Education*. Vol. 18:2, pp. 191–201.

Bergmann B. (1990) "Feminism and Economics". *Women's Studies Quarterly*. Vol. 18:3/4, pp. 68–74.

Bergmann B. (1995) "Becker's Theory of the Family: Preposterous Conclusions". *Feminist Economics*. Vol. 1:1, pp. 141–150.

Bergmann B. and Adelman I. (1983) "The Economic Report of the President's Council of Economic Advisors: The Economic Role of Women". *American Economic Review*. Vol. 73:4, pp. 509–514.

Bergmann B. and Lyle R. (1971) "Occupational Standing of Negroes by Areas and Industries". *Journal of Human Resources*. Vol. 6:4, pp. 411–433.

Blanchard O. (2017) *The Economics Job Market Rumors Site Needs to Clean Up Its Act*. As retrieved on September 25, 2018 at: https://piie.com/blogs/realtime-economic-issues-watch/economics-job-market-rumors-site-needs-clean-its-act.

Blau F. (2013) *Female Labour Supply: Why Is the US falling Behind?* Cambridge, MA: NBER Working Paper Series. As retrieved on June 12, 2019 at: www.nber.org/papers/w18702.pdf

Blau F. (2013) *Female Labour Supply: Why Is the US Falling Behind?* Cambridge, MA: NBER Working Paper Series. As retrieved on June 12, 2019 at: www.nber.org/papers/w18702.pdf

Blau F. and Ferber M. (1986) *The Economics of Women, Men, and Work*. 1st Edition. Upper Saddle River, NJ: Prentice Hall.

Blau F., Ferber M., and Winkler A. (2010) *The Economics of Women, Men, and Work*. 6th Edition. Upper Saddle River, NJ: Prentice Hall and Pearson.

Bodkin R. (1999) "Women's Agency in Classical Economic Thought: Adam Smith, Harriet Taylor Smith, and J. S. Mill". *Feminist Economics*. Vol. 5:1, pp. 45–60.

Bordo S. (1987) *The Flight to Objectivity: Essays on Cartesianism and Culture*. Albany, NY: Albany State University of New York Press.

Boserup E. (1970) *Woman's Role in Economic Development*. London: George Allen & Unwin.

Boxer M. (1988) "For and About Women: The Theory and Practice of Women's Studies in the United States". Minnich E., O'Barr J., and Rosenfeld R. (Eds.) *Reconstructing the Academy: Women's Education and Women's Studies*. Chicago: The University of Chicago Press, pp. 69–103.

Boxer M. (2002) "Women's Studies as Women's History". *Women's Studies Quarterly*. Vol. 30:3/4, pp. 42–51.

Braunstein E. (2008) "The Feminist Political Economy of the Rent-Seeking Society: An Investigation of Gender Inequality and Economic Growth". *Journal of Economic Issues*. Vol. 42:4, pp. 959–979.

Braunstein E. and Folbre N. (2001) "To Honor and Obey: Efficiency, Inequality and Patriarchal Property Rights". *Feminist Economics*. Vol. 7:1, pp. 25–44.

Buhle M.J. (2000) "Introduction". Howe F. (Ed.) *The Politics of Women's Studies: Testimony from 30 Founding Mothers*. New York: The Feminist Press at The City University of New York, pp. xv–xxvi.

Burggraf S. (1998) *The Feminine Economy and Economic Man: Reviving the Role of Family in the Postindustrial Age*. New York: Perseus Books Group.

Butler J. (1990) *Gender Trouble: Feminism and the Subversion of Identity*. New York and London: Routledge.

Butler J. (1993) *Bodies That Matter: On the Discursive Limits of 'Sex'*. New York and London: Routledge.

Cass B. et al. (Eds.) (1983) *Why So Few? Women Academics in Australian Universities*. Sydney: Sydney University Press.

Charusheela S. (2010) "Gender and the Stability of Consumption: A Feminist Contribution to Post-Keynesian Economics". *Cambridge Journal of Economics*. Vol. 34:6, pp. 1145–1156.

Cherrier B. (2017a) *'The American Economic Association Declares that Economics Is Not a Man's Field': The Missing Story*. As retrieved on September 25, 2018 at: https://beatricecherrier. wordpress.com/2017/03/31/the-american-economic-association-declares-that-eco nomics-is-not-a-mans-field-the-missing-story-of-women-economists/

Cherrier B. (2017b) "Classifying Economics: A History of JEL Codes". *Journal of Economic Literature*. Vol. 55:2, pp. 545–579.

Chesler P. (2018) *A Politically Incorrect Feminist: Creating a Movement with Bitches, Lunatics, Dykes, Prodigies, Warriors, and Wonder*. New York: St. Martin's Press.

Christensen K. (1998) "Economics Without Money; Sex Without Gender: A Critique of Philipson and Posner's '*Private Choices and Public Health: The AIDS Epidemic in an Economic Perspective*'". *Feminist Economics*. Vol. 4:2, pp. 1–24.

Chubb J.E. and Moe T.M. (1988) "Politics, Markets, and the Organization of Schools". *American Political Science Review*. Vol. 82:4, pp. 1065–1087.

Coase R. (1960) "The Problem of Social Costs". *The Journal of Law and Economics*. Vol. 3:2, pp. 1–44.

Code L. (1981) "Is the Sex of the Knower Epistemologically Significant?". *Metaphilosophy*. Vol. 12:3/4, pp. 267–276.

Colander D. and Woos J. (1997) "Institutional Demand-Side Discrimination Against Woman and the Human Capital Model". *Feminist Economics*. Vol. 3:1, pp. 53–64.

Conrad C. and Doss C. (2008) "The AIDS Epidemic: Challenges for Feminist Economics". *Feminist Economics*. Vol. 14:4, pp. 1–18.

Crenshaw K. (1989) "Demarginalizing the Intersection of Race and Sex: A Black Feminist Critique of Anti-Discrimination Doctrine, Feminist Theory and Antiracist Politics". *University of Chicago Legal Forum*. Vol. 1989:1, pp. 139–167.

Crouch B. (2012) "Finding a Voice in the Academy: The History of Women's Studies in Higher Education". *The Vermont Collection*. Vol. 33, article 3.

Danby C. (2004) "Toward a Gendered Post Keynesianism: Subjectivity and Time in a Nonmodernist Framework". *Feminist Economics*. Vol. 10:3, pp. 55–75.

Dawson M. (1965) *Graduate and Married*. Sydney: Sydney University Press.

Dewan R. (1995) "Gender in Neoclassical Economics: Conceptual Overview". *Economic and Political Weekly*. Vol. 30:17, pp. WS46–WS48.

Duggan L. (1995) "Restacking the Deck: Family Policy and Women's Fall-back Position in Germany Before and After Unification". *Feminist Economics*. Vol. 1:1, pp. 175–194.

Duncan S. and Edwards R. (1997) "Lone Mothers and Paid Work – Rational Economic Man or Gendered Moral Rationalities?". *Feminist Economics*. Vol. 3:2, pp. 29–61.

Dymski G. and Nembhard J. (2002) "Rhonda M. Williams: Competition, Race, Agency, and Community". *The Review of Black Political Economy*. Vol. 29:4, pp. 25–42.

Eastwood M. (1972) "Fighting Job Discrimination: Three Federal Approaches". *Feminist Studies*. Vol. 1:1, pp. 75–103.

Eichler M. (2014) *Women's Studies*. As retrieved on September 22, 2018 at: www.thecana dianencyclopedia.ca/en/article/womens-studies.

Eisenstein Z. (1979) *Capitalist Patriarchy and the Case for Socialist Feminism*. New York: Monthly Review Press.

Elchos A. (1990) *Daring to Be Bad: Radical Feminism in America, 1967–75*. Minneapolis, MN: University of Minnesota Press.

Engels F. ([1884] 1992) *The Origin of the Family, Private Property, and the State*. Chicago: Charles H. Kerr & Co.

England P. (1992) *Comparable Worth: Theories and Evidence*. New York: Aldine de Gruyter.

England P. (1993) "The Separative Self: Androcentric Bias in Neoclassical Assumptions". Ferber M. and Nelson J. (Eds.) *Beyond Economic Man: Feminist Theory and Economics*. Chicago: The University of Chicago Press, pp. 37–53.

England P. (2003) "Separative and Soluble Selves: Dichotomous Thinking in Economics". Ferber M. and Nelson J. (Eds.) *Feminist Economics Today: Beyond Economic Man*. Chicago: The University of Chicago Press, pp. 33–57.

England P. and Farkas G. (1986) *Households, Employment, and Gender: A Social, Economic, and Demographic View*. New York: Aldine Publishing Co.

England P. and Folbre N. (2003) "Contracting for Care". Ferber M. and Nelson J. (Eds.) *Feminist Economics Today: Beyond Economic Man*. Chicago: The University of Chicago Press, pp. 61–79.

England P., Farkas G., Kilbourne B., and Dou T. (1988) "Explaining Occupational Sex Segregation and Wages: Findings From a Model With Fixed Effects". *American Sociological Review*. Vol. 53:4, pp. 544–558.

Fukuda-Parr S. (2003) "The Human Development Paradigm: Operationalizing Sen's Ideas on Capabilities". *Feminist Economics*. Vol. 6:2–3, pp. 301–317.

Fukuda-Parr S., Heintz J., and Seguino S. (2013) "Critical Perspectives on Financial and Economic Crises: Heterodox Macroeconomics Meets Feminist Economics". *Feminist Economics*. Vol. 19:3, pp. 4–31.

Fausto-Sterling A. (1985) *Myths of the Gender*. New York: Basic Book.

Feiner S. (1990) "Hidden by the Invisible Hand: Neoclassical Economic Theory and the Textbook Treatment of Race and Gender". *Gender & Society*. Vol. 4:2, pp. 159–181.

Feiner S. (1995) "Reading Neoclassical Economics. Toward an Erotic Economy of Sharing". Kuiper E. and Sap J. (Eds.) *Out of the Margin: Feminist Perspectives on Economics*. London: Routledge, pp. 151–166.

Ferber M. (1987) *Women and Work, Paid and Unpaid: An Annotated Bibliography*. Shrewsbury, MA: Garland Publishing.

Ferber M. (1995) "The Study of Economics: A Feminist Critique". *The American Economic Review. Papers and Proceedings of the 107th Annual Meeting of the American Economic Association*. Vol. 85:2, pp. 357–361.

Ferber M. (1999) "Guidelines for Pre-College Economics Education: A Critique". *Feminist Economics*. Vol. 5:3, pp. 135–142.

Ferber M. and Nelson J. (Eds.) (1993) *Beyond Economic Man: Feminist Theory and Economics*. Chicago: The University of Chicago Press.

Ferber M. and Nelson J. (Eds.) (2003a) *Feminist Economics Today: Beyond Economic Man*. Chicago: The University of Chicago Press.

Ferber M. and Nelson J. (2003b) "Introduction: Beyond Economic Man, Ten Years Later". Ferber M. and Nelson J. (Eds.) *Feminist Economics Today: Beyond Economic Man*. Chicago: The University of Chicago Press, pp. 1–31.

Ferber M. and O'Farrell B. (1991) *Work and Family: Policies for a Changing Work Force*. Washington, DC: National Academy Press.

Ferguson M. (1994) *Feminism and Postmodernism*. Durham, NC: Duke University Press.

Figart D. (2001) "In Pursuit of Racial Equality: The Political Economy of Rhonda M. Williams". *The Review of Black Political Economy*. Vol. 28:4, pp. 13–29.

Figart D. and Mutari E. (1999) "Feminist Political Economy: Paradigms". O'Hara P.A. (Ed.) *Encyclopedia of Political Economy*. Vol. 1. London: Routledge, pp. 335–337.

Fine B. (2000) "Economics Imperialism and Intellectual Progress: The Present as History of Economic Thought". *History of Economics Review*. Vol. 32:2, pp. 10–35.

Folbre N. (1986) "Cleaning House: New Perspectives on Households and Economic Development". *Journal of Development Economics*. Vol. 22:1, pp. 5–40.

Folbre N. (1993a) "How Does She Know? Feminist Theories of Gender Bias in Economics". *History of Political Economy*. Vol. 25:1, pp. 167–184.

Folbre N. (1993b) "Micro, Macro, Choice, and Structure". England P. (Ed.) *Theory on Gender: Feminism on Theory*. New York: Aldine de Gruyter, pp. 323–31

Folbre N. (1994a) "Children as Public Goods". *American Economic Association Papers and Proceedings*. Vol. 84:2, pp. 86–90.

Folbre N. (1994b) *Who Pays for the Kids? Gender and the Structure of Constraint*. London: Routledge.

Folbre N. (1995) "Holding Hands at Midnight: The Paradox of Caring Labor". *Feminist Economics*. Vol. 1:1, pp. 73–92.

Folbre N. (2001) *The Invisible Heart: Economics and Family Values*. New York: New Press.

Folbre N. (2008) *Valuing Children Rethinking the Economics of the Family*. Cambridge, MA: Harvard University Press.

Folbre N. (2009) *Greed, Lust, and Gender: A History of Economic Ideas*. Oxford: Oxford University Press.

Folbre N. and Himmelweit S. (2000) "Introduction: Children and Family Policy: A Feminist Issue". *Feminist Economics*. Vol. 6:1, pp. 1–3.

Folbre N. and Nelson J. (2000) "For Love or Money – Or Both?". *The Journal of Economic Perspectives*. Vol. 14:4, pp. 123–140.

Folbre N., Shaw L., and Stark A. (2005) "Introduction: Gender and Aging". *Feminist Economics*. Vol. 11:2, pp. 3–5.

Forget E. (1997) "The Market for Virtue: Jean Baptiste Say on Women in the Economy and Society". *Feminist Economics*. Vol. 3:1, pp. 95–111.

Forget E. (2001) "Saint-Simonian Feminism". *Feminist Economics*. Vol. 7:1, pp. 79–96.

Forget E. (2011) "American Women and the Economics Profession in the Twentieth Century". *Oeconomica*. Vol. 1:1, pp. 19–30.

Fraser N. (2009) "Feminism, Capitalism, and the Cunning of History". *New Left Review*. Vol. 56:56, pp. 97–117.

Friedan B. (1963) *The Feminine Mystique*. New York: W.W. Norton and Co.

Friedman M[arilyn]. (2000) "Feminism in Ethics: Concept of Autonomy". Fricker M. and Hornsby J. (Eds.) *The Cambridge Companion to Feminism in Philosophy*. Cambridge: Cambridge University Press, pp. 205–224.

Friedman M[ilton]. (1953) *Essays in Positive Economics*. Chicago: The University of Chicago Press.

Fuller C. (1996) "Elements of a Post Keynesian Alternative to Household Production". *Journal of Post Keynesian Economics*. Vol. 28:2, pp. 595–607.

Funk N. (2013) "Contra Fraser on Feminism and Neoliberalism". *Hypatia*. Vol. 28:1, pp. 179–196.

Galindo M. and Ribero D. (Eds.) (2012) *Women's Entrepreneurship and Economics: New Perspectives, Practices and Politics*. Dordrecht, Heidelberg, London, and New York: Springer.

Gammage S., Kabeer N., and Meulen Rodger Y. (2016) "Voice and Agency: Where Are We Now?". *Feminist Economics*. Vol. 22:1, pp. 1–29.

Garnett R. (2015) "Beyond Chalk and Talk: A Feminist-Austrian Dialogue". *International Journal of Pluralism and Economics Education*. Vol. 6:2, pp. 151–164.

Gasper D. (2007) "Dialogue. Adding Links Adding Persons, and Adding Structures: Using Sens' Frameworks". *Feminist Economics*. Vol. 13:1, pp. 67–85.

Gasper D. and Van Staveren I. (2003) "Development as Freedom v-v and as What Else?". *Feminist Economics*. Vol. 9:2–3, pp. 137–161.

Gelbach S. (2006) "A Formal Model of Exit and Voice". *Rationality and Society*. Vol. 18:4, pp. 395–418.

Gershuny J., Bittman M., and Brice J. (2005) "Exit, Voice, and Suffering: Do Couples Adapt to Changing Employment Patterns?". *Journal of Marriage and Family*. Vol. 67:3, pp. 656–665.

Giddens A. (1984) *The Constitution of Society: Outline of the Theory of Structuration*. Cambridge, MA: Polity Press.

Goetz A.M. and Jenkins R. (2016) "Agency and Accountability: Promoting Women's Participation in Peacebuilding". *Feminist Economics*. Vol. 22:1, pp. 211–236.

Gordon L., Kerber L., and Kessler-Harris A. (2013) "Gerda Lerner (1920–2013). Pioneering Historian and Feminist". *Clio*. Vol. 38:2, pp. 258–259.

Grapard U. (1995) "Robinson Crusoe: The Quintessential Economic Man?". *Feminist Economics*. Vol. 1:1, pp. 32–52.

Grapard U. (1999) "Methodology". Peterson J. and Lewis M. (Eds.) *The Elgar Companion to Feminist Economics*. Cheltenham: Edward Elgar, pp. 544–555.

Grasswick H. (Ed.) (2011) *Feminist Epistemology and Philosophy of Science: Power in Knowledge*. Dordrecht, Heidelberg, London, and New York: Springer.

Grossbard S. (1995) "Do Not Sell Marriage Short: Reply to Strober". *Feminist Economics*. Vol. 1:1, pp. 207–214.

Haack S. (1996) "Science as Social? Yes and No". Nelson L. and Nelson J. (Eds.) *Feminism, Science, and Philosophy of Science*. Dordrecht: Kluwer Academic Publishers, pp. 79–94.

Hammond M. (2016) "Contrast Effects in Social Evolution and Schumpeter's Creative Destruction". Turner J., Machalek R., and Maryansi A. (Eds.) *Handbook of Evolution and Society: Toward an Evolutionary Social Science*. London and New York: Routledge, pp. 609–628.

Hanmer L. and Klugman J. (2016) "Exploring Women's Agency and Empowerment in Developing Countries: Where Do We Stand?". *Feminist Economics*. Vol. 22:1, pp. 237–263.

Harding S. (1982) "Is Gender a Variable in Conceptions of Rationality? A Survey of Issues". *Dialectica*. Vol. 36:2–3, pp. 215–232.

Harding S. (1986) *The Feminist Science Question*. Ithaca, NY: Cornell University Press.

Harding S. (1987) "Introduction: Is There a Feminist Method?". Harding S. (Ed.) *Feminism and Methodology*. Bloomington, IN: Indiana University Press, pp. 1–14.

Harding S. (1995) "Can Feminist Thought Make Economics More Objective?". *Feminist Economics*. Vol. 1:1, pp. 7–32.

Harding S. (1999) "The Case for Strategic Realism: A Response to Lawson". *Feminist Economics*. Vol. 5:3, pp. 127–133.

Harding S. (2003) "Representing Reality: The Critical Realism Project". *Feminist Economics*. Vol. 9:1, pp. 151–159.

Harding S. (2004) "Rethinking Standpoint Epistemology: What is 'Strong Objectivity?'". Harding S. (Ed.) *The Feminist Standpoint Reader*. London: Routledge, pp. 127–140.

Harding S. and Hintikka M. (Eds.) (1983) *Discovering Reality Feminist Perspectives on Epistemology, Metaphysics, Methodology, and Philosophy of Science*. Dordrecht, Heidelberg, London, and New York: Springer.

Hartmann H. (1981) "The Unhappy Marriage of Marxism and Feminism". Sargent L. (Ed.) *Women and Revolution: A Discussion on the Unhappy Marriage of Marxism and Feminism*. Boston: South End Press, pp. 1–41.

Hawk T. (2011) "An Ethic of Care: A Relational Ethic for the Relational Characteristics of Organizations". Hamington M. and Sander-Staudt M. (Eds.) *Applying Care Ethics to Business*. Dordrecht, Heidelberg, London, and New York: Springer, pp. 3–34.

Hayek F. (1948) *Individualism and Economic Order*. London: Routledge.

Hill M. (2003) "Development as Empowerment". *Feminist Economics*. Vol. 9:2/3, pp. 117–135.

Hill M. and King E. (1995) "Women's Education and Economic Well-Being". *Feminist Economics*. Vol. 1:2, pp. 21–46.

Himmelweit S., Bergmann B., Green K., Albelda R., and Koren C. (2004) "Dialogue. Lone Mothers: What Is to Be Done?". *Feminist Economics*. Vol. 10:2, pp. 237–264.

Hirschman A. (1970) *Exit, Voice, and Loyalty: Responses to Decline in Firms, Organizations, and States*. Cambridge, MA: Harvard University Press.

Hopkins B. and Duggan L. (2011) "A Feminist Comparative Economic Systems". *Feminist Economics*. Vol. 17:3, pp. 35–69.

Hoppe H. (2002) *Feministische Ökonomik*. Berlin: Sigma.

Horodecka A. (2015) "The Concept of Human Nature as Driving Force for Changes in Economics Exemplified by Feminist and Neoclassical Economics". *Ekonomia.* Vol. 401, pp. 155–165.

Horwitz S. (1995) "Feminist Economics: An Austrian Perspective". *Journal of Economic Perspective.* Vol. 9:2, pp. 259–279.

Howe F. (1987) *Myths of Coeducation: Selected Essays, 1964–1983.* Bloomington, IN: Indiana University Press.

Iversen V. (2003) "Intra-Household Inequality: A Challenge for the Capability Approach?". *Feminist Economics.* Vol. 6:2–3, pp. 93–115.

Jaggar A.M. (2002) "Challenging Women's Global Inequalities: Some Priorities for Western Philosophers". Philosophical Topics. *Vol.* 30:2, pp. 229–252.

JEL. (1991) "Classification System: Old and New Categories". *Journal of Economic Literature.* Vol. 29:1, pp. xviii–xxviii.

Jennings A. (1994) "Toward a Feminist Expansion of Macroeconomics: Money Matters". *Journal of Economic Issues.* Vol. 28:2, pp. 555–565.

Jones K. (2004) "Gender and Rationality". Mele A. and Rawling P. (Eds.) *The Handbook of Rationality.* Oxford: Oxford University Press, pp. 301–319.

Ju A. (2009) *Women's Studies at Cornell Evolves Over a 40 Year History to Include Sexual Minorities.* As retrieved on September 24, 2018 at: http://news.cornell.edu/stories/2009/11/cornell-looks-back-40-years-womens-studies.

Kabeer N. (1999) "Resources, Agency, Achievements: Reflections on the Measurement of Women's Empowerment". *Development and Change.* Vol. 30:3, pp. 435–464.

Kabeer N. (2008) *Mainstreaming Gender in Social Protection for the Informal Economy.* London: Commonwealth Secretariat.

Kabeer N. (2016) "Gender Equality, Economic Growth, and Women's Agency: 'The Endless Variety' and 'Monotonous Similarity' of Patriarchal Constraints". *Feminist Economics.* Vol. 22:1, pp. 295–321.

Kabeer N. and Natali L. (2013) "Gender Equality and Economic Growth: Is There a Win-Win?". *IDS Working Paper* 417, pp. 1–58.

Kaplan G. (2003) "Ardent Warrior for Women's Rights". *The Sydney Morning Herald.* July 31.

Katz E. (1997) "The Intra-Household Economics of Voice and Exit". *Feminist Economics.* Vol. 3:3, pp. 25–46.

Keller E. (1985) *Reflections on Gender and Science.* New Haven, CT: Yale University Press.

Kennedy E. (2008) "Socialist Feminism: What Difference Did It Make to the History of Women's Studies". *Feminist Studies.* Vol. 34:3, pp. 497–525.

King M. and Saunders L. (1999) "An Interview with Marianne Ferber: Founding Feminist Economics". *Review of Political Economy.* Vol. 11:1, pp. 83–98.

Klasen S. and Wink C. (2003) "'Missing Women': Revisiting the Debate". *Feminist Economics.* Vol. 9:2–3, pp. 263–299.

Koggel C. (2003) "Globalization and Women's Paid Work: Expanding Freedom?". *Feminist Economics.* Vol. 9:2–3, pp. 163–184.

Kosnik L.R. (2018) "A Survey of JEL Codes: What Do They Mean and Are they Used Consistently?". *Journal of Economic Surveys.* Vol. 32:1, pp. 249–272.

Krueger A. (1974) "The Political Economy of the Rent-Seeking Society". *American Economic Review.* Vol. 64:3, pp. 291–303.

Kuiper E. and Sap J. (Eds.) (1995) *Out of the Margin: Feminist Perspectives on Economics.* London and New York: Routledge.

Laezar E. (2000) "Economic Imperialism". *Quarterly Journal of Economics.* Vol. 115:1, pp. 99–146.

Lamos C. (1995) "Open Questions". *Feminist Economics*. Vol. 1:2, pp. 59–62.

Lavoie M. (1992) "A Post-Keynesian Approach to Consumer Choice". *Journal of Post Keynesian Economics*. Vol. 16:4, pp. 539–562.

Lawson T. (1999) "Feminism, Realism, and Universalism". *Feminist Economics*. Vol. 5:2, pp. 25–59.

Lawson T. (2003a) "Ontology and Feminist Theorizing". *Feminist Economics*. Vol. 9:1, pp. 119–150.

Lawson T. (2003b) "Theorizing Ontology". *Feminist Economics*. Vol. 9:1, pp. 161–169.

Lerner G. (1972) (Ed.) *Black Women in White America: A Documentary History*. New York: Pantheon.

Lerner G. (1979) *The Majority Finds Its Past*. New York: Oxford University Press.

Lerner G. (1987) *The Creation of Patriarchy*. New York: Oxford University Press.

Lerner G. (1994) *Creation of Feminist Consciousness*. New York: Oxford University Press.

Levin L. (1995) 'Toward a Feminist, Post-Keynesian Theory of Investment'. Kuiper E. and Sap J. (Eds.) *Out of the Margin: Feminist Perspective on Economics*. New York: Routledge, pp. 100–119.

Lewis M. and McGoldrick K. (2001) "Moving Beyond the Masculine Neoclassical Classroom". *Feminist Economics*. Vol. 7:2, pp. 91–103.

Lloyd G. (1984) *The Man of Reason: "Male" and "Female" in Western Philosophy*. Minneapolis, MN: University of Minnesota Press.

Longino H. (1987) "Can There Be a Feminist Science?". *Hypatia: A Journal of Feminist Philosophy*. Vol. 2:3, pp. 51–64.

Longino H. (1990) *Science as Social Knowledge: Values and Objectivity in Scientific Inquiry*. Princeton, NJ: Princeton University Press.

Longino H. (2002) *The Fate of Knowledge*. Princeton, NJ: Princeton University Press.

Love B. and Cott N. (Ed.) (2006) *Women who Changed America: 1963–1975*. Urbana and Chicago: University of Illinois Press.

Lundberg S. (2018) "The 2017 Report on the Status of Women in the Economics Profession". *Reports from the American Economic Association's Committee on the Status of Women in the Economics Profession*. Vol. 46:1, pp. 1–16.

MacKinnon C. (1987) *Feminism Unmodified*. Cambridge, MA: Harvard University Press.

Matthaei J. (1992) "Marxist-Feminist Contributions to Radical Economics". Roberts B. and Feiner S. (Eds.) *Radical Economics*. Norwell, MA: Kluwer-Njhoff, pp. 117–144.

Matthaei J. (1996) "Why Feminist, Marxist, and Anti-Racist Economists Should Be Feminist-Marxist-Anti-Racist Economists". *Feminist Economics*. Vol. 2:1, pp. 22–42.

McCloskey D. (1993) "Some Consequences of a Conjunctive Economics". Ferber M. and Nelson J. (Eds.) *Beyond Economic Man: Feminist Theory and Economics*. Chicago: The University of Chicago Press, pp. 69–93.

McCloskey D. (1995) "The Discrete Charm of Bourgeoisie". *Feminist Economics*. Vol. 1:3, pp. 119–124.

McCrate E. (1988) "Gender Difference: The Role of Endogenous Preferences and Collective Action". *American Economic Review*. Vol. 78:2, pp. 235–239.

McFadden M. (2018) "Women's Studies". *New Dictionary of the History of Ideas*. As retrieved on September 16, 2018 at: www.encyclopedia.com.

Mead M. (1935) *Sex and Temperament in Three Primitive Societies*. New York: William Morrow and Co.

Mead M. (1949) *Male and Female: A Study of the Sexes in a Changing World*. New York: William Morrow and Co.

Meagher M. (1997) "Recreating Domestic Service: Institutional Cultures and the Evolution of Paid Household Work". *Feminist Economics*. Vol. 3:2, pp. 1–27.

Miller J. and Meulen Rodgers Y. (2008) "Economic Importance and Statistical Significance: Guidelines for Communicating Empirical Research". *Feminist Economics*. Vol. 14:2, pp. 117–149.

Millett K. (1970) *Sexual Politics*. New York: Doubleday and Co.

Mitchell J. (1971) *Woman's Estate*. London: Penguin.

Mohsen B., Galindo M., and Mendez M.T. (2012) "Women's Entrepreneurship and Economic Policies". Galindo M. and Ribero D. (Eds.) *Women's Entrepreneurship and Economics: New Perspectives, Practices and Politics*. Dordrecht, Heidelberg, London, and New York: Springer, pp. 23–34.

Moller Okin S. (1979) *Women in Western Political Thought*. Princeton, NJ: Princeton University Press.

Moller Okin S. (1989) *Justice, Gender, and the Family*. New York: Basic Books.

Nelson J. (1992) "Gender, Metaphor, and the Definition of Economics". *Economics and Philosophy*. Vol. 8:1, pp. 103–125.

Nelson J. (1993a) "Value-free or Valueless? Notes on the Pursuit of Detachment". *History of Political Economy*. Vol. 25:1, pp. 121–145.

Nelson J. (1993b) "Gender and Economic Ideologies". *Review of Social Economy*. Vol. 51:3, pp. 287–301.

Nelson J. (1993c) "The Study of Choice or the Study of Provisioning? Gender and the Definition of Economics". Ferber M. and Nelson J. (Eds.) *Beyond Economic Man: Feminist Theory and Economics*. Chicago: Chicago University Press, pp. 23–36.

Nelson J. (1995) "Feminism and Economics". *Journal of Economic Perspectives*. Vol. 9:2, pp. 131–148.

Nelson J. (1996) *Feminism, Objectivity and Economics*. London: Routledge.

Nelson J. (2003) "Once More, With Feeling: Feminist Economics and the Ontological Question". *Feminist Economics*. Vol. 9:1, pp. 109–118.

Nelson J. (2004) "Clock, Creation and Clarity: Insights on Ethics and Economics from a Feminist Perspective". *Ethical Theory and Moral Practice*. Vol. 7:4, pp. 381–398.

Nelson J. (2005) "Interpersonal Relations and Economics". Gui B. and Sugden R. (Eds.) *Economics and Social Interactions*. Cambridge: Cambridge University Press, pp. 250–261.

Nelson J. (2006) *Economics for Humans*. Chicago: The University of Chicago Press.

Nelson J. (2009) "Rationality and Humanity: A View from Feminist Economics". *Occasion: Interdisciplinary Studies in the Humanities*. Vol. 1:1, pp. 1–19.

Nelson J. (2011) "Care Ethics and Markets: A View from Feminist Economics". Hamington M. and Sander-Staudt M. (Eds.) *Applying Care Ethics to Business*. Dordrecht, Heidelberg, London, and New York: Springer, pp. 35–53.

Nelson J. (2014) "The Power of Stereotyping and Confirmation Bias to Overwhelm Accurate Assessment: The Case of Economics, Gender, and Risk Aversion". *Journal of Economic Methodology*. Vol. 1:3, pp. 211–231.

Nelson J. (2016) "Not-So-Strong Evidence for Gender Differences in Risk Taking". *Feminist Economics*. Vol. 22:2, pp. 114–142.

Nelson J. (2019) *A Caution About Sent and Van Staveren's Feminist Review*. As retrieved on April 1, 2019 at: https://julieanelson.com/2019/03/28/a-caution-about-sent-and-van-staverns-feminist-review/.

Nussbaum M. (1997) *Cultivating Humanity: A Classical Defense of Reform in Liberal Education*. Cambridge, MA: Harvard University Press.

Nussbaum M. (2000) *Women and Human Development: The Capabilities Approach*. Cambridge and New York: Cambridge University Press.

Nussbaum M. (2003) "Capabilities as Fundamental Entitlements: Sen and Social Justice". *Feminist Economics*. Vol. 6:2–3, pp. 33–59.

Nussbaum M. (2013) *Creating Capabilities: The Human Development Approach*. Cambridge, MA: The Belknap Press of Harvard University Press.

Oliver P. (1991) "What Do Girls Know Anyway?; Rationality, Gender, and Social Control". *Feminism & Psychology*. Vol. 1:3, pp. 339–360.

Olson P. (2007) "On the Contributions of Barbara Bergmann to Economics". *Review of Political Economy*. Vol. 19:4, pp. 475–496.

Pearse R. and Connell R. (2016) "Gender Norms and the Economy: Insights from Social Research". *Feminist Economics*. Vol. 22:1, pp. 30–53.

Peter F. (2003a) "Critical Realism, Feminist Epistemology, and the Emancipatory Potential of Science: A Comment on Lawson and Harding". *Feminist Economics*. Vol. 9:1, pp. 93–101.

Peter F. (2003b) "Gender and the Foundation of Social Choice: The Role of Situated Agency". *Feminist Economics*. Vol. 6:2–3, pp. 13–32.

Peterson J. and Lewis M. (1999) "Introduction". Peterson J. and Lewis M. (Eds.) *The Elgar Companion to Feminist Economics*. Cheltenham: Edward Elgar, pp. xv–xvii.

Phipps S. and Burton P. (1995) "Social/Institutional Variables and Behavior Within Households: An Empirical Test Using the Luxembourg Income Study". *Feminist Economics*. Vol. 1:1, pp. 151–174.

Polanyi K. (1944) *The Great Transformation. The Politicla and Economic Origin of Our Time*. New York: Rinehart.

Polanyi K. (1968) *Primitive, Archaic and Modern Economies: Essays of Karl Polanyi*. New York: Anchor Books.

Pollak R. (2003) "Gary Becker's Contributions to Family and Household Economics". *Review of Economics of the Household*. Vol. 1:1, pp. 111–141.

Pomeroy S. (1994) "The Contribution of Women to the Greek Domestic Economy". Stewart D. and Stanton A. (Eds.) *Feminism in the Academy*. Ann Arbor, MI: University of Michigan Press, pp. 180–195.

Power M. (2004) "Social Provisioning as a Starting Point for Feminist Economics". *Feminist Economics*. Vol. 10:3, pp. 3–19.

Pujol M. (1992) *Feminism and Anti-Feminism in Early Economic Thought*. Aldershot: Edward Elgar Publishing.

Qizilbash M. (2005) "Dialogue. Sen on Freedom and Gender Justice". *Feminist Economics*. Vol. 11:3, pp. 151–166.

Robbins L. (1927) "Mr. Hawtrey on the Scope of Economics". *Economica*. Vol. 7:20, pp. 172–178.

Robeyns I. (2003) "Sen's Capability Approach and Gender Inequality: Selecting Relevant Capabilities". *Feminist Economics*. Vol. 6:2–3, pp. 61–92.

Robeyns I. (2017) *Wellbeing, Freedom and Social Justice: The Capability Approach Re-Examined*. Cambridge: Open Book Publisher.

Rorty A. (1988) *Mind in Action: Essays in the Philosophy of Mind*. Boston: Beacon Press.

Rowbotham S. (1972) *Women, Resistance, and Revolution*. New York: Verso.

Samuelson P. (1947) *Foundations of Economic Analysis*. Cambridge, MA: Harvard University Press.

Saunders L. and King M. (2000) "An Interview With Barbara Bergmann: Leading Feminist Economics". *Review of Political Economy*. Vol. 12:3, pp. 305–316.

Schneider G. and Shackelford J. (2001) "Economics Standards and Lists: Proposed Antidotes for Feminist Economists". *Feminist Economics*. Vol. 7:2, pp. 77–89.

Schneir M. (1994) *Feminism in Our Time: The Essential Writings, World War II to the Present*. New York: Vintage Books.

Schönpflug K. (2008) *Feminism, Economics and Utopia: Time Travelling through Paradigms.* London: Routledge.

Scott J. (1988) *Gender and the Politics of History.* New York: Columbia University Press.

Seguino S. (2000) "Gender Inequality and Economic Growth: A Cross-Country Analysis". *World Development.* Vol. 28:7, pp. 1211–1230.

Seguino S., Stevens T., and Lutz M. (1996) "Gender and Cooperative Behavior: Economic Man Rides Alone". *Feminist Economics.* Vol. 2:1, pp. 1–21.

Seitz J. (1993) "Feminism and the History of Economic Thought". *History of Political Economy.* Vol. 25:1, pp. 185–201

Seitz J. (1995) "Epistemology and the Task of Feminist Economics". *Feminist Economics.* Vol. 1:3, pp. 110–118.

Sen A. (1987) "Gender and Cooperative Conflicts". *Working Paper 18*: World Institute for Development Economics Research (WIDER).

Sen A. (1989) *Hunger and Public Action.* Oxford: Clarendon Press.

Sen A. (1990a) "Development as Capability Expansion". Griffin K. and Knight J. (Eds.) *Human Development and the International Development Strategy for the 1990s.* London: Macmillan, pp. 41–158.

Sen A. (1990b) "Gender and Cooperative Conflicts". Tinker I. (Ed.) *Persistent Inequalities: Women and World Development.* Oxford: Oxford University Press, pp. 123–149.

Sen A. (1990c) "More Than 100 Million Women Are Missing". *The New York Review of Books.* December 20.

Sen A. (1992) "Missing Women". *British Medical Journal.* Vol. 304:6827, pp. 586–587.

Sen A. (1999) *Development as Freedom.* New York: Anchor Books.

Sen A. (2005) "Mary, Mary, Quite Contrary!". *Feminist Economics.* Vol. 11:1, pp. 1–9.

Sen A., Agarwal B., Humphries J., and Robeyns I. (2003) "Continuing the Conversation". *Feminist Economics.* Vol. 9:2–3, pp. 319–332.

Sent M. and Van Staveren I. (2019) "A Feminist Review of Behavioral Economics Research on Gender Differences". *Feminist Economics.* Vol. 25:2, pp. 1–35.

Shackelford J. (1992) "Feminist Pedagogy: A Means for Bringing Critical Thinking and Creativity to the Economics Classroom". *American Economic Review.* Vol. 82:2, pp. 570–576.

Shackelford J. (1999a) "International Association for Feminist Economics (IAFFE)". Peterson J. and Lewis M. (Eds.) *The Elgar Companion to Feminist Economics.* Cheltenham: Edward Elgar, pp. 486–489.

Shackelford J. (1999b) "International Association for Feminist Economics". O'Hara P. (Ed.) *Encyclopedia of Political Economy.* London: Routledge, pp. 561–562.

Slote M. (2007) *The Ethics of Care and Empathy.* London: Routledge.

Smith B. (2013) *Women's Studies: The Basics.* London: Routledge.

Solomon B. (1985) *In the Company of Educated Women: A History of Women and Higher Education in America.* New Haven, CT: Yale University Press.

Soloveitchik J. (1992) *The Lonely Man of Faith.* New York: Doubleday.

Staveren I. (2010) "Post-Keynesianism Meets Feminist Economics". *Cambridge Journal of Economics.* Vol. 34:6, pp. 1123–1144.

Strassmann D. (1993) "The Stories of Economics and the Power of Storyteller". *History of Political Economy.* Vol. 25:1, pp. 147–165.

Strassmann D. (1995) "Creating a Forum for Feminist Economic Inquiry". *Feminist Economics.* Vol. 1:1, pp. 1–5.

Strassmann D. (1998) "Editorial. Towards a More Accountable Economics". *Feminist Economics.* Vol. 4:1, pp. viii–ix.

Strassmann D. (1999) "Feminist Economics". Peterson J. and Lewis M. (Eds.) *The Elgar Companion to Feminist Economics*. Cheltenham: Edward Elgar, pp. 360–370.

Strassmann D. (2004) "Editorial. Feminist Economics: It Flourishes". *Feminist Economics*. Vol. 10:3, pp. 1–2.

Strassmann D. (2010) "Editorial: Toward a More Inclusive Feminist Economics". *Feminist Economics*. Vol. 16:1, pp. 1–2.

Strober M. (1984) "Toward a General Theory of Occupational Sex Segregation". Reskin B. (Ed.) *Sex Segregation in the Workplace: Trends, Explanations, Remedies*. Washington, DC: National Academy Press, pp. 144–156.

Strober M. (1987) "The Scope of Microeconomics: Implications for Economic Education". *The Journal of Economic Education*. Vol. 18:2, pp. 135–149.

Strober M. (1995) "Do Young Women Trade Jobs for Marriage? A Skeptical View". *Feminist Economics*. Vol. 1:1, pp. 197–205.

Strober M. (2003) "The Application of Mainstream Economics Constructs to Education: A Feminist Analysis". Ferber M. and Nelson J. (Eds.) *Feminist Economics Today: Beyond Economic Man*. Chicago: The University of Chicago Press, pp. 135–155.

Strober M. and Cook A. (1992) "Economics, Lies, and Videotapes". *The Journal of Economic Education*. Vol. 23:2, pp. 125–151.

Tollison R. and Congleton R. (Eds.) (1995) *The Economic Analysis of Rent Seeking*. Cheltenham: Edward Elgar Publishing.

Vaughn K. (1994) "Beyond Economic Man: A Critique of Feminist Economics". *The Journal of Economic Methodology*. Vol. 46:1, pp. 307–313.

Walker D. (1994) "Economics of Gender and Race". Boettke P. (Ed.) *The Elgar Companion to Austrian Economics*. Aldershot: Edward Elgar, pp. 362–371.

Walker D., Dauterive J., Schultz E., and Block W. (2004) "The Feminist Competition/ Cooperation Dichotomy". *Journal of Business Ethics*. Vol. 55:3, pp. 243–254.

Waller W. (1999) "Austrian Economics". Paterson J. and Lewis M. (Eds.) *The Elgar Companion to Feminist Economics*. Cheltenham: Edward Elgar, pp. 18–25.

Waller W. and Jennings A. (1990) "On the Possibility of a Feminist Economics: The Convergence of Institutional and Feminist Methodology". *Journal of Economic Issues*. Vol. 24:2, pp. 613–622.

Waller W. and Jennings A. (1991) "A Feminist Institutionalist Reconsideration of Karl Polanyi". *Journal of Economic Issues*. Vol. 25:2, pp. 485–497.

Weintraub R. (1993) "Editor's Introduction". *History of Political Economy*. Vol. 25:1, pp. 117–119.

Williams R. (1993) "Racial Inequality and Racial Conflict: Recent Developments in Radical Theory". Darity W. (Ed.) *Labor Economics: Problems in Analyzing Labor Markets*. Boston: Kluwer Academic Publishers, pp. 209–236.

Williams R. and Kenison R. (1996) "The Way We Were?: Discrimination, Competition, and Inter-Industry Wage Differentials in 1970". *Review of Radical Political Economics*. Vol. 28:2, pp. 1–31.

Willis E. (1984) *Radical Feminism and Feminist Radicalism: No More Nice Girls: Countercultural Essays*. Minneapolis, MN: University of Minnesota Press.

Wilson K. (2015) "Towards a Radical Re-appropriation: Gender, Development and Neo-liberal Feminism". *Development and Change*. Vol. 46:4, pp. 803–832.

Witte J.F. (2001) *The Market Approach to Education: An Analysis of America's First Voucher Program*. Princeton, NJ: Princeton University Press.

Wolfers J. (2017) "Evidence for a Toxic Environment for Women in Economics". *The New York Times*. August 18. As retrieved on September 25, 2018 at: www.nytimes.com/2017/08/18/upshot/evidence-of-a-toxic-environment-for-women-in-economics.html.

Woolf V. (1929) *A Room of One's Own*. London: Hogarth Press.

Woolf V. (1938) *Three Guineas*. London: Hogarth Press.

Woolley F. (1996) "Getting the Better of Becker". *Feminist Economics*. Vol. 2:1, pp. 114–120.

Woolley F. (2005) "The Citation Impact of Feminist Economics". *Feminist Economics*. Vol. 11:3, pp. 85–106.

Wu A. (2017) "Gender Stereotype in Academia: Evidence from Economics Job Market Rumors Forum". *Working Papers 2017–19*. Princeton, NJ: Princeton University Press.

Wylie A. (2007) "The Feminism Question in Science: What Does It Mean to 'Do Social Science as a Feminist'?". Nagy Hesse-Biber S. (Ed.) *Handbook of Feminist Research*. New York: Sage, pp. 544–556.

4 Latest developments of gender studies in economics

During the past decades, the use of the label 'gender' within economics had been expanded and adopted by both feminist economics and standard economics. Since 2005, the use of the word 'gender' has dramatically increased in articles hosted by *Feminist Economics*, while the label 'new home economics' had become a subset of gender economics that, as previously stated, was officially recognized in the 1990s by AEA with the JEL code J16 (today labeled 'economics of gender').

The issue may seem a trivial matter of nominalism, which can be explained as the adoption of the term 'gender' to replace 'feminist' in feminist economics and to replace 'new home' in the new home economics. Nevertheless, any semantic shift is rooted in a cultural transformation, and in this specific story it is related to the emergence of gender studies within social science, which were aimed to scrutinize, on one side, the differences between sex and gender and, on the other side, to analyze women's status as well as other sexual minorities' conditions.

Therefore, as a matter of fact, today the label 'gender' may be applied to two different economics approaches, which cope with gender issues within economics either from a neoclassical perspective (gender neoclassical economics, or economics of gender) or from a heterodox perspective (feminist economics as well as gender issues in other heterodox approaches to economics). Officially, the AEA's JEL classification regards 'gender economics' as a synonymous of 'economics of gender'; that is, the neoclassical economics' treatment of gender issues.

Before going into a more detailed description of the latest developments of gender neoclassical economics and feminist economics, it will be useful to make some reflections about the emerging of the notion of 'gender' as a cultural category, which was introduced in psychology and later adopted by social scientists in order to expose a more neutral analysis of sexual categories to overcome the distinction between male/masculinity/men and female/femininity/women, and to include all genders (Halberstam 2014). The description of gender as a cultural category (Section 1) allows to understand the latest development of gender issues in economics within both feminist economics and gender neoclassical economics and as well as the differences that still persist between the two approaches (Sections 2, 2.1, and 2.2). Nonetheless, beyond their theoretical and methodological differences, the two approaches converge in pointing out the persistence of gender inequality in the economy at any level. In general terms, the main manifestations of gender economic inequality are gender labor gap, gender wage gap, and gender entrepreneurship gap (Section 3).

4.1 Gender as a cultural category

The introduction of the notion of gender as a cultural category within the social sciences allowed for enrichment of the traditional biological distinction between sexes, without denying it. From a conceptual perspective, the difference between 'sex' and 'gender' was intended to clearly differentiate a natural and biological distinction between males and females (sex) from a constructed distinction between the different social roles of men and women (gender). Gender indicates the behavioral, cultural, and psychological traits typically associated with a specific sex.[1] The word 'gender' was coined in 1955 by the psychologist John Money, who tried to find a proper way to distinguish between bodily sex (male and female), sex category (men and women), and social roles (masculinity and femininity) (Money and Ehrhardt 1972). Gender studies had revealed that gender is a fundamental factor in shaping any kind of sexual orientation and vice versa (for example, LGBTQIA).

In the social sciences, the notion of gender is determinant in analyzing the conditions of minorities who are minorities because of their sexuality. The label 'minority' is usually applied to any social group whose social position is subordinated to the will of the majority group that rules the society. It is important to remark that majority and minorities are not merely a matter of numbers, but rather are a matter of power: members of the majority group may be more numerous than members of minorities, and it may happen that a small number of people gets the power and reaches the status of majority.

Traditionally, in any historical epoch as well as in any geographical region, patriarchy had always guaranteed men's dominance over women, which had to gender inequality. Gender studies consider the subjection of women not as a matter of mere biological differentiation between sexes, but as the effect of the domination of the majority group (men), which had shaped a set of values, habits, rules, social and cultural norms that had perpetually reinforced the minority status of their counterpart (women).

Gender studies emerged to understand the role of gender intended as a cultural category either to explain social phenomena or to denounce social distortions and discriminations. Gender studies emerged as a reaction the use of biological determinism, that is, the idea that biology may explain behavioral differences in an exhaustive way.[2] Against this view of biology as destiny, the term 'gender' was adopted by psychologists in order to define the phenomenon of transsexuals' sex and gender mismatch (Stoller 1968). Gender as a cultural category is related to the complexity of social constructions of sexual identities, hierarchies, and interactions. Essed et al. (2009) considered gender as "a complex and unfixed mix of significant structural and cultural or representational considerations both making and marking social distinctions [between sexes]" (Essed et al. 2009, 4).

Early feminist thinkers and activists, like Rubin (1975), used the label 'gender' to describe social impositions on both sexes that had originated by gender identity. They were influenced by the notion of 'social identity', that is, the individual's awareness to belonging to a particular social group, which had been introduced into social sciences by Tajfel (1972). Later, the social identity approach was extended by including the 'self-categorization theory' whereby individuals see themselves in terms of certain social categories (Turner 1985; Turner et al. 1987).

The definition of gender, as it is commonly accepted today, is based on the notion of 'social construction' of socialization, personality, and sexuality (Haslanger 1995). Gender socialization is grounded on the idea that gendered norms had reinforced women's subordination as well as men's dominance: women had learnt to be passive, docile, and emotional, while men had learnt to be active, aggressive, and logical thinkers. According to some feminists like Millett, gender is "the sum total of the parents', the peers', and the culture's notions of what is appropriate to each gender by way of temperament, character, interests, status, worth, gesture, and expression" (Millett 1971, 31). Feminist thinkers had been influenced by social learning theorists who stressed the role of social stereotypes in raising children. More specifically, boys have been depicted as adventurers and leaders, while girls have been depicted as quiet and helpers, and this gender stereotype had been massively represented within children's books and movies. The same process had been reproduced in the manufacture of toys and games as well as in marketing strategies (Renzetti et al. 2012).

According to some psychologists, the reinforcement of gender stereotypes may be explained by following intra-household dynamics: given that women tend to be the primary caretakers of their children, mothers identify themselves with their daughters and train them in caretaking, while encouraging their sons to be like their fathers, who traditionally are more self-focused and less caring. This process is based on a gender self-reinforcement of some kind of ego boundaries which had been unconsciously developed (Chodorow 1978, 1995).

MacKinnon (1989) developed a notion of gender as a theory of sexuality based on men's dominance: gender stereotypes arose as effects of the sexual objectification of women for satisfying men's desires, and the consequent eroticization of men's dominance and women's submission had justified and reinforced the hierarchy of power relations between them. Hence, according to MacKinnon, any gender difference is neither a matter of psychological orientation nor of behavioral scheme, rather gender stereotypes are effects of a hierarchal sexuality which had been socially conditioned, which is well testified by the phenomena of pornography and prostitution (MacKinnon 1989, 2006).

The spread of poststructuralism reinforced the connection between knowledge and gender by intending knowledge to be a form of power built up by a male-dominated culture and by intending gender to be "the primary way of indicating and conveying inequalities of power (of all kinds) in society" (Hudson 2008, 23). In this scenario, gender studies analyzed gender stereotypes in order to explain gender inequality at any level: the social construction of gender and sexuality had made heterosexual men dominant and women oppressed and repressed, along with other minorities (Lorber 2006). Rooted on the idea that gender stereotypes had always shaped social power, gender studies aimed to promote a balance among men, women, and other gender identities, into different aspects of the cultural, political, and economic sphere (Lerner 1986, 1991; Haraway 1991; Butler 1990; Nussbaum 2000).

Some criticism about the introduction of gender as a cultural category arose among scholars. For instance, Stacey and Thorne (1985) had argued that feminism had added gender as another variable without being able to transform the existing conceptual frameworks of social sciences, economy, politics, religion, and education. The sex/gender distinction had been criticized by some feminists as well because it seems to perpetuate the oppositions between mind/body, culture/nature, and reason/emotion, which traditionally had been adopted to justify women's oppression. In fact, those dichotomies usually entailed the superiority of one term (mind, culture, reason), associated with men, over the weaker terms (body, nature, emotions), associated with women (Lloyd 1993; Grosz 1994; Moi 1999; Prokhovnik 1999).

From a philosophical perspective, gender studies may be grounded either on gender realism or on gender nominalism. Gender realism implies that *all* women are thought to differ from *all* men, while gender nominalism considered racial, cultural, and class differences between women and refused to adopt a normative ideal of womanhood. According to gender nominalism, gender is not separable from race and class – otherwise all women would experience womanhood in the same way, which is false – and is based on 'white solipsism', which conforms womanhood to a particular racial and cultural background, while marginalizing others. An example of this white solipsism was Friedan's concept of domesticity as the main vehicle of gender oppression (Friedan 1963): Friedan did not consider that less-privileged women already worked outside the home (Armstrong 1989; Spelman 1988; Harris 1993; Stoljar 1995; Young 1997; Stone 2004, 2007). The normative ideal of womanhood carried on by gender realism had created new normative stereotypes, based on a notion of femininity that is constructed as if it was natural, while it is functional only within a heterosexist social order (Butler 1993, 1999; Heyes 2000).

More recently, neo-gender realism emerged in order to define a social and not biological notion of *woman* that may be useful and effective to fight against sexism (Haslanger 2005; 2006). Witt (2011, 2011) argued for a Another gender theory, known as essentialism, or 'uniessentialism' recently emerged. It is based on the distinction among *persons* (those who possess self-consciousness), *human beings* (those who are biologically human) and *social individuals* (those who have a social role), and it assumes that social individuals would be different persons if their sex/gender would have been the other.

Gender studies had a great impact on disciplines that are focused on the importance of balancing power and responsibilities among individuals. In fact, if gender roles are recognized as socially constructed, they may be changed in order to make a society more just and equitable; and if all social interactions are gendered, discrimination is the result of gender stereotypes. Gender stereotypes have been explained by functionalism, focused on how gender roles had contributed to social order and equilibrium; by conflict theory, focused on the level of power associated with gender; by symbolic interaction, focused on the ability of gender roles to be persuasive; and by feminism, focused on women's empowerment (Kramer and Beutel 2014).

Over the past several decades, the presence of gender studies has increased within and outside academia. Economic theory and political economy were involved in this story too. As we know, feminist economics accused standard economics of ignoring the role of gender stereotypes as a plausible origin of discriminatory preferences (Keller 1985; Longino 1990; Harding 1991; Beneria 1995; Figart 1997; Mutari et al. 1997). Feminist critiques of gender neoclassical economics led to the latest developments of gender issues within standard economics (namely, economics of gender).

4.2 Gender feminist economics

Gender theory applied to economics highlighted that gender is the primary way to indicate inequalities of power, which affected both microanalysis of decision making and macroeconomic policy measures. Two possible attitudes had been developed in order to analyze how gender influenced political economy and economics. The first attitude claimed that the androcentric notion of economics, mainly focused on competition, should be replaced by a gynocentric notion of economics, much more centered on cooperation. An alternative attitude avoided the dualism of androcentrism versus gynocentrism and promoted the creation of an economics for humans able to overcome any gender dichotomy (Nelson 2015, 2018).

As seen in the previous chapter, feminist economics considers economics as a socially constructed discipline influenced by many elements, including gender. Lately, feminist economics has preferred to adopt the label 'gender' in order to include all gender identities in the analysis of inequality; however, some internal critiques arose. For example, according to Beneria (1995), the use of gender within human capital theory was not transformative of the discipline: it followed what Harding (1987) had called the 'add women and stir' approach without giving a new emphasis on the peculiarity of women's work in the market as well as in nonmarket sector. Barker agreed with Beneria: according to Barker (1999), the introduction of the label 'gender' within feminist economics had been often regarded as redundant, the label 'feminist' being already able to connote the need to introduce women's issues into economics and political economy.

Economic history, economic demography, and social capital theory also were deeply affected by the introduction of gender as a cultural category. In economic history, the analysis of the neglected contribution by women and the study of female identity was promoted. In economic demography, Folbre (1983) and Ferber and Nelson (1993) showed that the marriage age of women had been wrongly analyzed by assuming that men and women would react to economic stimuli in the same manner. In social capital theory, traditionally based on families, gender studies revealed that, although the legal position of women had prevented them from being the recipient of funds to open up business, many wealthy widows and spinsters invested in financial products and in manufacturing and got some outstanding results (Hudson 2008; see also Chapter 1). Moreover, female entrepreneurship in secondary and tertiary activities has been recently investigated against the supposed risk-aversion bias which affects women (Owens 2002; Barker 2006).

In the 1990s, along with feminist economics, gendered political economy emerged to contrast wth gender neoclassical economics. Gender political economy shared with feminist economics the necessity to understand gendered structures within the economy and to explain women's subordination in the economic realm (Cook et al. 2000; Cook and Roberts 2000). In 1997, the Gender and Political Economy cluster of the Political Economy Research Centre at the University of Sheffield organized a workshop, 'Towards a Gendered Political Economy'. The workshop aimed to scrutinize the methodology and the contents of gender political economy as well as the relationship between gender political economy and other disciplines (Waylen 1997, 1998).

From a methodological perspective, gendered political economy criticized neoclassical economics, but many researchers believed that some new developments within neoclassical economics might be integrated in gendered political economy. Possible examples are the new neoclassical institutionalism (Humphries 1995, 1998) as well as Gardiner's attempt to develop a socially constructed human capital theory (Gardiner 1997, 1998). Against the standard model of individual rationality able to maximize, gendered political economy focused its attention on the role of social structures and agency. For instance, Folbre (1993b) advocated the notion of a purposeful choice as a valid tool to understand the relationship between structures and agency.

The contents of gendered political economy have been identified around three main themes: the analysis of households, markets, and states as gendered structures; the division between production and reproduction in different contexts as a central point of investigation; and the adoption of international comparative research able to replace the category of development.

In mid-1990s, feminist economist Joyce Jacobsen published a seminal handbook about the treatment of gender within economics. Although Jacobsen's book was not intended as a neoclassical way to deal with gender issues in economics, her book's title was *Economics of Gender* (Jacobsen 1994, 1998), which is the official label that will be adopted later by AEA to denote gender neoclassical economics. Jacobsen described economics of gender as a threefold inquiry on "theoretical models that include two sexes; empirical work that addresses similarities and differences between the sexes; and analysis of economic policies that affect the sexes differently" (Jacobsen 1998, 3). Aware that gender inequality is not the same everywhere and that it depends on political structures as well as on cultural differences, Jacobsen's approach adopted a historical and cross-societal comparative analysis in order to understand variations among similar countries as well as possible effects of a state-imposed gender equality.

In Jacobsen's terms, the economics of gender may shed new light on:

1) The gendered composition of labor market sectors which is reinforced by social conventions;
2) The ratio in labor force participation: some relevant differences between men and women persist in pink ghettoes and in some sectors in which men are preferred;
3) Divorce rates and fertility rates, which are often analyzed as directly connected to the rise of female labor force participation, which had increased the former and decreased the latter;
4) Gender segregation and discrimination, which are major causes of the gender wage gap, are intended as prejudices reinforced by gender-biased norms;
5) The debate over nature versus nurture in assessing the origin, either biological or environmental, of the differences between men and women behavior;
6) The cost of gender inequality in macro-sectors, including business;
7) The role of gender assumptions in global policy;
8) The role of gender in sustainability, health and innovation.

Furthermore, according to Jacobsen, the economics of gender is aimed to find some possible policies to reduce inequalities, including the possibility to introduce quotas: they may imply specific investments on women's education in order to increase women's empowerment.

Jacobsen's definition of the nature and the scope of economics of gender was endorsed by many other feminist economists, who underlined the importance of women's empowerment and the strict and direct correlation between women's empowerment and economic development (Duflo 2012; Bohnet 2016; Cassar and Katz 2016). Nonetheless, Jacobsen's description of the economics of gender may be endorsed by gender neoclassical economists as well, even though their approach is different and is grounded on standard economics. For example, gender neoclassical economists consider the gendered composition of labor market sectors as the effect of the theory of comparative advantages: men have comparative advantages in some labor market sectors, while women have comparative advantages in nonmarket sectors. Gender segregation may by intended by gender neoclassical economists as a response to market imperfections, while gender discrimination in workplace may be intended as an effect of imperfect information about women's productivity as well as an effect of fewer investments in human capital by parents who have fewer incentives to invest in their daughters' education.

As Jacobsen recently wrote:

> Women and the labor market can be regarded as a big umbrella to cover both economics of gender and feminist economics, without ignoring that the differences between the two approaches are relevant: the economics of gender is specifically concerned with how gender differences lead to different economic outcomes, as encapsulated in terms of such standard economics measures as earnings, income, wealth, poverty rates, hours of work, and time use. Feminist economics is a much broader intellectual project that encompasses this concern and these measures but also considers how economics, both as a field and as a body of theory and methodology, has been shaped by those who have chosen to work in it, which historically and currently has been mostly men. Labor economics, because it has been the main area in economics where gender differences have been studied extensively, has been the area where both of these projects have been most extensively developed.
>
> (Jacobsen 2018, 623)

4.3 Gender neoclassical economics

Gender within neoclassical economics had been studied in relation with markets, especially labor market and marriage markets. More recently, access to the credit market, especially in relation to entrepreneurship as well as the effects of globalization on women, has been central in the economics of gender, which aims to analyze interpersonal relations within households.

Gender neoclassical economics adopts a standard analytical framework to cope with gender issues in economics, unlike feminist economics, which calls for a revision of both neoclassical economics' vision and analysis. The use of the label 'gender' had been preferred by gender neoclassical economists to avoid accusations of being biased against men and to get a more neutral position about gender inequality. Claiming to be neutral about gender identities, gender neoclassical economics incorporates gender studies within mainstream economics in order to raise awareness of gender gaps and to develop new solutions which may be able to erode gender barriers (Moore 2015).

As earlier reminded, in the 1990s, the American Economic Society assigned JEL code J16 to gender economics (today, labeled as 'economics of gender'). This made it a subset of area J: 'Labor and Demographic Economics', which "covers studies about macro- and micro-issues in demographic economics and studies about microeconomic issues in labor economics". More specifically, gender neoclassical economics; that is, the economics of gender, covers the following subjects: "Non-labor Discrimination, Bias, Discrimination, Family Economics, Female, Feminism, Gender, Gender Discrimination,

Gender Segregated, Maternity, Minorities, Motherhood, Mothers, Pregnancy, Pregnant, Sexism, Sexual Harassment, Single Mother, Women".[3]

In the neoclassical economics' framework, gender identity had been adopted in order to establish its impact within households and to understand the dynamics of power among households' members: starting from the comparative advantage theory, gender neoclassical economics had argued that two people are better off within a family rather than remaining single. Furthermore, it provided a marriage theory based on costs and benefits, by refining Becker's model and the human capital theory: gender neoclassical economics had shown that women usually acquire less human capital than men do (a possible origin for the gender labor gap and consequently for the gender wage gap). Moreover, according to gender neoclassical economics, women usually get qualitatively different human capital that is less demanded in the labor market (another likely source of the gender wage gap). Gender neoclassical economics explains that men's aversion to earning less than women, as well as women's role in taking care of domestic labor, had impacted marriage formation, marriage satisfaction, and divorce rates. For instance, in the early 1980s, Manser and Brown (1980) and McElroy and Horney (1981) applied Nash's bargaining model to households: spouses cooperate in the process of bargaining to get a Pareto efficient (optimal) solution, but if they do not cooperate a thread point can be reached and separation and divorce may occur.

As gender neoclassical economics is focused on the capacity of human rationality to maximize an expected utility function, it adopts a positive approach that considers gender equality as a rational outcome in terms of growth and well-being for the society as a whole, and regards any gender gap as a market failure as well as gender inequality as a nonoptimal situation. Hence, gender neoclassical economics promotes gender equality if it will be increasing social utility. It is a matter of efficiency, not of fairness or justice. According to gender neoclassical economics, the gender division of labor within families, which includes the allocation of caring mainly to mothers, may be able to explain the gender labor gap as well as gender specialization in household production. Gender specialization, which must be intended as either consequences of biological differences or of different investments in human capital, may be efficient. Furthermore, any gender-specific premarital investments, intended as a social norm aimed to educate boys and girls in different ways, may be a valid tool to coordinate the proper matching in the marriage market. Matchmaking is a perfect example to understand the main difference between gender neoclassical economics and feminist: traditional matchmaking may be efficient from a gender neoclassical economics' perspective, but it is unfair from a feminist economics' vision if it worsens women's conditions, as it traditionally did (Baker and Jacobsen 2007).

Gender neoclassical economics is the latest development and the further enrichment of Becker's new home economics. As described in Chapter 2, Jacob Mincer (1962) had considered the trade-off between housework and paid work in analyzing married women's time. In Becker's model of time allocation, the household was considered able to maximize a single utility function (Becker 1964), while in Becker (1976), a decision process that involves several agents "can produce household demand functions that are no longer equivalent to those obtained by maximizing a single well-behaved household utility function" (Chiappori and Lewbel 2015, 411). Giuliano's review of the literature on gender roles and gender gaps within neoclassical economic theory allows an understanding of the way the inclusion of the notion of gender had somehow modified standard economics (Giuliano 2018). Giuliano pointed out that the introduction of gender roles had been determinant in several fields and that empirical research had shown that cultural differences related to gender roles emerged as a consequence of specific historical situations that tended to persist even when those circumstances change, especially in a very stable environment. Examples include the role of religion,[4] family structures,[5] and language.[6] Since the contributions of Manser and Brown (1980), McElroy and Horney (1981), and Lundberg and Pollak (1996), the allocation of family resources had been modelled as a Nash bargaining game with exogenous preferences; later, Lundberg and Pollak (2003) and Basu (2006) introduces endogenous preferences. In this perspective, the traditional division of labor between partners may be reinforced even when men and women have the same preferences and endowments. This condition explains the bias against women in the division of the benefits of marriage as well as the lesser amount of education provided to daughters with respect to sons (Cigno 2008).

In theoretical framework of gender neoclassical economics, gender gaps are the results of asymmetrical allocations of efforts and rewards between men and women, who are considered identical. The asymmetry in favor of men had inevitably led to a so-called rational and efficient solution, which increased home-work for women and enlarged the gender labor gap in favor of men. Although a cooperative solution between the two groups to involve equity at home as well as in the marketplace would be optimal, it would be risky and costly because the family and market may behave unfairly (Elul et al. 2002; Chichilnisky 2008).[7]

Lundberg (2008) had modified the previous gender neoclassical economics' model of the household, which considered the family as a single decision-making agent, by introducing distribution within household, transition costs, and inequalities between partners.

The original and unitary model assumed the maximization of household's utility function as follows:

$$max \ U(c_m, c_f, G)$$

subjected to a budget constraint:

$$c_m + c_f = y_m, \ y_f + w_m(T - l_m) + w_f(T - l_f)$$

Household production function is determined by:

$$G = g(l_m, l_f)$$

or simply:

$$G = h_m l_m, + h_f l_f$$

where G is the consumption of a household public good; l_m and l_f are inputs of the husband's and wife's time; c_m, and c_f are market goods; w and y are wages and income.

The model has been criticized mainly because it was unable to explain internal distribution among families' members as well as the dissolution of families, and it was based on a unitary demand function which was an inconsistent assumption. So the model was modified by introducing a nonunitary form, in which husband's and wife's utility functions, described as U^m (c_m, G) and U^f (c_f, G), that allowed to analyze gender inequalities in the relationships among family members.

The latest developments in gender neoclassical economics had been mainly focused in embedding the notion of gender as a determinant element in ranking preferences and in considering social norms in relation with gender identity as influential for economic behavior. Akerlof and Kranton (2000, 2002, 2005, 2008, 2010) combined the two notions of 'gender' and 'identity' within economics, by introducing the concept of 'identity economics'. They considered gender identity a concept of social identification that performs men and women as social categories. When applied to economic matters, gender identity becomes identity economics: it shapes men's and women's economic lives by impacting gender economic gaps and gender economic inequalities. According to authors, the notion of identity economics is rooted in the idea that gender discrimination as well as racial discrimination do not arise from purely personal preferences; rather, they reflect social codes that had become social norms. Akerlof and Kranton incorporated gender identity into a general model of economics behavior to demonstrate that identity economics largely impacts economic issues. For instance, gender identity influences payoffs because it can explain harmful behavior. Identity economics is useful to reveal preferences' ranking, and it can be a conscious or an unconscious motivation in the process of decision making. Authors pointed out that any deviation from standard behavior based on gender identity is highly costly. More specifically, they considered the role of gender discrimination in the labor market and within the household.

As Davis (2007, 2011a, 2011b) suggested, Akerlof and Kranton's model was a refined version of Becker's model and did not explain how individuals' different social identities are related. According to Davis, although Akerlof and Kranton claimed to have brought greater realism into economics, their model was simply a more sophisticated version of the traditional utility function model, grounded on 'identity utility' which incorporates social group norms:

individuals gain 'identity utility' if they conform to social group norms and vice versa. Against their model, Davis adopted a model based on a sociological approach which allows individuals' multiple identities or multiple social identities to emerge. As Davis wrote:

> An interactive reciprocal relation between the self and society in the sense that each influences the other. Individuals always act in social contexts and influence society through the groups, organizations and institutions, while society influences individuals through shared language meanings and other inherited social structures that enable individuals to interact, and take on social roles.
>
> (Davis 2007, 355)

Fine (2009) further criticized Akerlof and Kraton by pointing out that adding identity to the neoclassical utility function may be problematic because of the limits of individuals' rationality, which are the following: finite perception, incomplete expression, multiple criteria, interdependent preferences, and strategic decision making.

The literature on the role of gender differences in ranking individual preferences ad involved psychologists and economists.[8] Recently, it was developed mainly by experimental economists who work the different different attitudes between genders to competition as well as to altruism and risk aversion (Eckel and Grossman 1998, 2001, 2008; Hyde 2005; Niederle 2015).[9]

Gneezy et al. (2003) explained gender differences in ranking preferences as the results of discrimination in human capital's investments as well as of women's competition aversion: they observed that an increase in the competitiveness of the environment raises men's performance, while it had no effect on women's performance, especially when women have to compete against men.

Niederle and Vesterlund (2007) tried to scrutinize gender gaps in many high-profile professions by arguing that men and women respond differently to competitive environments: in mixed-gender competitions, women may not enter the competition at the same rate as their male counterparts because, on one side, men are more overconfident than women, and, on the other side, men and women differ in their preferences for performing in a competition (for a critique to this specific point, see Nelson's contribution as described in Chapter 3, paragraph 4).

Croson and Gneezy (2009) identified gender differences in risk preferences, social (other-regarding) preferences, and competitive preferences. More specifically, they used some experiments to show that women are more risk-averse and more averse to competition than men and that women's social preferences are more malleable and more situationally specific than men's social preferences. In their model, women's risk aversion had been described by using the old-fashioned argument of women's emotional reactions to risky situations versus men's overconfidence under uncertainty and over challenging and risky situations (Lowenstein 2001). Gender differences towards competition often have been explained by a combination of nature and nurture. Regarding social preferences, Croson and Gneezy (2009) had claimed that women's behavior is more context-dependent than men's behavior. Although both genders maximize their utility function, men's function is less influenced by any possible information about the other party. In another paper by Gneezy et al. (2009), authors explored whether there are gender differences in selecting into competitive environments across matrilineal societies (Khasi in India) and patriarchal societies (Maasai in Tanzania). They observed that the gender gap in leadership positions may suggest that men are much more competitive than women. Their observations led them to affirm that, in the patriarchal Maasai society, women are actually less competitive than men, while in the matrilineal Khasi society women are more competitive than men.

According to Niederle and Vesterlund (2011), although differences in overconfidence and in attitudes toward competition affect gender differences in labor market, gender differences in risk aversion play a smaller and less robust role than expected.

Alesina et al.'s article (2013) endorsed Boserup's hypothesis (1970) that the form of agriculture traditionally practiced in the preindustrial period had influenced the gender division of labor and the evolution of gender norms, that had an influential role that persists among today's new generations of immigrants, whose ancestors had practiced plough agriculture.

Niederle's survey (2015) pointed out that, while gender differences play a large and robust role in explaining different attitude to competition and risk aversion between men and women, they play a less strong role in explaining altruism.

As mentioned earlier, gender neoclassical economics is mainly focused on two broad inquiries: women's status in the labor market, and the theory of marriage and fertility.[10]

Many labor economists have dealt with the gender wage gap, sex segregation, and their mutual correlation (Blau and Kahn 2017; Cortes and Pan 2018). Many others had analyzed how female labor force participation might have affected social environment and they had scrutinized the effects of some economic policies, such as antidiscrimination legislation and welfare programs devoted to reducing gender inequality. Recently, Guidi and Schmidt (2018) have been interested in the effects of taxation on labor supply: they asserted that transfer programs on women's labor supply had largely affected women's choice, given that women usually are the second earner within families.

Regarding marriage and fertility in gender neoclassical economics, Becker's model adopted the notion of gains from specialization, according to which the principal role of marriage is to protect the spouse who entirely invests in household capital. Lately, Lam (1988) developed a model based on a joint public good; that is, couples' agreement on the public aspects of marriage (where to live, how many children to have and the kind of education reserved to them, and so forth). Additional contributions by Lundberg (2012) refused to consider gender specialization in marriage by adopting a joint consumption model. Hirsh et al. (2010) had defined marriage as a stable match when it is not possible to find another partner who is willing to abandon the current one.

Some models of spouse sorting have been described by considering the role of preferences and research costs, age, education, race and ethnicity, and income inequality. For instance, there is a massive literature on assortative matching based on preferences, which often may result unrealistic (Mansour and McKinnish 2014). Gender neoclassical economists claimed that evidence was provided asserting that individuals match well when husbands are a few years older than their potential wives and, in general terms, a small age gap is preferred because it implies that spouses share similar preferences (Lee and McKinnish 2018). The tendency to get married with a same-level educated partner had been explained as an effect of a lower cost in researching and meeting potential partners (which usually occurs while people are attending college, at least for the first marriage) rather than as an effect of shared preferences, which are expected among partners with the same level of education. This phenomenon is more likely among higher-skilled professionals (Mansour and McKinnish 2018b) and involves interracial and interethnic marriage, which seems to be related to meeting opportunity. Furthermore, some inquiries into possible interactions between marital sorting and income inequality included returns on education, on the cost of marrying down, and on the decline in marriage rates (Schwartz 2013; Autor 2014). More recently, Mansour and McKinnish (2018) have adopted cost–benefi analysis combined with the availability of new data sets to online dating websites in order to explain modern marriage: they consider marital sorting depending on the gains from marriage regarded as an alternative to single status.

An interesting approach to marriage within neoclassical gender economics had been developed by Shoshanna Grossbard (1984, 1993, 2015, 2018) who proposed a 'work in household' (WiHo) model: in WiHo, exogenous variations in sex ratios and their effects are taken into account, partners may conflict about allocations, and both psychological and physical care of the spouse are included.

Grossbard's model belongs to gender neoclassical economics: she always admitted to having been deeply influenced by her formation at the University of Chicago, especially by Becker's new home economics (Becker 1973, 1981), and by Friedman, who had considered marriages as nonprofit firms able to organize household production in a manner that is similar to central authority employed in a collectivistic society (Friedman 1976). Differently from Becker and Friedman, Grossbard's WiHo model distinguished between couples' economic decisions within household activities that may benefit a spouse and couples' economic decisions that do not benefit a spouse. Inspired by African marriage dynamics, analyzed by Grossbard at the beginning of her career, the WiHo model applied price theory to households by considering households as firms, husbands as employers, and wives as workers. Furthermore, the WiHo model assumed that there are markets for different types of men and women and that an 'equilibrium price of WiHo' may be reachable in each sub-market. Moreover, in the WiHo model, optimization is not rejected but is pursued by individuals rather than by households as in the new home economics approach.

The original element in Grossbard's model is the fact that family members are independent decision makers, and they do not necessarily cooperate. In fact, the WiHo model rejects Becker's benevolent husband able to optimize on behalf of the family. Furthermore, the institutional framework may provide exchanges of WiHo for WiHo, or WiHo for money as well as in-kind gifts. The WiHo model was later expanded by including public goods along with private goods (Grossbard 2003). According to Grossbard, a major advantage of WiHo is that it included the old distinction between home production and leisure introduced by Margaret Reid.

In some other works, Grossbard shed light on how institutions related to marriage and divorce influenced the share of children born to a single mom and how out-of-couple births vary with community property and alternative property division schemes in case of separation. Based on a rational choice model of marriage and assuming that, on average, women earn less than men, Grossbard showed that women are less likely to have an unpartnered birth when rules for the division of joint property are more advantageous to spouses with lower earnings (Ekert-Jaffe and Grossbard 2008).

The WiHo model is an effort to embed feminist economics' concerns within a neoclassical economics framework. The history behind Grossbard's efforts is emblematic of the narrative of the relationship between gender neo-classical economics and feminist economics and their strong divergence, at least in the 1990s.

Grossbard recently published an entry in her blog, *Economics of Love*, which allows readers to understand the problematic attitude of feminist economists towards gender neoclassical economists. The story began in 1994, when Grossbard published an article, "Young Women May Trade Jobs for Marriage" in the *Wall Street Journal*. Grossbard's article considered how the marriage market had influenced individuals' value of time in marriage. Her analysis showed that a rapid increase in women's labor force participation had coincided with a rapid growth of the population entering marriage markets: the trend started in the late 1930s in the United States and later involved Baby Boomers. Therefore, the slow growth in women's labor force participation overlapped the coming of age of successive generations of shrinking size born during the baby-bust and the marriage market had become unbalanced by favoring men (Grossbard and Granger 1998).

Classical liberal and feminist economist Barbara Bergmann (see Chapter 3) harshly criticized Grossbard's model, accusing it of being based on the assumption that married women decided individually about whether to get a job, after having compared costs and benefits, without taking account of social and peers' pressure on them. Bergmann attacked Grossbard by defining her as a "female economist who told the Wall Street Journal editors that women do not want to get a career on their own, if they can be spouse of a wealthy man". Surely, Bergmann continued, "Wall Street Journal editors were very happy to publish her article", and she invited Grossbard "to grow up and try a little harder to shake the dust of sexist Chicago from shoes".[11]

In her online blog post, Grossman published some private letters she had received from Gary Becker, Nancy Folbre, and Deirdre (still Donald at that time) McCloskey in defense of her work, after Bergmann's harsh critique. Becker assured Grossbard that Bergmann's voice would have been surely isolated because no feminist economist may deny that there is an economic bargaining component within marriage. Much more interesting was feminist economist Folbre's message. In a letter dated July 7, 1994, Folbre wrote:

> I think that Barbara's reading of Shoshanna's argument is wrong. It's not about women embracing traditional sex roles, but about them considering the costs and benefits of marriage. One can agree, *à la* Bergmann, that the costs of economic dependence are high, and still argue *à la* Grossbard, that when those costs go down slightly, (as when husbands have more money and good jobs are harder to find) more married women will drop out. Yes, the decline seems negligible, and yes, it's probably due in part to more women staying in school, but I don't have any problem with Shoshanna's argument. And I'm happy to see some discussion of these issues on the Wall Street Journal.[12]

McCloskey reacted by writing a letter directly addressed to Bergmann:

> Barbara, please desist from bullying Shoshana, IN BLOCK CAPITALS, about 'sexist Chicago'. You are a reasonable person, I know, and will surely want to note sexist Harvard, sexist MIT, sexist Massachusetts, sexist NYU, sexist Cambridge, sexist Stanford, sexist Illinois, and so forth. There is no case, none, zero, to be made that the Chicago School is more sexist than the X school. Chicago comes in sexist and nonsexist colors. For instance, Theodore Schultz, who was hiring and encouraging in every way women economists, in the 1930s. It's from him and from his colleagues and the Iowa State and Chicago, Margaret Reid, that I learned to respect the American tradition in home economics, which invented Becker style home economic before Becker was out of diapers. And from him and Jean Bowman, I (and Shoshana) learned the importance of education of women for economic growth. ... The world is not simple. It does not happen to be so that the people one most admire for their politics are also the people with the most admirable views on the Woman Question. It's a mathematical point: you cannot maximize more than one thing at time. And it's a point of human wisdom, as Montaigne said in a less statistical way, that no human characteristic is reliably correlated with another. It does not line up this way: conservative = antifeminist = stupid. Life would be simpler if it were true.[13]

McCloskey's letter looks more like a defense of the Chicago school of economics than an endorsement of Grossbard's contribution. Nevertheless, it is useful to understand the complexity of the influence of institutional framework in building up a research field within economics. McCloskey's words are a clear and useful example of the proper attitude that should be adopted by historians: any oversimplified vision of a problem within a discipline (in this case marriage theory within neoclassical economics) must be rejected in favor of an attitude which takes account of the complexity of factors which converge in determining the rise of a theory or a new research field.

4.4 Beyond labels: some data about gender gaps in the world economy

This final paragraph aims to go beyond the methodological and theoretical divergences and affinities between feminist economics and gender neoclassical economics in order to offer a glance at the present state of women's economic conditions in the world economy. Data provide evidence of a persistent gender inequality, as both feminist and gender neoclassical economics highlight.

As mentioned earlier, the development of gender studies in social sciences shed new light on the role of gender equality, gender equity, and women empowerment as tools able to increase the well-being of society as a whole. Gender equality requires that women and men equally share responsibilities in the decision-making process and in getting access to opportunities aimed to better their lives. Gender equity is the process of being fair to women and men and it requires finally compensating women who have been disadvantaged for ages in terms of access to resources, independence, and leadership. Given that women's position is still subordinated to men's position, the promotion of both gender equality and gender equity leads to women's empowerment and ensures that both women and men are able to take part fully as equal partners in private and public life.

Equity and equality between women and men have been declared an ineludible aim in many official documents issued by international organizations, as in the *incipit* of the first Human Development Report (1990): "people are the real wealth of a nation and inequality amongst genders can no longer be accepted". Gender equity and equality were fundamental principles of the European Union's treaties (Rome 1957; Amsterdam 1997; Lisbon 2007/09); in 1995, The United Nations organized the United Nations Development Program to compile the Gender-Related Development Index (GDI) and the Gender Empowerment Measure (GEM); in 2010, The United Nations Entity for Gender Equality and the Empowerment of Women was founded. In the 2030 Agenda for Sustainable Development, Goal 5 is entirely devoted to gender equality. The aim and intent of these organizations are to measure gender inequality, to consider its negative externalities; to indicate possible measures to reduce it; and to promote gender equity (Human Development Report 2014, 2018).

Time series data sets about gender inequality are fundamental tools that aimed to understand the phenomenon, to test theories, and to establish connections among factors which had determined gender inequality. The Historical Gender Equality Index (HGEI) is the most recently adopted index for measuring gender inequalities: it captures data between 1950 and 2003. HGEI covered the following indicators: the access to health resources; the autonomy within the household in decision on education, marriage, and labor force; the political representation of women; and the socioeconomic status of women linked to the access to material resources (Dilli et al. 2019).

Data reveal that gender inequality persists overall in spite of decades of political and social battles against it. Programs to implement gender equality and to integrate women and men are known under the general label of 'gender mainstreaming': a strategy for the integration of gender issues in analyzing, proposing, and monitoring possible policies to promote new opportunities and to reduce social pressure on both women and men. For instance, women may assume a more competitive and leadership role, while men may assume a more nurturing role.[14] From an economic perspective, women's under-representation may be regarded as a constraint to human progress. The phenomenon of women's under-representation had generated several gender gaps: in education, in politics, in the economy, in leadership role, and so forth. The most significant gender gaps in the economy are gender labor gap, gender wage gap, and gender entrepreneurship gap.

In 2006, the World Economic Forum published a data set to measure gender disparity on a scale from 0 (disparity) to 1 (parity) that allows the measurement of progresses towards gender parity in many countries. Gender gaps are outlined across four thematic dimensions: economic participation and opportunity (female over male ratio in labor force participation, gender wage gap at the same level for similar work, female over men ratio at the top positions); educational attainment (female literacy rate over male literacy at any educational level); health and survival (sex ratio at birth and female healthy life expectancy over male value), and political empowerment (the ratio of females to men in parliaments and governments as well as number of years of women as heads of a state).[15]

The World Economic Forum's last report (2018) benchmarks 149 countries. The Index ranks countries is based on their gender gaps, not on their development level. Key findings include the following results:

1) The largest gender disparity appears in political empowerment, which maintains a gap of 77.1%: on average, at global level, 18% of ministers and 24% of members of parliaments are women;

2) The second-largest gap, measured at 41.9%, is in economic participation and opportunity: women have as much access to financial services as men in just 60% of the countries assessed and to land ownership in just 42% of the countries assessed; among the 29 countries with available data, on average, women double men in spending their time on housework and other unpaid activities;

3) Both the gender educational gap and gender health gap are significantly lower, at 4.4% and 4.6 respectively % (at the present moment, in 44 countries the percentage of illiterate women is more than 20%).

The report ranks countries according to gender equality rather than women's empowerment; it measures gender gaps rather than levels; and it considers gender gaps in outcome variables rather than in input variables. To prefer gaps over levels allows the measurement of gender gaps while accessing resources and opportunities, rather than to measure the actual levels of the available resources and opportunities in any country. The evaluation of countries based on outcomes rather than inputs provides a snapshot of those sectors in which men and women stand with regard to some fundamental outcome indicators related to basic rights. Although policies, rights, culture, or customs that are "input" indicators are not included in the Index, they are analyzed in the report. The Index's focus on gender gaps rather than on women's empowerment allows better measurement of gender inequality and how it performs. Hence, the report neither rewards nor penalizes cases in which women are outperforming men in particular indicators in some countries.

The report divides the world in the eight geographical regions. According to the most recent data, Western Europe has the highest level of gender parity (75.8%), followed by North America (72.5%), Latin America (70.8%), Eastern Europe and Central Asia (70.7%), East Asia and the Pacific (68.3%), Sub-Saharan Africa (66.3%), South Asia (65.8%), and the Middle East and North Africa (60.2%). The most gender-equal country today is Iceland (85%), followed by Norway (83.5%), Sweden, and Finland (82.2%). Among the top 10, there are Nicaragua (5th), Rwanda (6th), New Zealand (7th), Philippines (8th), Ireland (9th), and Namibia (10th).

Focusing our attention more on economic parameters that measure gender inequality, we must consider three gender economic gaps: the gender labor gap, which includes the access to labor market as well as the possibility and facility of promotions; the gender wage gap, which includes wage discrimination in same-level jobs; and the gender entrepreneurship gap, which includes the possibility of access to financial resources either to work as freelancer or to open a business, by taking account of the distinction between traditional entrepreneurship (serial entrepreneurship and portfolio entrepreneurship) and social entrepreneurship. Gender economic gaps depend on several historical and cultural factors and they are strictly related with gender education gap and gender political gap. The gender educational gap includes the possibility of access to any stage of education, and the gender political gap includes the number of women in charge in any political position, either at local level or at international level.

The following subparagraphs offer a glance of the present situation for any gender economic gap which reveals the persistence of gender inequality worldwide.

4.4.1 Gender labor gap

According to the OECD Report (2017), gender gap in labor market persists despite girls and young women's gains in education. Women, especially migrant, often experience lower job quality across OECD countries.[16] Although women's employment rates increased by an average of almost 3 percentage points across the OECD countries, the gender labor gap remained at 11% between 2012 and 2016. This is mainly due to women's relative gains in the labor market during and immediately after the 2007–2009 recession.

Gender stereotypes persist and are a serious obstacle to gender equality in the labor market. Boys and girls are expected to get a job and to purse their careers in gender-stereotyped fields, regardless of the subjects in which they have been more proficient at school. Moreover, many parents still have different expectations for their sons and daughters (OECD 2016a). The OECD report confirms that self-ghettoization is another relevant element in gender labor gap: women still prefer to get a part-time job, and consequently to get a lower pay, in fields such as the public sector, especially education and health, in order to take care of their families, while men prefer to work full time in sectors such as finance, banking, and insurance, as far as they are not involved in taking care of their families. The major consequence of this self-ghettoization is the gender wage gap (OECD 2017).

Other important factors which influence the gender gap in the labor force are age and marriage status. The gender labor gap increases in laborers over the age of 45 and in married workers. In fact, across the OECD countries, the gender gap in the employment rate between childless men and women is relatively small (4.8 percentage points on average). The gender labor gap becomes 22.6 percentage points when comparing men and women who have at least one child aged 0–14. The negative effects of motherhood on labor force participation are particularly pronounced for women with low levels of education. Moreover, as women are more likely to take care of their children as well as of elder relatives, some employers are less inclined to invest in female employees. Many OECD governments consider the best way to reduce barriers to women's employment by proposing a more accessible childcare system and by increasing flexible work arrangements for a better-quality job.

Women's lower labor force participation, the higher probability of interrupting their careers to take care of their family, and the higher likelihood of working part-time significantly reduce the number of women who get a promotion to advance in their career or who reach top positions in workplace. The phenomenon is known as 'leaky pipeline', or 'glass ceiling', and it involves top jobs positions in both private and public companies, including academia.

Many studies showed that a leaky pipeline for women in academic economics is significantly high (Ginther and Kahn 2004; McDowell et al. 2001). In accordance with the content of this book, some results on leaky pipeline in economics departments will be provided. Although between 1972 and 1993, the number of women in top Ph.D. departments had increased, during the past 20 years, that trend had stopped. According to a CSWEP report (2014), shares in academia have dropped since early 2000 from 25% to less than 16% in 2014. Furthermore, women in the economic professions are disproportionately concentrated in a few fields. The latest annual Committee on the Status of Minority Groups in the Economics Profession Report (2018) shows that, in 2016–2017, only one-third (380) of the 1,150 Ph.D. degrees in economics achieved in the United States had been awarded to women. Minority women were the recipients of 5.1% of all economics degrees conferred in 2017 (to women and men) and 17.1% of all degrees in economics had been conferred to women. Minority representation amongst women was the highest at the bachelor's level (17.3%) and master's level (15.9%), while it was the lowest at the Ph.D. level (7.4%) (CSMGEP 2018, 5). In a recent interview, Bayer pointed out that the female percentage of students in economics at the undergraduate level is well below the female percentage in other social sciences, in business, in humanities, and is even below the female percentage in STEM fields; however, many economists either are not really aware of these disparities or simply underrate it.[17]

A possible reason of this trend is that women usually have fewer academic publications than men on average because of their responsibilities as mothers. Nonetheless, the gender gap in economics and physical science departments seems to be unrelated to the fact of having or not having children (Ceci et al. 2014). The gender gap in academic publications recently has been deeply scrutinized by some prominent economists. Although Card et al. (2018) claimed that there is no evidence of differential gender bias in publishing, Hengel (2017) found out that papers written by women spend six months longer under review at one top journal than papers submitted by men. Moreover, some other elements emerge: women's coauthorship patterns are predictive of lower output (Ductor et al. 2018); women receive significantly less credit than men for coauthored work, especially when coauthored with men; and discrimination against women in manuscript review requires that female authors commit to higher standards. In a recent paper, Lundberg and Stearns (2019) have analyzed trends in the gender composition of academic economists over the past 25 years, and they have reviewed women's relative position in the discipline, including research productivity and income. The authors have pointed out that differential assessment of men and women are reflected in gendered institutional policies and in an apparent implicit bias in editorial review processes, and they may explain the gender disparity in promotion rates in economics' departments. Furthermore, the gender gap in tenure tracks, in tenure positions, and in promotions in economics departments are much greater than those in the other social sciences departments (Ginther and Kahn 2014).

Bayer and Rouse (2016) argued that implicit attitudes and institutional practices may have contributed to the underrepresentation of women and minorities at all stages of their academic careers. Authors suggested that broadening the pool by including more women and minorities in the economic profession would ensure the achievement of a more robust and relevant knowledge. It is not just a matter of fairness, but efficiency. They also proposed some initiatives and some new educational approaches, such as active learning and some specific program of mentoring, as well as some measures to support women in their early-career stage. Antecol et al. (2018) pointed out that when universities offered some extra time to do research to be published, male professors benefited while women are punished.

4.4.2 Gender wage gap

The gender wage gap is not intended as a situation that involves men and women who are working exactly the same job at exactly the same place, but are paid differently. This discrimination is illegal in many countries. The gender wage gap, which is commonly reported as a woman earning 80 cents for every dollar earned by a man, refers to the median annual pay of all women who work in a year compared to the pay of a similar cohort of men. Hence, the gender wage gap depends directly on the gender labor gap, on women's preference for part-time jobs, on the pink ghetto that usually includes lower-paid jobs, and on glass ceiling.

According to the OECD Report (2012, 2017), the gender wage gap among full-time workers across OECD countries is slightly below 15%; it has been unchanged since 2010 and is especially large among high earners. Measuring the size of the gender pay gap, the type of earnings used (hourly, weekly, monthly, or annual earnings) matters. On average, across the 29 OECD countries with available data on both the monthly and hourly gender gaps, the gap in median monthly earnings for full-time employees is 18.6%, while the gap in median hourly earnings for full-time employees is 12.5%. Like the gender labor gap, the gender wage gap is larger among older workers and tends to be wider among parents than among nonparents. Again, like in the gender labor gap, women are penalized: as far as they usually take care of families, they are forced to work less and, consequently, are paid less than men who work full time.

Across OECD countries, the gender wage gap is higher in the information and communications technology sectors, in finance, and in personal services. The relationship between the gender wage gap and high- or low-skilled jobs is not linear. In some countries, including Austria, Chile, Portugal, Switzerland, the Czech Republic, and Spain, the gender wage gap for workers in high-skilled sectors is more than 20% and often is smaller in low-skilled sectors. In some other countries, including Italy, Hungary, Luxembourg, and Slovenia, the gender wage gap is in favor of men working in low-skilled occupations. Possible causes for the gender wage gap in very high salaries include the underestimation of women's skills and the persistence of unpaid care work and discrimination in hiring, career progression, and opportunities in the labor market. Measures to reduce the gender wage gap may include pay transparency, pay gap calculator, and anti-discrimination laws (Goldin 2002, 2014).

4.4.3 Gender entrepreneurship gap

Besides the gender labor gap and gender wage gap, the other economic factor that is determinant in gender economic gaps is the number of women entrepreneurs or self-employed, which is overall smaller than the number of men entrepreneurs, albeit with some relevant differences amongst geographical areas and countries. The gender entrepreneurship gap depends on macroeconomic elements such as the general institutional framework; on cultural elements, such as gender stereotypes; and on governmental policy (Welter 2010; Doe 2017) as well as on microeconomic elements such as individual expectations and motivations and self-exclusion (Jamali 2009; Klyver et al. 2013).

Self-employed laborers work either alone in their own businesses or they may create jobs by hiring employees (OECD 2016b). Self-employment has usually been thought as a full-time labor market activity, but lately it has taken a number of different forms, known as hybrid or informal entrepreneurship (that is, forms of self-employment combined with employment, education and/or volunteer work), group entrepreneurship (that is, self-employment in a team), and freelancers (that is, self-employed people who undertake project-based work, often in creative industries). Informal entrepreneurship is growing especially in developing countries where women's access to capital is heavily limited (ILO 2016).

Blomqvist et al. (2014) estimated that the elimination of gender entrepreneurship gap could raise global GDP as much as 2%. According to OECD Report (2017), in 2016, the self-employed women rate ranged from 4.1% in Norway to 23.5% in Mexico; Chile registered the smallest gender gap (1.9 %), and Turkey the largest (14.5%). The gender entrepreneurship gap widened in Japan, Latvia, and Luxembourg, while in the Middle East and North Africa, or MENA region, the gap was even greater.[18]

The Global Entrepreneurship Monitor (2017) reveals some key findings about the gender entrepreneurship gap, which confirm some aspects which are determinant in other gender economic gaps.[19] Women are more likely than men to work as entrepreneurs in sectors that are less competitive and less profitable. This process reinforces the phenomenon of pink ghettoization even in entrepreneurship. Self-employed women are less likely than self-employed men to have employees, because they prefer to run small business, better if lone-firms. The direct consequence is that they tend to earn less, making the gender pay gap wider in entrepreneurship as well. The gender entrepreneurship gap is narrower among young and unmarried people and higher among older people.

Some important differences appear in analyzing different geographical areas. Women are much prone to choose self-employment than men in low-GDP countries, mainly because this is the best way for them to sustain their families, in spite of much more difficulties they have to face to get their business set. Difficulties are subjective, such as self-exclusion and lack of financial education, and objective, such as a persistent lack of an adequate policy aimed to promote the access to credit and their financial independence.

In five economies, the number of women entrepreneurs is equal to or higher than the number of men entrepreneurs: Vietnam, Mexico, Indonesia, the Philippines, and Brazil. The highest ratio is in Vietnam, where women are one-third more likely to start a business than men. Lately, in the United States, a rapid and impressive increase of women entrepreneurs occurred as well: it reached 45% on an average of 9%. This phenomenon is mainly due to African American female entrepreneurs' rate, which had increased 126%. Only 13% of female entrepreneurs in North America start an activity out of necessity, while in sub-Saharan Africa, the percentage is 36%. In the European Union, female entrepreneurs prefer small-sized firms, which often involve family members; they are less innovative but more reliable in terms of credit accountability (Peris-Ortiz et al. 2012). In Europe and the MENA region, on average, women start their business at less than 60% the rate of men.

Innovation-driven economies in the most economically advanced countries show that women start their own business often because they need a source of income and have no other job options. In developing countries, women's entrepreneurship is concentrated in tertiary sectors such as manufacturing, farming, and tourism; and entrepreneurship often attracts women without high education. Education levels among female entrepreneurs is directly related to economic development: in factor-driven economies, 14% of women entrepreneurs have a post-secondary degree or higher, but in innovation-driven economies, the rate of educated women entrepreneurs is 61%.

According to the *World Bank Gender Action Plan 2016–2021* (2016), women entrepreneurs are forced to face numerous difficulties to get access to capital, especially in very remote places, where it is hard to find a bank.[20] Furthermore, the lack of networks and knowledge resources limits market linkages; legal, regulatory, and policy obstacles make access to finance even harder.

Since 1995, the World Bank has a special program to provide regular credit and microcredit aimed to promote entrepreneurship among women. As reported by the World Bank, microcredit is especially dedicated to the "poorest", and women represent 85.2% of the poorest. The World Bank report points out that in developing countries, married women are more prone to becoming entrepreneurs and family leaders (Gaméz-Gutiérrez and Saiz-Álvarez 2012). They are 'portfolio entrepreneurship' rather than 'serial entrepreneurship', that is, they devote their ability to several microfirms in order to raise the chance to get a sufficient income for their family rather than concentrate their entrepreneurial activity in a specific firm. Cultural factors, such as migration as well as the fact that in rural communities and villages women are helped in taking care of children by other members of the community, make portfolio entrepreneurship easier for women, in spite of a persistent cultural discrimination against them.

Things are different when shifting the attention from traditional entrepreneurship to social entrepreneurship. Social entrepreneurship has been defined as an "entrepreneurial activity with an embedded social purpose" (Austin et al. 2006, 2) or as "the pursuit of sustainable solutions to neglected problems with positive externalities" (Santos 2012, 335).[21]

Both the Global Entrepreneurship Monitor (2009) and the LSE-SELUSI Database (2010) suggested that gender gap in social entrepreneurship is generally smaller than gender gap in business entrepreneurship and even in traditional firms, women entrepreneurs seem to emphasize social goals more than their male counterparts (Hechavarria et al. 2012; Humbert 2012; Huysentruyt 2014; Nicolás and Rubio 2016). The difference in proportions of women as traditional entrepreneurs and social entrepreneurs is 10% with a 5.3% margin of error.

The number of women social entrepreneurs is increasing overall in developed countries, but it is less significant in developing countries. Although in some countries, like Argentina, Iceland, Israel, Lebanon, and Russia, women social entrepreneurs outnumber their male counterparts, in other countries, such as Brazil, Bosnia, and Morocco, the situation is opposite; and in countries like China, Finland, Latvia, and the United States, the proportion is the same (Terjesen et al. 2011). Possible reasons to explain the fact that the gender gap in social entrepreneurship is smaller than in business entrepreneurship might be that women are either generally more altruistic and socially minded than men, or that women seem to be more averse to competition (Benavides-Espinosa and Mohedano-Suanes 2012; Huysentruyt 2014), although, as seen in Chapter 3, Nelson (2014, 2016) had recently shown the methodological fallacy in this gender stereotype.

Notes

1 According to the American Psychological Association, "gender is the condition of being male, female, or neuter. In a human context, the distinction between gender and sex reflects the usage of these terms: sex usually refers to the biological aspects of maleness or femaleness, whereas gender implies the psychological, behavioral, social, and cultural aspects of being male or female (i.e., masculinity or femininity)" (American Psychology Association, 2013, 6). Hence, gender identity refers to one's sense of oneself as male, female, or transgender. When gender identity and biological sex are not congruent, the individual may identify as transsexual or as another transgender category.

2 Pioneers of biological determinism were Geddes and Thomson (1889) who claimed that metabolism in women makes them passive and uninterested in social and political matters while it makes men passionate and interested in political and social matters.

3 As retrieved on May 19, 2019 at: www.aeaweb.org/econlit/jelCodes.php?view=jel.

4 By reinforcing Woodberry and Shah's argument that Protestant missions worked especially on minorities (2004), Nunn (2014) pointed out that while Protestant missions in Africa during colonial period had a positive impact on female education and a small impact on male education, the situation in Catholic missions was the opposite.

5 Alesina and Giuliano (2010) pointed out that societies with strong family ties have a greater home production made by women and a lower female participation in labor market.

6 Galor et al. (2016) studied how gender-based language had reinforced gender stereotypes and had affected economic outcomes.

7 Some institutions, such as pre-nuptial agreements and legislation for equal pay, may improve fairness (Waldfogel 1998).

8 Woolley (1914) provided the first review of the literature on gender differences in psychology.

9 Swineford (1941) provided the first experimental test on gender differences in risk aversion in psychology; while Schubert et al. (1999) published the first article in an economic journal about this issue.

10 The most recent literature on both issues includes Blau and Winkler (2018) and Antecol et al. (2018).

11 As retrieved on January 30, 2019 at: https://static1.squarespace.com/static/59af966b49 fc2bd0f750a72a/t/5b84a2a20e2e721b341bac99/1535419043941/barbara+bergmann+ on+femecon.pdf.

12 As retrieved on January 30, 2019 at: https://static1.squarespace.com/static/59af966b49 fc2bd0f750a72a/t/5b8586ae21c67c0c1333238b/1535477423112/nancy+ folbre+in+ defense+of+SG+model+of+labor+supply+by+individuals+who+are+ married.pdf.

13 As retrieved on January 30, 2019 at: https://static1.squarespace.com/static/59af966b49fc 2bd0f750a72a/t/5b859857cd8366c6feec18b4/1535481944594/Don+McCloskey+in+ defense+of+SG+%26+crit+of+Bergmann.pdf.

14 Gender mainstreaming was first introduced in 1985 at the United Nations Conference on Women held in Nairobi. Ten years later, in 1995, during the United Nations Fourth World Conference on Women held in Beijing, it has been established that policies and political programs should ensure a gender perspective. In 1998, the Council of Europe defined gender mainstreaming as: "the (re)organisation, improvement, development and evaluation of policy processes, so that a gender equality perspective is incorporated in all policies at all levels and at all stages, by the actors normally involved in policy-making" (Council of Europe 1998).

15 As retrieved on February 3, 2019 at: www.weforum.org/reports/the-global-gender-gap-report-2018.

16 The OECD Gender Initiative examines existing barriers to gender equality in education, employment, and entrepreneurship. The OECD report monitors the progress made by governments to promote gender equality in both OECD and non-OECD countries. As retrieved on February 3, 2019 at: www.oecd.org/gender/.

17 As retrieved on February 2, 2019 at: www.aeaweb.org/research/gender-gap-economics-profession-interview-with-amanda-bayer.

18 In the MENA region, less than one quarter of working-age women participate in the labor force, and less than 10% of incorporated businesses are women-owned, in fact, only one in eight is an entrepreneur, while men entrepreneurs are 1/3 of the male labor force.

19 Since 1999, GEM has collected data about entrepreneurship in more than 100 economies. GEM adopts a multi-phase measure of entrepreneurship which includes potential entrepreneurs, intentional entrepreneurs, nascent entrepreneurs, established business owner, discontinued entrepreneurs, and new entrepreneurs. As retrieved on February 5, 2019 at: www.gemconsortium.org/report/49860.

20 As seen in Chapter I, gender discrimination in getting access to financial resources which make women able to start and run a business had been a central topic within both liberal feminist theory and socialist feminist theory (Carter and Williams 2003; Galindo et al. 2012).

21 The notion of social entrepreneurship has been introduced in the 1950s (Bowen 1953). During the past decade, the number of researches on social entrepreneurship is dramatically increased, and it was especially analyzed in relation with poverty (Bloom 2009; Ghauri et al. 2014), and with women empowerment (Datta and Gailey 2012) either in developed countries or in developing areas (Saebi et al. 2018).

References

Akerlof G. and Kranton R. (2000) "Economics and Identity". *The Quarterly Journal of Economics.* Vol. 115:3, pp. 715–753.

Akerlof G. and Kranton R. (2002) "Identity and Schooling: Some Lessons for the Economics of Education". *Journal of Economic Literature*. Vol. 40:4, pp. 1167–1201.

Akerlof G. and Kranton R. (2005) "Identity and the Economics of Organizations". *Journal of Economic Perspectives*. Vol. 19:1, pp. 9–32.

Akerlof G. and Kranton R. (2008) "Identity, Supervision, and Work Groups". *American Economic Review*. Vol. 98:2, pp. 212–217.

Akerlof G. and Kranton R. (2010) *Identity Economics: How Our Identities Shape Our Work, Wages, and Well-Being*. Princeton, NJ: Princeton University Press.

Alesina A. and Giuliano P. (2010) "The Power of the Family". *Journal of Economic Growth*. Vol. 15:2, pp. 93–125.

Alesina A., Giuliano P., and Nunn N. (2013) "On the Origins of Gender Roles: Women and the Plough". *Quarterly Journal of Economics*. Vol. 128:2, pp. 469–530.

American Psychology Association (2013) "The 2012 Annual Report of the American Psychology Association". *The American Psychologist*. Vol. 68:5, pp. 6–48.

Antecol H., Bedard K., and Stearns J. (2018) "Equal But Inequitable: Who Benefits From Gender-Neutral Tenure Clock Stopping Policies?". *American Economic Review*. Vol. 108:9, pp. 2420–2441.

Armstrong D. (1989) *Universals: An Opinionated Introduction*. Boulder, CO: Westview Press.

Austin J.E., Stevenson H., and Wei-Skillern J. (2006) "Social and Commercial Entrepreneurship: Same, Different, or Both?". *Entrepreneurship Theory and Practice*. Vol. 30:1, pp. 1–22.

Autor D. (2014) "Skills, Education, and the Rise of Earning Inequality Among the 'Other 99 Percent'". *Science*. Vol. 344, pp. 304–330.

Baker M. and Jacobsen J. (2007) "Marriage, Specialization and the Gender Division of Labor". *Journal of Labor Economics*. Vol. 108:4, pp. 663–679.

Barker D. (1999) "Gender". Paterson J. and Lewis M. (Eds.) *The Elgar Companion to Feminist Economics*. Cheltenham: Edward Elgar, pp. 390–396.

Barker H. (2006) *The Business of Women; Female Experience and Urban Development in Northern England*. Oxford: Oxford University Press.

Basu K. (2006) "Gender and Say: A Model of Household Behavior with Endogenously Determined Balance of Power". *The Economic Journal*. Vol. 116:211, pp. 558–580.

Bayer A. and Rouse C. (2016) "Diversity in the Economic Profession: A New Attack on an Old Problem". *Journal of Economic Perspectives*. Vol. 30:4, pp. 221–242.

Becker G. (1964) *Human Capital: A Theoretical and Empirical Analysis, with Special Reference to Education*. Chicago: The University of Chicago Press.

Becker G. (1973) "A Theory of Marriage: Part I". *Journal of Political Economy*. Vol. 81:4, pp. 813–846.

Becker G. (1976) *The Economic Approach to Human Behavior*. Chicago: Chicago University Press.

Becker G. (1981) *A Treatise on the Family*. Cambridge, MA: Harvard University Press.

Benavides-Espinosa M. and Mohedano-Suanes A. (2012) "Linking Women Entrepreneurship with Social Entrepreneurship". Galindo M. and Ribeiro D. (Eds.) *Women's Entrepreneurship and Economics*. Dordrecht, Heidelberg, London, and New York: Springer, pp. 53–71.

Beneria L. (1995) "Toward a Greater Integration of Gender Economics". *World Development*. Vol. 23:11, pp. 1839–1850.

Blau F. and Kahn L. (2017) "The Gender Wage Gap: Extent, Trends, and Sources". *Journal of Economic Literature*. Vol. 55:3, pp. 789–965.

Blau F. and Winkler A. (2018) *The Economics of Women, Men, and Work*. 8th Edition. New York: Oxford University Press.

Blomqvist M., Chastain E., Thickett B., Unnikrishnan S., and Woods W. (2014) *Bridging the Entrepreneurship Gender Gap: The Power of Networks*. Boston: Boston Consulting Group Report.

Bloom P. (2009) "Overcoming Consumption Constraints Through Social Entrepreneurship". *Journal of Public Policy & Marketing*. Vol. 28:1, pp. 128–134.

Bohnet I. (2016) *What Works: Gender Equality by Design*. Cambridge, MA: Harvard University Press.

Boserup E. (1970) *Woman's Role in Economic Development*. London: George Allen and Unwin Ltd.

Bowen H. (1953) *The Social Responsibilities of the Businessman*. New York: Harper & Brothers.

Butler J. (1990) *Gender Trouble: Feminism and the Subversion of Identity*. London: Routledge.

Butler J. (1993) *Bodies that Matter*. London: Routledge.

Butler J. (1999) *Gender Trouble*. 2nd Edition. London: Routledge.

Card D., DellaVigna S., Funk P., and Iriberri N. (2018) "Are Referees and Editors in Economics Gender Neutral?". *Working Paper*. As retrieved on September 17, 2018 at: https://eml.berkeley.edu/~sdellavi/wp/EditorGender_Dec17.pdf.

Carter N. and Williams M. (2003) "Comparing Social Feminism and Liberal Feminism". Butler J. (Ed.) *New Perspectives on Women Entrepreneurs*. Greenwich, CT: Information Age Publishing, pp. 25–50.

Cassar A. and Katz E. (2016) "Gender, Behavior, and Women's Economic Empowerment". *CDG Background Paper*. Washington, DC: Center for Global Development, pp. 1–27.

Ceci S., Ginther D., Kahn S., and Williams W. (2014) "Women in Academic Science: A Changing Landscape". *Psychological Science in the Public Interest*. Vol. 15:3, pp. 75–141.

Chiappori P. and Lewbel A. (2015) "Gary Becker: A Theory of Allocation of Time". *The Economic Journal*. Vol. 125:583, pp. 410–422.

Chichilnisky G. (2008) "The Gender Gap". Bettio F. and Verashchagina A. (Eds.) *Frontiers in the Economics of Gender*. London: Routledge, pp. 57–76.

Chodorow N. (1978) *Reproducing Mothering*. Berkeley, CA: University of California Press.

Chodorow N. (1995) "Family Structure and Feminine Personality". Tuana N. and Tong R. (Eds.) *Feminism and Philosophy*. Boulder, CO: Westview Press, pp. 199–216.

Cigno A. (2008) "A Gender-neutral Approach to Gender Issues". Bettio F. and Verashchagina A. (Eds.) *Frontiers in the Economics of Gender*. London: Routledge, pp. 46–56.

Cook J. and Roberts J. (2000) "Towards a Gendered Political Economy". Cook J. et al. (Eds.) *Towards a Gendered Political Economy*. London: Palgrave MacMillan, pp. 3–13.

Cook J., Roberts J., and Waylen G. (Eds.) (2000) *Towards a Gendered Political Economy*. London: Palgrave MacMillan.

Council of Europe (1998) *Gender Mainstreaming*. As retrieved on August 30, 2019 at: https://rm.coe.int/1680630394

Cortes P. and Pan J. (2018) "Occupation and Gender". Averett S., Argit L., and Hoffman S. (Eds.) *The Oxford Handbook of Women and the Economy*. New York: Oxford University Press, pp. 425–452.

Croson R. and Gneezy U. (2009) "Gender Differences in Preferences". *Journal of Economic Literature*. Vol. 47:2, pp. 448–474.

CSMGEP (2018) *Report of the Committee on the Status of Minority Groups in the Economic Profession*. As retrieved on April 2, 2019 at: www.aeaweb.org/content/file?id=9030.

Datta P. and Gailey R. (2012) "Empowering Women Through Social Entrepreneurship: Case Study of a Women's Cooperative in India". *Entrepreneurship: Theory & Practice*. Vol. 36:3, pp. 569–587.

Davis J. (2007) "Akerlof and Kranton on Identity in Economics: Inverting the Analysis". *Cambridge Journal of Economics*. Vol. 31:3, pp. 349–362.

Davis J. (2011a) "Review of *Identity Economics* by Akerlof and Kranton". *Economics and Philosophy*. Vol. 27:3, pp. 331–338.

Davis J. (2011b) *Individuals and Identity in Economics*. Cambridge: Cambridge University Press.

Dilli S., Carmichael S., and Rijpima A. (2019) "Introducing the Historical Gender Equality Index". *Feminist Economics*. Vol. 25:1, pp. 31–57.

Doe H. (2017) "Gender and Business. Women in Business or Businesswomen? An Assessment of the History of Entrepreneurial Women". Wilson J.F., Toms S., de Jong A., and Buchnea E. (Eds.) *The Routledge Companion to Business History*. London and New York: Routledge, pp. 347–357.

Ductor L., Goyal S., and Prummer A. (2018) "Gender and collaboration". *Cambridge-INET Working Paper* 1807.

Duflo E. (2012) "Women Empowerment and Economic Development". *Journal of Economic Literature*. Vol. 50:4, pp. 1051–1079.

Eckel C. and Grossman P. (1998) "Are Women Less Selfish than Men?: Evidence From Dictator Experiments". *The Economic Journal*. Vol. 108:448, pp. 726–735.

Eckel C. and Grossman P. (2001) "Chivalry Versus Solidarity in Ultimatum Game". *Economic Inquiry*. Vol. 39:2, pp. 171–188.

Eckel C. and Grossman P. (2008) "Forecasting Risk Attitudes: An Experimental Study Using Actual and Forecast Gamble Choice". *Journal of Economic Behavior and Organization*. Vol. 68:1, pp. 1–17.

Ekert-Jaffe O. and Grossbard S. (2008) "Does Community Property Discourage Unpartnered Births?". *European Journal of Policy Economy*. Vol. 24:1, pp. 25–40.

Elul R., Silva-Reus J., and Volij O. (2002) "Will you Marry Me? A Perspective on the Gender Gap". *Journal of Economic Behavior and Organization*. Vol. 49:4, pp. 549–572.

Essed P., Goldberg D., and Kobayashi A. (2009) "Introduction: A Curriculum Vitae for Gender Studies". Essed P., Goldberg D., and Kobayashi A. (Eds.) *A Companion to Gender Studies*. Chichester: Wiley-Blackwell, pp. 1–25.

Ferber M. and Nelson J. (1993) *Beyond Economic Man: Feminist Theory and Economics*. Chicago: The Chicago University Press.

Figart D. (1997) "Gender as More than a Dummy Variable: Feminist Approaches to Discrimination". *Review of Social Economy*. Vol. 55:1, pp. 1–32.

Fine B. (2009) "The Economics of Identity and the Identity of Economics?". *Cambridge Journal of Economics*. Vol. 33:2, pp. 175–191.

Folbre N. (1983) "Of Patriarchy Born: The Political Economy of Fertility Decision". *Feminist Studies*. Vol. 9:2, pp. 261–284.

Friedan B. (1963) *Feminine Mystique*. New York: Norton.

Friedman M. (1976) *Price Theory*. Chicago: Aldine Publishing Company.

Galindo M., Ribeiro D., and Rubio J. (2012) "Women's Approach to Economics and Firms". Galindo M. and Ribeiro D. (Eds.) *Women's Entrepreneurship and Economics*. Dordrecht, Heidelberg, London, and New York: Springer, pp. 9–19.

Galor O., Özak Ö., and Sarid A. (2016) "Geographical Origins and Economic Consequences of Language Structures". *CESifo Working Paper Series* No. 6149.

Gámez-Gutiérrez J. and Saiz-Álvarez J. (2012) "Microcredits for Women Entrepreneurship: Are They an Effective Tool to Avoid Family Impoverishment?". Galindo M. and Ribeiro D. (Eds.) *Women's Entrepreneurship and Economics*. Dordrecht, Heidelberg, London, and New York: Springer, pp. 167–177.

Gardiner J. (1997) *Gender, Care and Economics*. London: Macmillan.

Gardiner J. (1998) "Beyond Human Capital". *New Political Economy*. Vol. 3:2, pp. 209–221.

Geddes P. and Thomson A. (1889) *The Evolution of Sex*. London: Walter Scott.

Ghauri P., Tasavori M., and Zaefarian R. (2014) "Internationalisation of Service Firms Through Corporate Social Entrepreneurship and Networking". *International Marketing Review*. Vol. 31:6, pp. 576–600.

Ginther D. and Kahn S. (2004) "Women in Economics: Moving up or Falling off the Academic Career Ladder?". *Journal of Economic Perspectives*. Vol. 18:3, pp. 193–214.

Ginther D. and Kahn S. (2014) "Academic Women's Careers in the Social Sciences". Lanteri A. and Vromen J. (Eds.) *The Economics of Economist*. Cambridge: Cambridge University Press, pp. 285–315.

Giuliano P. (2018) "Gender. A Historical Perspective". Averett S., Argit L., and Hoffman S. (Eds.) *The Oxford Handbook of Women and the Economy*. New York: Oxford University Press, pp. 645–671.

Global Entrepreneurship Monitor (2017) "Women's Entrepreneurship 2016/2017 Report". *Global Entrepreneurship Research Association (GERA)*. As retrieved on February 20, 2018 at: www.gemconsortium.org/report/49860.

Gneezy U., Leonard K., and List J. (2009) "Gender Differences in Competition: Evidence from a Matrilineal and a Patriarchal Society". *Econometrica*. Vol. 77:5, pp. 1637–1664.

Gneezy U., Niederle M., and Rustichini A. (2003) "Performance in Competitive Environments: Gender Differences". *The Quarterly Journal of Economics*. Vol. 118:3, pp. 1049–1074.

Goldin C. (2002) *A Pollution Theory of Discrimination: Male and Female Differences in Occupations and Earnings*. Cambridge, MA: NBER Working Paper Series.

Goldin C. (2014) "A Grand Gender Convergence: Its Last Chapter". *American Economic Review*. Vol. 104:4, pp. 1091–1119.

Grossbard S. (1984) "A Theory of Allocation of Time in Markets for Labor and Marriage". *The Economic Journal*. Vol. 94:376, pp. 863–882.

Grossbard S. (1993) *On Economics of Marriage*. Boulder, CO: Westview Press.

Grossbard S. (2003) "A Consumer Theory with Competitive Markets for Work in Marriage". *Journal of Socio-Economics*. Vol. 31:6, pp. 609–645.

Grossbard S. (2015) *The Marriage Motive: A Price Theory of Marriage. How Marriage Markets Affect, Employment, Consumption, and Savings*. Dordrecht, Heidelberg, London, and New York: Springer.

Grossbard S. (2018) "Marriage and Marriage Markets". Averett S., Argit L., and Hoffman S. (Eds.) *The Oxford Handbook of Women and the Economy*. New York: Oxford University Press, pp. 55–73.

Grossbard S. and Granger C. (1998) "Women's Jobs and Marriage: Baby-Boom versus Baby-Bust (Travail des Femmes et Mariage: du baby-boom au baby-bust)". *Population*. Vol. 53, pp. 731–752.

Grosz E. (1994) *Volatile Bodies: Toward a Corporeal Feminism*. Bloomington, IN: Indiana University Press.

Guidi M. and Schmidt L. (2018) "Taxes, Transfers, and Women's Labor Supply in the United States". Averett S., Argit L., and Hoffman S. (Eds.) *The Oxford Handbook of Women and the Economy*. New York: Oxford University Press, pp. 453–480.

Halberstam J. (2014) "Gender". Brugett B. and Hendler G. (Eds.) *Keywords for American Cultural Studies*. 2nd Edition. New York: New York University Press, pp. 116–118.

Haraway D.J. (1991) *Simians, Cyborgs, and Women: The Reinvention of Nature*. London: Routledge.

Harding S. (1991) *Whose Science? Whose Knowledge? Thinking from Women's Lives*. Ithaca, NY: Cornell University Press.

Harding S. (Ed.) (1987) *Feminism and Methodology*. Bloomington, IN: Indiana University Press.

Harris A. (1993) "Race and Essentialism in Feminist Legal Theory". Weisberg D.K. (Ed.) *Feminist Legal Theory: Foundations*. Philadelphia, PA: Temple University Press, pp. 581–616.

Haslanger S. (1995) "Ontology and Social Construction". *Philosophical Topics*. Vol. 23:2, pp. 95–125.

Haslanger S. (2005) "What Are We Talking About? The Semantics and Politics of Social Kinds". *Hypatia: A Journal of Feminist Philosophy*. Vol. 20:4, pp. 10–26.

Haslanger S. (2006) "What Good Are Our Intuitions?" *Proceedings of the Aristotelian Society*. Vol. 80:1, pp. 89–118.

Hechavarria D., Ingram A., Justo R., and Terjesen S. (2012) "Are Women more likely to Pursue Social and Environmental Entrepreneurship". Hughes K. and Jennings J. (Eds.) *Global Women's Entrepreneurship Research: Diverse Settings, Questions and Approaches*. Cheltenham: Edward Elgar, pp. 135–151.

Hengel E. (2017) "Publishing While Female: Are Women Held to Higher Standards? Evidence From Peer Review". *Cambridge Working Papers in Economics* 1753, Faculty of Economics, University of Cambridge.

Heyes C. (2000) *Line Drawings*. Ithaca, NY: Cornell University Press.

Hirsh G., Hortaşçsu A., and Ariely D. (2010) "Matching and Sorting in Online Dating". *American Economic Review*. Vol. 100:1, pp. 130–163.

Hudson P. (2008) "The Historical Construction of Gender". Bettio F. and Verashchagina A. (Eds.) *Frontiers in the Economics of Gender*. London: Routledge, pp. 21–41.

Human Development Report (2014) "Gender Inequality Index Data". *United Nations Development Program*. As retrieved on December 26, 2018 at: http://hdr.undp.org/en/2014-report.

Human Development Report (2018) *Statistical Update*. As retrieved on December 29, 2018 at: http://hdr.undp.org/sites/default/files/2018_human_development_statistical_update.pdf

Humbert A. L. (2012). *Women as Social Entrepreneurs*. As retrieved on August 30, 2018 at: https://www.birmingham.ac.uk/Documents/college-social-sciences/social-policy/tsrc/working-papers/working-paper-72.pdf

Humphries J. (1995) *Gender and Economics*. Aldershot: Edward Elgar.

Humphries J. (1998) "Towards a Family-Friendly Economics". *New Political Economy*. Vol. 3:2, pp. 223–240.

Huysentruyt M. (2014) "Women's Social Entrepreneurship and Innovation". *OECD Local Economic and Employment Development*. OECD Publishing. As retrieved on December 28, 2018 at: http://dx.doi.org/10.1787/5jxzkq2sr7d4-en.

Hyde J. (2005) "The Gender Similarities Hypothesis". *American Psychologists*. Vol. 60:6, pp. 581–592.

International Labor Organization (2013) *Gender and Development Report*. As retrieved on December 27, 2018 at: www.ilo.org/global/topics/economic-and-social-development/gender-and-development/lang-en/.

International Labour Organization (2016) *Women at Work: Trends 2016*. Geneva: International Labour Organization.

Jacobsen J. (1994) *The Economic of Gender*. 1st Edition. Oxford: Blackwell Publishers Ltd.

Jacobsen J. (1998) *The Economic of Gender*. 2nd Edition. Oxford: Blackwell Publishers Ltd.

Jacobsen J. (2018) "Women and the Labor Market". Averett S., Argys L., and Hoffman S. (Eds.) *The Oxford Handbook of Women and the Economy*. New York: Oxford University Press, pp. 623–641.

Jamali D. (2009) "Constraint and Opportunities Facing Women Entrepreneurs in Developing Countries: A Relational Perspective". *Gender in Management: An International Journal*. Vol. 24:4, pp. 232–251.

Keller E. (1985) *Reflections on Gender and Science*. New Haven, CT: Yale University Press.

Klyver K., Nielsen S.L., and Evald M.R. (2013) "Women's Self-employment: An Act of Institutional (Dis)integration? A Multilevel, Cross-country Study". *Journal of Business Venturing*. Vol. 28:4, pp. 474–488.

Kramer L. and Beutel A. (2014) *The Sociology of Gender*. Oxford: Oxford University Press.

Lam D. (1988) "Marriage Markets and Assortative Mating with Household Public Goods: Theoretical Results and Empirical Implication". *Journal of Human Resources*. Vol. 23:4, pp. 462–487.

Lee W. and McKinnish T. (2018) "The Marital Satisfaction of Differently-Aged Couples". *Journal of Population Economics*. Vol. 31:2, pp. 337–362.

Lerner G. (1986) *The Creation of Patriarchy*. Oxford: Oxford University Press.

Lerner G. (1991) *The Creation of Feminist Consciousness: From the Middle Age to 1870*. Oxford: Oxford University Press.

Lloyd G. (1993) *The Man of Reason: 'Male' and 'Female' in Western Philosophy*. London: Routledge.

Longino H. (1990) *Science as Social Knowledge*. Princeton, NJ: Princeton University Press.

Lorber J. (2006) "Shifting Paradigms and Challenging Categories". *Social Problems*. Vol. 53:4, pp. 448–453.

Lundberg S. (2008) "Gender and Household Decision-Making". Bettio F. and Verashchagina A. (Eds.) *Frontiers in the Economics of Gender*. London: Routledge, pp. 116–133.

Lundberg S. (2012) "Personality and Marital Surplus". *IZA Journal of Labor Economics*. Vol. 1:3, pp. 1–21.

Lundberg S. and Pollak R. (1996) "Bargaining and Distribution on Marriage". *Journal of Economic Perspectives*. Vol. 10:4, pp. 139–158.

Lundberg S. and Pollak R. (2003) "Efficiency in Marriage". *Review of Economics of the Household*. Vol. 1:3, pp. 153–167.

Lundberg S. and Stearns J. (2019) "Women in Economics: Stalled Progress". *Journal of Economic Perspectives*. Vol. 33:1, pp. 3–22.

MacKinnon C. (1989) *Toward a Feminist Theory of State*. Cambridge, MA: Harvard University Press.

MacKinnon C. (2006) "Difference and Dominance". Hackett E. and Haslanger S. (Eds.) *Theorizing Feminisms*. Oxford: Oxford University Press, pp.

Manser M. and Brown M. (1980) "Marriage and Household Decision Making: A Bargaining Analysis". *International Economic Review*. Vol. 21:1, pp. 31–44.

Mansour H. and McKinnish T. (2014) "Couples' Time Together: Complementarities in Production Versus Complementarities in Consumption". *Journal of Population Economics*. Vol. 27:4, pp. 577–580.

Mansour H. and McKinnish T. (2018a) "Marriage Market Search and Sorting". Averett S., Argys L., and Hoffman S. (Eds.) *The Oxford Handbook of Women and the Economy*. New York: Oxford University Press, pp. 35–53.

Mansour H. and McKinnish T. (2018b) "Same-Occupation Spouses: Preferences or Research Costs". *Journal of Population Economics*. Vol. 31:4, pp. 1005–1033.

McDowell J.M., Singell L., and Ziliak J. (2001) "Gender and Promotion in the Economics Profession". *ILR Review*. Vol. 54:2, pp. 224–244.

McElroy M. and Horney M. (1981) "Nash-Bargained Household Decisions". *International Economic Review*. Vol. 22:2, pp. 333–349.

Millett K. (1971) *Sexual Politics*. London: Granada Publishing Ltd.

Mincer J. (1962) "Labor Force Participation of Married Women: A Study of Labor Supply". Lewis G. (Ed.) *Aspects of Labor Economics*. Princeton, NJ: Princeton University Press, pp. 63–106.

Moi T. (1999) *What Is a Woman?* Oxford: Oxford University Press.

Money J. and Ehrhardt A. (1972) *Man and Woman, Boy and Girl: The Differentiation and Dimorphism of Gender Identity from Conception to Maturity*. Baltimore, MD: John Hopkins University.

Moore S. (2015) "Gender Economics: An Introduction to Contemporary Gender Economics". Moore S. (Ed.) *Contemporary Global Perspectives on Gender Economics*. Hershey, PA: IGI Global.

Mutari E., Boushey H., and Fraher W. (1997) *Gender and Political Economy: Incorporating Diversity into Theory and Policy*. Armonk, NY: M.E. Sharpe.

Nelson J. (1995) "Feminism and Economics". *Journal of Economic Perspectives*. Vol. 9:2, pp. 131–148.

Nelson J. (2014) "The Power of Stereotyping and Confirmation Bias to Overwhelm Accurate Assessment: The Case of Economics, Gender, and Risk Aversion". *Journal of Economic Methodology*. Vol. 1:3, pp. 211–231.

Nelson J. (2016) "Not-So-Strong Evidence for Gender Differences in Risk Taking". *Feminist Economics*. Vol. 22:2, pp. 114–142.

Nelson J. (2018) *Economics for Humans*. 2nd Edition. Chicago: The Chicago University Press.

Nicolás C. and Rubio A. (2016) "Social Enterprise: Gender Gap and Economic Development". *European Journal of Management and Business Economics*. Vol. 25:2, pp. 56–62.

Niederle M. (2015) "Gender". Kagel J. and Roth A. (Eds.) *Handbook of Experimental Economics*. Vol. 2. Princeton, NJ: Princeton University Press, pp. 482–561.

Niederle M. and Vesterlund L. (2007) "Do Women Shy Away from Competition? Do Men Compete Too Much?". *The Quarterly Journal of Economics*. Vol. 122:3, pp. 1067–1101.

Niederle M. and Vesterlund L. (2011) "Gender and Competition". *Annual Review of Economics*. Vol. 3, pp. 601–630.

Nunn N. (2014) "Gender and Missionary Influence in Colonial Africa". Akyeampong E., Bates R., Nunn N., and Robinson J. (Eds.) *Africa's Development in Historical Perspective*. New York: Cambridge University Press, pp. 489–512.

Nussbaum M. (2000) *Women and Human Development: The Capabilities Approach*. Cambridge and New York: Cambridge University Press.

OECD Report (2012) *Closing the Gender Gap: Act Now*. Paris: OECD Library.

OECD (2016a) *2015 OECD Recommendation of the Council on Gender Equality in Public Life*. Paris: OECD Publishing. As retieved on August 30, 2019 at: https://doi.org/10.1787/9789264252820-en.

OECD Report (2016b) *Entrepreneurship at a Glance 2016*. Paris: OECD Library. As retrieved on March 21, 2018 at: http://dx.doi.org /10.1787/entrepreneur_aag-2016-en.

OECD Report (2017) *The Pursuit of Gender Equality: An Uphill Battle*. Paris: OECD Library. As retrieved on March 21, 2018 at: https://dx.doi.org/10.1787/9789264281318-en

Owens A. (2002) "Inheritance and the Life Cycle of Family Firms in the Early Industrial Revolution". *Business History*. Vol. 44:1, pp. 21–46.

Peris-Ortiz M., Palacios-Marqués D., and Rueda-Armengot C. (2012) "Women Entrepreneurship and Gender Accountability". Galindo M. and Ribeiro D. (Eds.) *Women's Entrepreneurship and Economics*. Dordrecht, Heidelberg, London, and New York: Springer, pp. 181–189.

Prokhovnik R. (1999) *Rational Woman*. London: Routledge.

Renzetti C., Curran D., and Maier S. (2012) *Women, Men, and Society: The Sociology of Gender*. 6th Edition. New York: Pearson.

Rubin G. (1975) "The Traffic in Women: Notes on the 'Political Economy' of Sex". Reiter R. (Ed.) *Toward an Anthropology of Women*. New York: Monthly Review Press, pp. 157–210.

Saebi T., Foss N., and Linder S. (2018) "Social Entrepreneurship Research: Past Achievement and Future Promises". *Journal of Management*. Vol. 45:1, pp. 70–95.

Samuelson P. (1956) "Social Indifference Curves". *Quarterly Journal of Economics*. Vol. 70:1, pp. 1–22.

Santos F. (2012) "A Positive Theory of Social Entrepreneurship". *Journal of Business Ethics*. Vol. 111:3, pp. 335–351.

Schubert R., Brown M., Gysler M., and Brachinger H. (1999) "Financial Decision-Making: Are Women Really More Risk-Averse?". *American Economic Review*. Vol. 89:2, pp. 381–385.

Schwartz C. (2013) "Trends and Variations in Assortative Mating: Causes and Consequences". *Annual Review of Sociology*. Vol. 39, pp. 421–470.

Spelman E. (1988) *Inessential Woman*. Boston: Beacon Press.

Stacey J. and Thorne B. (1985) "The Missing Feminist Revolution in Sociology". *Social Problems*. Vol. 32:4, pp. 301–316.

Stoljar N. (1995) "Essence, Identity and the Concept of Woman". *Philosophical Topics*. Vol. 23:2, pp. 261–293.

Stoller R. (1968) *Sex and Gender: On The Development of Masculinity and Femininity*. New York: Science House.

Stone A. (2004) "Essentialism and Anti-Essentialism in Feminist Philosophy". *Journal of Moral Philosophy*. Vol. 1:2, pp. 135–153.

Stone A. (2007) *An Introduction to Feminist Philosophy*. Cambridge, MA: Polity Press.

Swineford F. (1941) "Analysis of a Personality Trait". *Journal of Educational Psychology*. Vol. 32:6, pp. 438–444.

Tajfel H. (1972) "Social Categorization". Moscovici S. (Ed.) *Introduction a' la Psychologie Sociale*. Vol. 1. Paris: Larousse, pp. 272–302.

Terjesen S., Lepoutre J., Justo R., and Bosma N. (2011) *Global Entrepreneurship Monitor Report on Social Entrepreneurship*. London: Global Entrepreneurship Research Association.

Turner J. (1985) "Social Categorization and the Self-concept: A Social Cognitive Theory of Group Behavior". Lawler E. (Ed.) *Advances in Group Processes: Theory and Research*. Vol. 2. Greenwich, CT: JAI Press, pp. 77–122.

Turner J., Hogg M., Oakes P., Reicher S., and Wetherell M. (1987) *Rediscovering the Social Group: A Self-Categorization Theory*. Oxford: Blackwell.

Waldfogel J. (1998) "The Family Gap for Young Women in the United States and Britain: Can Maternity Leave Make a Difference?". *Journal of Labor Economics*. Vol. 16:3, pp. 505–545.

Waylen G. (1997) "Gender, Feminism, and Political Economy". *New Political Economy*. Vol. 2:2, pp. 205–220.

Waylen G. (1998) "Introduction". *New Political Economy*. Vol. 3:2, pp. 181–188.

Welter F. (2010) "Contextualizing Entrepreneurship – Conceptual Challenges and Ways Forward". *Entrepreneurship Theory and Practice*. Vol. 35:1, pp. 165–184.

Witt C. (2011) "What Is Gender Essentialism?". Witt C. (Ed.) *Feminist Metaphysics. Explorations in the Ontology of Sex, Gender and the Self.* Dordrecht, Heidelberg, London, and New York: Springer, pp. 11–26.

Witt C. (2011) *The Metaphysics of Gender.* Oxford: Oxford University Press.

Woodberry R. and Shah T. (2004) "The Pioneering Protestant". *Journal of Democracy.* Vol. 15:2, pp. 47–61.

Woolley H.T. (1914) "The Psychology of Sex". *Psychological Bulletin.* Vol. 11, pp. 353–379.

World Bank (2016) *World Bank Gender Action Plan 2016–2021.* As retrieved on August 30, 2018 at: http://documents.worldbank.org/curated/en/243921492664887890/pdf/114422-WP-PUBLIC-gender-action-plan-2016-2021.pdf.

World Economic Forum (2018) *The Global Gender Gap Report 2018.* As retrieved on August 30, 2018 at: www3.weforum.org/docs/WEF_GGGR_2018.pdf.

Young I.M. (1997) *Intersecting Voices: Dilemmas of Gender, Political Philosophy and Policy.* Princeton, NJ: Princeton University Press.

Appendix
Timeline

The woman question and political economy: the genesis of feminist economics and gender neoclassical economics

Forerunners

1405. Christine De Pizan published *Livre de la Cité des Dames* to urge an economic education for women in order to empower their social position.

1622. Mary de Gournay insisted on the fact that there are no neurological differences between women and men which may determine any different behavior between sexes.

1693. John Locke denied any mental difference between the sexes and advocated an identical program of education.

1756. In the *Encyclopedia*, the subjection of women was depicted to be a result of a constructed patriarchal system.

1791. Olympe de Gouges published *The Declaration of the Rights of Woman and the Female Citizen.*

1792. Mary Wollstonecraft published *A Vindication of the Rights of Woman.*

Woman question and political economy within classical liberalism, socialism, and abolitionism

1816. In London, Jane Marcet published *Conversation on Political Economy* to promote a free-market education for girls. In Vienna, The *Israelitische Frauenverein* was founded to promote girls' education.

1825. In Great Britain, William Thompson and Anna Doyle Wheeler published *Appeal of One Half the Human Race, Women, Against the Pretension of the Other Half, Men, to Retain Them in Political, and thence in Civil and Domestic, Slavery;* motherhood was presented as the primary source of women's social inferiority, which had forced them to be confined to unremunerated reproductive labor.

1832–1834. In London, Harriet Martineau published *Illustrations of Political Economy* to popularize economic knowledge among women.

1833. In Philadelphia, delegates of abolitionist movements founded the American Anti-Slavery Society. A few days later, a group of women, led by Sarah Moore Grimké, Sarah Douglass, Harriet Purvis, Sarah Forten, Margaretta Forten, and Lucretia Mott established the Philadelphia Female Anti-Slavery Society.

1837. Sarah Moore Grimké published *Letters on the Equality of the Sexes* to complain about the *miserably deficient* education imposed on women by the conservative American society.

1851. Harriet Taylor Mill published *The Enfranchisement of Women* to demand an *equal education* between sexes at any level; am effective *partnership* between spouses in labor-force; a significant *reduction* of any gender gap; and a *coequal share* in political institutions.

1851. In Akron, Ohio, at the Women's Convention, Sojourner Truth delivered her speech *Ain't I a Woman?* to strongly denounce the double discrimination of African American women in the United States of America.

1857. In London, Barbara Bodichon published *Women and Work* to support gender equal pay by introducing the principle that women and men share the same attitude and motivations (necessity, self-fulfillment, and greed) when they choose to work. She considered educational gender gap as well as job discrimination as effects of men's monopoly over the most remunerative jobs.

1858. Barbara Bodichon, Matilda Hays, and Bessie Parkes founded the monthly periodical *English Women Journal* to promote female employment.

1859. Jessie Boucherett, Barbara Bodichon, and Adelaide Procter founded the *Society for Promoting the Employment of Women.*

1860. Switzerland allowed female students to enroll in universities and colleges.

1866. In Vienna, The *Verein für erweiterte Frauenbildung* (the Viennese professional women's association) was founded to promote the admission of women to secondary school as well as to universities, and to prepare them to get access to some professions.

1868. In London, Josephine Grey Butler published *The Education and Employment of Women* to propose some measure for regulating prostitution.

1869. John Stuart Mill published *The Subjection of Women* to explore patriarchy and slavery as expressions of the collective self-interest of the dominant group in society (white men) over the dominated group (women and black population). Mill debated against Jevons-Marshall's conception of women's mental attitude, which had prevented them from being involved in scientific and artistic fields as well as in many other valuable professions.

1879. In Cambridge, Massachusetts, Harvard University created Radcliff College for female students.

1889. In Germany, during a meeting of the Second International, Clara Zetkin gave a speech about the connection between socialism and woman question which had been often neglected.

1891–1917. The *Economic Journal* hosted a debate between Sidney Webb and Millicent Garrett Fawcett around the origin of the gender wage gap as the effect of the general inferiority of women's labor in terms of quantity and quality (Webb) versus the effect of women's occupational segregation, mainly because of some distorted trade unions' policy of exclusion (Fawcett). The debate also involved socialist Beatrice Webb and classical liberal Eleanor Rathbone, who proposed a differentiated wage system and some state subsidy for motherhood that implicitly reinforced the stereotype of women as primarily mothers and wives.

1894. The Economic Journal hosted Ada Heather-Bigg's article, "The Wife's Contribution to Family Income": the first explicit attack on patriarchy ever published in an academic economic journal.

1895. In Germany, women students were admitted to the School of Philosophy and were enrolled in political economy curricula.

1898. In the United States, Charlotte Perkins Gilman published *Women and Economics* to promote an equal division of homework between men and women and to encourage women's self-determination in their professional activities.

1899. In Great Britain, Margaret Llewelyn Davies founded *The Women's Co-operative Guild* for the advancement of women in society, focused on the minimum wage for women employed in cooperatives.

1902. In Great Britain, Helen Bosanquet published a book about women's education and economic conditions, *The Strength of the People. A Study on Women's Wage* to promote major investments on women's education as a measure to rise social well-being.

1906. Helen Bosanquet published *The Family* to limit women's economic independence to unmarried women. Millicent Garrett Fawcett reacted by deploring parents' tendency to exclude their daughters from investments in education.

1907–1938: In Vienna, the first two generations of Austrian school women economists emerged, but anti-Semitism and racial bans against Jews prevented them from getting any official academic position.

1908. Beatrice Webb founded the Fabian Women's Group to study the relationship between women's economic independence and socialism.

1919. In Austria, female students were admitted to the School of Law and enrolled in political economy curricula.

Women economists entering academia

1873. At Lake Placid, New York, Ellen Swallow Richards organized the first Lake Placid Conference to promote home economics and the opening of the Woman's Laboratory at MIT to encourage female students to get enrolled in scientific and technological curricula.

1873. At Kansas State University, the first home economics department was established.

1886. The American Economic Association started an annual essay competition on papers about the economic conditions of women.

1896. At the University of Wisconsin–Madison, Helen Page Bates was the first woman to earn a Ph.D. in economics in the United States of America. At LSE, Gertrude Tuckwell was appointed the first adjunct professor of economics

1899. At the Lake Placid Conference, the term home economics was first introduced to denote the scientific management of the house, based on the interconnection between the cult of domesticity and the ideal of social responsibility.

1908. At the Lake Placid Conference, the American Home Economics Association (AHEA) was founded to make home economics available in primary, junior-high, and high schools' curricula, and to fundraise the expansion of the discipline. Ellen Richards served as its first president. The *Journal of Home Economics* was established.

1909. The University of California at Berkeley offered the course 'The Household as Economic Agent'.

1920. Lilian Knowles was appointed first full-time lecturer, then Professor in economic history, at the London School of Economics.

1920s–1930s. At the University of Chicago, Hazel Kyrk, Margaret Reid, and Elizabeth Hoyt founded household economics.

1923. At the University of Chicago, Hazel Kyrk published *A Theory of Consumption* to analyze whether welfare economics may actually prevent either inefficiency (by providing only necessary goods) or unfairness (by providing benefits only to people who actually need them).

1927. In the United States, the Bureau of Home Economics Act passed aimed to increase home economic education at any level. Ten years later, in 1937, the George-Dean Act increased funding for home economics.

1934. At the University of Chicago, Margaret Reid published *The Economics of Household Production*, which was especially focused on women's unpaid labor within households.

New research fields in economics: the role of women's studies and feminism in the split between gender neoclassical economics and feminist economics

1956. At the University of Sydney, Madge Dawson introduced women's studies by teaching 'Women in a Changing World', a course on Western European women's economic and political status.

1962–1964. At Columbia University, Jacob Mincer and Gary Becker founded the new home economics by publishing their first papers to model the home-based decision-making process, to emphasize human capital as the core of labor economics, and to consider the role of women in the labor market.

1965. Muriel Johnson introduced the first women's studies course, 'Women in Contemporary Culture' at Kansas State University.

1969. The first program of women's studies was established at San Diego State College.

1970. In the United States of America, the economist Ester Boserup published *Woman's Role in Economic Development* to criticize the stereotyped model of western family made up by the combination of a male 'breadwinner', a female 'homemaker', and their dependent children.

1971. The American Economic Association created the Committee on the Status of Women in the Economics Profession (CSWEP) to monitor the progress of women economists within academic departments and to reduce gender gaps in the profession. Women's studies curricula were established at Wichita State University, Kansas, and at Harvard University.

1972. McGeorge Bundy, President of the Ford Motor Company, announced the first $1 million national fellowship program for faculty members and doctoral dissertations on women's studies. At Columbia University, the journal *Feminist Studies* was founded.

1975. The feminist journal *Signs: A Journal of Women in Culture and Society* was founded.

1977. *The Journal of Consumer Research* hosted a debate on the nature of the new home economics, which involved Marianne Ferber and Bonnie Birnbaum, Margaret Reid, and the sociologist John P. Robinson. Critiques to the new home economics emerged among feminist economists who refused to adopt neoclassical economics to scrutinize gender issues.

1981. At the University of Chicago, Becker published his *Treatise on the Family* to examine family behavior in rational choice terms.

1990. The American Economic Association established JEL codes for household economics (D1), the new home economics (D13), and gender (neoclassical) economics (J16), later labeled 'economics of gender'.

1992. Foundation of the International Association of Feminist Economics (IAFFE).

1993. Marianne Ferber and Julie Nelson coedited the book *Beyond Economic Man: Feminist Theory and Economics* to explore connections between feminism and economics. *History of Political Economy* hosted a mini-symposium to consider the role of feminist economics in the history of economic theory and thought.

1994. Joyce Jacobsen published *The Economics of Gender* to scrutinize the cost of gender inequality in economic matters.

1995. Edith Kuiper and Jolande Sap edited *Out of the Margin: Feminist Perspectives on Economics* to criticize the narrow conception of rationality within neoclassical economics.

1995. Foundation of IAFFE's academic journal, *Feminist Economics*. The United Nations presented the first programs to eradicate gender inequality: the United Nations Development Program (UNDP), the Gender-Related Development Index (GDI), and the Gender Empowerment Measure (GEM).

1997. The Economic and Social Council of the United Nations included IAFFE among its members.

1999. Janice Peterson and Margaret Lewis edited *The Elgar Companion to Feminist Economics* that revealed the increasing and evolving literature of feminist economics.

2003. Marianne Ferber and Julie Nelson edited a revised and enlarged version of *Beyond Economic Man: Feminist Economics Today*, about the developments of feminist economics within the discipline, albeit neoclassical economics had remained silent or indifferent to its instances.

2006. Feminist economics got its official JEL code (B54) that denoted it as a heterodox approach to economics. The World Economic Forum started to publish its dataset to measure gender disparity in the world.

2007. IAFFE's first annual conference.

2010. The United Nations established the Entity for Gender Equality and the Empowerment of Women.

Index

Abbott, E. 61–63, 74
abolitionism 5, 55–56, 58–59, 217
accountability 142, 146, 205
Adams, W. 131
Adler, F. 46–47
Adler, V. 45
Aerni, A. 134, 138, 168
African American population 56, 58–59,
    63, 71, 126, 135, 153, 205, 218
Agarwal, B. 134, 150, 153, 157, 160–161,
    167–168, 179
agency 68, 123, 156–157, 160–161,
    166n34, 167n38, 187
Albelda, R. 134, 168, 174
Aleichem, S. 36
Allen, C. 127
Allen, R. 97, 100, 115
Allied Social Sciences Association (ASSA)
    134, 141
Altmann-Gottheiner, E. 73n24
American Economic Association (AEA) 4,
    9, 11, 59, 63, 113n24, 134, 165n15, 219,
    221–222
Anderson, E. 160–161, 168
Anderson Garrett, E. 7
androcentrism 69, 122, 140, 146, 151,
    162, 186
Anstey, V. 31, 72n10
Anthony, S.B. 57–58
anthropology 99, 107, 113n16, 125, 128
anti-Semitism 33, 35, 39, 40–41,
    128, 219
Aquinas, T. 66
Aristotle 66, 166n30
Arrow, K. 131
Atkinson, M. 30, 72n8
Atkinson, T.G. 164n2
Auspurg, A. 50
Austen, J. 19

Austrian economics 11, 72n19, 123,
    158–159
Ayer, H. 70

Bacon, F. 145
Baker, G.F. 61, 65–66, 73n26, 74
Barker, D. 10, 13n5, 134–135, 151, 155,
    160, 167n44, 186–187
Barre, P. de la 16
Bassi, L. 12n2
Bates, H. P. 61, 220
Bauer, H. 46
Bauer, O. 46
Beard, M. 123
Beauvoir, S. de 123–124
Becker, G. 9, 12, 87, 98, 100–106, 108,
    110–111, 112n2, 113n21, 113nn23–24,
    114nn25–32, 190–192, 194–197,
    220–221
Beecher, C. 88
Beecher, H. 88
behavior 11, 63, 97, 101–104, 107–111,
    112nn1–2, 113n18, 113n23, 114nn25–26,
    113, 141, 144, 149, 151–152, 156,
    166n32, 167n48, 183–184, 188, 192,
    194, 206n1, 217, 221
behavioral economics 11, 123, 156, 158,
    162–163, 167n48
Beneria, L. 142, 154, 166n31, 186
Bentham, E. 72n8
Bergmann, B. 100, 114n32, 130–131,
    134–136, 140, 150–151, 164n12,
    166n25, 196–197
Berik, G. 156
Berliner, C. 52–53
Bernfeld, S. 48
Bettauer, B. 38, 72n12
Bickford Gammon, S. 71
Bigg, H. 25–26, 219

Spencer, H. 21
Stanton Cady, E. 57–58
Starr, E. 89
Steindler, O. 38
Steinfeld Kuczynski, M. 52
Steuart, J. 19, 66
Stewart, M. 56
Stewart McKinney, S. 58, 73n25
Stigler, J. 111
Stimpson, C. 128
Stoctöcker, H. 50
Stolper, G. 42
Stolper Kassowitz, A. 41–42
Stone, L. 58
Strassmann, D. 123, 139–140, 143, 150, 153, 156
Strigl, R. 72n19
Strober, M. 131, 134, 138, 150
Stuart Campbell, H. 89
suffrage 4–5, 12nn3–4, 18, 20, 22–25, 29–33, 44–45, 50, 54–59, 62, 71n1
Sumner Woodbury, H. 61, 64
Swanwick, H.M. 73n8
sweating system 26, 28–29, 71n7

Talbot, M. 62, 94–95
Taussig, F. 60
Taylor Mill, H. 22–23, 166n35, 218
Terrell, M.C. 59
Thomas, C. 164n11
Thompson, W. 27–28, 217
Tisch, C. 52–54
Tobias, S. 127
Truth, S. 58, 218
Tubman, H. 58–59
Tuckwell, G. 31, 220
Turgot, A.R.J. 53

Ulmann, R. 38, 40
unionism 23, 29, 31, 62, 65, 72n9
United Nations (UN) 47, 96, 129, 134, 141, 198, 207n14, 221–222
unpaid work 3, 106, 141, 153, 162
utilitarianism 22

Veblen, T. 62, 69, 73n30, 96, 112n12
Victorianism 18–21, 23–24, 27, 29, 148, 152

wage gap 3–4, 9, 12, 23, 25–26, 30, 48, 52, 57, 63–66, 89, 105–106, 128, 135, 139, 142, 153, 183, 188–190, 194, 199–201, 203–204, 218
Wagner, A. 63
Wakefield, P. 19
Walker, C.J. Madame 71
Wallace, P. 61, 67, 73n28, 131
Walls, G. 28
Webb, S. 25, 28–29, 31, 51, 63, 218–219
Webb Potter, B. 6, 25–26, 28–29, 51, 60, 63, 71n7, 219
Weintraub, R. 139
Werfel, F. 72n12
Wheeler Doyle, A. 27–28, 217
Wieser, F. 40–43
Williams, R. 154, 167n36
Wilson, C. 71n8
Wittgenstein, C. 33
Wittgenstein, L. 33
Wollstonecraft, M. 18–19, 28, 51, 57, 217
woman question *see* (early) feminism; *see also* women, emancipation; women, subjection
women: economists 3, 7–9, 12, 12n1, 18–19, 24–25, 28–34, 40–41, 44–49, 51–52, 56, 59–61, 65, 68, 86, 91–95, 100, 105, 130–134, 166n34, 197, 219, 221; emancipation 1–8, 12n4, 17–21, 24, 27–59, 70, 71n6, 86, 88, 93, 123–125, 130, 143, 160; empowerment 3, 12, 94, 129, 157, 161, 167nn39–43, 186–188, 198–200, 207n21, 221–222; entrepreneurs 3, 7, 204–206; studies 4, 9–10, 40, 122–130, 132, 139, 164nn7–10, 220–221; subjection 1–2, 16–19, 22, 30, 39, 54, 57, 69, 123–124, 144, 149, 183, 217–218
Woolf, L. 31
Woolf, V. 7, 31, 123
Wortley Montague, M. 19
Wright, F. 56
Wright, H. 113n12
Wright Coffin, M. 57
Wunderlich, F. 52

Zetkin, C. 50, 54, 218
Zuckerkandl, B. 72n12
Zweig, S. 35

Printed in the United States
by Baker & Taylor Publisher Services